E

W

ONE YEAR DEVOTIONAL

A Fresh Vision of God

Further Study Compiled by Trevor J. Partridge

Foreword

Well over 30 years ago now, when I was pastor of a church in central London, I was asked by a member of my congregation how I went about the task of drawing spiritual strength and encouragement on a daily basis from the Word of God. I explained that every week I set out to explore a Scriptural theme like the bloodline in the Bible or looking at the encounters which some Bible characters had with the Lord on mountain tops.

He asked me if I would write on a card a few Scriptural references relating to the theme I was pursuing so that he could follow it with me. I responded to his request and after a few weeks more people were requesting the cards and soon I found myself writing a dozen of them a week. One night after a church service a group of people asked if I would add some of the comments and thoughts that came to me as I meditated on the theme. This is how the idea for *Every Day with Jesus*, a monthly study on a biblical theme, was born.

The first *Every Day with Jesus* was on the theme of Revival, a subject very close to my heart and one which has also been included in this book. Other themes followed that first edition in 1965 and it soon became clear that a month was too short to develop a subject so I decided to expand a theme over two months. Today these two-monthly themes are read daily by about half a million people around the world.

Devotional reading it needs to be said is designed not simply to inform the mind, but to fire the spirit. My prayer is that the six carefully selected themes in this first edition – themes which have nourished and fired my own soul – will nourish and fire yours also.

Selwyn Hughes

The Vision
of God

Needed - a new vision

"In the year that King Uzziah died, I saw the Lord ..." (v.1)
For reading & meditation – Isaiah 6:1-13

We begin by focusing on a theme of deep spiritual importance. It is my conviction that *the Christian Church needs a fresh vision of God*. Almost without our realising it, a spiritual myopia has afflicted us; we are not seeing life clearly because we do not see God clearly. A right perspective on God gives us the right perspective on everything else – life, work, money, service, relationships, and so on.

There is possibly no greater vision of God and His glory in the whole of the Bible (apart from John's encounter with the Almighty in the book of Revelation) than the vision we find recorded in Isaiah chapter 6. It is with this chapter that we are to be concerned. We shall depart from it at times to look at other related aspects, but the thrilling vision of God that was given to Isaiah is to be central to our study. Isaiah came face to face with the living God and found that his whole life was transformed. I trust the same thing will happen to us as we pursue this theme together.

The reason our problems often seem overwhelming is because we allow the things of time to loom larger in our gaze than the things of eternity. The tiniest of coins, when held close to the eye, can blot out the sun. I invite you, therefore, on this very first day of our journey to begin to lay hold on the truth that life works better when we know how to *glance at things but gaze at God*. Seeing Him clearly will enable us to see all other things clearly.

FURTHER STUDY

Psa. 99:1-9; 21:13;
57:11; Isa. 33:5

1. What does the psalmist affirm?

2. What does the psalmist exhort us to do?

Prayer

O God, give me, I pray, a fresh vision of Yourself. I need it and need it badly. Fill my whole horizon with the splendour of Your love, Your power and Your glory. In Christ's peerless and precious Name I ask it. Amen.

How sad!

"... for God is with us." (v.10)
For reading & meditation – Isaiah 8:1-10

Before concentrating on the dramatic vision given to Isaiah in the Temple, we must take a few moments to acquaint ourselves with his personal history.

We do not know exactly when Isaiah was born but we do know that he prophesied during the time of Uzziah, Jotham, Ahaz and Hezekiah. This puts his ministry from around 740 to at least 687 BC. The name "Isaiah" means "the Lord saves", and the passage before us today shows that he was married to a "prophetess" (v.3) and had two sons – Shear Jashub (7:3) and Maher-Shalal-Hash-Baz. The prophet, you remember, introduced his vision of God to us by informing us that "in the year that king Uzziah died, I saw the Lord." Just who was Uzziah? Uzziah was king of Judah from 791 to 740 BC. At first he was a godly king, but when he burned incense in the Temple (2 Chron. 26:16-21) he was struck with leprosy and remained leprous until his death.

When Uzziah died, a period of darkness descended on Judah. In the midst of this spiritual despondency Isaiah was given a vision of the Lord high and lifted up. Was the fact that Isaiah's vision occurred soon after Uzziah's death a mere coincidence? I don't think so. In some way Uzziah's death triggered in Isaiah a spiritual crisis that made him more ready to lift his gaze from earth to heaven. How true to life this is. We look up only when something happens that knocks us flat on our backs. How sad that sometimes earthly securities have to be removed before we can see the glory of Him who sits upon the throne.

FURTHER STUDY

Job 42:1-5;
Psa. 141:1-10

1. What did Job say after he saw God's greatness?

2. What did the psalmist say on observing the evildoers?

Prayer

Father, I am deeply sorry that I go through life with my gaze focused more on that which is around me than on that which is above me. Forgive me and help me develop a more heavenward gaze. In Jesus' Name I pray. Amen.

When props are knocked out

"The eternal God is your refuge, and underneath are the everlasting arms." (v.27)

For reading & meditation – Deuteronomy 33:20-29

Some commentators believe that many in the nation at that time, including Isaiah, had allowed their hopes and expectations for Judah to become so entwined around King Uzziah that when he died they were filled with despair. One modern-day commentator compares it to the shock that reverberated around the world when President Kennedy was assassinated in 1963.

If Isaiah had been pinning his hopes for the spiritual survival of Judah on Uzziah rather than on God then it is easy to see how disappointed and disillusioned he would have become on hearing that King Uzziah had died. Perhaps it wasn't until he came to recognise the impotency of the one who lay in the coffin that he was prepared to lift his eyes to gaze at the One who sat on the eternal throne. How we need to learn the solemn lesson that our trust must always be in God. If it isn't, then God will knock the props out from beneath our feet, not because He is angry at our lack of confidence in Him but because He knows we cannot function effectively unless we are fully dependent on Him.

I wonder, am I talking to someone right now who over the past year has had the props knocked from beneath their feet? The things you have depended on for so long are no longer there. Then listen to me: God is not angry with you. He just wants you to rest your weight fully on Him. You may have to be willing to see your earthly securities laid in a coffin, so to speak, before you can see the glory of the One who sits upon the throne.

FURTHER STUDY

2 Chron. 20:1-30;
Psa. 34:5; 123:1

1. What circumstances did Jehoshaphat find himself in?

2. What did he confess and affirm in his prayer?

Prayer

O Father, help me see that all Your actions toward me have my highest interest at heart. You allow things to happen not to demean me but to develop me. You strip me in order to sustain me. Give me a trusting heart. In Christ's Name I ask it. Amen.

Unchanging and Unshakeable

"Jesus Christ is the same yesterday and today and for ever." (v.8)

For reading & meditation – Hebrews 13:1-16

We saw yesterday that whenever God knocks the props from beneath our feet it is in order that we might rest more securely on Him. The sooner we learn how to make God our security the better, for we are going to face some dark and difficult days up ahead.

During the period when the newspapers were filled with reports of the upheaval in Europe and the great changes taking place in Russia, I turned to my Bible and read these words: "... let us be grateful for receiving a kingdom that cannot be shaken ..." (Heb. 12:28, RSV). The message seemed so appropriate. All around us right now nations are being shaken and almost everything is in the stage of upheaval and change. I am not a prophet, but I think more international unrest and change is on the way. This is a time when God wants His people to look up and see that He is still on the throne.

Every kingdom is shakeable except the kingdom of God. The kingdom of Communism is shakeable. It has to be held together by force. Relax the force and, as the world has witnessed, it goes to pieces. The kingdom of finances is shakeable. The stock market goes up and down with the events of the day. The kingdom of health is shakeable. The doctor says: "I am afraid you have an incurable illness." Shakeable! But in a world of flux be assured of this: Christians are people who belong to an unchanging Person and who dwell in an unshakeable kingdom. God is allowing kingdoms to be shaken so that they might discover the unshakeable kingdom – the kingdom of God.

FURTHER STUDY

Psa. 102:27;
Mal. 3:6;
Heb. 1:10-12;
James 1:1-18

1. What has the Lord declared?
2. What did James confirm?

Prayer

Father, what a comfort it is to realise that I belong to an unchanging Person and an unshakeable kingdom. Passing events cannot shake me. In You I am more than a match for anything. I am eternally grateful. Amen.

"I saw the Lord"

"... and saw the God of Israel." (v.10)
For reading & meditation – Exodus 24:1-18

I remind you that the thought occupying our minds in these opening days of our meditations is this: God allows the props to be knocked out from beneath our feet in order that we might rest our weight fully upon Him. And this is as true for nations as it is for individuals.

We are in the midst of a great international shake-up at the moment – ideologically, politically, and economically. Every programme for the running of God's universe which is an alternative to His own is being shown to be ineffective. I love the story of the little boy in Sunday school who, when asked to make an acrostic from the word Easter, came up with this: "Every Alternative Saviour Takes Early Retirement." All systems that leave out Jesus Christ are doomed to failure for they are not in harmony with the universe. Probably the greatest form of evangelism that is going on at the moment is the shaking of the nations. What is shakeable is being shaken so that the unshakeable might appear. God is preparing the world for the revelation of His kingdom in a way that many cannot discern.

But what about your own personal life? Is that being shaken? What kind of experiences have you had recently? Have you seen, as Isaiah did, your hopes and expectations put in a coffin? Then take heart – all this could be the prelude to a new vision of God. God has often to empty the throne of our hearts before He fills it with Himself. You may yet say: "In the year that all my hopes and expectations came crashing down, I saw the Lord."

FURTHER STUDY

Gen. 32:1-31;
Ex. 24:9-11

1. What did the man say to Jacob?

2. What did Jacob say of the place where he met the man?

Prayer

O Father, how I long that the months ahead will become for me ones of vision and venture. Show me Your glory, I pray, in a way I have never known before. I ask this in and through the Name of Christ my Lord. Amen.

Whose universe is this?

"But about the Son he says, 'Your throne, O God, will last for ever and ever ..." (v.8)

For reading & meditation – Hebrews 1:1-14

We move on now to consider the fact that when Isaiah received his vision of God he saw the Almighty "seated on a throne" (Isa. 6:1). Why a throne? Have you noticed in your study of the Scriptures that the seers and apostles in their times of perplexity were often sustained by a vision of the heavenly throne? When Ezekiel was comforting the forlorn exiles he saw the eternal throne (Ezek. 43:7). Daniel, during the rule of Belshazzar, saw the Ancient of Days sitting on His throne (Dan. 7:9). When John was exiled on the island of Patmos and had his great vision of the future, he too saw the throne many times. And in the year that King Uzziah died and Isaiah saw the Lord, he beheld Him "seated on a throne." Why was there given to these men in their hour of great need a vision of the eternal throne? To remind them whose universe it was.

A king reigns from his throne – the symbol of might, power and authority. By revealing His throne to Isaiah it was as if God was saying to him: "There may be no one on the throne of Judah at this moment, but My throne is never unoccupied." We too need at this critical hour in human history to be sustained by the vision of the Almighty seated upon the throne. Earlier this century Communist leaders were declaring: "We have deposed kings from their thrones; now we will depose the King from the skies." What foolishness. How can creatures whom God has made hope to pull the Creator from His throne? No rocket can ever reach it and no atomic bomb can blast it. The throne of God is unassailable.

FURTHER STUDY

Psa. 45:1-6; 103:19; Isa. 66:1

1. What did the psalmist declare?

2. What did the Lord declare about Himself?

Prayer

My Father and my God, just as You have sustained others with a vision of Your throne – sustain me too, I pray. Your throne is unassailable. I draw deep comfort and security from that. Thank You, Father. Amen.

Our God reigns!

"... you have sat on your throne, judging righteously." (v.4)

For reading & meditation – Psalm 9:1-20

We said yesterday that earlier this century Communist leaders were declaring: "We have deposed kings from their thrones; now we will depose the King from the skies." Following the Revolution in 1917, atheism was adopted in Russia – but what is the result? There are more Christians in the Russian Federation than there are in the British Isles! Not only that, many Christians feel Russia and Eastern Europe constitute some of the greatest spiritual harvest fields in the world at the moment.

The kingdoms of Europe have been shaken in order that from the dust the unshakeable kingdom might appear. Christians need ever to keep this in mind: it is from the throne of heaven that the final decisions are made regarding the world's affairs, not the thrones of earth. I am well aware that there are times when it looks as if the authority of heaven's throne has little to do with what transpires on planet earth. Murder, pillage, lust, greed, rape, selfishness, pride and jealousy are spread wide across it, and the battle between good and evil seems as sharp as ever. But don't be taken in by what you see with your eyes or read in your newspapers. Whatever the appearances, our trust must be in the Scriptures which are God's written Word. He tells us in its pages that this is His world – and that He reigns from the central throne of the universe.

God is King! See Him on the throne! And crown Him again in your heart.

FURTHER STUDY

Psa. 47:1-9; 93:1;
96:10; 97:1-2

1. Why can we rejoice?

2. What is the conviction of the psalmist?

Prayer

Father, I bow in Your presence and acknowledge You as the ruler of the universe and the captor of my heart. I have no crown of gold to cast at Your feet but I do more – I cast my heart. I am Yours and You are mine – for ever. Thank You, my Father. Amen.

Why doesn't God do something?

"Why, O Lord, do you stand far off? Why do you hide yourself in times of trouble?" (v.1)

For reading & meditation – Psalm 10:1-18

Many people, most of whom live their normal lives in neglect of God, complain in times of distress or national emergency that God never seems to do anything. Even Christians struggle and ask questions similar to the ones raised by the psalmist: "Why doesn't God intervene to prevent rail crashes, stop babies being battered, or prevent earthquakes wiping out whole communities?"

The problem is a very old one. It puzzled the psalmists, the prophets, and it has perplexed the people of God in every age. It baffled poor Peter in the Garden of Gethsemane. When he stood helpless and ineffectual, and watched soldiers march his betrayed Master away, something came nigh to bursting in his heart. He knew that it was devilry, but why should Christ allow Himself to suffer it? Surely the same word that cured the leper, gave sight to the blind, and summoned the dead to life could blast these evil men for their wickedness? Yet the Master allowed men to lead Him away. As Peter stumbled into the darkness, the question must have hammered in his reeling brain: "Why? … Why? … Why?"

There is only one answer to be given to this question: God does not work in our way. This may not satisfy some, but it is an answer nevertheless. His might finds fitting expression not in the power to wound but in the power to woo. His power does not coerce but constrain. Never does He violate the personalities He has made. It would be easy for Him to intervene, but another purpose is at work – the purpose of constraining love. Hard though it may be, we must have patience with the patience of God.

FURTHER STUDY

Isa. 55:1-11;
Psa. 18:30; 145:17;
Hosea 14:9

1. What is God's promise concerning His Word?

2. What conclusion did Hosea come to?

Prayer

O Father, help me understand this important truth, that in running the world You do not work our way. I am big enough to ask questions but not big enough to know the answers. Hold me fast even when I doubt. In Jesus' Name. Amen.

Unassailable – but accessible

*"Let us then approach the throne of grace with
confidence …"* (v.16)

For reading & meditation – Hebrews 4:1-6

We continue meditating on the fact that ultimate authority rests with God who sits upon His throne. Years ago congregations frequently sang a chorus that goes like this:

> *God is still on the throne,*
> *And He will remember His own;*
> *Though trials may press us*
> *And burdens distress us*
> *He never will leave us alone.*

The story is told of a little boy who, when introduced to this chorus for the first time in his Sunday school, came home and told his mother: "We learned a new song in Sunday school today." "Oh yes," said his mother, "what was it?" "God is still on the phone," said the little lad. Well that wasn't exactly what he had been taught, but the thought contained in those words was equally true. Though God reigns from a majestic throne, He is accessible to us at all times of day and night. The lines of communication that lead from us to Him are never blocked and never "down". When a man or woman, boy or girl says, "God be merciful to me a sinner," the message goes straight through to the throne and they receive this personal reply: "You are forgiven, redeemed, and set free from your sin."

FURTHER STUDY
Eph. 1:1-7; 2:7;
Phil. 4:19;
1 Tim. 1:14

1. What will God
meet according to His
riches?

2. What was Paul's
testimony?

The throne of God, you see, is not only a throne of righteousness but a throne of grace! Righteousness says: "Stay back until you are good enough to approach." Grace says: "I will put on you the robes of righteousness that are provided for you by Christ – now you are good enough." Too good to be true? Too good not to be true!

Prayer

Father, I draw near again today to Your throne of grace, and with the redeemed all around the world sing: "How marvellous, how wonderful, this my song shall ever be; how marvellous, how wonderful is my Saviour's love to me." Amen.

The sceptre of righteousness

"So Esther approached and touched the tip of the sceptre." (v.2)

For reading & meditation – Esther 5:1-14

We continue meditating on the fact that the throne of God is also a throne of grace. I know of no more wonderful picture to illustrate this than the passage before us today.

Queen Esther approaches the king in order to put into operation the first part of her plan to outwit Haman in his desire to massacre the Jews. In those days no one would enter into the king's presence uninvited, not even the queen. So she dresses as attractively as possible and stands where the king can catch sight of her. As soon as the king spots her in the entrance to the king's hall, he invites her to approach him and holds out the royal sceptre toward her as a sign that she is welcomed and accepted. Esther touches the top of the sceptre in acknowledgement of the king's welcome and proceeds to outline her request.

What a beautiful picture this is of the way we sinners are accepted into the presence of the King of kings. We are told in Hebrews 1:8 that God too has a sceptre – a sceptre of righteousness – which soiled sinners would never be able to touch. However, the good news of the gospel is this: we can approach the throne of a holy God with the assurance that through the sacrifice on the cross, God has given us His righteousness – the consequence of the finished work of Christ. As we move forward and touch it, in other words acknowledge our acceptance of it, we are welcomed into His presence as if we had never sinned. Can anything be more wonderful in earth or heaven than to be accepted at the throne of a righteous and holy God? And it's all because of Jesus. Blessed be His name for ever!

FURTHER STUDY

Psa. 65:1-13; 48:10; 97:2; 145:17-18

1. What are the foundations of God's throne?

2. What accompanies the righteousness of God?

Prayer

O Father, how can I sufficiently thank You for extending to me Your offer of salvation in Christ? What amazing mercy! What wondrous grace! Help me witness to it both by my lips and by my life. In Jesus' Name I pray. Amen

"His Majesty!"

"For the Lord is the great God, the great King above all gods." (v.3)

For reading & meditation – Psalm 95:1-11

What is the word that comes to mind when you think of a throne? Is it not the word "majesty"? Our word "majesty" comes from the Latin *majestas* and means greatness. Jim Packer says: "When we ascribe majesty to someone we are acknowledging greatness in that person and voicing our respect for it; as for instance, when we speak of 'Her Majesty, the Queen'." "Majesty" is a word that is often used of God. "The Lord reigns, he is robed in majesty" (Psa. 93:1). "They will speak of the glorious splendour of your majesty" (Psa. 145:5). Christ, we are told, at His ascension, "sat down at the right hand of the Majesty in heaven" (Heb. 1:3).

Why was it necessary for Isaiah to see God "seated on a throne"? Because his instincts of trust and worship would be stimulated by a vision of God's majesty. And so will it be with us. One of the reasons why our faith is so feeble is because our thoughts of God are not great enough. Do we picture God "seated on a throne" or just sitting upon a cloud?

The trouble with many in today's Church is that, although they cherish great thoughts about men, they have only small thoughts about God. I love the song written by Jack Hayford that begins "Majesty! Worship His Majesty". But it is possible to sing that with great gusto in church and then revert to our inadequate thoughts about God when we kneel down to pray. Learn to associate God with majesty. I promise you, filling your mind with thoughts of "His Majesty" will set your devotional life on fire!

FURTHER STUDY

1 Chron. 29:10-13;
Psa. 96:4-6;
Job 37:22-23

1. What did David proclaim in the presence of the whole assembly?

2. What did Elihu proclaim to Job?

Prayer

O Father, as I turn my gaze upward to focus on Your greatness and Your glory, stimulate my instincts of trust and worship and set my soul on fire. I look at You and my heart cries out in godly reverence and fear: "Your Majesty". Amen.

Difficulties are not almighty

"… the Lord, the Lord Almighty, has told me …" (v.22)
For reading & meditation – Isaiah 28:16-29

There can be little doubt that the vision Isaiah received in the Temple transformed his life. The young prophet might not have known it at the time but on the River Tiber a city was being built which was to be called Rome. As we know, that city became the focal point of a great empire which in 63 BC overcame Isaiah's beloved city of Jerusalem. The vision he saw of the One who was "seated on a throne", however, would remain with him throughout his entire ministry and give within the conviction that, no matter who or what would hold the centre stage of earth's affairs, the Lord alone was sovereign and ruled over all. After that, whenever other prophets drew back from speaking the Word of the Lord because of fear, Isaiah never hesitated. We have an example of this in the passage before us today.

Now that's an important lesson for your life and mine. It is so easy for us to allow the problems of life to loom large in our thinking. When we do so we soon lose the right perspective. Our obsession with our problems can become an issue that almost blots out God. Maybe someone you trusted has hurt you, and that problem has become so large that it reaches almost cosmic proportions. Well, I want to tell you today that, big though it may be, it is not bigger than God. Don't lose your perspective.

The Lord is on His throne, high and exalted. See how big God really is and set your problems over against that vision. Your difficulties are not almighty. The Lord alone is almighty.

FURTHER STUDY

Matt. 19:16-26;
Jer. 32:17;
Luke 1:37

1. What did Jesus say to the disciples?

2. What did Gabriel say to Mary?

Prayer

O God, fill my vision with Yourself for I see that when I do not view You as almighty I can so easily view my problems in that way. Keep my gaze and my focus fully on You. In Jesus' Name I ask it. Amen.

Seeing God as God

"Whom did the Lord consult to enlighten him … Who was it that taught him knowledge …?" (v.14)

For reading & meditation – Isaiah 40:1-20

We said yesterday that Isaiah's vision of God's majesty remained with him throughout his entire ministry. See how, in this fortieth chapter of his prophecy, Isaiah applies the truth of the majesty of God, which he learned in the vision in the Temple, to the lives of the disillusioned and downcast people of Judah. In God's Name he puts several questions to the people.

First: "Who has understood the mind of the Lord, or instructed him as his counsellor?" (v.13). This question is designed to correct false notions of God. Luther once said to Erasmus: "Your thoughts of God are too human." This may be our trouble too. We think of God in the same way that we think about ourselves – as limited and fallible, Because we are limited and require information and counselling, we think God does too. We think of God as too much like ourselves. Put the mistake right, says Isaiah. Learn to acknowledge the majesty and greatness of God.

A second and similar question is also posed: "To whom, then, will you compare God? What image will you compare him to?" (v.18). This question is also designed to correct wrong concepts of God. Isn't it sad that because we ourselves are limited and weak, we imagine that, at some points, God is too. Isaiah does here what a doctor would do when entering the room of a sick patient who has closeted himself behind shuttered windows. He opens the windows, lets in the fresh air and light, and says: "No wonder you are sick. You are not taking advantage of the resources that bring healing." Spiritual health comes from seeing God as He is.

FURTHER STUDY
Job 38:1-42:16
1. How does God bring perspective back to Job?
2. How did Job respond?

Prayer

My Father and my God, if I am mistakenly making You in my image instead of seeing that I am made in Yours then forgive me, I pray. Help me see You as You really are – ruling and reigning with all might, all power and all authority. Amen.

Strength like the eagle's

"They will soar on wings like eagles ..." (v.31)
For reading & meditation – Isaiah 40:21-31

We continue looking at the questions which Isaiah poses to the people of Judah and indeed to the whole nation of Israel, on behalf of God, here in this gripping fortieth chapter.

A third question is this: "Why do you say, O Jacob, and complain, O Israel, 'My way is hidden from the Lord; my cause is disregarded by my God'?" (v.27). The questions we looked at yesterday were designed to correct their false concepts of God; this one is designed to correct the wrong ideas they had concerning themselves. They were allowing themselves to think that God had abandoned them. How absurd! Let me ask you a personal question: Do you believe God has abandoned you? If you do, you ought to be ashamed of yourself. Such unbelieving pessimism dishonours the Almighty.

A fourth question is this: "Do you not know? Have you not heard? The Lord is the everlasting God, the Creator of the ends of the earth. He will not grow tired or weary, and his understanding no-one can fathom" (v.28). This question is intended to rebuke them for their slowness to believe in God's greatness and majesty. God talks to them in a way that is calculated to shame them out of their unbelief. How ridiculous it is for us to imagine that God can get old and tired. How slow we are to believe in God as God – sovereign, all-seeing, and all-powerful. The need to "wait upon the Lord" and contemplate His majesty is one of our greatest needs in the Church. For it is when we do so, and only when we do so that our strength will be renewed and we will soar on wings like eagles.

FURTHER STUDY

1 Kings 8:14-24;
1 Chron. 17:20;
Psa. 89:1-52

1. What was at the heart of Solomon's prayer of dedication?

2. In what ways does the psalmist describe God?

Prayer

My Father and my God, write these truths upon my heart, so that I shall be gripped and mastered by these important convictions. I don't just want to hold them as ideas, I want them to hold me. Help me, dear Father. In Jesus' Name. Amen.

"He is exalted ..."

"But you, O Lord, are exalted for ever." (v.8)
For reading & meditation – Psalm 92:1-15

We move on now to focus on a further phrase that Isaiah uses when describing his vision of God: "I saw the Lord ... high and exalted" (Isa. 6:1). These words take us beyond the fact that God is seated on a throne and show us that His throne is situated far above the boundaries of space and time. The words "seated on a throne" introduce us to the majesty of God; the words "high and exalted" introduce us to the transcendence and loftiness of God. Oh how desperately we need a new vision of the transcendence of God in the Church today.

Earlier this century A.W. Tozer shook the Church of his day when he wrote: "The Church has surrendered her once lofty concept of God and has substituted for it one so low, so ignoble, as to be utterly unworthy of thinking, worshipping men. This she has done not deliberately but little by little and without her knowledge, and her very unawareness only makes her situation all the more tragic." Tozer went on to point out that a low view of God is the underlying cause of many of our problems. He said: "A whole new philosophy of the Christian life has resulted from this one basic error of our thinking." I would have to agree.

When we lose our sense of God's transcendence then a hundred different ills arise within us. Take this for example: with the loss of the sense of God's transcendence comes the further loss of understanding the significance of worship. To truly worship God we need to see that we are worshipping Someone who is not only above us, but far above us. He is the Creator – we are merely creatures.

FURTHER STUDY

Ex. 15:1-21;
Job 36:22;
Isa. 33:5-6; 5:16

1. What did the song of Moses begin and end with?

2. What does the word "awesome" mean?

Prayer

Father, help me see that while You are nearer to me than the breath I breathe, You are also a God who is high and exalted. And help me understand that these two truths are not contradictory but complementary. In Jesus' Name I pray. Amen.

Immanent – yet transcendent

"I live in a high and holy place ... with him who is contrite and lowly in spirit ..." (v.15)

For reading & meditation – Isaiah 57:11-21

The thought occupying our attention at the moment is what theologians call the transcendence of God. The idea behind transcendence is that of distinctiveness, separateness – that God is uniquely other than everything in creation.

We said yesterday that the words "high and exalted" show us that God's throne is situated far above the boundaries of space and time. Too much must not be made of this, however, for although the transcendence of God is frequently expressed biblically in terms of time and space (see Psalm 90:2 and 1 Kings 20:28, for example), we must not think that God lives in a time and space like ours, only beyond that of creation.

Over against that thought we must hold the truth of God's immanence, and by that we mean that He dwells in the lives of those who have repented of their sin – a truth our text for today brings out so clearly. Yet the fact God indwells us must not be allowed to cloud the truth that He is above us, infinitely exalted above all creation. To think of God as transcendent inspires adoration and worship. Without this idea in our minds then worship is a mere ritual and a formality. In days past, men and women who knew what it was to walk in the fear of the Lord had, as a basis for their lives, the concept of God as "high and exalted". However intimate their communion with God, they were gripped by the fact that God was high and lifted up. Why is it that in the modern-day Church we do not meet many of this ilk?

FURTHER STUDY

Gen. 14:17-20;
Heb. 7:1; Psa. 21:7;
Mark 5:7

1. How was God described by Melchizedek?

2. How did the evil spirit address Jesus?

Prayer

O God, forgive me if, in my desire to have You close to me, I have lost sight of Your majesty, Your greatness and transcendence. Help me understand that to see You as high and exalted is not a loss but a gain. In Jesus' Name I ask it. Amen.

"The proper study of mankind ..."

*"Now this is eternal life: that they may know you, the only
true God ..." (v.3)*

For reading & meditation – John 17:1-19

We ended yesterday with the thought that, in days past, men and
women who knew what it was to walk in the fear of the Lord had,
as a basis for their lives, the concept of God as "high and exalted". We
finished with the question: Why is it that in the modern-day Church we
do not meet many of this ilk? The answer I think is that, notwithstand-
ing all the good things happening in the Church today, there is not
enough teaching and emphasis on the nature and character of God.

The great preacher C.H. Spurgeon made this statement: "It has been
said that the proper study of mankind is man. I will not oppose the idea,
but I believe it is equally true that the proper study of God's elect is
God." The contemporary Church, generally speaking, focuses more on
issues like "how to gain a good self-image", or "how to be more effective
in prayer" than it does on how to know God. Not that these other issues
are unimportant, but, as Jim Packer says in his book *Knowing God*:
"Knowing God is crucially important for the living of our lives. The
world becomes a strange, mad, painful place, and life in it a disappoint-
ing and unpleasant business, for those who do not know about God."

Of course, it takes time to know God. Determine
right now that in the coming months you will commit
yourself to knowing God in a deeper way; first by
spending more time with Him in prayer and meditation, and second by increasing your understanding of
Him through more thorough study of His Word.

FURTHER STUDY

Eph. 1:1-17;
Phil. 3:1-11

*1. What did Paul pray
for the Ephesians?*

*2. What did Paul
desire for himself?*

Prayer

Father, I see that knowing You better involves increased time – time to talk to You
and time to study Your Word. Guide me so that I can make the coming months yield
great gains in my knowledge of You. In Jesus' Name I pray. Amen.

Our prayers reveal us

"O Lord, the great and awesome God ..." (v.4)
For reading & meditation – Daniel 9:1-19

When dwelling on the fact that God is "high and exalted" we must be careful not to think of Him as highest in an ascending order of beings, starting with a single cell and going on up from, say, a fish to a bird, to a man, to an angel, to an archangel, and then – God. This would be to see God merely as eminent, perhaps even pre-eminent. He is so much more than that. He is transcendent.

That means He stands apart from creation. He is as high above an archangel as He is above an amoeba, for the gulf that separates the amoeba from the archangel is finite, whereas the gulf separating God from an archangel is infinite. The amoeba and the archangel, though far removed from one another in the scale of created things, are, nevertheless, one in that they are both created. They belong in the category of what one theologian describes as "that which is not God" – separated from God by infinitude itself.

Even a casual reader of the Scriptures could not help but notice that those who appear to have a great knowledge of God have lofty thoughts concerning Him. This comes out most clearly in the prayers of God's people – Daniel's prayer which we have ready today being just one example. If you want to know how a person views God, listen to him or her pray! It's interesting to note that those who know God intimately invariably begin by acknowledging His greatness. They know that when they accord God His rightful place then it is more likely that everything else will be put in its rightful place.

FURTHER STUDY

Neh. 1:1-11;
4:1-15; 9:32

1. What was Nehemiah's view of God?

2. How did this affect the rebuilding of the wall?

Prayer

O God, slowly the light is dawning – when You are not accorded Your rightful place then nothing else is in place. You can get along without me, but I can't get along without You. Help me never to forget this. In Jesus' Name I ask it. Amen.

God help grammar!

"Be still, and know that I am God ..." (v.10)
For reading & meditation – Psalm 46:1-11

A famous preacher once preached from the text that is before us today and entitled his message: "Have you a God you can be still with?" It was reported that most of the congregation, being well educated, tuned out a lot of what he was saying because they could only think of the fact that he ended a sentence with a preposition. How sad that when eternal issues were at stake their only thought was of grammar. The great preacher D.L. Moody often split an infinitive when preaching. Once, when a retired schoolteacher took him to task for this lapse of grammatical correctness, he replied: "Madam, when I see souls going to hell and grammar gets in the way – then God help grammar!"

At the risk of repeating the unfortunate mistake of the first minister to whom I referred, I would like to ask you that same question: Have you a God you can be still with? In other words, is your life such a ceaseless round of activity that when you come to focus your mind on God you cannot give yourself to the task for very long, so you blurt out a few prayers and then you are gone? You won't get to know God – really know God – that way.

You see, what our text is saying is this: you cannot get to know God until you are willing to stay still before Him. Knowing God means contemplating Him, worshipping Him, and studying Him. It should be a cause for deep spiritual concern that the words of our text mean next to nothing to the self-confident bustling worshippers who move in and out of our churches nowadays.

FURTHER STUDY

Job 37:1-24;
Psa. 131:2;
Isa. 30:15

1. What did Elihu counsel Job?

2. What was the psalmist able to say?

Prayer

Loving heavenly Father, how blessedly You put Your finger on our problems. Help me face up to the question "Have I a God with whom I can be still?" and not rush past it. Slow me down, dear Father, so that I face this issue. In Jesus' Name. Amen.

Knowing God as He is

"God is spirit, and his worshippers must worship in spirit and in truth." (v.24)

For reading & meditation – John 4:1-26

Modern-day Christianity, generally speaking, is not producing the kind of person who can appreciate what it means to withdraw from the hustle and bustle of life and focus on worshipping God. And one of the reasons for that is the loss of the concept of God's transcendence.

You see, it is impossible to keep up the practice of Christian principles and perform our Christian duties in the way they should be performed when our attitude to God or our view of Him is erroneous. If we are to see spiritual power flowing through our lives then we must begin to think of God as He is. "Worship is as pure or as base," said Tozer, "as the worshipper entertains high or low thoughts of God." Because of this the most important issue for the Church is not "How can we evangelise?", but "How can we know God better?" Evangelism is important, but not half as important as knowing God. Worship must always come first, and work must always come second. Today's Christian teachers should be focusing (among other things) on making clear who God is, for the Church of tomorrow will depend largely on what kind of concept of God we have today.

FURTHER STUDY

1 Cor. 3:1-11;
Eph. 2:19-20

1. What had Paul taken trouble over?

2. What are we to be careful about?

A true understanding of God is as important to our worship of God, our work for God and our witness to God as a foundation is to a building. If the foundation is not right then the building will be lopsided, or worse – topple over. Thus we must ask ourselves: What kind of building will the Church of the next generation inherit from us? A strong one or an unsteady one?

Prayer

O God, I long with all my heart to worship you "in spirit and in truth". And whatever the road blocks on that journey, help me remove them and overcome them. For your own dear Name's sake I pray. Amen.

Christian idolaters

"Within your temple, O God, we meditate on your unfailing love." (v.9)

For reading & meditation – Psalm 48:1-14

We touched yesterday on an issue which I now want to expand upon because I believe it to be one of the most crucial aspects of Christian living – seeing God as He is, not as we would like Him to be. Unless we have an understanding of God *as He is*, not as we wish Him to be, then our lives will lack spiritual force and power. This is because our lives will never rise higher spiritually than our vision of God.

Among the sins which are hateful to God is the sin of idolatry, for idolatry, at its heart, is a libel on His character. Yet consider how many of us in the Church may be committing the sin of idolatry without realising it. The idolatrous heart assumes that God is other than He is, and substitutes for the true God one made after its own imagining. But a god who is created out of darkness of our hearts is not the true God. The greatest affront we can give to the Almighty is to view Him other than He really is.

God has gone to great lengths in the Scriptures to give us a clear picture of Himself, but when we continue to hold wrong ideas of Him, preferring to see Him the way we think He should be rather than the way He is, we demean Him. If we try to worship the god of our own imagining we then commit idolatry, for we are worshipping our idea of Him drawn from the darkness of our minds. Credal statements about God are fine – I have nothing against them – but if, in the secret chamber of our soul, we have an image of God which differs from the one we profess with our lips, then it is that core image which will have the greatest influence on our lives.

FURTHER STUDY

Acts 17:29;
Gal. 4:1-11;
2 Tim. 3:1-5

1. What were the Galatians doing?

2. What did Paul ask the Galatians?

Prayer

O Father, forgive me if I have been thinking of You as I want You to be rather than as You really are. Help me draw my concept of You from Your Word and from Your revelation in Christ, not from my own imaginings. In Jesus' Name. Amen.

Our biggest single problem

"Anyone who has seen me has seen the Father." (v.9)
For reading & meditation – John 14:1-14

We continue with the thought that we have to see God as He is, not as we would like Him to be. In a radio interview I was asked this question: "Over the years in which you have been a minister and counsellor, what has been the biggest single problem you have come across in the lives of fellow Christians? And what is the cause of that biggest single problem?" Unhesitatingly I replied: "Disappointment with God because of something He did not do, or something He did not provide. The cause – a wrong understanding of God and His ways."

Multitudes of Christians go through life with suppressed disappointment and anger because at some point in their experience God did not come through for them in the way they thought He should. I have heard people say: "I asked God to give me patience and instead He allowed the pressures to increase." "I asked God to take away my anger toward my wife and children, but He failed to answer my prayer." Time, it is said, is a wonderful healer, and many Christians recover from these negative feelings about God. But so often there is no real healing, just a covering over of the emotions. Then when some crisis hits and God does not come up to expectations the submerged feelings break the surface and the problem begins all over again.

The sooner we learn to accept God as He is, and do not imagine Him as we would like Him to be, the sooner we will move from the path of confusion to confidence. I tell you, this is a matter of supreme importance.

FURTHER STUDY

Psa. 22:1-5;
Rom. 5:5

1. What did David say about his fathers?

2. What was the result?

Prayer

O Father, I confess that I struggle when You don't seem to move in the way I want You to or do the things I want You to do. Help me know You better so that my expectations are based on truth, not on wishful thinking. In Jesus' Name. Amen.

The bottom line

*"How long, O Lord, must I call for help, but you do not
listen ...?" (v.2)*

For reading & meditation – Habakkuk 1:1-17

We continue focusing on the importance of seeing God as He really is, not as we would like Him to be.

The reason so many Christians become disappointed with God is because they do not have what can best be described as a "bottom line" – a line we draw under God. When we cannot make sense of a situation, the "bottom line" explains Him. So what is this "bottom line"? Is it the fact that God is Healer? I suggest not, for, if it was, then everyone should be healed. Is it that God is our Deliverer? No, not even that, for there are times when, despite our demands to be delivered, He makes no attempt to rescue us. Now I am not saying that God does not heal, or that He does not deliver us, but these aspects of His character are not the "bottom line". If we make them the "bottom line", we will become as confused as Habakkuk was in today's passage, when he confessed that he could not understand why God did not come through for His people.

The "bottom line", as it relates to God, is not deliverance, or healing, or protection, or any similar thing. He demonstrates His ability to do these things from time to time, but they are not to be seen as inevitable. Sometimes He heals and sometimes He doesn't. Sometimes He delivers and sometimes He doesn't. Sometimes He protects us from afflictions and accidents, and other times He allows them to happen. How do we make sense of all this? We can't unless we have a "bottom line"? So what is this "bottom line"? I will tell you tomorrow.

FURTHER STUDY
Eccl. 7:15
Psa. 73:1-28;

1. To what point had
the writer of
Ecclesiastes come?

2. What was the
psalmist struggling
with?

Prayer

My Father and my God, help me move, as Habakkuk did, from confusion to confidence, and give me the understanding and convictions I need to trust You even when I cannot trace You. In Jesus' Name I ask it. Amen.

Steady as you go!

"The Sovereign Lord is my strength; he makes my feet like the feet of a deer ..." (v.19)

For reading & meditation – Habakkuk 3:1-19

We acknowledged yesterday that if we see the "bottom line" concerning God as the fact that He is a Healer, or Protector, or a Deliverer, then we are often going to be disappointed, because every one of us knows that there are times when He does not come through for us in the way we expect. If He lets something happen to us that we think He shouldn't have let happen, then we will find it very difficult to trust in Him should we have the same requirement again. Often in these situations we end up developing a deep rage or disappointment with God which, in the interests of the Christian faith, we learn to suppress. This is largely because we do not understand God's "bottom line".

So what is the "bottom line" as regards God? I suggest it is His justice. By that I mean the truth that whatever God does, He does because it is right. Not that it is right because God does it, but that God does it because it is right. There is a world of difference between those two things. Most Christians find it difficult to believe in the justice of God. They say they do, but when questioned it is clear they believe only in justice on their terms.

FURTHER STUDY

Jer. 12:1-17;
Psa. 98:8-9; 99:4

1. What issue did Jeremiah take up with God?

2. What motivates God's justice?

In the passage before us today, Habakkuk comes to see that whatever God does is just, and it is his new-found confidence in the justice of God that holds him steady as he contemplates the judgment that God is about to bring on His people. I tell you with all the conviction of my heart that unless we are gripped by the belief that God acts justly in everything – everything – then we will not have the sure-footedness we need to negotiate the rocky slopes that are up ahead.

Prayer

Father, I see that if I am to move upwards in my Christian life with the sure-footedness of a deer, then I can only do so as I am gripped by the conviction that everything You do is right. Burn that conviction into me. In Jesus' Name. Amen.

"My comfort is My justice"

*"They will come to you, and when you see their conduct and
their actions, you will be consoled..."* (v.22)
For reading & meditation – Ezekiel 14:12-23

We continue emphasising the point that the "bottom line" as regards God is justice – the fact that everything that God does is right.

In our reading today God tells Ezekiel that He is going to judge Jerusalem but that He would provide comfort during that destruction. But what was that comfort? It was to spare a few people and bring them before Ezekiel, so that he could see how evil they were and realise that God had a just cause for everything He did. In other words, God was saying: "My comfort is My justice." You see the point? If your "bottom line" is "comfort", if that is more important to you than anything else, then when God acts justly it will be no comfort to you. When you cry out for comfort and think that is the most important thing you need from God, it may be that, from His point of view, your biggest need is justice. Then, when God acts justly but not according to your idea of justice, you get totally confused. But the problem is not with God, it is with you. You have not got the "bottom line" drawn clearly enough. Your "bottom line" is being drawn at *your idea of justice,* not His, and therefore His actions are anathema to you.

Most of us don't really believe in God's justice, only justice on our terms. It is easy to believe in God's justice when other people or other families are on the receiving end; but the true test of spiritual maturity is when in our own lives things do not go the way we expect them to go, and we say with Abraham, when pleading with God for the deliverance of Sodom: "Shall not the Judge of all the earth do right?" (Gen. 18:25, AV)

FURTHER STUDY

Gen. 18:22-25;
Psa. 33:4;
Hosea 14:1-9

1. What question did
   Abraham ask?

2. What was Hosea's
   conviction?

Prayer

Father, help me resolve this tension between my idea of justice and Yours. For I see that if it goes unresolved then I shall continue to misunderstand – even rebel. Teach me to accept that Your way is right – always. In Jesus' Name I ask it. Amen.

"See His glory come down"

"I will not yield my glory to another." (v.11)
For reading & meditation – Isaiah 48:1-11

Why do we find it difficult to draw the "bottom line" concerning God at the level of His justice? Perhaps we are able to do it when things are going well, but immediately disaster strikes we draw the line at a different level – at the level of His compassion, His ability to heal or His power to deliver. We then tend to demand from God not real justice but justice on our own terms – our terms being deliverance, healing or divine protection.

Now I am not saying that God is disinterested in us, but we must never put our well-being before His. There is a much higher value in this universe than our glory – it is God's glory. This is why we read over and over again in the book of Ezekiel words to the effect that "My glory is at stake."

The nation of Israel didn't see things that way and took a different, even a rebellious attitude toward God, saying: "No, it is our glory that is at stake." Don't we do something similar? When our problems loom large, and our welfare is under threat, we tend to argue with God when He says, "My glory is at stake," and retort, "No, Lord, it is not Your glory that is at stake; it is mine." What arrogance! What insanity! I tell you, if we are to develop any degree of spiritual maturity in our lives we have to put a higher value on God's glory than our own well-being. If we don't, then we will never come to know the depth of trust that Job exhibited when he said: "Though he slay me, yet will I hope in him" (Job 13:15).

FURTHER STUDY

Isa. 42:1-9;
1 Chron. 16:28-29;
Psa. 29:1

1. What will God not give to another?

2. What did David exhort to be ascribed to the Lord?

Prayer

Father, help me understand that in putting Your glory before my well-being I do not demean myself but develop myself. For in glorifying You I too am glorified. Help me grasp this. In Jesus' Name. Amen.

Where is our trust?

"Trust in him at all times …" (v.8)

For reading & meditation – Psalm 62:1-12

We continue meditating on this matter of God's glory being more important than our own well-being. The serious problem is not the pain that others have inflicted upon us, but the pain we have inflicted (and continue to inflict) upon God. Let me spell out as clearly as I can exactly what I mean.

Many Christians are far more interested in focusing on how they can get God to comfort them when they have been hurt than considering how much they have hurt Him. Not that it is wrong to seek His comfort – Scripture encourages us to do this – but it is only one side of the picture. The most popular books in our bookshops today are titles such as these: *How to be Healed of Life's Hurts* or *How to Overcome the Pains of the Past*. I repeat that this is a legitimate emphasis, but we must not lose sight of the fact that the important issue is not how badly people have behaved toward us, but how badly we have behaved (and continue to behave) toward God.

Take this for example: someone hurts us or upsets us and we decide to become the architects of their judgment. But what does God say? "Do not take revenge, my friends, but leave room for God's wrath … 'It is mine to avenge; I will repay,' says the Lord" (Rom. 12:19). Don't you think God is hurt when He sees us ignoring His Word? We may have been sinned against, but is that any justification for sinning against God? Let's not mince words here, for any violation of a divine principle must be called by its rightful name – sin. And no sin ought to be treated lightly – especially a sin against God.

FURTHER STUDY

Matt. 21:12-13;
23:37-39;
Luke 19:41

1. What pain was inflicted on Jesus as He observed the Temple area?

2. What pain did Jesus feel as He approached the city?

Prayer

O God, forgive me that so often I am more concerned about how others have treated me than the way I treat You. I see that a failure to trust You is a failure in love. I say, "I love You," but only so far. Forgive me and help me. In Jesus' Name. Amen.

Close – but not close enough

"Teach me your way, O Lord ... give me an undivided heart ..." (v.11)

For reading & meditation – Psalm 86:1-17

W e continue with the important issue we raised yesterday, namely, that the significant problem is not the hurts that others have given to us, but the hurts that we have given (and continue to give) to God. We looked at one direction we might go when hurt by others; look with me now at another.

Instead of trying to get back at them, we withdraw from them and decide to never again give them an opportunity to hurt us. Hence, in future, we relate to them at a superficial level – close enough to be considered friendly or sociable, but not close enough to get hurt. Notice what God says we ought to do when we become victims of spitefulness or animosity: "If your enemy is hungry, feed him; if he is thirsty, give him something to drink ... Do not be overcome by evil, but overcome evil with good" (Rom. 12:20-21). What this text is saying, you see, is this: be concerned about the person who has hurt you and put that concern into action; get close to them again and risk being hurt again.

To cling to our hurts and use them as a justification for avoiding close relationships is tantamount to saying: "God expects too much of us." Such an attitude is sinful. Why sinful? Because it reflects self-interest more than God-interest. It says to God: "It is not Your glory that is at stake here – it's mine." How sad that we are more keen to preserve our own well-being than trust God and His Word. I tell you, if we don't correct this imbalance we are never going to know God as He really is. We will see His justice only in terms of what it means for us, not in terms of what it means for Him.

FURTHER STUDY

Matt. 5:38-48;
Ex. 23:4-5;
Prov. 25:21-22;
Luke 23:34

1. What did Jesus teach in His sermon on the mount?

2. How did He demonstrate this?

Prayer

O God, we do not see ourselves, for we look at the sins that others commit against us with open eyes and then turn a blind eye upon the sins we commit against You. Help us to be as honest about ourselves as we are about others – and more. In Jesus' Name. Amen.

"Come on Lord, act justly"

*"… all his ways are just. A faithful God … upright and just
is he." (v.4)*

For reading & meditation – Deuteronomy 32:1-12

Can you see now why it is so hard to draw the "bottom line" concerning God in terms of His justice? We feel much more passionate about how we have been sinned against than how we sin against Him. "To dwell only on the fact that we have been victimised," says psychologist Larry Crabb, "is to develop a demanding spirit." We tend then to say to God: "Come on Lord, start acting justly and defend me against my adversaries." Once we give up our demandingness, however, we are at the mercy of other people and have to go through life trusting God to deal with them on His terms. Can we handle that kind of vulnerability?

I am not suggesting, by the way, that people who experience serious physical or sexual abuse should not report it to the authorities. What I have in mind as I write is the kind of situation when someone wounds our spirit by an insensitive word or action. When we focus on the sins of others toward ourselves it becomes hard to give up our rebellion against God, because, in the light of how we are hurting, we see it as justified. But when we focus on how much we have hurt Him, and how we continue to hurt Him by our self-centredness and our refusal to trust His power and love, our rebellious spirit dissolves of its own accord. Then what others have done to us seems of much lesser significance than what we have done to Him. Our perspectives are corrected and we are more ready to recognise the universal rightness of things and make eternal justice the "bottom line".

FURTHER STUDY

Eccl. 3:1-14;
Psa. 18:30;
Matt 5:48

1. What did the writer of Ecclesiastes know?

2. What did Jesus exhort in His sermon on the mount?

Prayer

Gracious Father, forgive us for the wrongs we inflict upon ourselves by trying to live in ways other than Your ways. Your ways produce rhythm; our ways produce ruin. Your ways produce freedom, our ways produce folly. Help us to take Your ways unreservedly. Amen.

Hearing *and* seeing!

"My ears had heard of you but now my eyes have seen you." (v.5)

For reading & meditation – Job 42:1-17

Perhaps the person who best illustrates what we have been talking about over the past few days – a failure to understand God's justice – is God's servant Job.

Following his suffering received at the hands of Satan, Job came to believe that the whole of life was unfair. He makes this point to God in chapter 27 verse 2: "As surely as God lives, who has denied me justice, the Almighty, who has made me taste bitterness of soul …" What is God's response to this? He confronts Job with these words: "Where were you when I laid the earth's foundation? Tell me, if you understand. Who marked off its dimensions? Surely you know!" (Job 38:4-5). Then, after listening for a long time to God outlining His greatness and His majesty, Job responds with the marvellous words that form our text for today: "My ears had heard of you but now my eyes have seen you." Job begins to see that any movement against God's justice is sin. His previous problem of being mistreated is forgotten in the light of the greater problem that he had misjudged the Almighty.

Then came the moment when Job prayed for the friends who hadn't been much help to him, and as he turned the focus from himself to others something big and beautiful took place within him – his rebellion dissolved and he was delivered from all his problems. Job came to see God as He is, not as he wanted Him to be, and with all the conviction of which I am capable I tell you that same revelation must come to us if we are to worship God and serve Him correctly.

FURTHER STUDY

Psa. 17:1-15; 34:5; 123:1

1. What was David asking God to honour?

2. What result was David convinced of?

Prayer

O Father, to hear of You by ear is indeed wonderful, but to "see" You is bliss beyond compare. Bring me to the same place You brought Your servant Job – no matter what lies in between. In Jesus' Name. Amen.

Too far to turn back

*"Whom have I in heaven but you? And earth has nothing I
desire besides you." (v.25)*

For reading & meditation – Psalm 73:1-28

W e pause at this point to gather up some of the things we have been
saying.

The most important need for the Church at this present time is a
fresh vision of God. The vision which the young Isaiah received as he
entered into the Temple must also become ours. It transformed him and
it will also transform us too. Many Christians come to the Bible, however, not to discover God as He is, but to confirm their own view of Him.
Thus they hold fast to a concept of the Almighty that is completely false,
and so, lacking a true knowledge of God, they stumble through life
rather than striding through it. When God is accorded His rightful place,
"high and exalted", then we acknowledge our rightful place and worship
becomes not a mere ritual but a deep and rich encounter with our
Creator.

One of the things that prevents us from seeing God as He really is, is
our preoccupation with how others behave toward us, when we should
be worrying about the way we have behaved toward God. History shows
that those who have really known God seem to have
exhibited little concern about what others have done
to them; they have been too busy focusing on how
they could arrive at a better knowledge of Him. Every
one of us must get hold of the fact that a little knowledge *of* God is worth more than a great deal of knowledge *about* Him. Thus we must pursue the vision
which Isaiah received in the Temple still further. One
thing is certain, we have come too far to turn back
now.

FURTHER STUDY
John 6:53-71;
Matt. 19:21

1. What did Peter
respond to Jesus'
question?

2. Why?

Prayer

O God, at last the doors of my life are beginning to turn outward instead of inward.
I am beginning to focus more on You than on myself. This feels so right. Lead me
on, my Father. I shall follow. In Christ's Name I pray. Amen.

The exclusiveness of God

"… and the one who trusts in him will never be put to shame."
(v. 6)

For reading & meditation – 1 Peter 2:1-12

As we continue looking at Isaiah's vision we come to the phrase: "… and the train of his robe filled the temple" (Isa. 6:1). The thought being conveyed here is of the exclusiveness of God. There is no room for anyone else in this high-exalted place. God is all in all.

A.W. Tozer, in his book *The Pursuit of God*, said: "When religion has said its last word, there is little that we need other than God Himself." So many of us have a faith in God which expresses itself something like this: God and a good job; God and good health. These things are fine as desires, but when they become demands we are revealing where our real trust lies. Let me ask you: Is God sufficient in your life? Maybe you have just learned that you have a terminal illness and you feel desperately alone. Is God enough? Or perhaps you have worked all your life to build up a business that has come crashing down and now you feel absolutely alone. Is God sufficient? Maybe your spouse has walked out on you and all you have left is God. Is He sufficient? Is He enough? As C.S. Lewis once put it: "You will never know how much you believe something until it is a matter of life and death."

The moment comes to us all when we find that the gods of this world are not gods. When that moment hits us where is our trust to be placed? At the highest point of the universe there is room for no one else but the Lord our God. Is He sufficient? Is He enough? With all my heart I say – He is. I hope you are able to say it too.

Prayer

O Father, with all my heart I affirm You are my sufficiency. You are enough! Forgive me that so often I rely on my own self-sufficiency or the sufficiency of others instead of depending on You. Forgive me and release me now. In Jesus' Name. Amen.

God "and"...

"... and you have been given fulness in Christ ..." (v.10)
For reading & meditation – Colossians 2:1-15

If, as we said yesterday, we have a faith in God which maintains we need God plus something else, the result will be that we will never discover God in all His fulness. In the "and" lies our greatest woe. If we omit the "and" we shall make some discoveries about God that will surprise us, and one of those surprises will be that He is perfectly capable of sustaining us in the most difficult situations. And we need not fear that by putting our trust fully in God we restrict our potential. As Augustine put it: "Thou hast formed us for Thyself and our hearts are restless till they find their rest in Thee."

When the Lord divided Canaan among the tribes of Israel, the Levites received no share of the land. God said: "I am your share and your inheritance" (Num. 18:20). Those words made the Levites richer than all their brethren, and this principle holds good for every child of God. The man or woman who knows God has the world's greatest treasure. He or she may not have many earthly treasures, but it will not make much difference, for in having Him they have everything that matters.

Imagine the Levites saying to God: "That's fine Lord, I want You to be my portion ... but what about that lake over there. And that mountain. Could we just have those? Do we look at the Lord who promises to be our portion and find that He is sufficient? Or are we still caught up with the idea that we need God plus something else? If we do then we do not really know God. We simply know about Him.

FURTHER STUDY

Col. 1:1-29;
Eph. 3:19;
John 1:16

1. What was Paul's prayer for the Colossians and Ephesians?

2. What did John testify of Jesus?

Prayer

O Father, help me remember that I belong to You, the all-creative, all-sufficient God. Make this truth come alive for me, not just in my head but in my heart. Let it become a conviction, not just an opinion. In Jesus' Name I pray. Amen.

No other gods

"You shall have no other gods before me." (v.3)
For reading & meditation – Exodus 20:1-21

Continuing the thought we have been examining over the past two days – that God wants to be our sufficiency – we look today at the opening statement of the Ten Commandments.

Why did God say: "I am the Lord your God ... You shall have no other gods before me"? And why does He still challenge us with that word when we want to make our gods of wood or stone? Of silver and gold? Of fame or fortune? The reason is that there *are* no other gods. We are fooling ourselves. We can give ourselves to them but they can't give themselves to us. Many of you will have come to the point (perhaps even today) when you discovered that the gods of this world are no gods. You pinned your hopes on something, gave yourself to it with the same energy as you would in worship, but it has let you down. This is how it is with the gods of this world.

I remember hearing Golda Meir, when she was Prime Minister of Israel, say: "The Jews have a fundamental problem with Moses. He led them through the wilderness for forty years and then brought them to the only place in the Middle East where there is no oil." When I heard her make that remark I thought to myself: "That's exactly why God did that – He wanted the Israelites to be dependent on Him, not on the earth's natural resources." So I ask you again: Do you look to the Lord who promises to be your inheritance, your portion, and see Him as sufficient? Or do you sometimes look to other gods? Let this truth sink deep into your soul – there are no other gods.

FURTHER STUDY

Ex. 3:1-21;
Gen. 15:1-21

1. What was God's response to Moses' first question?

2. What was God's response to Moses' second question?

Prayer

O God, forgive me when I have turned from You to other gods. You alone are God, and all life, individual and corporate, must finally bow the knee to You. I do so now gladly and willingly. Keep me bowed before You – always. In Jesus' Name. Amen.

God – the Enough!

"… 'I am God Almighty [El-Shaddai] …' " (v.1)
For reading & meditation – Genesis 17:1-22

We have been seeing that the phrase "and the train of his robe filled the temple" taken from Isaiah's vision suggests to us that there is room for no other in this exalted place. God is all in all. The Hebrew term for God, "El Shaddai", means "God – the Enough!" I like the thought that underlies that name – the Enough – because it brings home the truth that there is no situation in which we will ever find ourselves where God will not be enough.

God is much more than enough, of course. His sufficiency so immeasurably surpasses our demands. Nevertheless, it is marvellously comforting to know that however much more than enough God is to meet our needs, He is at least enough; nothing less than that.

There are many things in the world of which we think we do not have enough – money, power, status, education, and so on. And it is generally assumed that if only it were possible to have a sufficiency of "things", satisfaction would immediately result. But that is not so. The real trouble is not that people do not have enough "things", but that "things" in themselves are not enough. The plain fact is that there is ultimately only one way in which the human heart can have enough, or to be more exact, one Being who is enough for men and women, and that is God! As Dr Henry Van Dyke expressed it: "There is absolutely nothing that man cannot do without – except God." Remember – God is Enough. Only He is sufficient for us; only He can truly satisfy our souls. He, and only He is enough.

FURTHER STUDY

Eph. 3:14-21;
2 Cor. 9:8;
Psa. 36:8;
John 10:10

1. What is the heart of the apostle's prayer?

2. What has God promised?

Prayer

O Father, save me from thinking that anything can ever be a substitute for You. Just as Your glory filled all the Temple in Isaiah's day, so let Your glory fill me – exclusively. In Jesus' Name I ask it. Amen.

An encounter with the holy One

"Who of us can dwell with the consuming fire?" (v.14)
For reading & meditation – Isaiah 33:10-24

We look now at the next section of Isaiah's vision: "Above him were seraphs, each with six wings: With two wings they covered their faces, with two they covered their feet, and with two they were flying" (Isa. 6:2).

Seraphs are heavenly beings who serve above the throne of God. The sixth chapter of Isaiah contains the only references to seraphs in Scripture, but many commentators link them with the "living creatures" described in Revelation 4:8. The Hebrew word for "seraphs" means "burning ones" or "noble ones" and their specific ministry is to lead the continuous worship at the throne of God. One commentator suggests that they are described as "burning ones" because they are illuminated with the glory that comes from God's holy presence. He says: "It is not their own glory they display. It is rather a reflected glory – the glory of incandescent eternal holiness."

Ancient Christian writers often likened a close encounter with God to entering a danger zone. What did they mean? A contemporary author interprets it thus: "If we are sinful and God is holy, if God is a fire and we are straw, how can it be safe for us to enter His presence? The fact is, it is not safe. It is exceedingly dangerous." Why dangerous? The word "dangerous" is used because we differ from seraphs in that they are pure and we are not. Hence, the closer we get to God the more we run the risk of all that is unlike Him being consumed and destroyed. But when you think of it – isn't that the very reason why we ought to yearn to draw close to Him?

FURTHER STUDY

1 Cor. 3:10-17;
2 Cor. 4:18;
Heb. 12:27-29

1. What will be revealed with fire?

2. What will God remove by shaking?

Prayer

O Father, I see that this is something I cannot have too much of – an encounter with the holy One. I cannot be too much like You or have too much of Your holiness. Draw me, for I want to get as close as I can to Your holy fire. In Jesus' Name. Amen.

Lost & found

*"…let us be thankful, and so worship God acceptably with
reverence and awe …" (v.28)*

For reading & meditation – Hebrews 12:14-29

We are told that the seraphs who stood above the throne in Isaiah's vision had six wings: "With two wings they covered their faces, with two they covered their feet, and with two they were flying" (Isa. 6:2). Why cover their faces? Clearly they dared not look upon this One whom they were worshipping. The implication here is that what we do for God must be done with reverence.

One of the tragedies of modern-day Christianity is that quietly and almost unnoticed we are losing the spirit of reverence. Holy things are becoming common and are losing their sacredness. This is not happening everywhere, of course, but there is no doubt in my mind that the cynicism of the age is making its impact on the Church. If we do not resist it, the generations that follow will feel its effect in a hundred different ways.

I remember, as a teenager attending a Christian youth camp and taking part along with some others in a humorous "send up" of angels. The youth director hit the roof. He said: "You young people have trivialised something that is deeply sacred. I doubt whether you will have a correct view of angelic ministry ever again." He was right. Deep within me there has been a cynicism toward the ministry of angels for several decades, and it was only quite recently, while in Malaysia, that it was overcome. I was privileged to experience some awesome supernatural encounters that convinced me of the ministry of angels. It took several decades to undo what a few flippant moments had etched into my heart and mind. We dare not lose our reverence for holy things.

FURTHER STUDY

1 Pet. 1:1-17; 2:17;
Psa.33:8

1. How are we to live
our lives?

2. What are all the
people of the world
to do?

Prayer

O God, help me develop respect and reverence for holy things, but not to become over-spiritual about these matters and bore my friends with my solemnity and heaviness. That is not healthy either. Keep me balanced. In Jesus' Name. Amen.

"God's beautiful people"

"How beautiful ... are the feet of those who bring good news ..." (v. 7)

For reading & meditation – Isaiah 52:1-15

We continue thinking about the seraphs who stood above the throne in Isaiah's vision. We saw yesterday that with two wings they covered their faces, and now we consider the fact that with two they covered their feet. What is the significance of this? The implication here is that what is to be done for God must be done with humility.

The passage before us today draws our attention to the truth that the feet of God's heralds have a special importance, presumably because they speed the messengers of God's love on their way. Someone has pointed out that the only thing that is said to be "beautiful" about the followers of the Lord in Scripture is not their faces, or their figures, but their feet! That ought to keep us humble – if nothing else does. When worldly individuals talk about "beautiful" people they usually mean film, television or pop stars who live hedonistic lives – here today and burnt out tomorrow. God has His "beautiful" people too – those who carry the good news of the gospel wherever they go.

But the seraphs seem to be saying: "Oh, don't look at our feet. We want to focus the attention not on ourselves but on the Lord whom we are serving." This is true humility. Humble believers, while glorying in their task, seek to turn attention away from self to the Saviour and maintain the attitude which John the Baptist demonstrated when he said: "He must increase, but I must decrease" (John 3:30, AV). We should never forget that as far as our service for Christ is concerned, our task is not to draw attention to ourselves but to Him.

FURTHER STUDY

Matt. 18:1-9;
Prov. 22:4; 29:23;
Rom. 12:3

1. Who is the greatest in the kingdom of heaven?

2. How are we to think of ourselves?

Prayer

My Father and my God, grant in all my service to You that I will be hidden behind the cross, and the voice that people hear will not be mine alone, but the still small voice of the Holy Spirit speaking to them. In Christ's Name I pray. Amen.

Pursuing with passion

"The sorrows of those will increase who run after other gods." (v. 4)

For reading & meditation – Psalm 16:1-11

Now that we have examined the fact that the seraphs in Isaiah's vision had two wings covering their faces and two wings covering their feet, we focus on the phrase that says "with two they were *flying*". The implication here is that our service for God must be done with urgency.

As I considered the verse that is before us today, which points out how the ungodly chase after their gods, I thought how different it is with Christians. Few chase after God; they choose rather to saunter after Him. Christian service, generally speaking, is characterised more by lethargy than urgency, more by indolence than inspiration, and more by fitfulness than fervour. We say: "Yes, Lord, I'm available to You, providing it's convenient, providing it doesn't cost me anything." Contrast this with the attitude of people who serve the gods of sex, pleasure, fame, money, and so on. There is hardly a demand their gods make upon them that seems to be too much. They are willing to give up sleep, stay out until the early hours, and spend any amount they have to in order to satisfy their gods. Many Christians are like the young man who told his girlfriend: "Darling, I would go through fire and water for you." Then a few minutes later he said: "I'll see you tomorrow night if it isn't raining."

The seraphs of Isaiah's vision remind us that what we do for God must be done with urgency and passion. There is something terribly wrong when our Christian lives lack those qualities. God moves toward us with urgency and passion; do we move with urgency and passion toward Him?

FURTHER STUDY

2 Cor. 5:1-15;
Psa. 42:1-2

1. What did Christ's love do to Paul?

2. How did the psalmist describe his spiritual desire?

Prayer

O God, how can I ever thank You enough for pursuing me with urgency and passion? It meant so much to You to win me to Yourself. Grant that my passion might match Your passion, if not in degree, in kind. In Jesus' Name. Amen.

Our primary task

*"Ascribe to the Lord the glory due to his name; worship the
Lord in the splendour of his holiness." (v.2)*
For reading & meditation – Psalm 29:1-11

We come now to a marvellous section of Isaiah's vision where he
speaks of the seraphs in this way: "... they were calling to one
another: 'Holy, holy, holy is the Lord Almighty; the whole earth is full of
his glory.' At the sound of their voices the doorposts and thresholds
shook and the temple was filled with smoke" (Isa. 6:3-4).

What a moment this must have been for Isaiah as he watched the seraphs darting and hovering above the throne, and listened to them calling to one another and worshipping God with voices so strong that the
sound shook the Temple! Is it any wonder that echoes of the time he
spent in the Temple are heard in almost every one of the later chapters
of his prophecy? The lofty throne, the attending seraphs and the words
they utter all combine to spell out one message: worship is the highest
function of any of God's created beings.

What is worship? The essential meaning of the word in both Old and
New Testaments is that of reverential service – a truth we see illustrated
by the conduct of the winged seraphs above the eternal throne. Our present-day English word "worship" has evolved from the Anglo-Saxon
weorthscipe which means to give worth to someone or
something. Worship can best be understood by thinking of the word in this way: worth-ship. The worship
of God, then, is attributing worth to Him – and only
Him.

The primary reason for our existence on this earth
is to worship God. When we understand all that is
involved in this then our faith will throb with a new
power and prove itself sufficient for any task.

FURTHER STUDY

Psa. 84:1-12;
95:1-7;
1 Chron. 16:29

1. What did the
psalmist say is
better?

2. How are we to
come in worship?

Prayer

Father, I ask myself in Your presence: How much of my life is spent in worship?
How much time do I give to thinking of You and only You? Help me draw near to
You, not to ask for things, but just to worship You. In Jesus' Name I pray. Amen.

"A constant pageant of worship"

"... and serve him day and night in his temple ..." (v.15)
For reading & meditation – Revelation 7:1-17

We pick up from where we left off yesterday when we considered the nature and importance of worship. We must be careful not to fall into the trap of differentiating between worship and service, and thinking to ourselves that when we kneel in private we are at worship and when active in the church – teaching, preaching, or being of some practical help – we are then engaged in service. All service is worship, and all worship is service.

This thought is brought out not only in the symbolism of the seraphs whom Isaiah saw above the throne but it is found also in the passage before us today. In the book of Revelation heaven is described as a place that is filled with worship, but it is also a place where the saints "serve ... day and night". I love the story of the young housewife who, having been converted to Christ and realising that everything she did was an act of worship, put a sign over her kitchen sink which read: "Divine service conducted here three times a day." Later she saw that her acts of worship were not confined to washing the dishes but included everything. So she took down the sign because it was too limiting.

Someone asked a friend of mine once: "Where do you worship?" He replied "I worship in Woolworths, in the bank, in my car, in the supermarket ... My life is a constant pageant of worship." The person got the message. Worship is not something we keep for special occasions or do at certain times and periods. We worship both day and night.

FURTHER STUDY

Rom. 12:1-8;
John 4:24

1. What is to be our
spiritual act of
worship?

2. How are we to
worship God?

Prayer

Father, forgive me that I have been thinking of worship as something that goes on only at certain times or seasons. Help me to worship You everywhere and in everything. May my life too be a constant pageant of worship. In Jesus' Name. Amen.

Worship, praise and thanksgiving

"Yet you are enthroned as the Holy One; you are the praise of Israel." (v.3)

For reading & meditation – Psalm 22:1-11

We ask ourselves now: What is the scriptural relationship between worship, praise and thanksgiving?

All the biblical words for worship, whether in Hebrew or Greek, indicate an attitude of the heart or a posture of the body. Worship starts as being spiritual but also affects us physically. This is why devout Jews rock backward and forward when they pray; they regard worship as both physical and spiritual. The Bible describes such physical postures as lying face downwards before the Lord, kneeling in His presence, or standing before Him with uplifted hands as worship. Praise, on the other hand, has to do with utterance, and while it is not exclusive to our lips (we can praise God in our hearts), it is generally related to the words of our mouth. When we come to thanksgiving we come again to the thought of utterance, the difference being this: we praise God for who He is, but we thank Him for what He does. These are only general categories, of course, and we must not think in rigid terms when we praise, give thanks, or worship. Nothing could be worse than saying to yourself: "I have spent enough time in praise now. Perhaps I should spend an equal time in thanksgiving."

FURTHER STUDY

1 Thess. 5:1-18;
Psa. 100:4; 107:22

1. What is the will of God for us?

2. In what circumstances are we to give thanks?

All three words relate very much to three characteristics of God – again, speaking generally. In worship we relate to God's holiness. In thanksgiving we relate to God's goodness. In praise we relate to God's greatness. Although the distinction between these three words can be clearly seen in Scripture, it must not be regarded as hard and fast. The three are tributaries that flow together to form one great river.

Prayer

Father, may all these three – worship, thanksgiving and praise – be present in my life not in a mechanical way but in a natural way. All I want, dear Lord, is for You to be glorified in me. Help me to do just that. In Jesus' Name. Amen.

"The joyful exchange"

"Give, and it will be given to you." (v.38)
For reading & meditation – Luke 6:27-38

Before leaving the subject of worship, we must come to grips with the question of why God requires us to worship Him. Many struggle with this thought, especially in the early days of their Christian life. I can remember as a young Christian wondering: Why does God insist on us worshipping Him? Is it because He has an ego problem?

One of those who grappled with this problem was C.S. Lewis. He recalled how at one stage he thought God was really saying: "What I want most is to be told I am good and great." He came to see, however, that, in asking for our worship, God has in mind our enjoyment more than His own. He wrote: "In commanding us to worship Him, God is inviting us to enjoy Him." He went on to point out that, because of the great respect God has for every human will, He will not force Himself upon us. He is, therefore, unable to give Himself to us until we first give ourselves to Him.

The law of giving and receiving is fundamental, and relates just as much to God as it does to us. As we go through the door of giving ourselves to God in worship we find that God comes through that same door and gives Himself to us. God's insistence that we worship Him is not really a demand at all but an offer – an offer to share Himself with us. When God asks us to worship Him, He is asking us to fulfil the deepest longing in Himself, which is His passionate desire to give Himself to us. It is what Martin Luther called "the joyful exchange".

FURTHER STUDY
Matt. 10:1-8;
Acts 20:35

1. What were the disciples to do?

2. Why?

Prayer

O Father, how can I thank You sufficiently for coming through the door of Your own self-giving to stand at the door of my heart? You have given Yourself to me; now I give myself to You. This is truly a "a joyful exchange". Amen.

The one thing

"I am the Lord, your Holy One, Israel's Creator, your King."
(v.15)

For reading & meditation – Isaiah 43:14-28

We continue focusing our thoughts on Isaiah's vision of the worshipping seraphs above the throne and today we ask ourselves: What is the one thing above all others that true worshippers think of when approaching God? His Almightiness? His goodness? His faithfulness? The answer is: His holiness! You have only to comb the record of the Scriptures – particularly the Old Testament – to discover that those who were closest to the Lord thought more about His holiness than about any other attribute.

What exactly do we mean when we talk about the holiness of God? Theologians tell us that, strictly speaking, we should not think of divine holiness as an attribute but as the essential ingredient that holds God together. "Holiness," says J. Muilenburg, "is the distinctive mark and signature of the divine. More than any other, the term 'holiness' gives expression to the essential nature of the sacred. It is therefore to be understood, not as one attribute among other attributes, but as the innermost reality to which all others are related." These are powerful words because they point out that holiness is the way God is. Because He is holy, all His attributes are holy. Whatever we think of as belonging to God must be thought of as holy. This is why theologians insist that, whenever we talk about the love of God, we talk about it as *holy* love. If we remove God's love from the thought of holiness we can easily come out with sentimentalism, and a clear example of that can be seen in the vapid theorising about God that goes on in some of the liberal churches of our day.

FURTHER STUDY

Rev. 15:1-8;
1 Pet. 1:15;
Lev. 11:44-45

1. What did the angels sing?

2. What is the standard God requires?

Prayer

O Father, as I survey the wonder of Your holiness I too, like the worshipping seraphs, want to join in the refrain and say: "Holy, holy, holy is the Lord Almighty. The whole earth is full of Your glory." I worship Your holy Name. Amen.

The divine emphasis

"I am the Lord ... your God; therefore be holy, because I am holy." (v.45)

For reading & meditation – Leviticus 11:26-47

Did it surprise you to discover yesterday that the holiness of God is emphasised more than any other aspect of His nature? Stephen Charnock, a renowned theologian, says this: "God is oftener styled Holy than Almighty and set forth by this part of His dignity more than by any other. This is more fixed on as an epithet to His name than any other. You never find expressed 'His mighty name' or 'His wise name' but His *great* name and most of all His *holy* name." He goes on to make a statement that I pray will make as deep an impression upon you as it did upon me:

"As it seems to challenge an excellency above all His other perfections, so it is the glory of all the rest; as it is the glory of the Godhead, so it is the glory of every perfection of the Godhead; as His power is the strength of them, so His holiness is the beauty of them; as all would be weak without almightiness to back them, so all would be uncomely without holiness to adorn them. Should this be sullied, all the rest would lose their honour, as at the same instant the sun should lose its light, it would lose its heat, its strength, its generative and quickening virtue. As sincerity is the lustre of every grace in a Christian, so is purity the splendour of every attribute in the Godhead. His justice is a holy justice. His wisdom a holy wisdom. His arm of power 'a holy arm' (Psa. 98:1). His truth or promise a 'holy promise' (Psa. 105:42). His name which signifies all attributes in conjunction is 'holy' (Psa. 103:1)."

FURTHER STUDY

Rom. 1:1-7; Ex. 16:23; Deut. 26:15; 1 Chron. 29:3; Neh. 11:1; 2 Thess. 1:10

1. What other things are described as holy?

2. Would you describe yourself as holy?

Prayer

O Father, if ever Your Church needed a fresh vision of Your holiness it is today. Fill our pulpits with prophets and teachers who have a knowledge of the Holy. This we ask in Christ's peerless and precious Name. Amen.

"The attribute of attributes"

"… 'Holy, holy, holy is the Lord God Almighty, who was, and is, and is to come'. " (v.8)

For reading & meditation – Revelation 4:1-11

We see from the threefold cry of the winged seraphs – "Holy, holy, holy" (Isa. 6:3) – that the holiness of God is celebrated as no other attribute is celebrated before the throne of heaven. God Himself singles out this perfection to be honoured in a way that shows it to be, as John Howe put it, "the attribute of attributes".

The cry of the seraphs is significant because this is the only place in Scripture, apart from the passage before us today, where the word "holy" is repeated three times. Emphasis in Hebrew (as in English) is sometimes conveyed by repeating a word. Jesus, you remember, often used this device when He introduced a subject by saying "Verily, verily, I say unto you …". But the word "holy" is repeated not just twice but three times – the implication being, we are in the presence of something profound. And indeed we are – the ineffable holiness of God.

Try something with me. Read slowly through the following texts, and see what happens. "Who will not fear you, O Lord, and bring glory to your name? For you alone are holy" (Rev. 15:4). "Who among the gods is like you, O Lord? Who is like you – majestic in holiness, awesome in glory, working wonders?" (Ex. 15:11). "For I am God, and not man – the Holy One among you" (Hosea 11:9). "'Do not be afraid, O worm Jacob … for I myself will help you,' declares the Lord, your Redeemer, the Holy One of Israel" (Isa. 41:14). Is it not a fact that the more you make yourself aware of God's holiness the more honour and respect you want to give Him?

FURTHER STUDY

Matt. 6:5-13;
Luke 1:49;
Psa. 30:4; 105:3

1. What is the first thing Christ focused on in His prayer?

2. What are we to glory in?

Prayer

O Lord my God, there is none like You in heaven above or in the earth beneath; glorious in holiness, mighty in splendour, and wondrous in majesty. I worship You my Father. Words die on my lips but my heart is Yours for ever. Amen.

Holiness is healthiness

"... let us purify ourselves from everything that contaminates body and spirit, perfecting holiness out of reverence for God." (v. 1)

For reading & meditation – 2 Corinthians 7:1-16

We said a few days ago that when we study the Scriptures, particularly the Old Testament, we find that those who got closest to God thought more of His holiness than any other thing. Why should this be? I think in the nature of things it cannot be any other way, because, more than anything else, God wants us to be holy. Over and over again in the Bible we are told: "Be holy even as I am holy." We are not directed to be omnipotent (all-powerful) or omniscient (all-wise) as God is, but we are to be holy. This is the prime way of honouring God. We do not glorify Him by eloquent expressions or pompous service, but by aspiring to converse with Him with unstained spirits and live to Him in living *like* Him.

Are you seeking to be holy? God has made holiness the moral condition necessary to the health of His universe. Sin's temporary presence in the world only accentuates this. Whatever is holy is healthy, and evil is a moral sickness that must ultimately end in death. The formation of the language itself suggests this, the English word "holy" deriving from the Anglo-Saxon *halig* meaning "well" or "whole". To be whole in Christian terms means to be holy. Can you say "I am holy – truly holy"? I am afraid I can't. I don't think any honest Christian would say "Yes" to that question. But neither would any honest Christian ignore these solemn words: "Make every effort to live in peace with all men and to be holy; without holiness no-one will see the Lord" (Heb. 12:14).

FURTHER STUDY

Luke 1:67-80;
2 Pet. 3:11;
2 Cor. 7:1

1. Why has God raised up a horn of salvation?

2. What kind of people ought we to be?

Prayer

O Father, help me to be as concerned for the moral health of the universe as You are. But more, help me to focus first on my own moral health and to be rid of all in my life that is contrary to You and Your nature. In Jesus' Name I ask it. Amen.

The divine X-ray

"The Israelites said to Moses, 'We shall die! We are lost, we are all lost!'" (v.12)

For reading & meditation – Numbers 17:1-13

We move on now to consider the fact that Isaiah's revolutionary vision of the holiness of God results in him crying out in great agony of soul: "Woe to me … I am ruined! For I am a man of unclean lips, and I live among a people of unclean lips …" (Isa. 6:5).

The thing that strikes Isaiah as he stands in the presence of God is not just the ineffable holiness of God, but, by contrast, his own personal depravity. Up to this moment Isaiah probably thought of himself as a good, upright, moral man. And no doubt he was. If someone was to compare the young Isaiah's character with that of most of the other men and women in Israel, I feel confident that he would have stood out head and shoulders above most of them. However, Isaiah is not being compared to the creatures whom God had made; he is being compared to the Creator Himself. He is face to face with the Holy One of Israel. Suddenly, all his goodness and everything he had esteemed falls to pieces, and he stands naked, exposed and afraid.

I have always thought it interesting that the people who are farthest away from the Lord are those who are impressed with their own goodness, while those who are closest to Him seem to be more conscious of their sin. Why, I wonder? Is it because the white light of God's holiness acts like an X-ray that enables people to see more clearly what is going on at the core of their beings? If so, then how vital it is that sin-sick human beings have an encounter with a holy God.

FURTHER STUDY

Eph. 5:1-20;
1 John 1:5-7;
2 Pet. 1:19

1. How are we to live?
2. What are we to pay attention to?

Prayer

O God, let the X-ray of Your holiness reveal the insidious disease of sin that is deep within me. Show up the pride and arrogance that lies hidden in my nature. Make me more like You, dear Lord. In Jesus' Name. Amen.

Invest now!

"But just as he who called you is holy, so be holy in all you do." (v.15)

For reading & meditation – 1 Peter 1:3-25

We acknowledged yesterday that those who see the holiness of God most clearly see themselves most clearly. The white light of God's holiness is like an X-ray that enables them to discern the sin that is deeply hidden in their nature. We all know in an intellectual way that to catch sight of God's ineffable holiness would make us conscious of our own sin, but how many of us are willing to draw near enough to God for Him to show us what His holiness is like? It is one thing to imagine what it might be like; it is another thing to experience it. Dr John White, in *The Shattered Mirror*, puts the same thought in this way: "We can get some idea of the matter by imagining what it would be like to find ourselves, say, at a royal garden party, surrounded by impeccably dressed royal guests, while we were still unwashed and wearing the old, rough clothes in which we had just finished gardening. The difference between that imaginary experience and Isaiah's encounter with God is not merely one of degree, but a quality we could know only by experiencing it ourselves."

How can we experience it ourselves? We can begin by looking at the nature of God's holiness as outlined in His Word. Then continue by waiting before God in fervent, believing prayer and inviting God to reveal Himself to you. This takes time, of course, but any time spent with God is spiritual investment. But remember, a vision of God and His holiness will be emotionally overwhelming. It will cause you not only to cry out "Holy, holy, holy," but also, "Woe to me! I am ruined!"

FURTHER STUDY

Luke 18:9-14;
1 Cor. 10:12;
Prov. 28:26

1. What did Jesus teach in this parable?

2. What did Paul warn the Corinthians?

Prayer

O Father, I am afraid as I draw near, yet I draw near because I am afraid. Show me even more clearly that the time I spend with You will yield more than it costs. Whatever sacrifice is needed, help me make it. In Jesus' Name. Amen.

Fearing for one's life!

"Anyone who even comes near the tabernacle of the Lord will die." (v.13)

For reading & meditation – Numbers 17:1-13

Today we ask ourselves: What did Isaiah mean when, following the vision of God's holiness, he said: "I am a man of unclean lips, and I live among a people of unclean lips …" (Isa. 6:5)? Some commentators believe he was confessing here to a struggle with profanity. Probably a more likely explanation is that Isaiah is acknowledging his unworthiness to be a prophet – the spoken word being a prophet's business.

Which of these is the true explanation we cannot be certain, but what we do know for sure is this: when Isaiah saw the holiness of God he feared for his life. This is evident in his statement: "My eyes have seen the King, the Lord Almighty" (Isa. 6:5). Why should such seemingly innocuous words reflect a fear for his life? To understand what is being said here we need to look at today's text once again: "Anyone who even comes near the tabernacle of the Lord will die." It was a well-known fact in Israel that no one could get close to God and live. Anyone who saw God expected to die immediately. In fact, God said on one occasion: "You cannot see my face, for no-one may see me and live" (Ex. 33:20).

Perhaps now we can understand something of the concern that reverberated beneath the words: "My eyes have seen the King, the Lord Almighty." Isaiah's cry reflects much more than an ordinary conviction of sin; it is one of unspeakable horror. He had seen the King, the Lord Almighty. Now he must die! But does he? No, for as we shall see, God is not only a God of holiness – He is also the God of grace.

FURTHER STUDY

Ex. 33:12-21;
1 Tim. 1:17;
6:11-16

1. What was Moses' prayer?

2. How did Paul describe the Lord to Timothy?

Prayer

Father, help me see even more clearly the principle that is at work here, namely that before I can be saved I must admit my lostness – my utter helplessness. I freely confess, Father, that salvation is all of grace. And I am deeply, deeply thankful. Amen.

"Surprised by joy!"

"For it is by grace you have been saved ..." (v.8)
For reading & meditation – Ephesians 2:1-22

One thing ought to be clear by now – the more we know of God the more we will discover that He is holy, and that we are unholy. It doesn't hurt us to know that; it helps us. Something occurs in the contrast that prepares us to open ourselves more fully to His grace. Listen to how Tozer put it: "No one can know the true grace of God who has not first known the fear of God. The presence of the Divine has always brought fear to the hearts of sinful men. Always there was something about any manifestation of God that ... struck them with a terror more than natural. Until we have been gripped by that nameless terror which results when an unholy creature is suddenly confronted by that One who is the holiest of all, we are not likely to be much affected by the doctrine of love and grace."

How illuminating are those words. It isn't that God delights in striking fear into our hearts by the revelation of His holiness; it is just that being who He is, He cannot reveal Himself to us without this happening. But always His mercy and grace come to our aid to sustain us and cleanse us. Watch now as God moves toward Isaiah, not in judgment, but in grace. In the vision He inspires one of the seraphs to take a live coal from the altar, place it on the prophet's lips and declare: "Your guilt is taken away and your sin atoned for." Isaiah does not tell us what effect the seraph's action had on him. But if it was anything like the experience I had when He cleansed me then Isaiah would have been, as C.S. Lewis expressed it, "surprised by joy".

FURTHER STUDY

Titus 3:1-8;
Lam. 3:22-23;
Micah 7:18

1. What is the basis of
   our salvation?

2. What does God
   delight to do?

Prayer

Thank You, my Father, that I too have been "surprised by joy". When I expected to be consigned to hell You showed me the way to heaven. How can I ever sufficiently thank You for Your grace? All honour and glory be to You for ever. Amen.

Forgiven!

"He himself bore our sins in his body on the tree ..." (v.24)
For reading & meditation – 1 Peter 2:11-25

We must spend at least one more day reflecting on the wonder of the grace and forgiveness that flowed toward Isaiah at that significant moment in the Temple. Listen to the words once more: "See, this has touched your lips; your guilt is taken away and your sin atoned for" (Isa. 6:7).

In Christian circles we talk so easily about forgiveness. But do we really understand what it cost God to forgive? David Seamands points out that forgiveness is always at great cost to the forgiving one. He says: "When someone hurts us and we forgive them we take the hurt and indignation we feel and turn it back upon ourselves. Instead of putting it upon them we bear it in ourselves." Some people require of others that they be put on probation before forgiveness is given. I knew a man who, whenever his wife hurt him, would make her almost beg for days for his forgiveness. How different is real forgiveness. No marriage can properly operate without it – and no friendship either. Forgiveness means taking your own pride, your own indignation, your own hurt, holding it to your heart and quenching it in the flame of your love. This is what God does with us when He forgives.

FURTHER STUDY

1 John 1:5-10;
Psa. 130:4;
Eph. 1:7;
Isa. 43:25

1. How do we deceive ourselves?

2. What is the condition for receiving forgiveness?

We are now moving beyond Isaiah's vision to consider the genius of the gospel, namely that in God there is not only holiness but forgiveness also. Divine forgiveness, however, is costly. It cost God His only Son. Our text for today puts it powerfully when it says: "He himself bore our sins in his body on the tree." Can anything in earth or heaven be more wonderful?

Prayer

O God, nothing that anyone has done or can do against me compares to what I have done against You. Yet You have forgiven me. Help me now to forgive others, and to forgive graciously, not grudgingly. In Jesus' Name I ask it. Amen.

"An ounce of experience"

*"Some time later God tested Abraham. He said to him,
'Abraham!' 'Here I am,' he replied." (v.1)*

For reading & meditation – Genesis 22:1-19

As soon as Isaiah has been cleansed, he hears God's voice crying out: "Whom shall I send? And who will go for us?" Isaiah immediately responds: "Here am I. Send me!" (Isa. 6:8).

It is always a mystery to me that God wants stubborn and recalcitrant human beings on His team when He has ranks of angels who delight to do His bidding. But when you think of it, angels are limited by the one thing that is needful for God's ambassadors on earth – experience. Angels could put God's truth more eloquently, and present the divine arguments more powerfully, but they know nothing of the experience of grace, at least subjectively. They witness it at work in our lives, but they have never experienced it at work in themselves.

An old saying goes like this: "An ounce of experience is worth a ton of theory." How true. I can almost guarantee that the person who influenced you to come to Christ was himself or herself someone who had experienced the grace of God. I know people have been converted when listening to other people talk about the gospel who were not converted themselves. However, that is more the exception than the rule. The implication behind the words "Who will go for us?" is that the task on earth has to be done by the men and women on earth. Isaiah didn't hesitate. What about you? Is God calling you to some task, and you feel hesitant and uncertain? Perhaps it is because you have not had a powerful enough vision of the Lord. Those who see Him – really see Him – cannot help but say: "Here am I. Send me!"

FURTHER STUDY

1 Cor. 1:18-31;
John 15:16;
Acts 9:15;
James 2:5

1. What sort of people
has God chosen?

2. What did the Lord
say to Ananias?

Prayer

O God, day by day I am seeing more of Your glory, but give me an overwhelming vision of Yourself that will shatter every one of my self-concerns. Help me say in response to whatever You are calling me to: "Here am I. Send me!" Amen.

"The strange predicament of God"

*"The Lord sent me to prophesy against this house and this
city ... " (v.12)*

For reading & meditation – Jeremiah 26:1-16

We spend another day reflecting on the cry of God: "Whom shall I send. And who will go for us?" Someone has described this as "the strange predicament of God" – the Almighty asking help of human beings. Probably nothing is more difficult to understand as regards Christian truth than this, that the Almighty God, who holds the world in the hollow of His hand, seeks to enlist our support in relaying His truth.

Did this confuse Isaiah, I wonder? He had seen a vision of the majesty of God, and now this Almighty God was asking for Isaiah's co-operation. Why does He suddenly appear to be so powerless? Well, it isn't because God is powerless that He asks our help. He chooses to do so because that is His way. He wants us to be involved with Him in redeeming the world.

But we ask again: Why has God tied His own hands in this way? What is His rationale for wanting us on His team? John Wesley is reported to have said: "God does nothing in the world redemptively except through prayer." He seems to be saying in this statement that in bringing about redemptive changes in the universe, God moves, and only moves, through the prayers of His people. These are staggering words of Wesley's but I am in agreement with them fully and wholeheartedly. God could do His redemptive work here on earth without us, but He chooses not to because He wants it to be a team effort. Does that mean that if you and I do not make ourselves available to Him then some things just might not get done? I wonder.

FURTHER STUDY

Haggai 2:20-23;
1 Pet. 2:1-10

1. What was Haggai
to tell Zerubbabel?

2. How does Peter
describe God's
people?

Prayer

Father, it humbles me to think that You want me on Your team. I am overwhelmed by the invitation, but my heart cries out "Yes, Yes, Yes!" Use me in any way You want to and to go anywhere You want me to go. Here I am. Send me!

A call to failure!

"Hear this, you … who have eyes but do not see, who have ears but do not hear." (v.21)

For reading & meditation – Jeremiah 5:18-31

Once Isaiah has responded to the call of God with the words "Here am I. Send me!" the task he has been set is given in these words: "Go and tell this people: 'Be ever hearing, but never understanding; be ever seeing, but never perceiving.' Make the heart of this people calloused; make their ears dull and close their eyes. Otherwise they might see with their eyes, hear with their ears, understand with their hearts, and turn and be healed!" (Isa. 6:9-10). What a depressing commission. This is none other than a call to failure! God clearly tells Isaiah that his message will have the ironic but justly deserved effect of hardening the callous hearts of the rebellious people of Judah, thus rendering the warnings of judgment sure.

How do you think Isaiah felt about the fact that after offering himself as a messenger of God he is told that his message will have a hardening rather than a softening effect? He is given not so much a saving word as a searing word. Whatever he felt, we know one thing for certain – he set out to faithfully preach the word he had been given.

How many of us, I wonder, would respond to God with the words "Here I am. Send me!" if we thought God would commission us to failure? Speaking personally, I think I would have a big struggle with that. When the chips are down, few of us are willing to do what God says when we don't know whether the outcome will be successful or not. Perhaps it is because we don't know God well enough. We have seen Him only in part.

FURTHER STUDY

Matt. 26:36-45;
6:10; Rom. 6:13

1. How did Jesus
respond to what
seemed a path to
failure?

2. What do we need to
continually echo in
the Lord's Prayer?

Prayer

O God, I am Your disciple, but sometimes I am afraid to follow where You lead me. Help me do Your bidding whatever the outcome. And help me evaluate success not by what my senses say, but by what You say. In Jesus' Name. Amen.

No excuse

"You will be ever hearing but never understanding; you will be ever seeing but never perceiving." (v.14)

For reading & meditation – Matthew 13:1-17

How are we to understand the strange words God spoke to Isaiah that we looked at yesterday: "Make the heart of this people calloused; make their ears dull … close their eyes"?

The full flavour of the Hebrew language is drawn upon to describe the condition of those who harden their hearts against the Word of the Lord. We have to understand that the gospel is not only good news but also bad news. Good news to those who receive it; bad news to those who reject it. The gospel heard and accepted is life; the gospel heard and refused is death. As Dr Martyn Lloyd-Jones put it: "The same sun that melts ice, hardens clay." It is interesting that these words of Isaiah are quoted by Jesus in our reading today, and they are applied by Him to the people of His time. In fact, these words of Isaiah (in part) are found in every one of the four Gospels. The apostle Paul also quotes these words in the last chapter of the Acts of the Apostles, when explaining that God was turning the focus away from Israel to the Gentiles, and outlining the fact that, unlike the stubborn Israelites, the Gentiles "will listen" (Acts 28:28).

FURTHER STUDY

Rom. 1:18-23;
John 15:22

1. Why does Romans say that people are without excuse?

2. Why did Jesus say that people are without excuse?

Now, it is important to realise that neither God in Isaiah 6:9 nor Jesus in the passage before us is saying that some hearers will not understand but, rather, that those who are not willing to hear the Word of the Lord will find the truth hidden from them. But why preach the gospel to those who will not receive it? It is to expose and highlight their hard-hearted resistance in such a way that no one will be able to say they did not hear, and so that they will be absolutely without excuse when judgment comes.

Prayer

O Father, I see even more clearly that Your Word is not only a saving Word but a searing Word; it heals but also hardens. Save me from allowing my own feelings to hinder its accomplishment – positively or negatively. In Jesus' Name. Amen.

One ray of hope

*"… there is hope for a tree: If it is cut down, it will sprout
again …" (v.7)*

For reading & meditation – Job 14:1-12

As we draw to the close of the great passage in Isaiah 6 we examine the final words: "Then I said, 'For how long, O Lord?' … 'Until the cities lie ruined and without inhabitant, until the houses are left deserted and field ruined and ravaged, until the Lord has sent everyone far away and the land is utterly forsaken. And though a tenth remains in the land, it will again be laid waste. But as the terebinth and oak leave stumps when they are cut down, so the holy seed will be the stump in the land' " (Isa. 6:11-13).

Clearly Isaiah is going to witness Israel becoming like a wasteland. He has a long hard job ahead of him, prophesying to a people who, in the main, just do not want to hear. There is one ray of hope which we see in the last phrase of the chapter. *The Living Bible* puts it most effectively: "Yet a tenth – a remnant – will survive; and though Israel is invaded again and again and destroyed, yet Israel will be like a tree cut down, whose stump still lives to grow again."

When would the people listen? Only after they had come to the end and had nowhere to turn but to God. This would happen when the land was destroyed by invading armies and the people taken into captivity. The remnant referred to are those who either remained in the land after the captivity, or those who returned from Babylon to rebuild Jerusalem.

Oh, why don't we listen to God? Will we, like Israel, pursue our own paths and come back to Him only when we have nowhere left to turn? Is God speaking to you about this today? If so, consider what He may be telling you and obey Him while there is time.

FURTHER STUDY

Rom. 9:22-10:1;
11:1-36

1. What has been the
result of Israel's
unbelief?

2. What was Paul's
prayer for the
Israelites?

Prayer

O Father, when will I learn that Your way is the only sure way. Forgive me for the times when I prefer my way to Your way, and kill within me all those desires that put self-interest before Your interests. In Jesus' Name I ask it. Amen.

Enjoying majority status!

"So too, at the present time there is a remnant chosen by grace." (v.5)

For reading & meditation – Romans 11:1-12

We linger a little longer on the last two sentences of Isaiah 6: "And though a tenth remains in the land, it will again be laid waste. But as the terebinth and oak leave stumps when they are cut down, so the holy seed will be the stump in the land."

The prophet is being told that Israel will become a sick society and will finish up like a wasteland, but there will be a remnant who will hold on to God and be faithful. He is told also that there will be one tree left, indeed, one stump, and out of that stump will come a new tree! Even a felled tree leaves a stump behind which may produce fresh growth. The phrase "the holy seed" refers, without doubt, to the coming of the Messiah, the One who would redeem Israel and extend the offer of salvation beyond its borders to the whole world.

We should never be concerned that those who uphold God's cause always seem to be in the minority. Those who were truly spiritual were in the minority in Old Testament times and in New Testament times too. I am not an alarmist, but I have to say that I see a parallel between Isaiah's day and the day in which we live. What a state we are in at the present moment – and things are destined to get worse. But God has His remnant in this age as He has had in every age. If you are a committed follower of Jesus Christ then you are part of that remnant. And God has always used a redeemed remnant to change the world. You and I may be in the minority as far as the world is concerned, but as someone once pointed out: "One person with God is in the majority." We are minorities with a majority status! Hallelujah!

FURTHER STUDY

Isa. 63:7-16;
Deut. 14:2;
John 1:12;
Rom. 8:15; Gal. 4:6

1. What have we received the Spirit of?

2. What does this cause us to do?

Prayer

Father, I am thankful that I am part of today's remnant but I am even more thankful that that remnant is part of You. By myself I am nothing but with You I am a number. And what a number! Amen.

It's Jesus!

"Isaiah said this because he saw Jesus' glory and spoke about him." (v.41)

For reading & meditation – John 12:37-49

On this, our final day of meditating on the sixth chapter of Isaiah, we look at something quite astonishing. John tells us in the passage we have just read that the vision Isaiah received that day in the Temple was really a vision of Jesus and His glory. John is telling us that hidden in the darkness and smoke of the Temple our Lord was present – and present in all His glory. Right now I want to challenge you to open yourself up to a new vision of the glory of the Lord. Why? Because it is only when we see God as He is that we can see ourselves as we are and then, and only then, are we equipped to move out and minister to others. Our God calls us to serve Him, but He calls us to serve Him in holiness.

We live in a day that is similar in many ways to that of Isaiah – times of great confusion, great strife and great uncertainty. The balance of power is shifting from one nation to another, and every day something appears in our newspapers that makes us wonder what will happen next. Personally, I do not know what the next few years are going to hold for the nations of the earth, or for our witness as the Christian Church around the world. But we do know that the Lord is Lord. He is sovereign. He rules over all. He is high and exalted. He is holy and supreme. And all our problems pale in the light of His sufficiency.

We need to remind ourselves over and over again – *there are no other gods*. The leaders of the nations may strut around on the world's stage but they are not gods – just creatures of whom the Creator can easily dispose. Lift up your eyes to the eternal throne – and keep them there. Our God reigns – but He reigns in holiness.

FURTHER STUDY

Rev. 1:10-18;
2 Cor. 12:2-4

1. How does John describe himself on the Lord's Day?

2. What was Paul's testimony?

Prayer

Father, may the vision of Your glory that transformed Isaiah also transform me. Help me to walk through the earth with my gaze firmly fixed on You. Thank You for what You have taught me. To You be all the honour, all the glory and all the praise. Amen.

From Confusion to Confidence

Sure-footedness

*"The Lord God ... will make my feet like deer's
feet ..." (v.19, NKJ)*
For reading & meditation – Habakkuk 3:17-19

Today we embark upon a journey that will reveal the steps we must
take in order to move from confusion to confidence, or from fear to
faith. There can be no doubt, to my mind at least, that we are facing one
of the most momentous times in human history. Millions of the earth's
inhabitants are bewildered. They are not sure that the political leaders
and scientists know what they are doing. One of the most recent scares
to hit humanity – the dreadful disease "AIDS" – is causing growing con-
sternation in all parts of the world. However we look at our generation,
something appears to have snapped and life is left dangling at loose ends.

The question that faces us at this hour is this: How can we, as God's
people, walk through life with confidence and poise? Is there some formula we can discover, that will prevent our feet from slipping and sliding as we traverse the rocky slopes of this sick and confused world? I
believe there is – and that formula is brought clearly into focus in the
prophecy of Habakkuk. Although he begins his book in utter confusion,
he ends, as we see from our text for today, in a spirit of abounding
confidence.

FURTHER STUDY

Psa. 40:2;
Eph. 6:10-18;
Isa. 52:7

*1. What was the
psalmist's testimony?*

*2. What is to be on
our feet?*

How did Habakkuk discover the formula that
enabled him to walk with the sure-footedness of a deer
across the rough terrain of his times? We shall discover the answer to that question in the days to come.
Permit me to give you a word of advice, however,
before we start: don't be too anxious to find that
answer. For the deeper the search the more joyous the
eventual discovery.

Prayer

O Father, help me to be patient and painstaking in my search for the answer to spiritual confusion. Show me that there are no quick answers to life's big problems.
Slow me down so that I keep pace with You. In Jesus' Name. Amen.

A serious stumbling-block

"How long, O Lord, must I call for help, but you do not listen?" (v.2)

For reading & meditation – Habakkuk 1:1-4

Yesterday we said that we are starting out on a journey that will reveal the steps we need to take in order to move from confusion to confidence, or from fear to faith. Our map for this special journey is a small but significant book of the Old Testament – the prophecy of Habakkuk. We know very little about the personal details of Habakkuk's life – his home, his parents or his occupation – but we do know that he was a Hebrew and a contemporary of the prophet Jeremiah.

Habakkuk, it seems, began his prophetic ministry by asking God a pointed question – the one posed in our text today. Like many other prophets of the Old Testament, Habakkuk was perplexed and frustrated by the continuance of evil. He could not understand why God did not intervene to restrain the godless nations around him. The Almighty's apparent slowness in dealing with this issue produced within him a good deal of confusion and concern. "Confusion," says Dr Clyde Narramore, "is one of the biggest stumbling-blocks in the Christian life. It has brought many a Christian to the edge of despair."

Some years ago I met a man in the United States of America wearing a badge on which were inscribed the initials B.A.I.K. When I asked him what they meant he said: "Boy Am I Confused". I countered: "But you don't spell 'confused' with a K." He promptly replied: "Well, that shows you how confused I am." Are you confused about something in your spiritual life at this moment? Then take heart – God helped Habakkuk to move from confusion to confidence. And what He did for Habakkuk, He will also do for you.

FURTHER STUDY
Psa. 71:1-24;
James 3:16;
1 Cor. 14:33

1. What was the psalmist's request?

2. What was his positive confession?

Prayer

Father, I am grateful that when confusion surrounds me and I stumble – I can stumble onto my knees. Drive deep into my consciousness today the truth that the darkest hour is always the hour that precedes the dawn. Amen.

The first vital step

"Be honest and you will be safe ..." (v.18: GNB)
For reading & meditation – Proverbs 28:16-28

Although it is my intention to take you verse by verse through the prophecy of Habakkuk, there will be times, such as today, when we will turn into a side road and pause to focus on a different, but relevant part of Scripture. This will add to our overall understanding of the theme.

We saw yesterday that Habakkuk was confused and frustrated over God's inaction in the face of evil. Perhaps a similar confusion exists in your heart as, day after day, you pick up the newspaper and read about the appalling things that are going on in the world – rape, murder, corruption, violence, political intrigue, lust, vice, lawlessness, and so on. What do we do when confusion hits us in the way it hit the prophet Habakkuk? How do we handle ourselves at those times when nothing makes sense?

The first step is this: we must honestly admit to ourselves that we are confused. That might seem to some to be stating the obvious, but you would be amazed how difficult it is for some Christians to acknowledge and admit to what is going on inside them. This is because there is a sub-conscious desire in the hearts of many believers to present to the world the image of being people who have the answer to all of life's problems – and so whenever they feel confused, they tend to deny the fact and pretend that everything is fine. But that is dishonest – and few things cause more anxiety than dishonesty. The first thing, then, is honesty – honesty with God, honesty with others and honesty with ourselves.

FURTHER STUDY

Psa. 51:1-17;
Eph. 4:25;
Prov. 12:19

1. What does God desire?

2. What are we to speak?

Prayer

My Father and my God, I open up my depths to Your honesty. Let it search me and try me and see if there is any devious way in me – anything that dodges or denies. Help me to be an honest person. Amen.

Four ways to cope with confusion

*"The Lord is my light and my salvation — whom shall I
fear? The Lord is the stronghold of my life ..." (v.1)*
For reading & meditation – Psalm 27:1-14

Whenever we are faced with confusion – or, for that matter, any difficult situation that confronts us – we will usually take one of four measures: 1. Flee it! 2. Fight it! 3. Forget it! 4. Face it! The first three end in failure – only the fourth will get us anywhere.

So fix it clearly in your mind that the first step in dealing with confusion is admit it. Acknowledge the fact that you are feeling confused. Don't be like the minister who, when faced with a difficult passage in Scripture, would say to his congregation: "This is an interesting text – and now having looked it full in the face, let us pass on!" Be careful that you don't pass on until you have looked confusion fully in the face, acknowledged its reality and felt its pain.

Why is it necessary to feel its pain? Because any unpleasant thought or situation will, of necessity, have some impact upon our feelings. Depending on the type of person we are (our temperament, early training, and so on), we will choose either to face that feeling in all its fullness or push it down inside us – unacknowledged. But note this: to the extent that an emotion is not acknowledged, to that extent it will stay within us and cause trouble at some future point in our lives. One of the laws of the personality is this: unacknowledged emotions stay within us to cause trouble, acknowledged emotions don't. How good are you at acknowledging your feelings? Believe me, if you are not in charge of them, they will soon be in charge of you.

FURTHER STUDY

2 Cor. 12:1-10;
Isa. 40:31;
Psa. 81:1

1. How did Paul
respond after
acknowledging his
situation?

2. What is the key to
facing life's pain?

Prayer

O Father, here I am entering an area where I need Your special help and direction. You have told me to "fear nothing". Help me to face all my feelings in the knowledge that You, not my feelings, are my Lord and Master. Amen.

The way to real growth

"Be strong and courageous. Do not be terrified; do not be discouraged, for the Lord your God will be with you ..." (v.9)

For reading & meditation – Joshua 1:1-9

We must spend another day looking at this important matter of being willing to acknowledge our feelings. The truth is, most of us are unwilling to "feel" a negative emotion and we try to get rid of it as quickly as possible.

Our personalities are equipped with adaptive devices called "defence mechanisms" which come to our aid at such times and help us rid ourselves of negative feelings by either suppressing them or repressing them. Suppression involves pushing them down just below the level of our conscious mind into the subconscious, where we say: "I won't think about that now – it's too hurtful." Repression involves pushing them down into the unconscious where they are completely forgotten. These "defence mechanisms" may get us temporarily off the hook by relieving the anxiety we feel at having to face an unacceptable emotion, but they don't really solve the problem.

The only way to real growth and wholeness is a willingness to face feelings, no matter how terrifying and threatening they may be. It's not easy, of course – I still struggle in this area myself. I know I am better at facing unacceptable feelings than I was, say, twenty years ago – but I still have a long way to go. Keep in mind what I said yesterday, for it is a vitally important matter: to the extent that we push an unacceptable emotion away from us, fearing to face it and feel it, to that extent it will go on working within us counterproductively. For the sake of our mental and spiritual health, we must realise that any emotion that is buried within us is never buried dead – but buried alive.

FURTHER STUDY

Psa. 32:1-5;
Jer. 14:20;
Hosea 5:15

1. What happened when the psalmist kept silent?

2. What happened when he acknowledged his position?

Prayer

My Father and my God, since it seems my emotions are a vital part of me, give me the courage to be able to face them in the knowledge that when I am mastered by You, I can be mastered by nothing else. Amen.

Stepping off the cliff

*"The eternal God is your refuge, and underneath are the
everlasting arms." (v.27)*

For reading & meditation – Deuteronomy 33:1-29

I know that some will feel threatened by the subject we have been looking at over these past few days because, by reason of past hurts and
traumas, they feel they do not have the inner strength to cope with any
more unpleasant and uncomfortable feelings. Such people find it far easier to repress unacceptable feelings than to face them. We have to face
the fact, however, that if Habakkuk had done this, he would never have
risen to the heights of confidence which we see him enjoying in his final
chapter.

If you are terrified to face your feelings, then let me encourage you
to make the conscious decision now that you will attempt to move forward in this matter – if only a little. Make up your mind the next time
an unacceptable feeling comes your way, you will choose to face and feel
it in the strength that God provides.

Picture yourself standing on the edge of a cliff, looking down into a
deep abyss. The abyss represents your fear of experiencing your emotions. Now visualise a strong rope tied securely to your waist – a rope
that represents God's love and that is held in His hands
directly above the abyss. While you remain on the
cliff, the rope hangs limp around your waist. Note, it
is the cliff, not the rope, that is supporting you. The
only way you can experience the tightness of the rope
and know the power of the Lord to uphold you in the
presence of unpleasant feelings is to jump off the cliff
and trust yourself to the rope. In other words, if you
face your feelings, you will not fall into the abyss – you
will be supported by God's unbreakable rope of love.

FURTHER STUDY

Isa. 41:1-10;
Ex. 19:4; Psa. 18:35

1. What was God's
promise to Israel?

2. Take a pencil and
paper and draw the
above illustration to
help you visualise it.

Prayer

O Father, the thought of facing the things I am afraid to face draws me to hold back
and remain on the cliff of safety. But I long to experience Your mighty strength and
power. Help me step off that cliff – today. In Jesus' Name. Amen.

Evasion solves nothing

"I can do everything through him who gives me strength."
(v.13)

For reading & meditation – Philippians 4:8-20

The advice I have been giving – to be willing to face your confusion and feel it – runs counter to the view that is held by many in the Christian Church. It is a view with which I am very familiar, for at one time I held it myself. It says: "Whenever you see a problem coming toward you, turn your back on it, begin to praise the Lord, and it will go away." Some go even further and say: "Once you confess you have a problem, you allow it to have a foothold in your life and you will not be able to get rid of it. Confession leads to possession – you will get what you confess."

I am heartily in agreement with the belief that we can look so long at our problems that we lose our spiritual perspective – the problem becomes bigger and God grows smaller. But we must not fall into the trap of thinking that refusing to acknowledge a problem makes it go away. Gene Autry, the famous singing cowboy (and a boyhood hero of mine) said: "I have always followed the rule of one hundred per cent honesty in everything – honesty toward God, honesty toward others, and honesty toward myself."

FURTHER STUDY

Matt. 26:36-45;
Luke 2:49;
John 5:19-20;
Heb. 4:15

1. What did Jesus do with His pain and confusing circumstances?

2. Why was He able to face them?

Once again I suggest that if we are not willing to admit to a problem, then we are denying reality and being dishonest. Those whose method of coping with problems is to pretend they don't have them are taking the first step toward mental ill-health. Nothing is solved by evasion, for whatever we try to evade comes back to pervade. It comes back as hidden complexes within – an undertow of discord that restrains our spiritual progress.

Prayer

O Father, drive this thought deep into my spirit – whatever I try to evade comes back to pervade. Make me a person of courage – able to face anything and stand up to anything. In Jesus' Name. Amen.

A dialogue with God

"Cast all your anxiety on him because he cares for you." (v.7)

For reading & meditation – 1 Peter 5:1-11

We pause to gather up what we have been saying over the last few days. The Christian way is a way of complete honesty – we must be willing to face and feel unpleasant situations and feelings. There must be no attempt to deceive ourselves or pretend that things are different from the way they really are – no attempt to entice the mind into a fool's paradise of make-believe. No one can play tricks on the universe – let alone the universe of a personality. So there must be no waving of a magic wand over negative feelings – no telling the mind they are not there. We must be willing to face things in the knowledge that when we are linked to Jesus Christ, nothing can master us or overwhelm us.

Now for the second step: bring all your questions, doubts and feelings directly to God and talk to Him about them. Some regard Habakkuk's direct questioning of God (1:1-4) as impertinent, but I do not see it in that light. God does not fall off His throne every time one of His children confronts Him with a searching question. Believe me, whatever question you ask of God – He can take it!

Habakkuk did what every one should do whenever they fail to comprehend the ways of the Almighty – he talked directly to God about it. So whenever you feel confused about the state of the world – and who doesn't? – don't become too concerned about entering into a dialogue with other people. First enter into a dialogue with God. Problems must always be talked out – and who better to talk to than God?

FURTHER STUDY

2 Kings 19:8-37;
Psa. 91:15;
Phil. 4:6

1. How did Hezekiah deal with his problem?

2. What was the result?

Prayer

O Father, forgive me for running to others with my problems when I should first be running to You. Help me in future to share my burdens and my problems with You before I share them with anyone else. In Christ's Name I pray. Amen.

"What have you done about it?"

"But may all who seek you rejoice and be glad in you …" (v.16)

For reading & meditation – Psalm 40:1-17

We continue thinking about the second step we must take – bringing all our questions and feelings to God and talking directly to Him about them. Dr Jay Adams, a well-known Christian counsellor, says that whenever anyone comes to him for counselling, he begins by asking three preliminary questions: (1) What is your problem? (2) What have you done about it? (3) What do you expect me to do about it?

He says that one of the things that has amazed him about the replies he gets to the second question – "What have you done about it?" – is the fact that although many say they have sought help from friends, family or even books, few say that they have talked to God about their problem. My own experience would bear this out. In the early days of my ministry I remember being somewhat nonplussed when I asked a brother or sister who had come to me with a personal problem, "Have you talked to God about this?" to hear so often this response: "No, I thought I would talk to you about it first."

I have often wondered whether there would be such a demand for Christian counselling if people made it a habit to talk to God about their problems before talking them over with anyone else. That does not mean, of course, that the ministry of counselling is invalid for, according to Scripture, it is a God-ordained gift (Rom. 12:8). I am convinced, however, that if Christians developed the habit of first going to God with their problems, they would make the surprising discovery that on most occasions, they would have no need to consult anyone else.

FURTHER STUDY

1 Chron. 28:9;
Psa. 27:8;
Prov. 8:17;
Jer. 29:13

1. What does it mean to "seek the Lord"?

2. What does God promise?

Prayer

My Father and my God, help me to develop a prayer-habit so that whenever I am faced with a problem, the first One I think of talking to is You. I ask this in and through Your Son's peerless and precious Name. Amen.

Why put God first?

"You shall have no other gods before me." (v.3)
For reading & meditation – Exodus 20:1-17

We are saying that if we would learn to bring our doubts, our fears and our confusion to God and talk to Him about them in believing prayer, there would be fewer problems in the Church and less need for personal counselling.

This does not mean, as we said, that the ministry of counselling is invalid for, as Scripture clearly shows, it ought to play a vital part in every Christian congregation: "I am satisfied about you, my brethren, that you yourselves are rich in goodness, amply filled with all spiritual knowledge and competent to admonish and counsel and instruct one another also" (Rom. 15:14, Amplified Bible). There will be times when, even though we have spoken to God about our problems and our confusion, the guidance and enlightenment we need will come not directly from Him but through the lips of a minister, a friend or a counsellor.

The point I am making is that we must learn the spiritual principle of having a dialogue with God before we enter into a dialogue with anyone else. Why is this so important? Because our spiritual dependence must be rooted in God and not in anyone else. It is so easy to move away from a sense of dependence on God, and anything that contributes to that must be resisted. After all, what is the essence of sin? Is it not independence – man seeking to find his own solutions to his problems rather than discovering God's perspective on them? Of course, if God directs us to another member of His family for help and advice, then fine. The roots of our dependence, however, must be firmly fixed in Him.

FURTHER STUDY

Psa. 27:1-14;
Hosea 12:6;
Isa. 8:17

1. What is the admonition of the psalmist?

2. How often do you "wait" on the Lord?

Prayer

O God, open my eyes to see the dangers of being centred in myself or in others. If I am to move from confusion to confidence, then I must be centred in You. Help me make You the centre of my life – today and every day. Amen.

More tolerant than His people

"How long, O Lord? Will you forget me for ever? How long will you hide your face from me?" (v.1)

For reading & meditation – Psalm 13:1-6

Now that we have seen the importance of bringing all our doubts and confusion directly to God, the next question we must settle is this: How do we go about the task of telling the Almighty exactly what is in our hearts? Do we address Him in ecclesiastical language and in pious tones? No, we must talk to Him naturally, openly and honestly – telling Him precisely what we think and how we feel.

Look again at the first four verses of Habakkuk's prophecy and what do we find? We find a man addressing God in a manner that at first seems irreverent and impertinent. We see something similar in the passage that is before us today. Have you noticed how, when some of the Old Testament personalities felt confused or angry with God, they told Him exactly what they thought and felt – sometimes in language that is blunt almost to the point of rudeness?

Habakkuk was upset because God had not answered his prayers. You can almost hear the anger and frustration in his words as he hammers on the door of heaven: "Lord, I'm confused. Why don't You answer my prayer? How much longer are You going to allow this? When will You do something about these tremendous problems?" Does God tell him to shut up or rephrase his questions in more acceptable language? Does He withdraw from the prophet in an attitude of disgust? No, for as I said before – God can take it. It may not have occurred to you before, but it is a truth that is exemplified over and over again in Scripture – God is more patient and tolerant than any of His people.

FURTHER STUDY

1 Kings 19:1–21;
Rom. 15:5;
Psa. 86:5

1. How did Elijah express himself to the Lord?

2. How did the Lord respond?

Prayer

My Father and my God, when I think how I react when people show anger toward me, I stand in awe and amazement at the way You respond to those who are angry with You. Teach me to be more like You, dear Lord. In Christ's Name. Amen.

Be real

"My God, my God, why have you forsaken me? Why are you so far from saving me, so far from the words of my groaning?" (v.1)
For reading & meditation – Psalm 22:1-24

We ended yesterday by saying that God is more patient and tolerant than His people. We have only to look at Habakkuk remonstrating with God to see this. One thing we must learn about God it is this: He would prefer us to be real rather than pretend to be what we are not. Be assured of this: beneath confusion there is usually an element of anger. It may not be recognised, but it is there nevertheless.

I remember on one occasion a man telling me that he had just come through "a spiritual revolution". When I pressed him to share it with me he told me that all his life he had been brought up to believe he must address God in polite tones, and on no account should he ever show any sense of frustration or annoyance. But one day, while going through a time of spiritual confusion, he forgot himself, and in language that was stripped of all pious phrases told God exactly what he thought about Him and the way He was handling His world.

For two hours he argued with God, and when he had finished the Lord said to him: "You would never let anyone talk to you like that, would you? Why? Because you cannot see into the depths of another's heart. But I see everything – the pain, the hurt and the anger. I love you and I understand." The tender response of the Lord broke him and there followed three days of communion with Him that produced in him a deep spiritual transformation. God always responds to reality – even when that reality is couched in feelings of anger and hurt.

FURTHER STUDY

Luke 24:13-36;
Rom. 12:17

1. Why was Jesus able to respond to these disciples?

2. What was the result?

Prayer

O God, something is being burned into my consciousness – You are a God who delights in reality. Help me to be a real person – with no subterfuge, no phoneyness, no pretence. I ask this in and through the precious Name of Jesus. Amen.

The pain of answered prayer

"I am raising up the Babylonians [or Chaldeans], that ruthless and impetuous people, who sweep across the whole earth …" (v.6)

For reading & meditation – Habakkuk 1:6-11

When the Lord announced that He was about to use the evil and cruel Chaldeans to prune His people and to bring them to heel, Habakkuk was astounded. The Chaldeans, a tribe from southern Babylonia, were terrorists who loved to plunder and torture their enemies. Listen to God's description of the Chaldean armies in the passage we are looking at today: "… they are a law to themselves and promote their own honour. Their horses are swifter than leopards, fiercer than wolves … They fly like a vulture swooping to devour …" (vv.7–8).

Habakkuk had his prayer answered, but not in the way he expected. The prophet is now more confused than ever. First, God took an exceptionally long time to answer him, and when He did, the answer He gave was more difficult to receive than the silence. People have often said to me: "What can be greater than the pain of unanswered prayer?" I usually respond: "the pain of answered prayer."

Habakkuk was quite clear in his mind what he wanted God to do – chastise the nation of Israel and send revival. But when God replied that He was going to use the evil and cruel Chaldean army to punish them, the prophet was nonplussed. This is not an uncommon experience in the Christian life – getting an answer we do not expect. When Augustine pleaded with God for light to overcome the dark problems he faced, God gave him light – but the first thing it revealed was Augustine's unchastity and sensuality. We take certain risks when we pray, for God sometimes tells us things we might not want to know.

FURTHER STUDY

Jonah 1:1 – 4:11

1. Why was Jonah disgruntled?

2. What was he expecting?

Prayer

My Father and my God, help me to understand that when my prayers are answered in ways that I do not expect, it is because You desire my highest good. And help me not simply to understand it – but accept it. In Jesus' Name. Amen

"We are not saved from hurt"

"When he heard this, he became very sad, because he was a man of great wealth." (v.23)

For reading & meditation – Luke 18:18-30

We are seeing that the answer our prayers receive is not always the answer our hearts desire. One preacher has said: "He who asks God for light must not complain if the light scorches at times with its fierce and naked heat, and he who asks for guidance must not be surprised if God points him to paths he would rather not tread."

Oliver Wendell Holmes says that it is a rule which admits of few exceptions that when people ask for our opinion, they really want our praise. God will not deal with us like that. If we plead for light, then providing He sees that it will not devastate us, He will grant us the petition we ask. Note, I use the word "devastate" and not "hurt". God will not save us from getting hurt – if that pain is part of His purpose for making us better.

We see that principle illustrated in the story of the rich young ruler. He said to Jesus: "Good teacher, what must I do to inherit eternal life?" And Jesus said: "Sell everything you have and give to the poor, and you will have treasure in heaven. Then come, follow me" (vv.18, 22). The young man delighted in his wealth. It was the most important thing in his life. That is why Jesus asked him to put it on one side. The first place in any person's life is God's place. The answer the rich young ruler got was not the one he wanted, but it was certainly what he needed. The account says that he "became very sad". He got his answer – but failed to receive it.

FURTHER STUDY

Mark 14:26-42;
Matt. 20:22;
Psa. 80:5; 126:5

1. What was the cup Christ faced?

2. How does God use suffering?

Prayer

O God, forgive me that so often I am like this rich young ruler – I ask for light, but when it comes I am not ready to receive it. Lord, teach me to pray – and also to receive. In Christ's Name I ask it. Amen.

Trembling in the light!

"My heart falters, fear makes me tremble; the twilight I longed for has become a horror to me." (v.4)

For reading & meditation – Isaiah 21:1-10

We continue discussing the subject of the pain that sometimes results from answered prayer. Not only Habakkuk, but also Isaiah knew something of this.

Isaiah asked for light on the political situation of his day – a religious matter to a Hebrew prophet as well as a political one. He asked God to give him insight and understanding that he might see and comprehend what was hidden from others. He prayed for a divine illumination whereby his gaze might pierce the future so that he might speak forth a prophetic word to his people. And God gave him light! His prayer was answered! The darkness turned to a growing twilight. He saw – but what he saw filled his soul with terror. When he knew, he almost wished he did not know. The light glimmered all around him, but the pain of its revelation made him wish that he was back in the darkness of ignorance once again.

What did he see? He saw the people he loved broken by the might of the enemy. He saw their homes and cities shattered by the most ruthless of foes. God had truly answered his prayer and given him the insight he desired, but he turned from it sick with foreboding and with his body quivering in fearful anticipation. Listen to how the Living Bible paraphrases our text for today: "My mind reels; my heart races; I am gripped by awful fear. All rest at night – so pleasant once – is gone; I lie awake trembling." Perhaps, at times, it is better to remain in the darkness of ignorance than to tremble in the light of illumination.

FURTHER STUDY

Daniel 10:1–21;
Lam. 3:22-23;
Rev. 1:17

1. How did Daniel and John respond to the vision of God?

2. How is God's mercy expressed?.

Prayer

O Father, help me to be in closer touch with Your ways and Your purposes. Teach me the difference between desiring and demanding – a desire to know may leave me wondering, but a demand to know may leave me trembling. Amen.

The light scorches ...

*"As the heavens are higher than the earth, so are my ways higher
than your ways and my thoughts than your thoughts." (v.9)*
For reading & meditation – Isaiah 55:1-13

Now that we have looked at how Habakkuk and Isaiah experienced
the pain of answered prayer, we turn to consider some examples
drawn from more modern times.

When the great Methodist preacher Thomas Champness was first
appointed district evangelist to Newcastle upon Tyne, he got on his
knees and asked God for further light and illumination. The Lord said:
"You are to concentrate exclusively on winning men to Me ... and you
must be careless of your reputation as a preacher." Thomas Champness
was known as one of the greatest preachers of his day – a reputation of
which, according to his biographer, he was mildly proud. And God said:
"Give it up." He asked for light but the light scorched with an intense
and fierce heat.

Have you heard of Hugh Price Hughes? He was another great preacher of modern times – and a man with a scholar's mind. When, as a young
man, he asked God for direction concerning his career, the Lord said: "I
want you to be a preacher of the gospel." He was quite startled, for he
had not expected that. He realised at once what the
call to the ministry meant – a lower income, the abandonment of the delights of scholarly research, and so
on. It took him some time to receive the divine call
and adjust to it, but once he had he became a mighty
preacher and a choice servant of God. Mrs Hugh Price
Hughes was once asked what was the greatest sacrifice
her husband had ever made, and she replied: "He
could have been a scholar, but he chose under God to
be a simple preacher of the gospel."

FURTHER STUDY
Psa. 40:1-17;
139:17; Jer. 29:11

*1. How did the
psalmist describe
God's thoughts?*

*2. What is the essence
of God's thoughts?*

Prayer

My Father and my God, day by day I am being exposed to the truth that You always
give the best to those who leave the choice to You. Help me to put Your way before
my way – for then, and only then, will I experience true freedom. Amen.

"I just won't do that"

"He cuts off every branch in me that bears no fruit, while every branch that does bear fruit he prunes ..." (v.2)

For reading & meditation – John 15:1-11

We are spending time meditating on the fact that the answers our prayers receive are not always the answers our hearts desire. This we are calling "the pain of answered prayer". A preacher tells how he preached a series of sermons to his congregation on the subject of guidance, and in the last message of the series he encouraged them to put the matter to personal test. "Follow the principles I have laid before you," he said, "and let me know what happens."

Several weeks later, he noticed that one woman who had attended the whole of the series on guidance no longer attended the services – so he decided to call on her. During the course of his visit, he asked what was the reason for her non-attendance at church. She said that it was due to the disappointment she had experienced after putting into operation the principles he had taught on guidance. "What happened?" asked the minister, anxiously. "Did you hear nothing?" "Oh, yes," she replied, "I heard something all right. It came to me that I ought to write to my sister-in-law, the cat, with whom I quarrelled seven years ago. I just won't do that ..."

FURTHER STUDY

James 4:1-17;
Psa. 52:3;
Prov. 2:14

1. How does James define sin?

2. What is the personal application?

The verse that comes to my mind as I tell that story is one I am sure you will know well: "This is the verdict: Light has come into the world, but men loved darkness instead of light because there deeds were evil" (John 3:19). At the risk of being repetitive, the point is so important that it must be made yet again: never forget that when you pray for light, it may reveal far more than you wish.

Prayer

"Dear Lord, these three things I pray: to see Thee more clearly, love Thee more dearly, follow Thee more nearly – day by day." In Christ's peerless and precious Name I ask it. Amen.

How to avoid panic

"I will establish my covenant as an everlasting covenant between me and you and your descendants ... to be your God ..." (v.7)

For reading & meditation – Genesis 17:1-9

The next attribute of God on which Habakkuk focuses is that of faithfulness: "We will not die" (Hab. 1:12). What is the significance of these interesting words? Habakkuk is recalling that God is the God of the covenant.

Although the Almighty is eternal and beyond time, He condescended to make a covenant with men. His original covenant was with Abraham and was later renewed with Isaac and Jacob. Later still, He renewed it with David. It was this covenant which entitled the people of Judah to turn to God and say: "Lord, You cannot let us die, for You have made a covenant with us, one that can never under any circumstance be broken." Whatever the Chaldean army might do, it could never exterminate Judah, because God was bound and committed to His people in a covenant relationship that could never be broken.

Having focused on these four aspects of God's character – His eternal nature, self-existence, holiness and faithfulness – Habakkuk is now able to see his problem from a different perspective: "... you have appointed them to execute judgment ... you have ordained them to punish ..." (v.12). Can you understand what he is saying? He is beginning to perceive an answer to his problem and reasons thus: "God must be raising up the Chaldeans for Judah's benefit. Of this I can be certain. It is not that God is incapable of restraining them. In the light of His nature and attributes, such a thing would be impossible. I am not able to understand it fully, but I know that God cannot and will not do anything that is contrary to His character." If that is true – then why panic?

FURTHER STUDY

Jer. 31:1-31;
Heb. 8:10; 12:24

1. What was the Old Testament promise?

2. What happens in the new covenant?

Prayer

O Father, I see You are trying to teach me Your ways – the ways written in Your Word and exemplified in the lives of Your servants. Help me to learn this lesson of how not to panic. In Christ's Name I ask it. Amen.

The importance of fixed points

"... the Father of the heavenly lights, who does not change like shifting shadows." (v.17)

For reading & meditation – James 1:12-25

Over these past few days we have been saying that one of the things we must do if we are to move from confusion to confidence is to establish a context in which to think through our problems – and that context, we said, must be the nature and character of God.

The art of navigation depends to a large extent on the existence of fixed points. The fixed point can be a star, a lighthouse, or a headland; it does not really matter what it is providing it is fixed and solid. Granted the certitude of a fixed point, the navigator can take his bearing and steer his course. He cannot take his bearing from a cloud: it moves – it is vaporous and changing and, in the course of time, disappears. Navigation is possible because of the existence of fixed points, and by constant reference to these points, seamen make their way around the world.

The voyage of life is like that – one must have fixed points from which to take a bearing. The attributes of God are fixed points. His love, faithfulness, justice, purity, holiness and power – to name but a few – are established parts of God's nature. And the more we focus on them and the more we understand them, the more safely and reliably we will make our way across the sea of life. Many things in this universe are subject to change – but not the attributes and nature of God. What He was, He is, and what He is, He was. And what He was and is He ever will be – world without end.

FURTHER STUDY

Heb. 13:1-8;
Psa. 102:27;
Mal. 3:6; Heb. 1:12

1. What is the foundation of our faith?

2. What was the psalmist's testimony?

Prayer

O Father, help me to grasp the exciting truth that is implied in the thought before me today, namely, that because Your nature cannot change, Your Word will never fail. I am eternally grateful. Amen.

"Only small thoughts of God"

"… ask for the ancient paths, ask where the good way is, and walk in it, and you will find rest for your souls." (v.16)

For reading & meditation – Jeremiah 6:16

We continue making the point that the more we understand the nature and character of God, the more secure we will feel and the better equipped we will be to handle life's serious problems. Unfortunately, few preachers today expound the great truths concerning God's nature. They prefer instead to give clever little talks – ten minutes and no more – on topical issues and current events. There are notable exceptions to what I am saying, of course, but as Jim Packer points out: "The trend these days is for Christian minds to conform to the modern spirit – the spirit that spawns great thoughts of man and leaves room for only small thoughts of God."

A century ago, pulpits were occupied by men who left their hearers in no doubt as to the nature of God. But not any more. When, for example, did you last hear a sermon on the attributes of God? But let me ask you a more pointed question: When did you last read a book on that important subject? When I asked one publisher why he was not producing books that come to grips with the basic issues of the faith, he answered: "People are not writing them, and if they did few people would want to read them." How sad.

Let me make a plea for the return to old-fashioned thinking on the nature and character of God. If you have not read the book *Knowing God* by J.I. Packer, then purchase a copy today. Focus on knowing who God is and you will never again be at the mercy of the winds of doubt and uncertainty.

FURTHER STUDY

Psa. 8:1-9;102:25; Job 26:7; Heb. 11:3

1. What question does the psalmist ask?

2. How was the universe formed?

Prayer

O Father, with all my heart I cry out today: "Take me deeper into You." I am tired of superficiality. Help me to know You and understand You – to deeply know and understand You. In Jesus' Name. Amen.

Pygmy Christians

"Do you not know? Have you not heard? ... Have you not understood ...? (v.21)

For reading & meditation – Isaiah 40:21-31

Yesterday we ended with the statement that the more we understand God's nature, the more certain we will be about the rightness of His decisions. Have you ever wondered how it is that over the centuries, men and women have stood for God in the most unenviable circumstances? The answer is this: they were familiar with the nature and character of God.

One of the things that concerns me about many modern-day Christians is that they know little about the nature of God. The very first series of Bible studies I attended after I became a Christian was on the subject of the attributes of God. It was tough going for a young Christian, but those weeks of teaching built under me a foundation which has stood solid over the years. It was there that I heard for the first time statements that have stayed with me all my life. Statements such as: "It is only when we understand who God is that we will understand what He does." And: "We must be careful not to interpret God's character by what we see, but what we see by God's character."

J.I. Packer, in his book *Knowing God*, says: "The ignorance of God – ignorance both of His ways and of the practice of communion with Him – lies at the root of much of the church's weakness today." I agree. The modern Church, generally speaking, looks at God through the wrong end of a telescope and ends up reducing the Almighty to pygmy proportions. And what is the result? Our pews are filled with pygmy Christians who have only a superficial knowledge of the God they are pledged to serve.

FURTHER STUDY

Isa. 6:1-8; 9:6;
Psa. 97:6

1. What aspect of God's character did Isaiah witness?

2. How did he describe Christ?

Prayer

Father, I begin to see the framework in which I must win or lose the battle of life. And that framework is Your nature and Your character. Help me to know You better – then I shall be better. In Christ's Name I ask it. Amen.

Knowing God

"Your eyes are too pure to look on evil; you cannot tolerate wrong." (v.13)

For reading & meditation – Habakkuk 1:12-14

Now we come to the fourth step we need to take to move from confusion to confidence: establish a spiritual context in which to think through the problem.

Look how Habakkuk sets about doing this as illustrated in the verses that are before us today. He focuses his attention, not on his feelings or his circumstances, but on the nature and character of God. One by one, he singles out some of the attributes of God and reminds himself of the characteristics of God's nature: "O Lord, are you not from everlasting?" – His eternal nature; "We will not die" – His faithfulness; "You have appointed them to execute judgment" – His justice; "Your eyes are too pure to look on evil" – His holiness; "You have made men like fish in the sea" – His omnipotence.

Some commentators believe that the reason Habakkuk identifies God's attributes here is simply to build up an argument that the course proposed by God is contrary to His character. I think there is some truth in that as evidenced by his question in verse 17, but another reason why he sets about identifying God's attributes – so I believe – is to attempt to steady himself by reminding himself who God is. You see, it is only when we understand who God is that we will understand what He does. Habakkuk was saying, in effect: "I don't know what You are doing, Lord, but I know this – You are a God of justice, of faithfulness, of holiness, of purity and of power." It is a law of the spiritual life that the more we understand God's character and nature, the more certain we will be about the rightness of His decisions.

FURTHER STUDY

Isa. 40:1–31;
Psa. 89:6;
1 Chron. 17:20

1. What question does Isaiah ask?

2. How does he answer it?

Prayer

My Father and my God, help me to know You better. I know You – yet I do not know You. Enable me over these next few days to build a spiritual context for my problems – one that will stay with me for the rest of my life. In Jesus' Name. Amen.

"March on ..."

"My grace is sufficient for you, for my power is made perfect in weakness." (v.9)

For reading & meditation – 2 Corinthians 12:1-10

We spend one more day discussing the "pain of answered prayer". What do we do when we receive an answer to our prayers that causes us to tremble in the blinding light of a new revelation? We must go into the light with God. Pain or no pain – there must be no going back – we must march on.

Augustine tried to run away from what God had shown him, but he was driven out of every false place of refuge. We must do what Thomas Champness – the preacher we referred to the other day – did: we must yield to what God has shown us and come to terms with the fact that, after all, God knows best. When God said to Thomas Champness: "You must be careless of your reputation as a preacher," he struggled for a while but eventually he yielded. Speaking of the effort it cost him, he said: "I threw my reputation into the Tyne as I crossed the high-level bridge." In return for his obedience, God made him a glorious harvester of souls.

I remind you again of the risks you take when you enter into dialogue with God. The light you ask for may reveal more than you wish. It may be turned to trembling within you. But I plead with you, when that happens – go on. If you will live up to the demands God makes and face squarely what the light reveals, the trembling will pass and you will prove the truth of Isaiah's words: He will "strengthen the feeble hands, steady the knees that give way; say to those with fearful hearts, 'Be strong, do not fear; your God will come ...' " (Isa 35:3–4).

FURTHER STUDY

1 John 1:1–10; 2:9;
Eph. 5:8;
2 Cor. 4:6

1. How are we to walk?

2. What will be the result?

Prayer

O Father, in those moments when I am overwhelmed by the light that I asked for but which brought answers I did not expect, help me not to pull back but to walk in the light ... as You are in the light. Amen.

Put it to the test

*"I am still confident of this: I will see the goodness of the
Lord in the land of the living." (v.13)*
For reading & meditation – Psalm 27:1-14

We now summarise what we have been saying over the past few days
in relation to the need to establish for ourselves a spiritual context
in which to think through a problem. The secret, as we have seen, is not
to focus on the immediate problem, but to take the indirect approach
and remind ourselves of the "fixed points" in God's nature – His eternal
nature, His self-existence, His holiness, His faithfulness, and so on.

What happens when we do this? Well, try it for yourself. If you are
confused about something that God is doing – or not doing – in your life,
then I invite you to apply the principles we have been discussing over
these past days. Take the indirect approach – focus not so much on your
problem as on the nature and character of God. Remind yourself of who
and what He is – and that He can do nothing contrary to His character.
Gaze one by one upon His glorious attributes. If you do exactly as I suggest, I promise you that you will see your problem from a different perspective. Gradually you will find it shrinking to its rightful proportions.

Believers in every age have been using this method of handling spiritual confusion – and it has never failed. If, on the voyage of life, we need fixed points from which to take
our bearings, then we Christians have the most reliable of them all – one of them being the goodness and
graciousness of God. As John Greenleaf Whittier put
it:

> *Here in this maddening maze of things,*
> *When tossed by storm and flood,*
> *To one fixed ground my spirit clings,*
> *I know that God is good.*

FURTHER STUDY
Psa. 57:1-7; 108:1;
112:7

1. Where was the
psalmist's heart
fixed?

2. On what is your
heart fixed?

Prayer

O Father, I stand in awe of Your goodness. Help me to know it and understand it
more and more. And not only this, but every other aspect of Your great and glorious character. In Christ's Name I ask it. Amen.

God answers every prayer

"And therefore the Lord earnestly waits – expectant, looking and longing – to be gracious to you …" (v.18, Amplified Bible)

For reading & meditation – Isaiah 30:15-26

We move on now to consider the fifth step we must take in order to move from confusion to confidence: recognise that sometimes God will keep you waiting for an answer.

First we must make the point that learning how to wait quietly for God to answer prayer and bring about His purposes is one of the hardest lessons in the Christian life, and can mean the difference between peace and panic in your life. I am not quite sure myself which is the more difficult situation to be in – getting an answer from God that one does not like, or having to wait interminably for the divine reply. Christian friends to whom I have put that question over the years are almost unanimous in saying that waiting is by far the most difficult thing to endure.

God answers every prayer, but it has been said that the answer may come in one of four forms: (1) Yes; (2) No; (3) Here is something better; (4) Wait to see what I will do. The first is easy to handle – we just open our hands and take what God gives. The second response is a little more difficult – but just as kind as the first. As Tagore, the great Indian thinker, said: "Sometimes the Lord has to save us by hard refusals." The third is also easy to receive. The fourth reply – "Wait" – is the most difficult to handle, but just as loving as the others. God delays His answers for many reasons but the most common reason is this: to deepen our characters so that we won't become spiritual crybabies when we don't get everything at once.

FURTHER STUDY

Acts 1:1-14; 2:1-4;
Psa. 37:7; 40:1

1. What was Jesus' instruction to His disciples?

2. What was the eventual result?

Prayer

O Father, I know in my intellect that the waiting time can prove transformative to my whole being, but I confess that I find it so hard to endure. You have helped me before – help me now with this. In Jesus' Name. Amen.

Still struggling

*"Why are you silent while the wicked swallow up those
more righteous than themselves?" (v.13)*
For reading & meditation – Habakkuk 1:13

Yesterday we said that those times when God leaves us waiting for an
answer to our prayers and questions are some of the most difficult of
our Christian life. Do the heavens seem like brass to you right now?
Have the urgent questions you have put to God gone unanswered? Then
look with me at how Habakkuk found himself in this same situation –
and how he came through it.

It is obvious from the verse before us today that although Habakkuk
had come a long way in dealing with the fact of spiritual confusion, his
perspective is still not clear. After affirming the fact that God is of "purer
eyes than to behold evil, and cannot look on wickedness" (v.13, NKJ),
he presents another provoking question. *The Living Bible* puts it like this:
"Will you, who cannot allow sin in any form, stand idly by while they
swallow us up? Should you be silent while the wicked destroy those who
are better than they?"

Clearly Habakkuk is still struggling with this idea that God is going
to use the cruel Chaldeans to punish His people. What he is really saying is this: "If it is true, O Lord, that Your eyes are too
pure to look on evil, then how can You allow the
Chaldeans to do this to Your people? Judah might be
bad, but the Chaldeans are a thousand times worse."
Habakkuk is not the only one to be perplexed over the
fact that God uses the unrighteous to refine the righteous. If God can't get to us one way, then He will try
another. He loves us too much to let us stay as we are.

FURTHER STUDY
Luke 18:1-8;
Isa. 25:9; 33:2;
Gen. 49:18

1. What did Jesus
teach in this parable?

2. What does this
encourage us to do?

Prayer

Father, I am so grateful that You love me too much to let me get away with things
that deprive and demean me. You will develop me – even though You may have to
resort to most unusual means to accomplish it. Thank You, Father. Amen.

A prophetic protest

"Are they going to use their swords for ever and keep on destroying nations without mercy?" (v.17, GNB)

For reading & meditation – Habakkuk 1:13-17

The words before us now show that the prophet is really getting worked up about the idea of God using the cruel Chaldeans to discipline the people of Judah. And he makes his protest in the most extravagant language: "Are we but fish, to be caught and killed? Are we but creeping things that have no leader to defend them from their foes? Must we be strung up on their hooks and dragged out in their nets, while they rejoice? Then they will worship their nets and burn incense before them! 'These are the gods who make us rich,' they'll say." His outburst comes to a head with this challenging question: "Will you let them get away with this for ever? Will they succeed for ever in their heartless wars?" (vv.14-17: TLB).

We said yesterday that the fact that God uses the unrighteous to discipline the righteous has always been a problem to the people of God. Throughout the ages, believers from all walks of life have grappled with it, and so now must we.

First, let's pose the question in its modern form: Why does God use unbelievers to discipline believers – non-Christians to refine Christians?

FURTHER STUDY

Luke 12:13-21;
Psa. 73:3; 73:12;
Jer. 5:28; 12:1

1. What is the end of seemingly prosperous but godless men?

2. What did Jeremiah find perplexing?

Why does He use an unconverted wife or husband to chasten a partner who is a believer, a non-Christian parent to discipline a Christian son or daughter? What possible reason can God have for taking up an impure instrument to accomplish a holy purpose? I am sure you will agree with me when I say that few things are more humbling than God using someone whom we know is godless and lacking in character to chasten and refine us. Humbling – but necessary.

Prayer

O God my Father, how relentless is Your love. You stop at nothing to make me what You want me to be. Help me see that Your humbling is not designed to cripple me but to correct me. In Jesus' Name. Amen.

Well worth waiting for ...

"I wait for the Lord, I expectantly wait, and in His word do I hope." (v.5, Amplified Bible)

For reading & meditation – Psalm 130:1-8

We continue pursuing the question: Why does God use an impure instrument to accomplish a holy purpose? Or to apply it more personally: Why does God use our non-Christian relatives, acquaintances or workmates to reprove and correct us? It is extremely humbling to be on the receiving end of God's discipline at any time, but more so when it is brought to us by someone whom we regard as being below us in character and integrity.

In the days when I was an engineering apprentice, I worked for a while alongside a man who became my pet hate. He was coarse, rude, loud-mouthed, boorish and blasphemous. One day I felt I could not put up with his behaviour any longer and went to a quiet place to pray. I said: "Lord, why have You put me in this position? This man greatly irritates me, and what is more – he delights in taking Your Name in vain. Get him away from me – or get me away from him. Or give me some explanation of why You are letting me go through this."

I had to wait twelve whole months for an answer. During that time I prayed that God would respond in a positive way to my request. Sometimes I would get so angry with God because He kept me waiting for a reply that I would refuse to read His Word. A year later the answer finally came, and when it did, God showed me that He had used the waiting time to prune me of a tendency to want my own way in everything. Believe me, the experience of that year yielded far more than it cost.

FURTHER STUDY

Gen. 15:1-17:27;
21:1-34

1. What happened as a result of Abraham's impatience?

2. What are we often tempted to do?

Prayer

O Father, I am so thankful that You are strong enough not to yield to my every demand. Help me understand that there is always a good and wise purpose behind everything you do. I ask this in Christ's peerless and precious Name. Amen.

What time is it?

*"... it is time to seek the Lord, until he comes and showers
righteousness on you." (v.12)*

For reading & meditation – Hosea 10:12

We are seeing that one of the surprising features of God's ways with us is that He sometimes uses the strangest instruments to discipline His people. This is a fact which is illustrated not just in the life and times of Habakkuk but throughout the whole of history. And we must not miss the point that He might well be doing the same in our own day and age.

Consider with me for a moment the state of the Church right now. Though there are evidences of spiritual advance in certain quarters and in certain countries, generally speaking, the Church is in a bad way. It is lethargic, indolent, prayerless, unrepentant and resistant to the Holy Spirit's control.

What can God do to bring it to the place of conformity to His will? Well, He can do many things, but one sure way of getting the Church's attention is to allow it to come under pressure from hostile forces. It is a sad admission to have to make, but the Church has always been at its best when fighting with its back to the wall.

We must now ask ourselves this piercing and pointed question: If God saw it necessary to discipline His Church by allowing hostile forces to put it under pressure, what could He use? Atheistic communism could be one possibility; humanism another. But one of the most hostile forces to Christianity in the world at the moment is that of Islam. I am not a prophet, but I suspect that this is one of the instruments the Lord will use to refine His people unless the Church moves quickly to repentance.

FURTHER STUDY

Isa. 55:1-6;
Deut. 4:29;
Psa. 105:4;
Matt. 7:7

1. What is the difference between seeking and asking?

2. What is the condition for finding the Lord when we seek Him?

Prayer

O Father, how foolish we are in that we have lived so long yet learned so little. Help us to see that we either take Your way – or take the consequences. And we know from history that the consequences can be costly. Save us, O Lord. Amen.

What do we learn from history?

"For it is time for judgment to begin with the family of God ..." (v.17)

For reading & meditation – 1 Peter 4:12-19

One person has said that "the only lesson we learn from history is that we learn nothing from history". That is certainly true of the Christian Church. You would think, with the truth of Scripture staring us in the face – namely, that when other means fail, God will use hostile forces to punish His people – we would be more careful with our spiritual inheritance. But what are the facts?

The Church, generally speaking, seems to have little or no concern about its spiritual condition. It is playing when it ought to be praying, compromising when it ought to be convicting. The Church must accept the fact that if it does not respond directly to the gentle reproofs of the Word and the Spirit, then it will have to face the harsher reproofs of circumstances. And as history records, those circumstances can be most bitter and severe. It may seem strange and contradictory to us that God will use the unrighteous to refine the righteous, but as Scripture and history both show, this is what He does. God uses the strangest instruments to discipline His people – sometimes the last we would expect.

This principle applies not only to the Church as a corporate body but we see it illustrated in our individual lives also. You may, at this very moment, be in the position where God is using the last person you would expect, such as a non-Christian relative, acquaintance or workmate, to chasten and correct you. It's humbling, isn't it, to see someone who doesn't know the Lord being used by Him to help you know Him better?

FURTHER STUDY

Deut. 8:1-8;
Zech. 13:9;
Mal. 3:3;
1 Pet. 1:6-7

1. What was God's purpose in the wilderness?

2. What is the purpose of the testing periods we experience?

Prayer

O God, forgive us that although we are Your followers, we fail to follow You. Help Your people, myself included, to stay in the place of yieldedness and repentance. For we would rather be chastened by You than by circumstances. Amen.

The willingness to wait

*"Let integrity and uprightness preserve me, for I wait for and
expect You." (v.21, Amplified Bible)*

For reading & meditation – Psalm 25:1-22

A ll of us have times when, although we feel we deserve a clear answer
from God in relation to a certain circumstance or situation, we do
not get it. Sometimes God gives us an answer and sometimes He does-
n't. Indeed, a Christian may be kept in the position of waiting for a week,
a month, a year – or even a lifetime. What does one do when this happens? We must do what Habakkuk did – leave the issue with God.

I feel myself that the division between chapters one and two of
Habakkuk's prophecy is misplaced. Scripture is inspired but the chapter
divisions are not. The first verse of chapter two is not the start of a new
section but a continuation of the previous chapter. In verse 17 of chapter 1, Habakkuk asks God a question to which he gets no reply. So what
does he do? He does not attempt to rationalise his position or form a pre-
mature conclusion. He certainly does not say: "I do not understand all
this so therefore I am bound to conclude that God doesn't have an
answer to give."

No, he acted in the way every one of us ought to act when faced with
this situation – he committed the problem to God and left it with Him.

Ignore the chapter division and you will see how naturally and easily Habakkuk moves from the place of
questioning to the place of waiting. There is no petu-
lance, no sense of being ignored by God. He simply
says: "I will climb my watchtower now, and wait to see
what answer God will give to my complaint" (2:1,
TLB). Habakkuk's willingness was the turning point in
his spiritual confusion. Today it can be yours too.

Prayer

Forgive me, dear Lord, that when answers do not come, I too quickly come to the
wrong conclusions about Your purposes and designs. I see the lesson Habakkuk
illustrates is a deeply important one. Help me to learn it. In Jesus' Name. Amen.

The example of Jesus

"Commit your way to the Lord; trust in him, and he will do this." (v.5)

For reading & meditation – Psalm 37:1-11

We spend one more day on the issue of learning how to commit a problem to God and wait for Him to answer in His own good time. Do you find it hard to take something you do not understand to God and leave it with Him? If you do, then believe me, you are not alone. Throughout time, as we said, the people of God have found this one of the most difficult lessons they have had to learn.

The method which Habakkuk employed of committing a problem to God and leaving it with Him was the same method Jesus used in that dramatic episode at Gethsemane. The problem which Jesus had to wrestle with was not just the problem of being crucified on a cross, but of being separated from His Father by being "made sin" for us. The thing from which the Son of God recoiled was separation from His Father. This was, without doubt, the greatest perplexity of His life.

What did He do in this situation? He prayed and said: "My Father, if it is possible, may this cup be taken from me. Yet, not as I will, but as you will" (Matt. 26:39). He took the problem with which He was wrestling – the problem of being "made sin" – and left it with God. Then He moved on in the confidence that God's will is always right and that a holy God will never command anything that is wrong. If you are struggling right now with something that you do not understand – something that is causing you considerable confusion – then get up into the watchtower and just keep looking to God. But don't just share it with Him – leave it with Him.

FURTHER STUDY

2 Tim. 1:1-12;
Psa. 31:5; Phil. 1:6;
1 Pet. 2:23; 4:19

1. Of what was Paul convinced?

2. Of what can we be confident?

Prayer

Gracious and loving Father, I see that if I am to enjoy peace in the midst of my problems, I must learn this lesson of leaving my problems with You. Help me begin practising it this very day. In Jesus' Name. Amen.

Write it down

"Write on a scroll what you see ..." (v.11)
For reading & meditation – Revelation 1:9-20

Now we move on to consider the sixth step we must take to move from confusion to confidence: understand what it means to live by faith. Remind yourself that the future is in God's hands and that He always knows the end from the beginning. First we shall focus on the manner in which God's answer came to the prophet. We do not know how long Habakkuk had to wait for his answer, but immediately prior to receiving it, the prophet is commanded to "write down the revelation and make it plain on tablets so that a herald may run with it" (Hab. 2:2).

The words "write down the revelation" indicate that God's answer is to be in the form of a supernatural revelation. The words "make it plain on tablets" indicate that the revelation is not only for Habakkuk, but for others as well – hence it has to be in a permanent form. And the words "so that a herald may run with it" indicate that it must be written clearly. A further reason why the revelation must be recorded in writing could be to emphasise the immutability of its content, for future circumstances can very often appear to deny a Word that God has given and suggest that He has changed His mind.

FURTHER STUDY

2 Pet. 1:1–21;
Jer. 36:2;
Deut. 6:6; 6:9

1. Why did Peter put his words in writing?

2. What were the Israelites commanded to do?

Arising out of this, let me make a practical suggestion: whenever you feel that God has spoken to you about anything to do with the future, do what Habakkuk did and write it down. Delay and changing circumstances can sometimes cause God's Word of promise to be forgotten. So I suggest, whenever God speaks a Word to your heart concerning the future that you record it in a permanent form.

Prayer

Heavenly Father, help me not to be so heavenly minded that I lose a sense of practicality. Help me remember that "the faintest ink can sometimes be better than the strongest memory". Amen.

A sure word of prophecy

"For prophecy never had its origin in the will of man, but men spoke from God ... by the Holy Spirit." (v.21)

For reading & meditation – 2 Peter 1:16-21

The words "write down the revelation and make it plain" (Hab. 2:2) show that God was about to reveal to Habakkuk something that was going to take place at a future time and, as you know, that is what we call "prophecy".

Prophecy occupies a large place in Scripture – in fact, over half the Bible is devoted to predicting future events. It is my conviction that nothing brings greater comfort and consolation to a Christian than to understand the nature of a prophecy. It is something that is basic to God's relationship with human beings and that is why those who have doubts about God's concern over humankind concentrate their attacks on the subject of prophecy. "Unbelief," said Dr Martyn Lloyd-Jones, "is always critical of Bible prophecy."

In today's Church, we have teachers who tell us that the Old Testament prophets were simply men of political genius who had clear insight into situations. They take exception to the view that God revealed things to them. Our text for today in the Amplified Bible reads: "No prophecy ever originated because some man willed it to do so – it never came by human impulse – but as men spoke from God who were borne along (moved and impelled) by the Holy Spirit." What would we get out of our Bible reading today, I wonder, if all it contained were the thoughts of men? I venture to say, no more than we would get out of reading the thoughts of Kipling or of Shakespeare. My writings are exhausted of meaning after a few years but you will never exhaust the meaning of divine revelation. God comes out of it because God has gone into it.

FURTHER STUDY

Heb. 1:1;
2 Tim. 3:1-17;
Job 32:8;

1. How has God spoken in the past?

2. How was the Scripture given to us?

Prayer

My Father and my God, I am thankful that the Bible is not just a book, but the Book. Help me to drop my bucket into the well of Scripture and drink from its clean and pure waters. In Jesus' Name I pray. Amen.

The elements of prophecy

"… being fully persuaded that God had power to do what he had promised." (v.21)

For reading & meditation – Romans 4:1-22

Yesterday we saw that prophecy is a revelation of God to humankind. Another element of prophecy is the fact that it will take place at exactly the right time: "For the revelation awaits an appointed time; it speaks of the end and will not prove false" (Hab. 2:3). The time for the fulfilment is fixed by God and it will come to pass at the exact moment that God foreordains.

Yet another element is that of foretelling the future. Here again, some Bible teachers object to this and say that prophecy is forth-telling rather foretelling. It is quite true, of course, that prophecy is a form of teaching and therefore contains an element of forth-telling (speaking out the truth), but the true nature of prophecy lies in the fact that it is predictive. God told Habakkuk things that would happen long before they came to pass.

The last element of prophecy is that it will be fulfilled: "Write down the revelation and make it plain … for the revelation awaits an appointed time." The events God foretells are certain to take place – and in God's time. The revelation may seem to be delayed, but nothing can prevent or frustrate its fulfilment.

FURTHER STUDY

Matt. 5:1-18;
1 Kings 8:56;
Psa. 111:7-8;
Ezek. 12:25

1. What did Christ promise concerning God's Word?

2. Reaffirm your trust in His ability to fulfil His promise to you.

How does all this relate to the more practical aspects of daily Christian living? Let me put the answer in the form of two questions: Has God given you a word or a promise that is yet to be fulfilled? And does the delay cause you to wonder whether or not He has forgotten His promise? Then take heart – there are trains on His line until 11:59. What God has promised, He will most certainly perform.

Prayer

O God, I bring to You my doubts and uncertainties for You to put them to rest – for ever. Today I want You to burn deep into me the conviction that nothing can ever stop Your Word from being fulfilled. Nothing. I am so thankful. Amen.

When tempted to doubt ...

"But I the Lord will speak what I will, and it shall be fulfilled without delay." (v.25)

For reading & meditation – Ezekiel 12:21-28

Once we grasp the principles that underly Biblical prophecy, they enable us to face the future with confidence and poise. What is the point of being unduly anxious when we know that God is committed to keeping His Word – not in just one thing, but in everything? Remember God's prediction concerning the Flood? It was 120 years before it happened (Gen. 6:3) – but it came to pass exactly as God foretold.

But perhaps the most striking illustration of this is found in the life of Abraham in Genesis 15:13-14: "Then the Lord said to him, 'Know for certain that your decendants will be strangers in a country not their own, and they will be enslaved and ill-treated four hundred years. But I will punish the nation they serve as slaves, and afterwards they will come out with great possessions.' " Later, in Exodus 12:40-42, we read: "The sons of Jacob and their descendants had lived in Egypt 430 years, and it was on the last day of the 430th year that all of Jehovah's people left the land. This night was selected by the Lord to bring His people out from the land of Egypt" (TLB).

The first text is a general statement, but then God narrows it down more precisely to not just the year, not just the month, but the very night on which the deliverance is to take place. Keep these remarkable texts in mind when next you begin to doubt the reliability of God's personal word to you. Wait upon God. Be assured – everything He has promised will come to pass. It will be difficult at times to understand the delay. But wait for the vision – it is certain, it is sure, it can never, never fail.

FURTHER STUDY

Mark 1:1-15;
Gal. 4:4; Eph. 1:10;
1 Tim. 2:6

1. What did John
declare?

2. When did God send
His Son?

Prayer

Father, help me to look out at the future, not through the eyes of chilling doubt, but through the eyes of ever-increasing faith. And when I cannot understand, help me just to stand. In Jesus' Name. Amen.

"The Great Divide"

"But my righteous one will live by faith ..." (v.38)
For reading & meditation – Hebrews 10:19-39

We come today to one of the most wonderful statements in Scripture: "the just shall live by his faith" (Hab. 2:4, AV). The verse is quoted several times in the New Testament and is familiar to almost every Christian. What is not so familiar is the statement prior to it: "See, he is puffed up; his desires are not upright ...". And if we fail to focus on that first statement, then we will miss the sense of what God is saying to Habakkuk. Join the two statements together and you will notice that they present two sides of a picture – the man who is full of unbelief and the man who is full of faith.

You see, there are only two basic attitudes we can adopt to life in this world – one is the attitude of faith, the other the attitude of unbelief. One commentator puts it like this: "Either we view our lives in terms of our belief in God and the conclusions we are entitled to draw from that; or our outlook is based upon a rejection of God and the corresponding denials."

It is quite clear that this verse is a Biblical watershed, or, as it is sometimes called, "a Great Divide", with every single person being on one side or the other. Our lives are either based on faith – or they are not. So this is what life comes down to: we accept the government of God in the universe or we do not. Those who reject His rule, whether they realise it or not, live lives that are shot through with doubt and fear. Those who receive His rule live lives of quiet confidence and faith.

FURTHER STUDY

Luke 17:1-5;
Mark 9:14-27;
Heb. 11:6

1. What was the apostles' request?

2. What was the request of the boy's father?

Prayer

Gracious Father, I see that whether I like it or not, I have to stand on one side of this Great Divide. I stand on Your side, dear Father, for nothing lies outside the domain of Your Kingdom – at least, nothing worth having. Amen.

What is faith?

"For as he thinks in his heart, so is he." (v.7, NKJ)
For reading & meditation – Proverbs 23:1-16

A man's belief," says Dr Albert Ellis, a well-known modern-day psychologist, "determines both his conduct and his character." Our text for today, written almost 3,000 years before Ellis, puts the truth in an even more succinct form.

There are two possibilities before each of us as we look at life: we can base our conclusions about the meaning of life on what the humanistic philosophers, poets and historians tell us, or we can base them on what God tells us in His Word. Either we take the Word of God and live by it – or we do not. If we take the attitude that the prophets didn't know what they were talking about and there are no such things as miracles in the universe, then we do what the writer to the Hebrews told us about yesterday – we draw back from the godly way of life. The Biblical way is living by faith.

Listen to the word given to Habakkuk once again: "The just shall live by his faith" (Hab. 2:4, AV). Faith is taking the Word of God and relying on it. It involves believing what God says, simply and solely because He said it. The heroes of faith listed in Hebrews 11 did just that – they had no real reason for believing what God told them, other than the fact that He had spoken. Why did Abraham take his son Isaac to Mount Moriah? Why did he prepare to offer him as a sacrifice? Simply because God had spoken. A little boy, when invited to comment on the statement, "Faith is having confidence in what God has spoken," said: "God has confidence in what He has said – so must we."

FURTHER STUDY

Heb. 11:1-40;
Gal. 3:6; Phil. 3:8-9

1. How does this chapter describe faith?

2. Write out your definition of faith.

Prayer

O Father, forgive my doubts and hesitancies – and help me to have an unshakeable confidence in the truth and power of Your Word. Show me how to link my littleness to Your greatness. In Jesus' Name I ask it. Amen.

The only way to live

"He follows my decrees and faithfully keeps my laws. That man is righteous; he will surely live ..." (v.9)
For reading & meditation – Ezekiel 18:1-18

We spend one more day looking at the text: "The just shall live by his faith" (Hab. 2:4, AV). Many think that the life of faith is reserved only for those Christians who go into full-time Christian work, trusting God to meet their financial and physical needs. The life of faith, however, means much more than that – it is living day by day under the controlling principle that God is true to His Word. And that is to be the position of every Christian – at all times.

Permit me to ask this personal question: What is the controlling principle in your life? Is it the expertise you have gained from years of education and training? Is it a shrewd understanding of finances? Or is it the Word of God and its clear portrayal of the fact that the things of time are merely a preparation for what is to come?

The Bible, of course, does not encourage us to turn our backs on the world, but it does tell us that we must have a right view of the world. It categorically states that what really matters is the eternal kingdom of God. Living by faith means that we live on God's side of the Great Divide that we talked about the other day. In other words, we take our view of life and the world not from what the politicians or the scientists say about them but from what God says about them. And when we are willing to stake everything on the fact that what we read in the Bible is true, then and only then will we fulfil the statement: "the just shall live by his faith". This is the only true way to live – anything else is just existence.

FURTHER STUDY

Matt. 8:1-13; 9:29-30; 17:20;
Mark 11:22

1. What did Jesus say to the centurion?

2. What did he say to the blind men?

Prayer

O Father, now I see that faith is not something that comes in fits and starts but something that underlies the whole of my life, help me understand it even more clearly. For I want to live, dear Lord, truly live – not just exist. Amen.

"The five woes"

*"Woe to him who ... makes himself wealthy by extortion! ... Woe
to him who builds his realm by unjust gain ..." (vv. 6, 9)*

For reading & meditation – Habakkuk 2:5-11

We continue examining the steps we must take in order to move
from confusion to faith, and now we come to the seventh: keep in
mind that no matter how dark and difficult things may appear, God is
always in control.

The verses before us today are the first of "the five woes" (2:5–20).
These "woes" spell out not only the doom of the Chaldeans, but the end
of all those who choose the way of sin. Everything that is evil is under
God's judgment. Though the Chaldeans would rise up and flourish, the
boundaries of their prosperity were clearly drawn up by God.

The first woe (vv. 6-8) has to do with the way in which the
Chaldeans will find their attempts at the sequestration of God's people
flung back in their faces as they themselves experience what it means to
be stripped of their possessions. The second woe (vv. 9-11) spells out
the punishment the Chaldeans will receive for getting rich at the expense of
the poor. The very houses they have built through unjust gain will cry
out against them and the eventual cost of their sinful lifestyle will be the
forfeiture of their own lives.

The Chaldeans would learn – and through them
the other nations – that righteousness always has the
last word. I once heard a young man say on television:
"I would like to get this generation acquainted with
this guy called 'Kick' – he gives you lots of thrills." I
felt like saying: "Young man, I suggest you get
acquainted with another guy called 'Kick Back'. He is
always a little behind the first guy – and always has the
last kick."

FURTHER STUDY

John 5:1-30;
Psa. 103:6;
Rom. 2:2

1. What did Jesus
declare about His
judgment?

2. What governs the
judgment of God?

Prayer

O Father, I know You have designed the universe to respond with either results or
consequences. When I obey Your laws I get results, when I break them I get consequences. I am determined to get results. Help me. In Jesus' Name. Amen.

"As surely as night follows day"

" For the earth will be filled with the knowledge of the glory of the Lord, as the waters cover the sea." (v.14)

For reading & meditation – Habakkuk 2:12-14

We continue looking at the five woes which God pronounces on the evil Chaldeans. The third woe (vv.12-14) pronounces God's verdict on them for the prosperity they have gained through murdering and plundering other nations.

We cannot read these woes without once again thinking: Why does God allow it? Why does He permit nations to rise up and inflict such cruelty and horror on others? He allows it for a wise and particular purpose – a purpose that many find difficult to comprehend. What is that purpose? This: He allows evil nations to arise so that the rest of the world might see in them a visual aid of what happens when people attempt to pit their strength against God and His moral laws. And what does happen? They are brought down and smashed into the ground.

Isn't this the reality of history? Think of great and powerful empires such as Egypt, Babylon, Greece and Rome. What happened to them? They rose in great glory but eventually they fell. Nation after nation has risen, only to fall. The time came when God's woe was pronounced against them and put into effect. And remember this: that principle is still in effect today. God's woe is still being pronounced

FURTHER STUDY

2 Sam. 1:1–27;
Prov. 14:12;
Judg. 17:6

1. What was David's lament?

2. What is the end of our natural thinking?

on all those nations who have chosen their own way instead of God's. They may have temporary success – we must be prepared for that – but as surely as night follows day, they will fall. The ultimate triumph of good over evil is certain. Let there be no doubt about it: "For the earth will be filled with the knowledge of the glory of the Lord, as the waters cover the sea."

Prayer

My Father and my God, something is quietly being burned into my consciousness – You are the One who has the last word in everything. Help me to face all that comes in the light of this great and glorious fact. Amen.

Finding out how not to live

*"What profit was there in worshipping all our man-made idols?
What a foolish lie that they could help! ..." (v.18, TLB)*

For reading & meditation – Habakkuk 2:15-19

Today we look at the last two woes which God pronounced on the evil and cruel Chaldeans. The fourth woe (vv.15-17) had to do with the "scorched earth" policy operated by the Chaldeans, which involved deforestation and the destruction of animals. (Both are a matter of divine concern – see Deuteronomy. 20:19 and Jonah 4:11.) Such outrage, says God, carries within it the seeds of its own destruction: "You cut down the forests of Lebanon – now you will be cut down! You terrified the wild animals ... Now terror will strike you" (v.17, TLB).

The recurrent theme of the five woes, namely that sin recoils upon the sinner, sounds once more in the fifth and final one (vv.18-19). This woe is uttered upon the idolater and exposes the inexplicable folly of his practice. The words, "Woe to those who command their lifeless wooden idols to arise and save them, who call out to the speechless stone to tell them what to do" (v.18, TLB), demonstrate that idolatry is not something that is innocuous; indeed, it is deeply injurious because it destroys man's basic intelligence. As someone has put it: "The worst thing about idolatry is to be the one who practises the idolatry."

How sad that, right before our eyes, we see history repeating itself as, once again, humanity looks to the idols which it has set up in the world to save itself from death and destruction. We cannot trust ourselves to any other power but God – not even the United Nations. The world has had so many lessons in how not to live, you would think its people would now be ready to try the Way.

FURTHER STUDY

Rom. 1:18-32;
Ex. 20:4-5;
Lev. 26:1;
Deut. 11:16

1. For what did men exchange the glory of God?

2. What was the result?

Prayer

O Father, how sad it is that despite the fact that people have had so many lessons in how not to live – lessons that have left them exhausted and frustrated – they still do not turn to the Way. Help them find it – and find it soon. In Jesus' Name. Amen.

Sin has no future

"... you may be sure that your sin will find you out." (v.23)
For reading & meditation – Numbers 32:20-33

No one can read the five woes which God pronounced upon the Chaldeans without coming to the conclusion that sin has no future. The Moffatt translation of Amos 2:13 says: "I will make your steps collapse." Is this fact or fiction? It is fact. The more evil advances the more its "steps collapse".

The same thought comes across in 1 Kings 21:21: "Because you have sold yourself to no purpose in doing what is evil in the sight of the Eternal" (Moffatt). Note the phrase, "to no purpose". Does the doing of what God cannot approve always end in futility? Is it all "to no purpose"? Most certainly. Take another text: "Your doom appears; your sin has blossomed, your pride has budded" (Ezek. 7:10, Moffatt). Notice how sin blossomed and pride budded – and the fruit? Doom!

Look with me at one more Scripture: "The Beast which was and is not" (Rev. 17:11, Moffatt). Note the words, "was and is not": evil has a past, but it has no future. It "was", but it will not be. No matter if "the Beast" is spelled with a capital "B": it will shrivel; it is under the law of decay. Give evil enough rope and it will hang itself. If it is not being constantly bolstered up by the surrounding good, it will go to pieces. All evil is a parasite upon good. You have to throw enough good around evil to keep it going. When it is total "Beast", it is total blight. Sin has no future. It may get away with things at the moment, but inevitably it is doomed. The seeds of its own destruction are carried within its bosom.

FURTHER STUDY

1 Cor. 4:1-5;
Job 20:27;
Eccl. 12:14;
Luke 12:2

1. What will God bring to light?

2. What does the verse at the top of the page actually say?

Prayer

Gracious Father, this age through which we are passing has looked upon evil until its eyes are tired. Turn people's gaze in the direction of Yourself, I pray. Help them see that evil is the great illusion – and God the great Illumination. Amen.

"The long view"

"… no weapon forged against you will prevail …" (v.17)
For reading & meditation – Isaiah 54:4-17

Having now considered the five woes which God pronounced on the cruel Chaldeans, what is our conclusion? We come back to what we said at the beginning of this section – no matter how dark and difficult things may appear, God is always in control. The Chaldeans would rise and be permitted to commit great atrocities, but God would use those atrocities to discipline Judah. The Chaldeans had no direct knowledge of God's will. They would plan their attacks, ravage the cities, marshall their armies simply to satisfy their own lust for power, but God would use their purposes to carry out His. When, however, it was all over, they would have to face the judgment of God for their inhuman practices.

It is of the utmost importance that we, the people of God, learn how to become people of what has been described as "the long view". What does it mean to have "the long view"? It means, quite simply, to see things from God's perspective. If you take the short view of what is happening around you, then you come to your own conclusions. If you take the long view, then you come to God's conclusions.

God takes the long view of history and is quietly bringing all things to a predetermined end. My Christian friend, don't be a human ostrich – burying your head in the sand because you are afraid to face tomorrow. Nothing can happen in the future that God cannot control. Catch the sweep of His mind and the glory of His long-range purposes, and realise, as our text for today says, that no weapon forged against you can prevail.

FURTHER STUDY

Col. 1:13-22;
John 1:1-3;
1 Cor. 8:6

1. Where should we focus our gaze?

2. What does Colossians 1 reveal to us?

Prayer

O God, help me to look at life with "the long view". Drive deep into my spirit the thought that because You know the end from the beginning, nothing that is evil can work successfully against me. I am so thankful. Amen.

Ask "what?" not "why?"

"But the Lord is in his holy temple; let all the earth be silent before him." (v.20)

For reading & meditation – Habakkuk 2:20

The last part of God's answer to Habakkuk is as forceful as it is brief. It is that He knows what He is doing, even when circumstances seem to be speeding downhill like a car out of control. The phrase "let all the earth be silent before him" includes everything and everybody – the godly as well as the heathen. Sometimes God speaks pretty straight to us – just as He is doing here – and tells us things that we might not want to know, but things we certainly need to know.

If I understand this verse correctly, God is saying, in effect: "Stop asking endless questions such as: 'Why does God do this?' and 'Why does God do that?' Understand the fact that I know what I am doing and that I am the Lord of history." Once we make up our minds that God knows what He is doing, then all confusion vanishes. And that applies not only to the personal issues of life but to the global ones as well.

The same Word that brought comfort and illumination to Habakkuk's heart can, if we let it, comfort our own hearts. If you look at almost any day's newspaper you will find reports of rape, murder, crime, injustice and corruption. But if you turn from your newspaper and look up at God you will find yourself looking at the Ultimate, the Absolute. And what will happen? Instead of your heart being filled with fear, it will become strangely peaceful. Why? Because you will realise that God is at the centre of His universe and He is working out His purposes. And as someone said: "He who knows what God is doing need never ask why."

FURTHER STUDY

Matt. 19:16-26;
Job 42:2;
Psa. 115:3;
Isa. 43:13;
Luke 1:37

1. What did Jesus declare?

2. What can you declare today?

Prayer

Gracious and loving heavenly Father, help me this day to catch the sweep of Your purposes and become a part of them. Deepen my conviction that You are in control, for I see that then I will focus more on the "what" than the "why". Amen.

Focusing on God

"O Lord, I have heard the report of You and was afraid ..."
(v.2, Amplified Bible)
For reading & meditation – Habakkuk 3:1-2

Having examined the nature of God's revelation to Habakkuk, we now ask: What is the prophet's response to the divine unfolding? He draws near to God in an attitude of reverential worship and praise. This suggests the eighth step we must take if we are to move from confusion to confidence: make it a daily habit to worship the Lord and open your heart to Him in fervent prayer and praise.

Habakkuk confesses himself to be overwhelmed by the things which God has revealed to him: "I worship you in awe for the fearful things you are going to do" (v.2, TLB). One of the inevitable results of spending time in God's presence, contemplating Him and listening to His voice is that there arises within the heart a spontaneous desire to worship Him.

It was this thought that inspired me to launch the *Every Day with Jesus* study notes in the beginning. I realised that if I could focus people's minds on to a small portion of God's Word every day, it would inevitably result in a greater understanding and devotion to Him. The results have been astonishing. Someone who wrote to me said: "My life has been turned right around since I have begun to focus my thinking on God before I focus on the day."

You see, it is one of the laws of life that you become like the thing on which you focus. Focus on money and you will become like it – hard and metallic. Focus on getting even with those who act spitefully toward you and you will become like them – mean and inconsiderate. Focus on God and you will become like Him – good, gracious and generous.

FURTHER STUDY
John 4:1-24;
1 Chron. 16:29;
Psa. 96:9

1. How are we to worship?

2. Spend time today focusing your worship on Christ.

Prayer

O Father, if it is true that I become like that on which I focus, then help me to focus fully on You. Help me to maintain daily contact with You – through worshipping You and reading Your Word. In Jesus' Name I ask it. Amen.

"Worth-ship"

"I want to know Christ and the power of his resurrection ..."
(v.10)

For reading & meditation – Philippians 3:1-14

Yesterday we saw that one of the inevitable results of contemplating God and listening to His voice is a spontaneous desire to worship Him. Habakkuk, after having been closeted with God and receiving the staggering revelation of His power and sovereignty, finds his heart filled to overflowing.

You have only to read the third chapter of Habakkuk to see how his emotions are set on fire. It's interesting to notice that so strong is the emotional content in this chapter that it begins with the words: "A prayer of Habakkuk the prophet. On *shigionoth*." The word "*shigionoth*" (plural of *shigaion*; see heading to Psalm 7) is believed to indicate the tempo at which this prayer was originally meant to be sung. The tempo was to be strong one, corresponding to the profound emotions raised through the words and concepts of this chapter.

Why were Habakkuk's emotions so aroused? Because his soul had been set ablaze by a thrilling revelation of God. One of the things we must understand about the Christian life is that our worship of God is largely determined by our understanding of Him. So permit me once again to ask you a personal question: How do you see God? What is the depth of your understanding of Him? Today, comparatively few know how to really worship God. This is a direct result of the superficial preaching and teaching that comes from so many modern pulpits. Our worship of God depends, as the word suggests, on how much "worth" we ascribe to Him. The greater "worth" you see in Him, the greater worship you will give to Him.

FURTHER STUDY

Col. 1:1-12;
Jer. 9:24;
Hosea 6:3;
John 17:3

1. What was Paul's desire for the Colossians?

2. Write a psalm describing what your God is like.

Prayer

O God, if it is true that my worship of You flows from my understanding of You, then help me to know You more. As I spend time reading Your Word and in prayer, reveal Yourself to me – in a fresh and living way. In Christ's Name I ask it. Amen.

The highest form of prayer

"O Lord, listen! O Lord, forgive! O Lord, hear and act! ... do not delay, because your city and your people bear your Name." (v.19)
For reading & meditation – Daniel 9:1-19

We look now at how Habakkuk moves from worship to prayer – a prayer, by the way, which has become one of the best-known petitions of Scripture: "O Lord, revive Your work in the midst of the years! In the midst of the years make it known; In wrath remember mercy" (Hab. 3:2, NKJ).

We cannot help but notice, in this prayer the prophet's attitude toward God has completely changed. There is no longer any questioning of His way. He does not even protest at what God has told him about the terrible things that are going to happen. Nor does he petition God to reverse His judgment. Instead, there is a humble recognition that what God says He is about to do is perfectly proper and that the punishment that is to come upon Judah is one that she deserves. Habakkuk's prayer contains an attitude of complete submission to the will of God.

I have chosen the prayer of Daniel for today's reading because he too displays this attitude. Like Habakkuk, Daniel also came to a place of humiliation and submission to the divine will. But how did Habakkuk arrive at this position? I think it was because he had changed his spiritual focus from gazing at Judah to gazing at God. When Habakkuk focused his gaze on Judah and the Chaldeans he was troubled, but when he focused his gaze on God, he moved into the realm of spiritual light and illumination. He saw things from God's point of view. Thus he is concerned for the glory of God – and nothing else. We practise the highest form of prayer when our concern for God's glory transcends all other priorities.

FURTHER STUDY

Eph. 6:1-7;
Psa. 40:8; 143:10

1. How are we to carry out the will of God?

2. How did the psalmist respond to God's will?

Prayer

O God, help me lift my praying to this high place. Teach me how to bring my priorities in line with Your priority and how to make my primary concern the glory of God. In Jesus' Name. Amen.

A plea for revival

"Why don't you tear the sky apart and come down? ..."
(v.1, GNB)

For reading & meditation – Isaiah 64:1-8

We ended yesterday with the thought that the highest form of prayer is when we are concerned about the glory of God – and nothing else. Habakkuk did not petition God to give up the idea of using the Chaldeans to refine the people of Judah. Nor did he ask that there would be no sacking of Jerusalem. There was no such petition because he had come to see that the forthcoming events were well deserved.

Now that the prophet had begun to see the whole issue from God's point of view, his burden was for God's cause and God's glory. His petition – so I believe – can be paraphrased in these words: "Lord, whatever we, Your people, have to put up with is of no concern so long as Your work is revived and kept pure." His one great plea is that God will "revive [His] work in the midst of the years!" (Hab. 3:2, NKJ). Most commentators believe that the expression "in the midst of the years" means "while these terrible things that are predicted are going on among us".

Oh, that we could hear more of this kind of praying in our churches today. Most prayers we hear are concerned with topical issues – the nuclear threat, world economy, violence, corruption, and so on. These issues are important, of course, and most certainly there is a need to keep them in the focus of our praying. But these matters should not be our biggest concern. I have no hesitation in saying that the chief concern of the Church in this present age should be the spiritual restoration of God's people through a worldwide Holy Spirit revival.

FURTHER STUDY

Isa. 26:1-9;
2 Chron. 15:15;
Psa. 38:9; 73:25

1. Why did Isaiah seek God?

2. What was the psalmist's confession?

Prayer

My Father and my God, forgive us that we have allowed ourselves to slip into the depths of spiritual poverty and emptiness. Breathe once again into the midst of us – and begin, dear Lord, in me. Amen

"In wrath remember mercy"

*"Correct me, Lord, but only with justice – not in your anger,
lest you reduce me to nothing." (v.24)*

For reading & meditation – Jeremiah 10:12-25

We are seeing that Habakkuk's chief concern in prayer was not that God should call a halt to His plans, but that there should be a spiritual revival in Judah. The prophet's great fear was that Judah might be overwhelmed, and so he prays, in effect: "Preserve Your witness in our midst, O Lord – keep it alive, don't let it be destroyed."

The Hebrew word "revive" contains the idea of God bending down to the dying embers of a fire and breathing into them until they burst into flame. What an appropriate prayer this is for the Church today. If, like Habakkuk, we would make the Name and glory of God, rather than world events, the prime focus of our praying, we would come closer to the Biblical pattern and be more likely to see His glory revealed.

Before we turn aside from Habakkuk's great prayer and examine the final section of this chapter, we must spend a few moments looking at the final statement in his prayer: "In wrath remember mercy" (Hab. 3:2). The great devotional Bible commentator Matthew Henry says of this phrase: "Habakkuk does not say 'Remember our merit', but 'Lord, remember Thy own mercy'." The prophet uses a method which seems to be characteristic of that of many of the Old Testament saints when at prayer, namely, to remind God of His own nature. This was not a technique but showed a deep and profound understanding of the nature of importunate prayer. Modern-day praying lacks the depth and understanding that we see illustrated in the lives of the ancient prophets. When the Church gets back to powerful praying, then and only then will it get powerful results.

FURTHER STUDY

Micah 7:1-18;
Psa. 103:18; 108:4

1. How did Micah
view God?

2. Write out a
definition of "mercy".

Prayer

Gracious and loving heavenly Father, breathe on the dying embers of Your Church this day – myself included – until out of the ashes comes a new and living flame. This I ask in Christ's peerless and precious Name. Amen.

"Self-talk"

"… let your mind dwell on these things." (v.8, NASB)
For reading & meditation – Philippians 4:1-9

We come now to the ninth step in our progression from confusion to confidence: remind yourself of the evidences of God's faithfulness in the past and constantly talk to yourself about them.

At this point, we are going to leave Habakkuk just for a moment to lay down a foundation for our thinking over the next few days. Let me ask you: Do you ever talk to yourself? No? Then permit me to correct you. Although you don't realise it – because it goes on just below the threshold of awareness – you talk to yourself almost every minute of your waking day. Whatever event takes place in our lives, we respond to that event by talking to ourselves about it. Psychologists call this the "theory of propositional control" – we talk to ourselves in sentences. And what we tell ourselves, even subconsciously, will determine the way we feel about issues.

Have you heard someone ask the question: Why do I feel this way? Well, why do people feel a particular way about things? It is because our feelings are largely the direct consequence of our thinking. If you respond to a negative or unpleasant event by saying to yourself "Why should this happen to me?" then it is not difficult to predict how you will feel – sad and depressed. But if you respond by telling yourself, "God loves me and will never allow anything to happen to me unless it accords with a wise and loving purpose", you will feel quite different. Why? Because your feelings follow your thinking – just like little ducklings follow their mother.

FURTHER STUDY

Psa. 42:1-11; 94:19;
Prov. 23:7
(footnote)

1. What are some of the statements the psalmist made to himself?

2. What are some of the statements you make to yourself?

Prayer

O Father, if what I say to myself is powerful and determinative in my personality, then help me to control my self-talk so that it serves me rather than enslaves me. In Christ's Name I ask it. Amen.

Feeling better!

"You came out to deliver your people, to save your anointed one ..." (v.13)

For reading & meditation – Habakkuk 3:3-15

Now we have established the idea that what we tell ourselves, consciously or unconsciously, greatly influences how we feel, we look at how this is illustrated in the prophet Habakkuk's life and experience. The section before us today is dominated by remembrances of God's deliverances in the past. It is helpful to take in the whole section at one time so that we catch the sweep and force of the prophet's thinking.

First, he consciously focuses on the thought that God is mighty and all-powerful (vv. 3-7). He says: "His splendour was like the sunrise; rays flashed from his hand, where his power was hidden ... He stood, and shook the earth; he looked, and made the nations tremble." Next, he concentrates on the facts which surrounded Israel's deliverance from Egypt (vv. 8-15): "You split the earth with rivers; the mountains saw you and writhed ... the deep roared ... Sun and moon stood still ... you strode through the earth ... in anger ... You trampled the sea with your horses ...".

Can you see what Habakkuk is doing here? He is calling to mind the way in which God has come to the aid of His people in times past, and the more he focuses on God's faithfulness and power, the more the remaining mists of fog and confusion are dispelled. This, then, is the divinely provided way of handling all fear and confusion – consciously to focus on the facts of God's deliverances in the past. When the prophet did this, he began to feel better. And why? Because positive thoughts about God led to positive feelings about God. They always do.

FURTHER STUDY

Psa. 89:1;
2 Tim. 2:1-13;
Deut. 7:9;
1 Cor. 1:9

1. What was the psalmist able to sing about?

2. List some ideas of God's faithfulness in your own life.

Prayer

Father, help me not to view this principle merely as an interesting idea, but help me put it to the test in my daily life and experience. Show me even more clearly that how I think greatly influences how I feel. Amen.

Happy remembrances

"… a scroll of remembrance was written in his presence concerning those who feared the Lord and honoured his name." (v.16)

For reading & meditation – Malachi 3:8-18

Yesterday we looked at some of the things which the prophet brought to mind concerning God's past deliverances and we saw how these remembrances filled his heart with hope and consolation.

Today we are in a better position than Habakkuk, for we have even more wonderful facts on which to focus our thinking. We can see, for example, how everything that was revealed to the prophet was literally fulfilled. The Chaldeans did indeed invade Judah and carried people into captivity in Babylon. But at the appointed time, God brought judgment on the Chaldeans and destroyed them and caused a remnant of His people to return to Jerusalem.

However, we can go still further. We can focus not just on the fact of how God made a way for His people to come out of Egypt and Babylon, but on the greater deliverance which He engineered when He made a path to bring us from the dominion of Satan to the very doors of heaven. In the Old Testament, a sacrificial lamb could provide redemption for an individual or a family. But in the New Testament, the Lamb of God purchased redemption not just for an individual or a family but for the sins of the whole world!

FURTHER STUDY

Rom. 8:1-39;
2 Cor. 9:15;
Eph. 2:8

1. What can we now cry out to God?

2. What is available to us through Christ's sacrifice?

And there is yet more. We can focus on the glorious fact that our Lord has overcome the darkness of death, and by His glorious resurrection has given us the eternal pledge that because He lives, we shall live also (John 14:19). Keep these thoughts in mind throughout this day, and I promise you – you will know the effect of them in your feelings.

Prayer

Glorious Father, I come to You to ask for Your help in keeping these remembrances of Your faithfulness and power before me this day. I give You my mind – so that You can give me Yours. In Christ's Name I ask it. Amen.

On being human

"I heard and my heart pounded, my lips quivered ... and my legs trembled ..." (v.16)

For reading & meditation – Habakkuk 3:16

It seems strange that after recalling and reciting so many of the facts relating to God's strength and power, Habakkuk should be in the state we see him in at the moment. *The Living Bible* puts it thus: "I tremble when I hear all this; my lips quiver with fear. My legs give way beneath me and I shake in terror. I will quietly wait for the day of trouble to come upon the people who invade us."

If it is true that what we think about greatly influences the way we feel, then why, after focusing on such a catalogue of good things, does Habakkuk feel the way he does? The answer, I believe, is this: although calling to mind God's goodness is a proven and reliable method of dealing with fear and producing positive feelings within us, it does not completely eliminate all negative emotions.

It is terribly important that we understand this. Some preach that once we become Christians, we need never experience any negative or uncomfortable feelings. That simply is not so. The Christian faith does not promise us that once we become Christians we will never again experience negative emotions, but it does promise that the negative emotions will be manageable and brought under control. Habakkuk has been brought to the place where he sees everything perfectly clearly, but as he contemplates the trouble that is coming upon Judah, he trembles like a leaf. We should note, however, that though he feels strong emotions, he is not overcome by them. If this ever happens to you, don't see it as a lack of faith. Like Habakkuk, you are simply being human.

FURTHER STUDY

Phil. 2:1-13;
1 Cor. 2:3;
2 Cor. 7:15

1. How are we to work out our salvation?

2. What feelings did Paul admit to?

Prayer

Thank You, Lord, for reminding me that fear and trembling do not cancel out my faith, but serve as a reminder of my humanity. Help me to understand this – and not be overwhelmed by it. In Jesus' Name. Amen.

How to treat trouble

*"Yet I will rejoice in the Lord, I will exalt in the victorious God
of my salvation!" (v.18, Amplified Bible)*
For reading & meditation – Habakkuk 3:17-18

We have now reached the tenth and final step in our progression
from confusion to confidence: decide to face everything that
comes not in a spirit of resignation but in a spirit of rejoicing. The passage before us today shows quite clearly that it is possible to rejoice, even
in the face of the most disturbing circumstances: "Though the fig-tree
does not bud and there are no grapes on the vines ... yet I will rejoice in
the Lord, I will be joyful in God my Saviour."

There are three responses we can make in the presence of trouble: we
can rebel against it, resign ourselves to it, or we can rejoice in it. Many
take the way of rebellion when confronted by trouble – they cry out
against the heavens and question the justice of God, believing they have
good cause to do so. It is an understandable reaction, of course – but it
is not the Christian way. Others resign themselves to the situation and
say such things as: "Well, what will be will be." "There's no point in crying over spilt milk." "I will just have to grin and bear it." But resignation
is not the Christian way either – although many believers think it is.
Beneath all resignation simmers an unconscious resentment. It cannot
always be observed and it is sometimes so deeply
repressed that it cannot even be felt – but it is there
nevertheless.

FURTHER STUDY
Acts 16:16-40;
5:41; 2 Cor. 6:10

*1. How did Paul and
Silas respond to their
circumstances?*

*2. What was the
result?*

The Christian way of facing trouble is the way of
rejoicing. When the worst comes to the worst, we are
not just to put up with it, but rejoice in it. And if we
can't – then we still have a vital lesson to learn.

Prayer

O Father, I have learned so many lessons through the life of Your servant Habakkuk
– help me not to miss this last but vital one also. Teach me how to rejoice in all things.
For Jesus' sake. Amen.

"All times" – a mistranslation?

"Rejoice at all times." (v.16, Moffatt)
For reading & meditation – 1 Thessalonians 5:12-24

Many Christians find this text so challenging that they cannot allow their minds to focus on it. But as we have been saying – evasion will never get us anywhere. A letter I once received asked: "Did Paul really mean we should rejoice at all times? Didn't he mean sometimes? Can this be a mistranslation?" No, it is not a mistranslation – it is a true and accurate translation of the apostle's words.

But is it really possible to rejoice at all times? I believe it is. Here's the secret: we can rejoice in everything only to the extent that we see God in everything. Some might have difficulty with this, and respond: "There are some things which come from the devil; how can what you say be applied to that?" It is true that God may not be in the genesis of something, but He can certainly be in its exodus. Your circumstances or problems may have begun with the devil, but by the time they get to you and through you, they have a divine purpose running through them.

An old lady was praying for bread. Some boys, hearing her, decided to play a trick on her. They climbed up on her roof and threw some loaves down the chimney. "Praise the Lord," shouted the old lady, "God has heard my prayer." The boys then knocked on her door and said: "But it was not God who gave you the bread – it was us." She laughingly replied: "Well, the devil may have brought it, but it was God who sent it." Wherever an event comes from, by the time it gets to you, you can be sure it has got God's permission – and thus has the potential of becoming not a source of trouble but a source of triumph.

FURTHER STUDY

1 Pet. 4:1-13;
Phil. 4:4; Psa. 33:1;
James 1:2-3

1. Why does God allow us to go through trials?

2. Why can we rejoice in our trials?

Prayer

O Father, thank You for imparting to me the secret of continuous rejoicing – we can rejoice in everything when we see God in everything. Imprint these words indelibly on my spirit so that I may for ever live in the light of them. In Jesus' Name. Amen.

Hinds' feet on high places

*"… He makes my feet like hinds' feet, and will make me to walk
… upon my high places …" (v.19, Amplified Bible)*
For reading & meditation – Habakkuk 3:18-19

What a transformation has taken place in the heart of Habakkuk. Now he no longer stumbles in the darkness of doubt and spiritual confusion, but leaps from one revelation to another with the sure-footedness of a deer. He walks on high places where others fear to tread. By climbing his watchtower and entering into a dialogue with God, and by listening to His replies, Habakkuk has learned and discovered so much that his soul is lifted above the doubts and uncertainties that once plagued his mind. The prophet began in confusion – but ends in confidence.

What made the difference? Summing it all up in a single sentence – he saw that God was in charge of earth's affairs, no matter how things looked to the contrary, and he trusted Him to do what was right. When we learn to drop our anchor into the reassuring depths of God's nature and character and learn to trust Him even when we cannot trace Him, then we too will know the sustaining joy that Habakkuk experienced back there long centuries ago.

If we believe in God, really believe in Him, then we will not disintegrate when world events take a disastrous course, or when our newspapers tell us that society is falling apart at the seams. We believe in God's Word and therefore have inside information about the future that no news commentator (unless he is Christian) can possibly possess. Christ is Lord of history – and nothing can hinder His perfect purposes from coming to pass. So step out with confidence on the high places of life. God is the One with the last Word.

FURTHER STUDY

Psa. 37:1-40; 118:8;
Prov. 3:5; Isa. 50:10

1. How does David depict the short-lived prosperity of the wicked?

2. Where is your trust placed?

Prayer

Father, how can I sufficiently thank You for showing me the ten steps which brought Habakkuk from confusion to confidence? Help me ever to remember them and thus turn theory into fact. In Christ's Name I ask it. Amen.

The
Beatitudes

A prescription for health

"His disciples came to him, and he began to teach them…"
(vv.1-2)

For reading & meditation – Matthew 5:1-11

Today we begin a study of one of the most powerful and profound passages in Scripture – the Beatitudes. They form the first part of the Lord's teaching in what is known as the Sermon on the Mount and were addressed to His disciples. My hope is that our study of the Beatitudes will have a great impact on our spiritual lives and that we will be blessed by the discoveries we make together.

We begin our theme by laying down the thought that the eight principles which comprise the Beatitudes are the best prescription for mental and spiritual health it is possible to find. Dr James Fisher, a well-known and widely travelled psychiatrist, went throughout the world looking for the positive qualities that make for good mental health. He said: "I dreamed of writing a handbook that would be simple, practical, easy to understand and easy to follow; it would tell people how to live – what thoughts and attitudes and philosophies to cultivate, and what pitfalls to avoid in seeking mental health. And quite by accident I discovered that such a work had been completed – the Beatitudes."

What an amazing admission! I would go so far as to say that once a person absorbs the principles which underlie the Beatitudes – and lives by them – then that person will never again fall prey to serious depression or despair. How sad that so often the Christian Church has to refer its depressed and discouraged people to the mental experts of the world when we hold in our hands the blueprint for healthy and abundant living.

FURTHER STUDY

Luke 6:20-38;
Psa. 32:1-2; 41:1

1. What does "blessed" mean to you?

2. How would you define the word "beatitude"?

Prayer

My Father, help me to come to You at the beginning of these studies like a little child – open and receptive. Show me how to open my heart and my hands to receive Your prescription for mental and spiritual health. Amen.

"The psychology of Jesus"

"He did not need man's testimony about man, for he knew what was in a man." (v.25)

For reading & meditation – John 2:12-25

Yesterday we touched on the statement of a psychiatrist, Dr James Fisher, who said that when searching for the positive attitudes which made for good mental health, he came across the Beatitudes and realised that he need search no longer.

After nearly fifty years' experience of helping people with mental, emotional and physical problems he concluded: "If you were to take the total sum of all authoritative articles ever written by the most qualified of psychologists and psychiatrists on the subject of mental hygiene – if you were to combine them and refine them and cleave out the excess verbiage – if you were to take the whole of the meat and none of the parsley, and if you were to have these unadulterated bits of pure scientific knowledge concisely expressed by the most capable of living poets, you would have an awkward and incomplete summation of our Lord's Beatitudes – and it would suffer immeasurably through comparison."

Dr Raymond Cramer, a minister and a Christian psychologist, says something similar when he describes the Beatitudes as "the psychology of Jesus". Some may find that expression unacceptable when applied to the Beatitudes, but remember, this is a scientist who is speaking. In studying the laws of human behaviour and seeking to discover what brings a person to his highest point of integration, he came to see that the words of Jesus in the Beatitudes are the clearest and most succinct expression of the principles by which a person can know contentment and inner happiness. In an age which is fascinated with the study of human behaviour, there is only one true psychology – the psychology of Jesus.

FURTHER STUDY

Col. 1:1-20; 2:9-10;
John 1:16;
Eph. 1:22-23

1. Where is fulness found?

2. What does this mean for us?

Prayer

Father, I see that psychology, as well as all other "-ologies", are only valid as they are brought to Your feet. Show me, dear Lord, not just how to live, but how to live abundantly. In Jesus' Name I pray. Amen.

"The beautiful attitudes"

*"Rather, clothe yourselves with the Lord Jesus
Christ ..." (v.14)*

For reading & meditation – Romans 13:7-14

We continue considering on the fact that the Beatitudes are the finest prescription for mental and spiritual health that has ever been given. It is helpful to keep in mind at this stage in our meditations that the Beatitudes are *be*-attitudes, not *do*-attitudes; the doing comes out of the being. Some ministers and commentators refer to them as "the beautiful attitudes" – a description I find greatly appealing.

Our attitudes have a tremendous and powerful influence upon every part of our being – physical as well as emotional. A missionary from the Philippines tells how, during the war, he and his wife were ordered into prison camps by the Japanese, and were instructed that they could take with them all they could carry in their suitcases and no more. His wife, weighing just over 100 pounds, and not at all strong, carried a load of 200 pounds, mostly tinned food, a distance of five miles – a load neither of them could even lift after they arrived. Mannheim, a famous scientist, says that we normally use about one-eighth of our physical reserves, and that these reserves are only called upon when we employ the right attitudes.

If our attitudes can help tap hidden physical reserves, then think of what our experience can be if we adopt the "beautiful attitudes" which our Lord expounds for us in His Sermon on the Mount. We can maximise our potential and multiply our effectiveness, not only in the physical area of our being, but in our mental and emotional areas also. Many doctors and scientists agree that it is not our arteries but our attitudes which have the biggest say in our personal well-being.

FURTHER STUDY

1 Pet. 2:21;
Matt. 11:29;
John 13:15;
Heb. 12:2

1. What did Jesus do
besides expounding
these attitudes?

2. How should our
lives be?

Prayer

Loving heavenly Father, help me to do as Your Word commands and "clothe myself with the Lord Jesus Christ". Show me how to have His attitudes – the "beautiful attitudes" – so that I might live fully and abundantly. Amen.

The inner affects the outer

" 'All things are lawful for me'? Yes, but not all are good for me ..." (v.12, Moffatt)

For reading & meditation – 1 Corinthians 6:12-20

We are still focusing on this important thought that our attitudes play an important and determinative part in our physical health. One doctor told me that immediately he receives the current edition of *Every Day with Jesus*, he quickly scans it to see if I have written anything along the line of the relationship between attitudes and health – a favourite topic of mine – and then orders a small supply for those of his patients who need to have their attitudes changed. He wrote to me on one occasion and said: "Keep coming back to this subject every time you can – you just don't know how much good you are doing in my medical practice."

According to an article in the *British Medical Journal*, "there is not a tissue or an organ in the body that is not influenced by the attitude of mind and spirit". Man is a unit made up of spirit, soul and body, and he cannot be sick in one part without passing on the sickness to other parts. The attitudes we hold in our minds do not stay merely as attitudes – they pass over into definite physical effects.

God has so designed our beings that the right attitudes produce the right effects in our bodies. Suppose they produced the wrong effects. Then the body and morality would be alien to one another. An outstanding surgeon said: "I've discovered the kingdom of God at the end of my scalpel; it's in the tissues. The right thing morally is always the right thing physically." The laws of morality and the laws of health are written by the same God for the same purpose – healthy and happy living.

FURTHER STUDY

2 Cor. 4:1-16;
Prov. 20:27;
Matt. 15:18-19;
Mark 7:21-23

1. How did Paul need to be daily renewed?

2. What is it that defiles a man?

Prayer

O Father, You have made us so that we can either damage or deliver ourselves in this matter of health. Help me to have Your attitudes in everything I say and everything I do. For Your own dear Name's sake. Amen.

Christ's first word ...

"Be happy ... at all times." (v.16, Phillips)
For reading & meditation – 1 Thessalonians 5:12-24

Now that we have spent a few days meditating on the fact that the Beatitudes provide us with the right mental and spiritual attitudes for healthy and abundant living, we are ready to begin focusing on the first of these profound statements: "Blessed are the poor in spirit, for theirs is the kingdom of heaven." (Matt. 5:3).

Some translations read, "Happy are the poor in spirit ...", and one goes so far as to say, "Congratulations to the poor in spirit ..." It is important to keep in mind that the word "happy" (Greek *makarios*) carries a far richer tone than we commonly attach to the word. It suggests a deep, abiding happiness, not just a temporary emotional lift.

In the very first words of the Sermon on the Mount, therefore, Jesus puts His finger on one of life's most vital issues – individual and personal happiness. We all want to be happy – and rightly so. The longing for lasting happiness is a deep-rooted instinct that has been built into us by the Creator Himself. The God who made the sunset, painted the rose, put the smile on a baby's face, gave the gift of playfulness to a kitten and put laughter in our souls is surely not happy when we are unhappy.

Although it is a God-given instinct to be happy, we must also see that it is only God who can make us happy. Apart from Him and His redemptive love as expressed through the cross and the resurrection, we would be "most miserable" (1 Cor. 15:19, AV). As someone once confessed: "Now that I know Christ, I'm happier when I'm sad than before when I was glad."

FURTHER STUDY

Rom. 14:1-18;
Isa. 12:3;
John 16:24;
1 Pet. 1:8

1. What is the kingdom of God?

2. What is this joy full of?

Prayer

Thank You, my Father, that You not only command me to be happy but provide me with the resources which make it gloriously possible. One touch of Your gladness and my heart sings for ever. I am so deeply, deeply thankful. Amen.

You cannot *make* happiness

"And he saw them toiling in rowing ..." (v.48, AV)
For reading & meditation – Mark 6:45-51

Yesterday we said that we all want to be happy – and rightly so. This is a deep-rooted instinct which God has built into us. But happiness is not something you make but something you receive. You cannot make happiness any more than you can make love. You can express love but you cannot make love.

So it is with happiness. You cannot make it. She is a coquette: follow her and she eludes you; turn from her and interest yourself in something or someone else and you may win her. The Scriptures and psychology are at one here, and the experience of millions confirms their findings. The most miserable and fed-up people I know are those who are most bent on being happy. They are saying to themselves what the old lady said to the frightened child whom she had taken to the circus: "Now enjoy yourself, do you hear? I brought you here to have a good time, so make sure you do" – as she shook him till his teeth rattled.

In the passage before us today, it is said that the disciples were toiling, rowing in the dark and getting nowhere. The wind and the waves were against them and the whole venture was ending in futility. Then Jesus came. In John's account of the same event, we are told that they took Him into their boat and immediately the boat reached the shore where they were heading (John 6:21). This is the way it is with happiness. We strive to achieve it, but we "toil in rowing". Then we let Christ in – and lo, we reach the shore where we were going.

FURTHER STUDY

Isa. 61:1-10;
Luke 10:21;
John 15:11;
Psa. 16:11;
Neh. 8:10

1. What was Isaiah's testimony?

2. Where does our strength come from?

Prayer

Father, I see that to get happiness, I must for-get it. It is not an achievement, but a by-product – a by-product of knowing You. Help me to know You better, not just today but every day. In Jesus' Name I pray. Amen.

"Poor enough to receive"

*"I tell you the truth, anyone who will not receive the kingdom of
God like a little child will never enter it." (v.15)*

For reading & meditation – Mark 10:13-31

Today we ask ourselves: If happiness is not something we can create
but something we receive, how do we go about receiving it? Listen
again to the words of Jesus: "Blessed are the poor in spirit, for theirs is
the kingdom of heaven."

What does it mean to be "poor in spirit"? There are those who tell us
that the words should read, "Blessed in spirit are the poor" – an idea
derived from Luke 6:20, which reads: "Blessed are you who are poor, for
yours is the kingdom of God." Our Lord, however, is not thinking here
of material poverty, but spiritual poverty: "Blessed are the poor in spirit." The word for "poor" in the Greek is *ptochos* and refers to a chosen
poverty. It implies a voluntary emptying of the inner being and is used
of those who by choice are so poor that they become poor enough to
receive. One translation puts it: "Blessed are those who are receptive in
spirit" – those who are willing to empty their hands of their own possessions and have them filled with the riches of God.

Jesus' first prescription for happiness, then, is a voluntary act of self-
renunciation. This reverses the usual prescriptions for
happiness, which begin with words such as "assert",
"take", "release" or "affirm". The first step, therefore
toward mental and spiritual health is self-renunciation. It is the decision we must take to reach out and
receive Christ – with empty hands. Note that – with
empty hands. The reason why so many fail to find
Christ is because they are so unreceptive. Christ cannot give Himself to them because they do not give
themselves to Him.

FURTHER STUDY

Mark 9:30-37;
Matt. 10:40;
Luke 8:40;
John 1:12

1. What was the
attitude of the
disciples?

2. What was Jesus'
response?

Prayer

O Father, help me to fling everything else away so that I might find You. I will take
this first prescription: I will be humble enough to acknowledge my need and receive.
In Jesus' Name I pray. Amen.

Receptivity – the first law of life

*"… as many as received him, to them gave he power to become
the sons of God …"* (v.12, AV)

For reading & meditation – John 1:1-14

We ended yesterday by saying that the first step toward mental and spiritual health is self-renunciation and receptivity. I must be willing to acknowledge my need of Christ, stop striving to find happiness and instead receive Him into my life then, like the disciples we talked about the other day, I have reached the shore where I was going.

It should not be considered strange that entrance into the kingdom of God begins with receptivity – isn't that where all life begins? Our scientists tell us that the ovum and the sperm have to receive each other before they can begin the positive business of producing active life. The seed in the ground receives moisture and nutrition from the earth before it can begin to give forth in flower and fruit. If it doesn't begin with receptivity, it doesn't begin. The scientist who doesn't sit down before the facts as a little child and who is not prepared to give up every preconceived notion and follow to whatever end nature will lead him will know nothing.

The first law of life is receptivity, and that is also the first law of the kingdom of God. Look at our text once again: "As many as received him, to them gave he power to become the sons of God."

FURTHER STUDY

Matt. 13:1-23;
Acts 17:11;
1 Thess. 2:13

1. To what must we be receptive?

2. What was said of the Bereans?

How do we get power? First by receptivity: "as many as received him". At the very threshold of Christ's kingdom, then, we are met with the demand for self-emptying and receptivity. Have you made your own personal response to this demand? If not, I urge you to do so today. If you are not willing to do this, then nothing else can follow; if you are willing, then everything else follows.

Prayer

O God, You wrap me around as the atmosphere wraps itself around my body. Help me to respond to You as my physical body responds to its environment and lives. Through Jesus Christ my Lord. Amen.

Flinging away your garment

*"And throwing aside his garment, he rose and came to
Jesus." (v.50, NKJ)*

For reading & meditation – Mark 10:46-52

We are seeing that the first step to mental and spiritual health is
receptivity – we must be willing to empty our hands of whatever
we are holding and receive Christ.

Life has been defined as response to environment. You and I live
physically when we respond to our physical environment – we take in
food, light and air. When response is shut off, we die physically. Our
spiritual environment is the kingdom of God. When we respond to it,
surrender to it, receive our very life from it – then we live happily and
abundantly. Take a plant – how does it live? By being proud, self-sufficient, unrelated and unresponsive? No; it lives by surrendering, adjust-
ing, receiving. Suppose a plant tried to live by asserting itself, by trying
to "lord" it over the other plants – what would be the result? It would
lose its life, for it lives only as it responds to its environment. When it is
properly adjusted, it takes in from the air, sun and soil and lives abundantly.

The plain truth of what Christ is saying, then, in the words, "Blessed
[or happy] are the poor in spirit", is that we must
choose to give up whatever we are holding and allow
Him to fill our lives with His forgiveness, love and
power. A highly cultured and beautiful woman, after
reviewing her life, said with a sigh: "I have everything
– and nothing." Everything in the way of comfort and
riches – yet she was empty in heart. To find happiness,
we must find Christ. And how do we find Him? We do
what the blind man did in the passage today – fling
away our "garment" and run to Jesus.

FURTHER STUDY

Matt. 19:16-29;
16:25; John 12:24

1. What was the
young man's
problem?

2. What did Jesus
teach must come
before life?

Prayer

Blessed Lord Jesus, where else can I run? If I run from You, I shall run away from
life, from release, from forgiveness, from freedom and from eternal happiness. So I
come, humbly, willingly – and receive. Amen.

As many as *touched* Him ...

"She came up behind him and touched the edge of his cloak ..." (v.44)

For reading & meditation – Luke 8:40-56

We continue meditating on Christ's first prescription for happiness: "Blessed are the poor in spirit, for theirs is the kingdom of heaven." Over the past few days we have seen that the phrase "poor in spirit" refers not to material poverty, but spiritual poverty – a willingness to throw away our own self-sufficiency and open our hands to receive Christ.

The passage before us today shows how on one occasion as Jesus passed along the road, a multitude thronged around Him. A woman in deep need came timidly through the crowd and touched His garment. "Who touched Me?" asked Jesus as He felt power go forth from Him. The disciples replied: "Master, the multitudes throng You, so why do you say, 'Who touched Me?' " "Somebody touched me", said Jesus. He knew that there was a great difference between thronging Him and touching Him. Those who throng Jesus get little, those who touch Jesus get everything.

Sunday after Sunday, thousands of people go to church and listen; they throng Jesus but never touch Him. If you are one of those who con-

FURTHER STUDY

Mark 10:1-16; Matt. 14:35-36; 8:3; 8:15; 9:29-30; Luke 6:19

1. What are some of the occasions when Jesus touched people?

2. What was the result?

stantly throng Jesus but never touch Him, then I pray that over these few days in which we are meditating on the opening words of the Beatitudes, you will reach out and touch Christ in a definite and personal way. Touch Him now – today. Touch Him for forgiveness, for cleansing, for power over temptation, over fears, over anxieties, over everything that stands in the way of your personal happiness. As Christ gave Himself to those who needed Him when He was here on earth, so He does today. Cease thronging Him – touch Him.

Prayer

O Lord Jesus, as You pass by I move up from those who throng You to boldly touch You – and I do it now. By the touch of faith I receive into my being Your forgiveness and Your power. Thank You, dear Lord. It's done. Amen.

Come ... today

"For the Son of Man came to seek and to save what was lost." (v.10)

For reading & meditation – Luke 19:1-10

We spend one more day meditating on the first of the Beatitudes: "Blessed are the poor in spirit, for theirs is the kingdom of heaven." Dr Raymond Cramer, the minister and psychologist whom I mentioned earlier, says that in the psychology of Jesus, it is the one who has a problem that gets the Master's attention.

When our Lord was here on earth, everyone needed Him, but only those who realised their need got His attention. It is often said that God rushes to the side of a person in need. That is not quite true. It would be more correct to say that God rushes to the side of the person who recognises and acknowledges their need. Those who recognise their need are to be congratulated, they are to be envied – they are candidates for the kingdom of heaven.

We could translate this first Beatitude in the following manner without doing any injustice to the original statement of Jesus: "Congratulations to those who are humble and willing enough to recognise their need – for they are candidates for the help of God." Take it from me, there is no one in the kingdom of God who is not "poor in spirit". You cannot be filled until you are first empty. Salvation is not something earned, but something received. It is by grace we are saved, through faith, and that not of ourselves, it is the gift of God (Eph. 2:8). The old hymn puts it in a way that is powerful and effective:

> *Nothing in my hand I bring,*
> *Simply to Thy cross I cling ...*
> *Foul, I to the fountain fly;*
> *Wash me, Saviour, or I die.*

FURTHER STUDY

Phil. 3:1-9;
Mark 10:28;
Luke 5:27-28;
18:29-30

1. What was Paul's attitude?

2. What did Jesus require of the first disciples?

Prayer

Father, thank You for helping me understand that to be "poor in spirit" is to recognise my utter helplessness in trying to save myself. I have nothing to give, but everything to receive. Humbly I bow and receive You now. Amen.

Not just a code of ethics

"I have been crucified with Christ and I no longer live, but Christ lives in me ..." (v.20)

For reading & meditation – Galatians 2:15-21

We turn now to consider the second of our Lord's Beatitudes: "Blessed are those who mourn, for they will be comforted" (Matt. 5:4). It is important to note that there is a very definite order in these sayings of Christ. Every one is carefully thought out and is given a precise place in the spiritual sequence. Once we see that entrance into the kingdom of God is through the acknowledgement of one's spiritual poverty and the acceptance of Christ's riches and resources, we are then ready to consider the next: "Happy are those who know what sorrow means, for they will be given courage and comfort" (Phillips).

Before pondering the meaning of this Beatitude, we pause to make clear that the Beatitudes must not be viewed simply as a code of ethics, but as a description of character. Many people view these sayings of Jesus, as well as the rest of the Sermon on the Mount, as a set of regulations which they must follow in order to become a Christian – a kind of New Testament "Ten Commandments".

The simple truth is that to try to live out these principles in our own unaided strength would be about as possible as trying to move the Rock of Gibraltar with a pea-shooter. Dr Martyn Lloyd-Jones said: "We are not told, 'Live like this and you will become a Christian', but rather, 'Become a Christian and you will live like this.'" Advocates of the "social gospel" – the belief that we become Christians by attempting to live out Christ's principles – are seriously in error. We must first know Christ as a Person before we can fully live out His principles.

FURTHER STUDY

Eph. 3:1-19;
John 14:20;
Col. 1:27;
1 John 3:24

1. Of what does the indwelling Christ bring a full knowledge?

2. What is the "hope of glory"?

Prayer

Father, how tragic that, down the centuries, so many have got Your truth the wrong way round – they have tried to follow Your principles before first knowing You in Person. Help me never to go wrong here – ever. Amen.

The purpose of sorrow

"... the Father of our Lord Jesus Christ ... who so wonderfully comforts and strengthens us ..." (vv.3-4, TLB)

For reading & meditation – 2 Corinthians 1:1-11

We continue meditating on our Lord's second Beatitude: "Blessed [or happy] are those who mourn, for they will be comforted." The word "mourn" has reference to more than just sorrowing over the death of a loved one; it includes all those experiences in life where we may feel crushed, broken or sorrowful. I feel the best translation of this verse is the one given by J. B. Phillips which I quoted yesterday. Permit me to quote it once again: "Happy are those who know what sorrow means, for they will be given courage and comfort."

Why should people who are caught up in the throes of distressing and sorrowful experiences be congratulated? The conclusion of the verse gives the answer: "for they will be comforted". And what then? Out of the comfort they receive, they are able to give comfort to others. Examine the text at the top of this page again, or listen to it as J. B. Phillips paraphrases it: "For he gives us comfort in all our trials so that we in turn may be able to give the same sort of strong sympathy to others in their troubles."

One of the things which often intrigues me in my work of training Christian counsellors is the fact that the best counsellors are those who have known the deepest hurts. Has the Lord allowed you to go through deep waters? Congratulations! You are a candidate for receiving the divine comfort which, in turn, will deepen your sensitivity to others and enrich your ministry in the Body of Christ. Don't, whatever you do, ask God to deliver you from painful or sorrowful experiences – they are worth much, much more than they cost.

FURTHER STUDY

John 16:1-16; 14:26; 15:26; 1 Cor. 14:31; 1 Thess. 5:11-14

1. From where do we receive our comfort?

2. What does the word "comfort" mean to you?

Prayer

Blessed Lord, help me to grasp this fact, not just with my mind, but with the whole of my spirit. I see that if I can learn this truth, my entire approach to problems can be transformed. In Jesus' Name I pray. Amen.

"It's not worth an argument"

*"Dear brothers, is your life full of difficulties and temptations?
Then be happy."* (v.2, TLB)

For reading & meditation – James 1:1-12

We are meditating on the second of Christ's Beatitudes: "Blessed are those who mourn, for they will be comforted." Yesterday we saw that the meaning of this statement is that when we are willing to experience sorrow and grief, then God is able to use these encounters to sensitise our spirits and make our ministry to others more effective and more fruitful.

I am afraid, however, that the majority of Christians, myself included, greatly fear this truth. Some years ago after I had expressed this same truth a woman wrote to me thus: "I am terribly afraid of what you said concerning grief and sorrow being the means in God's hands of deepening our sensitivity to others. I have not found this to be so. I find that grief and sorrow make me more concerned about myself than about others. Thus I cannot pray the prayer you suggested: 'Lord, put all the pressure on me You want; I know that the pressure You permit is all part of Your purpose – to make me the kind of person You want me to be.' "

We must always be careful that we do not interpret Biblical truth by human experiences; we must interpret human experiences by Biblical

FURTHER STUDY

Job 23:10;
1 Pet. 1:1-9;
Isa. 48:10;
2 Cor. 4:17

1. What was Job's testimony?

2. What does our suffering bring about?

truth. Scripture tells us that God permits pressure for a purpose, and that sorrow and grief will produce tremendous benefits in our lives – providing we let them. There's the rub! Whenever Biblical principles don't seem to work for us, then don't question the principle – question whether or not you are open to it, and whether you are applying it in the way God directs. There is very little point in arguing with God – He's *always* right.

Prayer

O Father, help me to see that when things are not working out the way Your Word decrees, the problems are not on Your side – but on mine. And help me to side with You and against myself in such issues – for You are always right. Amen.

The dangers of denial

"Surely you desire truth in the inner parts ..." (v.6)
For reading & meditation – Psalm 51:1-12

We are looking at the Beatitudes as containing the principles which enable us to experience good mental and spiritual health. I cannot think of anything more psychologically in harmony with the best thinking of today's social scientists than the words of Jesus: "Happy are those who mourn, for they will be comforted." We would not be taking any undue liberty with the text of Matthew 5:4 if we translated it thus: "Congratulations to those who are willing to face and feel sorrow, for they will discover in and through the comfort that I impart to them a new ministry and a new joy."

A mentally and spiritually healthy person is someone who is willing to face and feel sorrow, and recognise that it can be made to deepen one's life – not devastate it. You are familiar, I am sure, with the terms "neurotic" and "psychotic". A "neurotic" is someone who is afraid to face reality, while a "psychotic" is someone who is unaware of reality.

If we draw back from being willing to face and feel any emotion that rises up within us, then the denial of this feeling will have negative results within our personality. A woman once said to me: "I have problems with the second Beatitude because I don't know how to mourn; I am too happy to mourn." As we talked, it became clear to her that it wasn't so much that she didn't know how to mourn, but that she didn't want to mourn. She was afraid to face or feel any negative emotions – grief, sorrow, and so on – and thus, despite her claim to happiness and lightheartedness, she was a stunted soul.

FURTHER STUDY

Psa. 139:14-24;
1 Chron. 28:9;
Jer. 17:10

1. What was David's prayer?

2. Make that your prayer today.

Prayer

Loving heavenly Father, how wonderfully You help me to put my finger on my need. Help me, I pray, to be willing to feel and face my emotions, and show me that when You are by my side I need be afraid of nothing – myself included. Amen.

Why pretend?

*"For we do not have a high priest who is unable to sympathise
with our weaknesses ..." (v.15)*

For reading & meditation – Hebrews 4:12-16

Yesterday we ended with the case of the woman who said that she didn't know how to mourn, when in reality her problem was she didn't want to mourn. Whenever we are unwilling to face a negative emotion, it implies that we are not in control of it, but that it is in control of us.

Christians are often taught to pretend that they feel joyful when really they are miserable. Our text today, however, tells us that we have a great High Priest who can sympathise with us in our weaknesses. How pointless it is to conceal our weaknesses from the Lord and deny ourselves the comfort of His uncritical compassionate understanding. This is very important, for I would say that eight out of ten Christians have a completely wrong view of how to handle hurts and sorrows.

The typical Christian reaction to negative emotions is either denial or expression. We dealt yesterday with the issue of denial – refusing to face them and feel them – so let's consider for a moment what we mean by the term "expression". The expression of emotions is the act of letting our emotions out. This is a popular approach with many of today's counsellors and therapists. They say, when you feel upset, hurt or angry, then shout and scream or punch a pillow until you have released those pent-up emotions. There is no doubt that some relief can be gained in this way, but it is not a very Biblical or mature way of dealing with our negative feelings. The right way of handling negative feelings is neither to deny them or express them, but to acknowledge them. But more of that tomorrow.

FURTHER STUDY

Luke 10:25-37;
7:13; Matt. 9:36;
20:34; Mark 1:41

1. What was Jesus
always
demonstrating?

2. How did He
graphically illustrate
this?

Prayer

O Father, I see that this whole issue of emotions is a minefield in which I must tread carefully and cautiously. Take my hand as I move through this area and lead me to clear and Biblical conclusions. For Jesus' sake. Amen.

Moving toward maturity

"Search me, O God, and know my heart; test me and know my anxious thoughts." (v.23)

For reading & meditation – Psalm 139:1-24

We continue meditating on the right way to handle our negative feelings. We said yesterday that the two wrong ways to handle hurting emotions are to deny them or express them. Denial pushes them down inside us, while expression dumps them on to other people or things. Neither of these, in my view, is a Biblical way of dealing with negative emotions. In fact, recent research by some psychologists shows that the uncontrolled expression of negative feelings can compound, rather than clear up, one's emotional difficulties.

In my judgement, the correct and Biblical way to handle negative emotions is to acknowledge them fully before God and share with Him how we feel. Now understand clearly what I am saying, for at this point many have responded to this advice by coming to God when they are hurt or sorrowful and saying: "Lord, please forgive me for feeling hurt." That misses the point entirely. A Christian psychologist puts the issue most effectively when he says: "We are not to pretend that we feel penitent when we feel hurt."

When our stomachs are churning with grief, sorrow or hurt, we must come before the One who sees and knows everything, and pray a prayer something like this: "Lord, right now I am hurting more than I think I can endure. I feel like screaming, running away or hitting somebody. I don't want to feel like this, dear Lord – but I do. Thank You for loving me as I am. Help me now to handle my feelings in a way that glorifies You and honours Your Name." When we pray a prayer like that – *and mean it* – we are on the way to maturity.

FURTHER STUDY

Psa. 51:1-19; 69:1-36; 46:1-11

1. How did David deal with his feelings?

2. Write a short psalm expressing your true feelings.

Prayer

O Father, help me not just to receive this concept into my mind and do nothing about it, but enable me to put it to work in my daily Christian living. I ask this for the honour and glory of Your peerless and precious Name. Amen.

"Wounded healers"

"I, even I, am he who comforts you ..." (v.12)
For reading & meditation – Isaiah 51:1-16

We spend one last day meditating on Jesus' words: "Blessed [or happy] are those who mourn, for they will be comforted." Facing negative feelings such as grief, sorrow, hurt and emotional pain is essential if we are to know our Lord's purpose for our lives. When we are willing to go down into the hurt and feel it, then something glorious and transformative happens – we experience the loving comfort and compassion of our Lord. "Blessed are those who mourn, *for they will be comforted.*" Comforted? By whom? By the Triune God. He comes alongside us in our pain, and through the comfort He pours into our beings, enables us to become more sensitive to Him, to ourselves, and to others.

After a lifetime of dealing with people and their problems, I have no hesitation in saying that the happiest people on earth are those who have been hurt but have had those hurts healed through the power of Christ's transforming love. They are what someone has called "wounded healers". Having been healed themselves, they go out to heal others. Going down into the pain of hurt feelings is not a very pleasant journey, but coming back from it with the comfort of God in your soul is an experience that is positively exhilarating and enriching. You return, not only with a new sensitivity in your soul, but with a new potential for ministering to others.

Remember this: great sorrow leads to great happiness – and without the sorrow, there can be no genuine happiness. This might sound to many like a contradiction in terms. It is not a contradiction, but a paradox – and a blessed one at that!

FURTHER STUDY

2 Cor. 1:1-7;
Psa. 86:17;
Isa. 12:1; 66:13

1. What has God promised?

2. How are we to respond?

Prayer

O Father, I take again this second prescription for happiness and ask that You will enable me to take the "medicine", not just today, but every day of my life. Then I will be whole – truly whole. In Jesus' Name I pray. Amen.

"Subdued puppies"?

"For the Lord taketh pleasure in his people: he will beautify the meek with salvation." (v.4, AV)

For reading & meditation – Psalm 149:1-9

We come now to Christ's third prescription for happiness: "Blessed are the meek, for they will inherit the earth" (Matt. 5:5). How we have shied away from that word "meek". We have thought of meekness as weakness and thus have a totally wrong concept of what Jesus meant. The Amplified Bible translates it thus: "Blessed are the meek (the mild, patient, long-suffering), for they shall inherit the earth."

The dictionary defines "meek" as "humble, compliant and submissive". Does this mean that Jesus expects the children of the kingdom to be like subdued puppies who crawl into their master's presence and cower at his feet? Or to become the type of people who lack inner fortitude and gumption, who can be easily pushed around and manipulated?

The truly meek person – in the Biblical sense of the word – is not timid, shy, hesitant and unassuming, but trusting, confident and secure. The root meaning of the word "meekness" is that of yieldedness or surrender – a characteristic without which no real progress can be made in the Christian life. What happens, for example, to the scientist who approaches the mysteries of the universe in a manner that is aggressive and belligerent? He discovers nothing. But what happens to the scientist who approaches the mysteries of the universe in a spirit of meekness? He finds its richest secrets unfolding themselves to him and he is able to harness the mighty forces around him to advantage. The Christian who approaches life in the same spirit – the spirit of meekness and submission – discovers the true meaning of his existence and the purpose of God in all his affairs.

FURTHER STUDY

James 1:12-21;
Zeph. 2:3;
Gal. 5:22-23;
1 Pet. 3:4

1. What are we to receive with meekness?

2. Does the Biblical definition of meekness fit you?

Prayer

Gracious Father, help me to understand clearly the difference between meekness and weakness. And show me how to apply this principle in all I say and in all I do. This I ask in Christ's powerful and precious Name. Amen.

Meekness – a *spiritual* quality

"And that is what some of you were. But you were washed, you were sanctified ..." (v.11)

For reading & meditation – 1 Corinthians 6:1-11

Yesterday we touched on the point that the universe will not respond to the aggressive, who approach it in a demanding spirit. It is the meek – those who are yielded, submissive and compliant – who inherit the earth. Thomas Huxley is quoted as saying something which we commented on earlier: "Science says to sit down before the facts like a little child, be prepared to give up every preconceived notion, be willing to be led to whatever end nature will lead you, or you will know nothing."

Today we must focus our thinking on the fact that the quality of meekness (sometimes translated as humility or gentleness) described in the Beatitudes is not the result of natural temperament, but comes from knowing Christ and abiding in Him. That goes, of course, for all the qualities enunciated in the Beatitudes – they are spiritual characteristics, not natural ones. This point needs elaborating, for there are many Christians who say: "I am aggressive by nature, so it is not possible for me to be a meek and mild person."

Every Christian, whatever their natural temperament, is meant to be meek. It is not a matter of natural disposition; it is a quality produced by

FURTHER STUDY

Num. 12:1-13;
Psa. 22:26; 147:6;
Luke 6:29

1. What was Moses'
great characteristic?

2. How does
meekness reveal itself
in practice?

the Spirit of God. Think of the powerful and extraordinary nature of a man like David – and yet observe his meekness. Look at a man like Paul the apostle, a master mind, a powerful and outstanding personality, yet consider his great humility and gentleness. How did these men get to be like this? Not because of a natural proneness toward meekness, but because they were indwelt by Christ and the Holy Spirit. It is not a matter of genes; it is a matter of grace.

Prayer

My Father and my God, help me to face up to the fact that whatever I am by nature, I can be changed by the power of Your grace. Show me how to absorb that grace so that I become more and more like You. For Your own dear Name's sake. Amen.

What meekness is not

*"… the unfading beauty of a gentle and quiet spirit, which is
of great worth in God's sight." (v.4)*
For reading & meditation – 1 Peter 3:1-12

We are seeing that meekness is not a natural quality, but a spiritual one, and by reason of this all Christians should possess it. Over the past couple of days we have examined the importance of meekness and seen something of its nature; today, we examine what meekness is not.

First, meekness (or humility) is not indolence. There are people who appear to be spiritually meek, but really they are not so at all – they are indolent. Again, meekness is not an easy-going type of attitude – the attitude seen in those who just take life as it comes. That is not meekness; that is flabbiness. There are some Christians who have such a casual air about them that one can easily mistake this for the quality which Jesus is referring to in the Beatitudes.

Another thing that meekness ought not to be confused with is niceness. There are people who are nice by nature. Dr Martyn Lloyd-Jones said of such people: "Natural niceness is something biological, the kind of thing you get in animals. One dog is nicer than another, one cat nicer than another." Finally, meekness is not passivity, or a desire to obtain peace at any price. How often is the person regarded as meek who adopts the attitude that anything is better than a disagreement. This is the kind of passivity which does not make for good mental or spiritual health. The most greatly used men and women of God down the ages have been people who were meek without being weak – strong men and women, yet meek men and women. They were meek enough to absorb the resources of God.

FURTHER STUDY

2 Tim. 4:1-16;
Psa. 37:11; 149:4;
Isa. 29:19

1. How did Paul display meekness?

2. What does meekness increase?

Prayer

O Father, I see that so much depends on my understanding of what meekness really is. I pray yet again for Your continuing light to be shed around me as I pursue these thoughts day by day. I ask this in Jesus' Name. Amen.

The meek are the assured

"Put on then, as God's chosen ones … meekness …"
(v.12, RSV)

For reading & meditation – Colossians 3:1-15

It is time now to focus more precisely on what Jesus meant when He said: "Blessed are the meek, for they will inherit the earth." Meekness, as Jesus is using the word here, refers to an attitude of heart and mind that is entirely free from a spirit of demandingness and accepts the will of God in its entirety.

I think J.B. Phillips gets close to the meaning in Jesus' mind when he translates His statement thus: "Happy are those who claim nothing, for the whole earth will belong to them." I must stress once again that the thought here is not of passivity, but of active compliance and obedience to the will of God. If I might be permitted to embark upon a translation of my own, I would put it this way: "Congratulations to those who do not feel the need to be over-assertive, for they will inherit the earth."

The meek are so sure of their resources and their goals that they can afford to be meek. Others have to become aggressive simply because they are unsure of themselves and their goals – hence the universe is closed to them. The meek could be called the assured, for they are meek enough to rest confidently in the resources of God. I realise, of course, that this is directly opposite to the world's view of things. The world thinks of strength, power, ability, self-confidence and self-assurance as the keys to success. The more you assert yourself and the more you affirm yourself, says the worldly person, the more you will get. But such people do not inherit the earth: they just inherit dirt.

FURTHER STUDY

Isa. 53:1-7;
Matt. 26:62-63;
27:14; Luke 23:9

1. How did Jesus display meekness?

2. How do you display meekness?

Prayer

O Father, more and more as I hang upon Your words, I realise that You have "hidden these things from the wise and learned, and revealed them to little children." Unfold Your truth in even more new and exciting ways to my heart. In Jesus' Name. Amen.

"All things serve"

*"... By his good life let him show his works in the meekness
of wisdom." (v.13, RSV)*

For reading & meditation – James 3:1-18

We continue meditating on the meaning of the word "meek" as used by Jesus in His third Beatitude. "Meekness," said one commentator, "is essentially a true view of oneself, expressing itself in attitude and conduct with respect to others."

If that is so, then meekness involves two things: (1) our attitudes towards ourselves, and (2) our attitudes toward others. The meek person is so sure of himself that he does not need to demand anything for himself. He does not see his rights as something to be rigidly held on to, but follows the spirit of Jesus as outlined in Philippians 2:6-7: "Who, although being essentially one with God ... did not think this equality with God was a thing to be eagerly grasped or retained; but stripped Himself of all privileges ... and was born a human being" (Amplified Bible).

That is the place to which you and I must come if we are to understand the principle of meekness. The Christian who is meek will not be over-sensitive about himself, or defensive; he realises that he has no rights at all and delights to leave everything in the hands of God. When he is called upon to suffer unjustly, he remembers the Word of the Lord that says, "It is mine to avenge; I will repay" (Rom. 12:19), and trusts God to work out the situation in His own time and in His own way. The poet Browning put the same truth in these words: "He who keeps one end in view makes all things serve." When that one end is the purpose of God, then indeed – all things serve.

> **FURTHER STUDY**
>
> 1 Pet. 2:18-25;
> Matt. 11:29; 26:52
>
> 1. What was Peter's exhortation?
> 2. Why was Jesus able to display meekness?

Prayer

O Father, instil into me such a spirit of meekness that such things as anger, impatience, irritation, distrust, suspicion and unbelief die within me. Help me to see that only meekness must survive. For Jesus' sake. Amen.

What an example!

"Take my yoke upon you ... for I am gentle and humble in heart, and you will find rest for your souls." (v.29)

For reading & meditation – Matthew 11:28-30

Today we ask ourselves: What is there about this famous saying of Jesus which engenders good mental health? Mental health, after all, is more than a medical term. It is a concept that goes beyond the walls of a hospital or a doctor's clinic and applies also to the home, the church and the world of everyday living.

Mental health is concerned with the dynamics of relationship and adjustment – the way we handle such things as anxiety, hostility and frustration. "Mental health," says one authority, "concerns itself with the everyday troubles of everyday people – helping them to solve their problems or face them bravely when they cannot be warded off." The statement of Jesus we are focusing on at the moment contributes to good mental health because it encourages us to be free from the attitude of demandingness – the attitude that says: "Things must go my way", "I ought to have some consideration", "People should respect my rights."

One psychologist goes as far as to say that if we could eliminate the *shoulds* and the *woulds* from our vocabulary and our inner attitudes, we could become transformed people overnight. He was not referring, of course, to the moral compass which God has placed within us that cries out for obedience to that which is right ("I ought not to lie", "I should always do right", and so on) but to the attitude of demandingness that insists on having one's rights irrespective of any other considerations. One of the biggest causes of mental and emotional illness is the attitude of demandingness and over-concern. Do we wonder any longer why Christ congratulates the meek and promises them the earth?

FURTHER STUDY

2 Cor. 10:1-18;
11:18-21;
Phil. 4:11-12

1. Why could Paul be bold?

2. How did Paul highlight the difference between weakness and meekness?

Prayer

Blessed Lord Jesus, deliver me, I pray, from a spirit of demandingness that insists on having my rights rather than being willing to give them up for the sake of others. Help me to take Your yoke upon me and learn from You. Amen.

"Sand in the machinery"

*"For by him all things were created: things in heaven and on earth
… all things were created by him and for him." (v.16)*

For reading & meditation – Colossians 1:15-27

We spend one more day meditating on the text: "Blessed are the meek, for they will inherit the earth." Today we ask ourselves: What did Jesus mean by the phrase, "for they will inherit the earth"? It means, so I believe, that when we develop the attitude of meekness, the whole universe is behind us. If, for example, we decide to manifest the attitude of anger and hostility rather than cultivating a meek and quiet spirit, then the anger and hostility becomes, as someone put it, "sand in the machinery of life".

The universe has been made in a Christlike fashion. Our text for today shows that when God made the world, He made it to work in the way of Christ: "All things were created by him [Christ] and for him." Edison, the scientist, tried eleven hundred experiments, all of which turned out to be failures. Someone said to him: "You must feel that you have wasted your time." "Oh no," answered Edison, "I simply found out eleven hundred ways how not to do things."

This is what is happening in the world right now – humanity is finding out how to live. People are discovering that there are some things which the universe will not approve and some things it will approve. The meek are those who have come to terms with reality and know that they cannot twist it to their own ends or make it approve of what cannot be approved. Whoever has the first word in this universe must always remember that the universe has the last word. The Christian who adopts the attitudes of his Master finds the universe backing him in everything he does.

FURTHER STUDY

Phil. 2:1-11;
John 1:3;
1 Cor. 8:6;
Heb. 1:1-2

1. How did Jesus
   demonstrate
   meekness?

2. How does this
   apply to you?

Prayer

Father, thank You for reminding me that life works in one way only – Your way. When I live life as You designed it, then the whole universe works with me. I inherit all things – all that is Yours is mine. Blessed be Your Name for ever. Amen.

What's your goal?

"But seek first his kingdom and his righteousness, and all these things will be given to you as well." (v.33)

For reading & meditation – Matthew 6:19-34

We turn now to the next of our Lord's Beatitudes: "Blessed are those who hunger and thirst for righteousness, for they will be filled" (Matt. 5:6). One of the axioms of life is this: everyone thirsts after something. Some thirst for success, some thirst for fame, some thirst for stable relationships, and some thirst for financial security. But there is a thirst which is common to every human heart – the thirst for happiness. Notice, however, that Jesus does not say: "Happy are those who thirst for happiness", but "Happy are those who thirst for righteousness."

Happiness, therefore, is a by-product – to get it, you must focus on something else. Dr W.E. Sangster, the famous Methodist preacher, when dealing with this point in one of his sermons, gave this illustration: "Do you enjoy a game of golf or tennis? Then this pleasure is strictly proportioned to the degree to which you lose yourself in the game. While it lasts, it must absorb you: your whole mind should be on the game. If you stop in the midst of it and ask yourself precisely what degree of pleasure you are deriving from this particular stroke, the pleasure will evaporate and you will begin to feel rather foolish in following a wee white ball over a mile or two of turf."

FURTHER STUDY

John 4:1-14; 6:35;
Psa. 36:8; Isa. 55:1

1. What did Jesus promise?

2. What do you thirst for?

To experience happiness, one must forget it and focus on something other than its pursuit. Those who reach out for happiness are for ever unsatisfied – the more they strive, the less they find. Happiness, I say again, is a by-product; it is not something you find, but something that finds you.

Prayer

My Father and my God, I see so clearly that if my goal is wrong, then all of life turns out wrong. Help me to make my goal, not the pursuit of happiness, but the pursuit of righteousness. In Jesus' Name I pray. Amen.

An important key to living

*"And we pray this in order that you may live a life worthy of
the Lord and may please him in every way ..." (v.10)*

For reading & meditation – Colossians 1:1-14

Yesterday we saw that when we make it a goal to hunger and thirst
after happiness, we get nowhere, but when we make it our goal to
hunger and thirst after righteousness, we get everywhere.

Once again Jesus touches on an aspect of good mental health when
He teaches us through these words to focus on right goals. Those who
study human behaviour tell us that everything we do has a goal. "We are
not conditioned animals that act automatically and unthinkingly in pro-
grammed response," says a psychologist, "... neither are we the hapless
victims of internal forces that drive us relentlessly in unwanted direc-
tions." It may sometimes feel as if we do things we don't want to do, but
the truth is that everything we do represents an effort to reach a goal that
somehow, albeit at an unconscious level, makes sense. In fact, one of the
ways in which you can better understand why you do the things you do
is to ask yourself: What's my goal?

A woman I once counselled and who was extremely frustrated
because her husband would not change to meet her requirements said to
me: "My husband is so stubborn and obstinate that I
just can't see any future for us together." I shared with
her the concept that everything we do represents a
goal, and asked her to put into words what she
thought her goal might be in her marriage. Without a
moment's hesitation she replied: "To change my husband." Her daily prayer was: "Lord, You love my husband and I'll change him." I suggested she altered her
goal to: "Lord, You change my husband and I'll love
him." She did, and instantly found a new freedom –
and a new happiness in her marriage.

FURTHER STUDY

Eph. 5:1-16;
Rom. 6:4;
2 Cor. 5:7;
Gal. 5:16

1. How are we to live?

2. Do you make the
most of every
opportunity?

Prayer

O Father, I see what I need – I need to bring my goals in line with Your goals. Unfold
more of this important truth to me as I pursue it over the next few days. In Jesus'
Name I ask it. Amen.

Why we get angry

"Run in such a way as to get the prize." (v.24)
For reading & meditation – 1 Corinthians 9:15-27

We continue meditating on the idea that everything we do represents a goal. In fact, most of the frustration we experience in life comes from wrong goals and blocks to those goals. Let me illustrate. Cast your mind back to the last time you were angry. If you can identify your goal and what blocked your goal, then you have the clue to what produced your anger and frustration.

A man once asked me if I could explain what caused his deep-seated anger. It soon became apparent that his anger was due to a blocked goal. His goal in life was to make money. He reasoned: "If I can make plenty of money, then everyone will see that I am a successful and important person." When he encountered blocks to this goal, such as his wife's insistence that he cut down on the amount of time he was spending in his business, he would erupt in anger.

I pointed out that the way to deal with the anger was to establish a goal that no-one could block. And what was that? To please the Lord. He resisted that idea at first, but when he came to realise that his goal in life was unbiblical and that his anger resulted from others blocking his unbiblical goal, he made a new commitment to God and found happiness and release. From then on his goal was not to make money, but to please the Lord. I hasten to point out that there is nothing wrong with wanting to make money – it is a legitimate human desire – but it must remain a desire and never become a goal.

FURTHER STUDY

James 1:9-20;
Psa. 37:8;
Prov. 14:17; 16:32

1. What does an impatient man do?

2. Who will "take the city"?

Prayer

O God my gracious Father, help me never to turn what can be a legitimate human desire into a life goal. Save me from pursuing unbiblical objectives, and guide me toward the truth which alone can make me free. In Jesus' Name. Amen.

Desires versus goals

*"… who for the joy set before him endured the cross,
scorning its shame …"* (v.2)

For reading & meditation – Hebrews 12:1-13

We ended yesterday by saying that some things in life, such as the desire to have money, can be legitimate concerns but they must be looked upon as desires and never become goals.

Permit me to differentiate between the two. A goal is a purpose to which a person is unalterably committed and something for which he or she assumes unconditional responsibility. A desire is something wanted and which cannot be obtained without the co-operation of another human being. A desire must never become the motivating purpose behind our behaviour, for if it does, then it becomes a goal – and a goal that is likely to be blocked, causing negative emotions to arise. Remember the man we talked about yesterday? His goal, we said, was to make money. Once he changed his goal to pleasing the Lord and then saw his concern to make money as merely a desire, he found instant release.

Keep in mind that what causes emotional problems to arise is invariably a blocked goal. Take another illustration that might help to mark the difference between goals and desires more clearly.

Have you ever found yourself talking to another Christian who seems to have difficulty in applying what seems to you a simple biblical principle? You point out the need to do as God says, but your friend fails to see the truth that to you is as clear as daylight. If you get frustrated, the chances are that you are allowing a desire to become a goal. To want your friend to listen is a legitimate desire, but to get frustrated over it means you are determined to make him listen – and that becomes a goal.

FURTHER STUDY

Psa. 37:1-11; 21:2;
73:25; Prov. 10:24

1. What was the psalmist's desire?

2. What happens when we delight ourselves in the Lord?

Prayer

Gracious Father, I come to You again to help me sort out this important issue of desires versus goals. I see that if I can resolve this problem, then a new chapter in my life is about to be written. Help me, dear Lord. In Jesus' Name. Amen.

Happiness is a by-product

"… in Your presence is fullness of joy, at Your right hand there are pleasures for evermore." (v.11, Amplified Bible)

For reading & meditation – Psalm 16:1-11

Having seen the importance of differentiating between goals and desires, we return to the thought that we can experience happiness only as a by-product. If we make obtaining happiness a goal, it eludes us like a will-o'-the-wisp, but if we give up the chase and hold it only as a desire, then it takes up residence in our heart.

Let me repeat: there is nothing wrong in wanting to be happy; it is a natural and valid desire. But the paradoxical truth is that I will never be happy if I am primarily concerned with becoming happy. My overriding goal in every circumstance must be to respond biblically, to put the Lord first and seek to behave as He would want me to. The wonderful truth is that as we devote our energies to the task of becoming what Christ wants us to be – righteous – He responds by filling us with unutterable happiness and joy. I must, therefore, firmly and consciously by an act of the will, refuse to make obtaining happiness my goal, and instead adopt the goal of becoming more like the Lord.

An obsessive preoccupation with "happiness" will obscure our understanding of the biblical route to eternal peace and joy. And what is that route? Our text for today tells us: "At Your right hand there are pleasures for evermore." It follows that if we are to experience those pleasures, then we must learn what it means to be at God's right hand. Paul tells us that Christ has been exalted to God's right hand (Eph. 1:20). Can anything be clearer? The more we abide in Christ, the more we shall experience true happiness.

FURTHER STUDY

Psa. 139:1-12;
140:13; Ex. 33:14;
Isa. 43:2

1. What did the psalmist feel about God's presence?

2. How much time are you spending in His presence?

Prayer

O God, forgive us that we have made the pursuit of happiness our goal, and the pursuit of righteousness merely a desire. Help us to get our values straightened out, and to set the goal of becoming more and more like You. In Jesus' Name. Amen.

At God's right hand

"Therefore let us ... go on to maturity ..." (v.1)
For reading & meditation – Hebrews 6:1-12

Quietly we are coming to see that it is only as we learn to dwell at God's right hand in fellowship with Christ that we can experience true happiness and joy. Despite the clear teaching true of Jesus that happiness is a by-product of righteousness (becoming more and more like Christ), there are still thousands of Christians paying no more than lip service to this truth. Happiness is their goal, righteousness merely their desire.

I am speaking generally when I make this next point, but sit down with any Christian who does not experience true happiness and you will find, deep within that person's heart, that they have never come to a clear understanding of this important principle uttered by Jesus: "Blessed are those who hunger and thirst for righteousness, for they will be filled." The same condition can be noted in nine out of ten people who seek help through Christian counselling. Ask them what they want to experience as they go through counselling, and they say, "I want to feel good", or "I want to feel happy."

I imply no criticism or condemnation of these people, for I know that the same tendency exists in my own heart. Whenever I am struggling or hurting over some issue, my immediate desire is to get rid of the negative feelings and recover my lost happiness. But to try to find happiness is like trying to fall asleep. As long as you consciously and zealously try to grasp it, it fails to come. There is only one way: it is to do whatever you have to do in the situation to glorify Christ. Then happiness inevitably bubbles upward – as it must.

FURTHER STUDY

Phil. 3:1-11;
2 Cor. 13:11;
Eph. 4:13;
Col. 1:28

1. What was Paul's desire?

2. What was Paul's goal?

Prayer

Father, I am so grateful that, as my Lover and my Redeemer, You corner my soul. Don't let me wriggle and apologise and slip past You. Help me to take my medicine, however bitter to the taste of self it may be. In Jesus' Name. Amen.

Spiritual/psychological problems

"I want to know Christ and the power of his resurrection ..."
(v.10)

For reading & meditation – Philippians 3:7-21

Today we ask: What happens to those who hunger and thirst after righteousness? The answer is clear: they will be filled. Make righteousness your goal and you will be eternally satisfied. If, once again, I might venture upon a paraphrase of my own, I would put it like this: "Congratulations to those who ardently crave to become more and more like Me and to know My righteousness, for they shall find a satisfaction that will never vanish or be destroyed."

May I be permitted to ask you this personal question: What are you most hungering and thirsting for? Is it health? Is it relief from pain? Is it freedom from anxiety? Is it financial security? All of these are legitimate cravings, but if your primary hunger and thirst is not to become more and more like Christ, then you will experience an inner emptiness that nothing you chase after can fill.

Let me point out one more thing – something that might astonish you: to the extent that your deepest hunger and thirst is not for God, to that extent you will experience spiritual and psychological problems. If you are not hungering and thirsting after Him, you will hunger and thirst after something else. When we make it our goal to glorify God, then we will enjoy Him. We must not make it our goal to enjoy Him in order to glorify Him. Remember the goal of happiness is elusive, regardless of how well-thought-out is our strategy. But the by-product of happiness is freely available to those whose goal is to know God and be found in Him.

FURTHER STUDY

Psa. 38:9; 73:25;
Isa. 26:1-9;
1 Pet. 2:2-3

1. What was the psalmist's confession?

2. What did Isaiah's desire cause him to do?

Prayer

Father, You are teaching me Your ways – written in Your Word and also in me. Help me to surrender to Your purposes so that I might be the vehicle of victory. Amen.

The meaning of mercy

"Mercy and truth are met together ..." (v.10, AV)
For reading & meditation – Psalm 85:1-13

We continue our study of the Beatitudes – the study of Jesus' decla-
rations of how to become "the happy ones". Today we come to the
fifth of Christ's famous sayings: "Blessed are the merciful, for they will be
shown mercy" (Matt. 5:7).

What does our Lord mean when He uses the word "merciful"? The
thought underlying the word is that of compassion and concern for the
plight of others. The Greek word used in this fifth Beatitude is also used
to describe the high priestly ministry of Christ in Hebrews 2:17. One
authority, W.E. Vine, says that a "merciful" person is "not simply pos-
sessed of pity but actively compassionate".

It is important to stress once again that the characteristic of being
merciful of which our Lord spoke here is not something that arises from
our natural temperament, but something that is endowed on us when we
abide in Christ. As Dr Martyn Lloyd-Jones said: "This is not a gospel for
certain temperaments – nobody has an advantage over anybody else
when they are face to face with God." Again, mercy is not turning a blind
eye to moral violations – the attitude that pretends not
to see things. This can be seen most forcefully when
we consider that the term "merciful" is an adjective
which is applied especially and specifically to God
Himself. This means that however the word applies to
God, it applies equally to man. God is merciful, but He
is also truth: "Mercy and truth are met together." If we
think of mercy at the expense of truth and law, then it
is not true mercy; it is merely a caricature.

FURTHER STUDY

Titus 3:1-7;
Psa. 103:17; 108:4;
Lam. 3:22

1. What is the quality
of God's mercy?

2. How merciful are
you?

Prayer

O God, help me, I pray, to have within me the right blend of mercy and truth. Save
me from becoming a lopsided Christian – someone who manifests one characteristic at the expense of another. In Jesus' Name I pray. Amen.

Grace and *mercy*

"… and when he saw him, he took pity on him. He went to him …" (vv.33–34)

For reading & meditation – Luke 10:25-37

We continue focusing our thoughts on what it means to be "merciful". One of the best ways to understand the word is to compare it with grace. Have you ever noticed, that the introduction to every one of Paul's epistles from Romans through to 2 Thessalonians, includes the words: "Grace and peace to you from God our Father and the Lord Jesus Christ"? The phrase usually appears in the second or third verse of these epistles. However, when he comes to what are described as the pastoral epistles (1 and 2 Timothy and Titus), he changes the phrase to read: "Grace, mercy and peace from God the Father and Christ Jesus our Lord."

When Paul inserted the word "mercy" after the word "grace", he implied an interesting distinction. Someone has defined the two words thus: "Grace is especially associated with men in their sins; mercy is especially associated with men in their misery." While grace looks down upon sin and seeks to save, mercy looks especially upon the miserable consequences of sin and seeks to relieve. This helps us to see mercy in a wider dimension. *Mercy is compassion plus action.*

FURTHER STUDY

Prov. 3:3; 11:17;
Micah 6:8;
John 8:1-11

1. What does the Lord require?

2. How did Jesus show mercy without compromising truth?

A Christian who is merciful feels such compassion and concern that he is not content until he does something about the plight of the one with whom he comes in contact. The story of the Good Samaritan is a classic illustration of being merciful. Others saw the man but did nothing to help him in his plight. The Samaritan, however, crossed the road, dressed the man's wounds, took him to an inn and made provision for his comfort. I say again: mercy is compassion *plus* action.

Prayer

Merciful and loving heavenly Father, make me in Your own image. One thing is sure – I cannot be a merciful person without Your help. So come and think in me, love in me and live in me. For Your own dear Name's sake. Amen.

Most misunderstood Beatitude

"Give, and it will be given to you ..." (v.38)
For reading & meditation – Luke 6:27-40

The fifth Beatitude – "Blessed are the merciful, for they will be shown mercy" – is quite different from the ones that precede it. In the first four, there is a contrast between the need and the fulfilment. The "poor in spirit" receive the kingdom; those "who mourn" are comforted; "the meek" inherit the earth; those who "hunger and thirst" are satisfied; but in the fifth Beatitude the theme changes: "the merciful will be shown mercy". It is as though we cannot receive mercy without first giving it.

We must move carefully here, for no Beatitude has been more misunderstood than this one. There are those who take these words to mean that we can only be forgiven by God to the extent that we forgive others. They bring alongside this Beatitude such passages as: "Forgive us our sins, for we also forgive everyone who sins against us" (Luke 11:4), and "This is how my heavenly Father will treat each of you unless you forgive your brother from your heart" (Matt. 18:35).

Putting all these Scriptures together, they claim that it is the clear meaning of the Bible that we are forgiven by God only to the degree that we forgive others. If this is so, then salvation is by works and not by grace. We must never interpret Scripture in a way that contradicts other Scriptures. What our Lord means in this fifth Beatitude is that when we demonstrate mercy to others, we make it possible for God's mercy to penetrate deeper into our own lives and personalities. The act of giving makes us more able to receive.

FURTHER STUDY

2 Cor. 9:1-6;
Prov. 11:25; 22:9;
Matt. 10:8

1. What is the law of sowing and reaping?

2. What was Jesus' instruction to the disciples?

Prayer

O Father, help me not to stumble over this truth. Show me that although my forgiveness of others is not a condition of salvation, it must be a consequence of it. In Jesus' Name I pray. Amen.

Forgiven!

"... forgiving each other, just as in Christ God forgave you." (v.32)

For reading & meditation – Ephesians 4:17-32

We must spend another day considering whether or not it is a condition of our salvation that we first forgive those who have sinned against us. We said yesterday that to believe this contradicts the teaching that we are saved by grace, through faith. What, then, is Scripture getting at when it seems to encourage us to forgive in order that we might be forgiven? I think it refers to the matter of realised forgiveness.

I know many Christians, as I am sure you do, who, although they have been forgiven by God, are never really sure of it. And one of the major reasons for this is that they have never taken the steps to get rid of the resentment they hold in their hearts toward others. The problem they experience in not feeling forgiven is not God's fault, but their own. He has forgiven them on the basis of their own personal repentance, but His forgiveness is unable to reach the centre of their spirit and dissolve their feelings of guilt because they harbour an unforgiving attitude toward others.

C.S. Lewis said something similar in relation to praise. He explained that we do not really receive something unless we give thanks for it. The

FURTHER STUDY
Luke 17:1-4; 23:34;
Mark 11:25;
Col. 3:13

1. How often should we forgive?

2. How did Jesus set us an example?

very action of saying "thank you", and meaning it, opens up the spirit to a true sense of appreciation. In giving thanks, something moves inside the centre of our spirits and allows the wonder of what has been done for us to invade us. It is the same with mercy and forgiveness. When we adopt these attitudes toward others, we not only express mercy and forgiveness – we experience it.

Prayer

O Father, I see that You have fashioned me in my inner being for mercy and forgiveness, and when I demonstrate it, I allow it to invade me to my deepest depths. I am so grateful. Amen.

Some things bitter to digest

"Woe to them! They have brought disaster upon themselves." (v.9:)

For reading & meditation – Isaiah 3:1-11

Now we pause to ask ourselves how this fifth Beatitude, when prac-tised, engenders within us good mental and spiritual health. Psychologists have shown that those who lack the qualities of mercy and compassion are more likely to develop physical problems. Harsh, judg-mental attitudes may bring a sense of satisfaction to the person who does not know the meaning of mercy, but it is a false sense of satisfaction.

A verse that, strictly speaking, does not apply to what I am saying here, but nevertheless has some application is this: "It did taste sweet, like honey, but when I had eaten it, it was bitter to digest" (Rev. 10:10, Moffatt). That is what happens whenever we adopt any attitude that is not in harmony with Jesus Christ. At first it does "taste sweet, like honey" – its beginnings are apparently sweet, but it is "bitter to digest" – it cannot be assimilated. Our human constitution is not made to func-tion effectively on any attitude that is foreign to the spirit of Jesus Christ.

A Christian doctor says: "We are allergic to wrong attitudes just as some people are allergic to shrimps." I am physically allergic to red and green peppers. I have tried them scores of times, but the result has always been the same – I get sick. I am just as allergic to harsh, judgmental attitudes. I can't assimilate them. They disrupt me – body, soul and spirit. And what goes for me goes also for you When we fail to practise the principles which our Lord out-lined for us in the Beatitudes, then our sense of well-being is lowered, depleted and poisoned. Goodness is good for us – spiritually, mentally and physically.

FURTHER STUDY

Psa. 23:1-6; 31:9;
Ex. 34:6; Gal. 5:22;
Eph. 5:9

1. Of what is goodness a characteristic?

2. Can you make the same declaration as the psalmist?

Prayer

Father, something is being burned into my consciousness: there is only one healthy way to live – Your Way. When I break with You, I break with life. Help me always to maintain a close connection with You. In Jesus' Name. Amen.

Getting back what you give

"He who seeks good finds goodwill, but evil comes to him who searches for it." (v.27)

For reading & meditation – Proverbs 11:16-31

Those who know how to be merciful are men and women to be envied. They get back what they give. Psychologists are always pointing out that our attitudes and emotions are contagious. Scripture puts the same truth in these words: "A man that hath friends must shew himself friendly" (Prov. 18:24, AV). And what's more, a merciful attitude can encourage others to themselves be merciful. People who are merciful are not so apt to arouse harsh feelings or awaken enmities – they receive what they give.

Within the act of mercy is the power to effect change. When you demonstrate mercy toward someone, it calls forth the same feeling tones from the other person, and there will be an exchange that will reinforce the importance of the quality of mercy in your own spirit. So you do not lose anything, for they, in turn, give you something of themselves that can enrich your life.

It does not always happen, of course, that the demonstration of mercy evokes a positive response in others, but whether it does or not, you are all the better for being merciful. The pay-off is in you. Have you noticed how a person with this quality always seems to have good personal relationships? And when he or she has need of mercy from others, then it is instantly forthcoming – for as we give, so shall we receive. And not only do they enjoy good personal relationships – they enjoy (other things being equal) good physical health. The right thing morally is always the healthy thing physically. For morality is one – whether it is written in our tissues, or whether it is written in the Testaments.

FURTHER STUDY

Matt. 18:23-35;
6:15; James 2:13

1. What was Jesus teaching in this parable?

2. How is this sometimes a picture of us?

Prayer

Gracious Father, I am finding Your way amid my own ways. Daily, hourly, it is being disclosed before my astonished gaze. Help me to follow Your way, Your attitudes and Your lifestyle. For all other ways defeat me. Yours develops me. Amen.

Through Christian eyes

*"Each of you should look not only to your own interests, but
also to the interests of others." (v.4)*

For reading & meditation – Philippians 2:1-13

As we conclude our study of the phrase, "Blessed are the merciful, for they will be shown mercy", we ask ourselves: What would happen if we really put into practice this important principle? It would mean that we would look at everyone through Christian eyes. We would see sinners, not merely as the victims of sin and Satan, but as men and women who are to be pitied. We would see a fellow Christian who falls by the way, not as someone to come down on, but as someone to be lifted up.

Far too many of us walk about with judgmental attitudes, and whenever anyone slips up, we either harangue them with a Bible text or wither them with a look of scorn. We have the philosophy of an eye for an eye and a tooth for a tooth. Failure is met with derision and wrong is met with contempt. I have no hesitation in saying that such attitudes ought not to be found among the people of God. Wherever they are present, they will eat like acid into the soul. Being merciful means letting Christ have control of our lives so that His gentleness overcomes our vindictiveness, His kindness our unkindness, and His bigness our littleness.

Are you a merciful person? Do you look upon those who have fallen with concern and compassion – or is your attitude one of contempt and scorn? Can you feel pity for those who have been duped by the world and the devil? If so, then – congratulations! You have passed the test and are on your way to experiencing spiritual health and happiness. Blessed indeed are those who are merciful – for they will obtain mercy.

FURTHER STUDY

Luke 18:1-14;
2 Cor. 8:1-9;
Heb. 2:17-18

1. How did Jesus
   show mercy?

2. How do you show
   mercy?

Prayer

O my Father, with all my heart I cry out – help me to be a merciful person. Touch my whole being today by Your blessed Holy Spirit so that I might be changed into Your image. In Jesus' Name I pray. Amen.

Spiritual heart surgery

"But the things that come out of the mouth come from the heart, and these make a man 'unclean'." (v.18)

For reading & meditation – Matthew 15:1-20

Today we come to the Beatitude which is considered by many to be the most sublime of them all: "Blessed are the pure in heart, for they will see God" (Matt. 5:8).

First we ask: What is meant by the term "heart"? According to the general use of the word in Scripture, it has reference to what goes on in the core of our being. The heart is more than just the seat of the emotions; it is the fount from which everything proceeds. In our reading today, our Lord put it thus: "For out of the heart come evil thoughts, murder, adultery, sexual immorality ..." and so on (v.19). Dr Oswald Chambers said: "If a sinner really wishes to understand his heart, then let him listen to his own mouth in an unguarded frame for five minutes." Luke put it this way: "... the evil man brings evil things out of the evil stored up in his heart. For out of the overflow of his heart his mouth speaks" (Luke 6:45).

It has been pointed out that the gospel is a religion of new things. It offers us all a new birth, a new life, a new hope, a new happiness, and, at the end of time – a new name. However, out of all these fascinating new things which Christ offers His children, none is perhaps more intriguing than His offer of a new heart. The promise is first given in the prophecy of Ezekiel: "I will give you a new heart and put a new spirit within you" (Ezek. 36:26). Quite clearly, when it comes to spiritual things, the heart of the matter is the matter of the heart. Christ's offer of changing our hearts is one of the greatest promises of the Bible. Be encouraged: our Lord is not content with tinkering about on the surface of our lives – His goal is to purify our hearts.

FURTHER STUDY

Psa. 51:1-10;
19:12-13; 79:9

1. What was the psalmist's prayer?

2. Make it your prayer today.

Prayer

My Father and my God, slowly but surely I am coming under the sway of Your "beautiful attitudes". But I see You have more for me to discover. Hold me close as I go through your spiritual heart surgery. In Jesus' Name I pray. Amen.

Purity – not a popular thought

"… he purified their hearts by faith." (v.9)
For reading & meditation – Acts 15:1-11

Now that we understand what Scripture means by the term "heart" – the core of our being – we ask ourselves another important question: What does our Lord mean when He uses the word "pure"? "Blessed are the pure in heart, for they will see God."

The word "pure" (Greek: *katharos*) means a heart that is clean or clear. Unfortunately, purity does not seem to be popular in contemporary Christianity. The emphasis nowadays seems to be more on power than on purity. Most Christians I talk to want to know how they can possess and develop spiritual gifts. Few, generally speaking, want to know how to experience the blessing of what our text today calls a heart purified by faith.

Sixteen hundred years ago St Augustine expressed a sentiment in words which might well sum up the thoughts of many – thankfully, not all – in today's Church: "Lord, make me pure … but not just yet." Most of us would be willing to identify ourselves with the conditions laid down in the first five of our Lord's Beatitudes, but how do we feel about the condition of being pure in heart? Are we ready and willing to pray:

> *I want, dear Lord, a heart that's true and clean*
> *A sunlit heart, with not a cloud between.*
> *A heart like Thine, a heart divine.*
> *A heart as white as snow.*
> *On me, dear Lord, a heart like this bestow.*

FURTHER STUDY

John 13:1-17;
2 Cor. 7:1;
James 4:8;
1 John 3:3

1. What was Peter's request?

2. Make it your request today.

Prayer

O yes, dear Father, from the depths of my being I cry – make me clean. I have come so far with You – how can I turn back now? I'm a candidate for both power and purity. Give me the deep inner cleansing I need – today. For Jesus' sake. Amen.

Whiter than snow!

"Cleanse me with hyssop, and I shall be clean; wash me, and I shall be whiter than snow." (v.7)

For reading & meditation – Psalm 51:1-15

A s we continue discussing what it means to be pure in heart, we ask: How do we ensure that our hearts are made pure? Great controversy has raged over this issue in every century of the Church. Those who see sin as having made deep inroads into human nature say that the only thing God can do with sin is to forgive it. Others see the soul as a battleground on which long-drawn-out hostilities take place between the flesh and the Spirit. And there are those who claim, as did John Wesley, that inner purity can be imparted by a sudden influx of divine grace.

Adherents of these views fall into three main groups: (1) those who believe that purity is imputed; (2) those who believe that purity is imparted; and (3) those who believe that purity is developed. Those who believe that purity is imputed say that Christ flings His robe of righteousness around a sinner and then God for ever sees him in the spotless garments of His Son. Those who believe purity is imparted claim that there is an experience awaiting all believers, usually subsequent to conversion, whereby, through a crisis experience, God imparts the gift of purity. This belief received great prominence under John Wesley. Those who believe purity is developed see the work of God in the soul proceeding along the lines of a slow but steady improvement.

Which of these is right? I believe that each view has something to contribute; it is when the emphasis is disproportionately placed that problems arise. God both imputes and imparts purity, and then helps us apply and develop these truths in our daily life and experience.

FURTHER STUDY

1 Pet. 1:1-22;
Psa. 24:3-4;
1 Tim. 1:5; 5:22

1. To what else does Peter relate purity?

2. What was Paul's exhortation to Timothy?

Prayer

O God my gracious Father, I am so thankful that You have provided for my deepest needs – and especially my need for inner cleansing. Wash me so clean on the inside that I will be whiter than the whitest snow. Amen.

Lord – make me clean

*"… through Christ Jesus the law of the Spirit of life set me
free from the law of sin and death." (8:2)*

For reading & meditation – Romans 7:14-8:4

Yesterday we ended by saying that God can impart purity as well as impute it, and He then helps us apply it in our daily life and experience. Permit me to share my own personal experience in this connection, not as a model for you to follow, but simply to illustrate how God revealed Himself to me.

Following my conversion in my mid-teens, friends assured me that I ought to ask God to baptise me in His Holy Spirit. This, they told me, would give me the power I needed to become an effective witness for Him. I asked God to do this – and in a remarkable encounter with Him, I found the power I sought. But although this experience transformed me overnight from a shy, timid follower of Christ into a fearless witness for Him, I still felt deeply troubled by sinful forces. I fought hard with such things as lust and sensuality until one night, worn down by the inner conflict, I got down on my knees and prayed: "Lord, reach deep inside me and make me truly clean."

Again, something wonderful took place – not so much an invasion of power as an invasion of purity. It did not result, I found, in placing me beyond the possibility of a carnal thought, a stab of pride, a trace of envy, but it meant that from that moment to this, I have been more conscious of the Holy Spirit's presence than I have been of sin's presence. Evil was not eradicated in me, as some proponents of imparted holiness believe, but I found that the eagerness for it had gone, and the hunger for it was no longer a clamour. Now, fifty years later, I never cease to thank God for His Spirit's cooling and cleansing touch.

FURTHER STUDY

Gal. 5:1-26;
Matt. 5:29;
Rom. 6:6; 13:14

1. How did Paul
exhort the Galatians?

2. How drastically
did Jesus put it?

Prayer

My Father and my God, although I realise I have to walk my own personal path to holiness and inner cleansing, help me to know at last that same cooling, cleansing touch in the depths of my heart. I ask this for Your own dear Name's sake. Amen.

A divine catharsis

"And he will be called Wonderful Counsellor ..." (v.6)
For reading & meditation – Isaiah 9:1-7

We continue meditating on the word "pure" as used by Jesus in His sixth Beatitude. I discovered when researching this theme that the word "catharsis" – meaning to cleanse or make pure – is derived from the same Greek root as the word "pure".

In psychology, the word "catharsis" is used to describe the feeling of release and cleansing a person experiences in the presence of a trusted friend or counsellor when they empty out many of their repressed feelings or ideas. In the right circumstances and under the right conditions, a person who does this often feels purged, renewed and released. I have seen this happen myself on countless occasions when counselling. A person comes with deep hurts, and when they are sure they are in the presence of someone who understands them, someone they can trust, they open up their repressed feelings in such a way that afterwards they sit back and say: "I feel so different. It's like someone has reached deep down inside me and scraped my insides clean."

What produces this feeling of purging and release? It is difficult to explain because the inner release a person feels is not obtained simply by sharing; it comes only in the atmosphere of mutual confidence and trust. When a counsellor shows signs of disapproval or shock, then no release (catharsis) is experienced. If, as mental health experts claim, this only happens when a counsellor is warm and accepting, as opposed to harsh and judgmental, then it becomes immediately obvious that in the presence of Jesus, the Wonderful Counsellor, we have the possibility of experiencing the deepest catharsis it is possible to know.

FURTHER STUDY

1 John 1:1-7;
Psa. 65:3;
Ezek. 36:25;
Zech. 13:1

1. How are we to walk?

2. What does this result in?

Prayer

Blessed Lord Jesus, my Counsellor and my Friend, help me to open up the whole of my being to You so that I might experience a divine catharsis. I long not just to be clean – I long to be wholly clean. For Your own dear Name's sake. Amen.

"No condemnation now I dread"

"So if the Son sets you free, you will be free indeed." (v.36)
For reading & meditation – John 8:21-36

We saw yesterday that the phenomenon of catharsis comes about not simply through telling someone else our troubles, but when that other person is a warm, accepting and understanding individual. Psychologists believe the explanation for this to be the fact that the warm, accepting manner of the helper is so directly opposite to the harsh, judgmental attitudes of those who caused the hurts that repressed feelings easily surface and are released.

What has this law of the personality to do with the subject now under discussion? A great deal, I believe. In Jesus Christ we find Someone who not only yearns for our trust, but is worthy of our trust. To sit in His presence is to hear words similar to those He spoke to the woman caught in adultery: "Neither do I condemn you … go now, and leave your life of sin" (John 8:11). Such acceptance, such compassion, such concern, cannot fail to produce within every heart a willingness to open up those hurts and fears which have been so deeply repressed.

As I said yesterday, I have witnessed on countless occasions this strange and mysterious phenomenon of catharsis take place as, in the presence of love and acceptance, repressed hurts and ideas are discharged from the personality. But beautiful and wondrous as this natural phenomenon is, it is as nothing compared to the glory and radiance that a person shows when they stand in the presence of Jesus Christ, the Wonderful Counsellor, and experience a catharsis that reaches, not merely into the outer regions of the heart, but to its greatest depths. To have such an experience is not just to be free – it is to be free indeed.

FURTHER STUDY

John 3:1-18; 5:24;
Rom. 8:1; 8:34;
Rev. 12:10

1. Who brings condemnation?

2. What is the promise to the believer?

Prayer

My Father and my God, slowly things are coming into focus. I am beginning to understand what You mean when You say: "If the Son sets you free, you will be free indeed." Purge me to the depths of my being. In Jesus' Name. Amen.

Seeing God

"Who may ascend the hill of the Lord? Who may stand in his holy place?" (v.3)

For reading & meditation – Psalm 24:1-10

We spend one more day meditating on the words: "Blessed are the pure in heart, for they will see God." The concluding words of this Beatitude are often misunderstood. Many believe them to have reference to the saints' eternal reward in heaven. Tennyson expressed this thought in his famous lines: "I hope to see my Pilot face to face when I have crossed the bar."

The thought contained in this phrase, however, is not so much related to seeing God in heaven, but to seeing God *now*. Seeing God means seeing God in everything. Let me put it another way: not to see God is to fail to find the meaning of life and to see no purpose in anything. Such a condition, one must admit, produces an emotional overload on the personality that leads inevitably to despair. Some who fall prey to this mood can end up committing suicide. As one person commented: "Those who can't see the why have little energy to cope with the what."

Seeing God is being acquainted with Him, sensing His acceptance, comprehending what it means to be forgiven and made anew. Raymond Cramer puts it beautifully when he says: "To the pure in heart, seeing God is viewing a stained glass window from the inside rather than the outside. The pure in heart are aware of a reality which most people miss. They are sure of God." Seeing God must be connected with purity of heart, for we must see and sense God first in our own inner being before we can see Him and sense Him elsewhere. See Him within and you will not fail to see Him without.

FURTHER STUDY

Isa. 6:1-8;
Psa. 99:9;
Heb. 12:14;
Rev. 15:4

1. What was Isaiah's experience?

2. What is a prerequisite for seeing the Lord?

Prayer

Gracious and loving Father, I recognise that an uncleansed heart causes more ill health and more unhappiness than anything else. Help me take the prescription You have given me with a thankful heart. Amen.

Peace in our time

"Therefore, since we have been justified through faith, we have peace with God through our Lord Jesus Christ." (v.1)

For reading & meditation – Romans 5:1-11

We have come now to the seventh positive attitude that makes for good spiritual and mental health: "Blessed are the peacemakers, for they will be called sons of God" (Matt. 5:9). This Beatitude seems to have a special relevance to the age through which we are passing, for if there is one thing the world needs at this moment, it is peacemakers.

Our generation has never known peace worldwide. One authority says: "During most of our recent history the air has been filled with rumblings of pending war until today, at the so-called peak of scientific enlightenment, the menace of a global conflict threatens our atomic age with suicide." The uncertainty caused by being on the brink of nuclear confrontation, despite the end of the cold war between the East and West, has taken its toll on people of all nations, spiritually and psychologically. Studies show that living in a generation which has the power to annihilate itself in global destruction has a crippling effect upon the minds of thousands, if not millions, of people.

There was never a time when peacemakers were as important as they are now. And more and more are standing up to be counted on the side of peace. The peace organisations report increasing memberships and their attempts to alert the world to the need for international treaties continues to gain the attention of every section of the media. Yet how strange that most of those who are so concerned for peace between nations fail to see the need for peace between themselves and their Creator. The solemn truth is that no man or woman can become a peacemaker – at least in the biblical sense of the word – until they have found peace within their innermost being.

FURTHER STUDY
Rom. 12:9-18;
14:19; Prov. 12:20;
Mark 9:50

1. What are we to do?

2. Are you a peacemaker?

Prayer

O my Father, help people to come to the realisation that before they can enjoy the peace of God, they must first enjoy peace with God. In Jesus' Name. Amen.

How much do we "project"?

"Search me, O God, and know my heart; test me and know my anxious thoughts." (v.23)

For reading & meditation – Psalm 139:1-24

We ended yesterday by saying that no one can become a peacemaker – in the biblical sense of the word – until they have found peace within their innermost self. As we are looking at the Beatitudes from the point of view of how effective they are in producing good spiritual and mental health, it is interesting to see how the psychology of Jesus is always ahead of the findings of those who study human behaviour. The view of many psychologists and psychiatrists is that much of the talk and activity by the masses in relation to international peace is actually a projection whereby they take the pressure off themselves. I am not convinced that all the concern can be dismissed in this way, but a lot of it can be explained in terms of the mechanism known as psychological projection.

Listen to what Louis Linn and Leo Schwartz say in their book *Psychiatry, Religion and Experience:* "A psychological origin of an adolescent's social idealism lies in his yearning for peace within himself. He tends to project his feelings of helplessness and turmoil on to the outer world, so that his yearning for peace may take the form of a wish for world peace." Many of the activists who work for world peace may find this difficult to accept, but the truth is that if they did not have a world crisis on which to project their feelings, they would have to create some other condition. As long as we are not at peace within ourselves, we will create situations on which we project our insecure feelings.

FURTHER STUDY

Lam. 5:1-5;
Isa. 48:22; 57:20;
Deut. 28:67

1 Which of these statements could be written about this generation?

2 Make this a matter for prayer today.

Prayer

Dear Father, help me to understand this strange mechanism of projection. For I see that I can do the right things for the wrong reasons. Only You can probe my heart. I pray today with the psalmist, "Search me, O God, and know my heart." Amen.

Discord within – discord without

" 'There is no peace,' says the Lord, 'for the wicked.' " (v.22)
For reading & meditation – Isaiah 48:12-22

We are seeing that the reason why people get caught up in activist measures to gain the attention of world leaders in relation to the need for securing international peace is due, in part, to the mechanism of projection. If we do not know peace within, then we will tend to focus on finding ways of securing peace in our outer circumstances and environment.

I hasten to add that not everyone who is involved in peace movements is motivated by this reason. I know a number of genuine Christians – people who already have the peace of God in their hearts – who are active in such organisations and have a genuine concern to bring pressure on world governments to do everything that must be done to address these problems. Nevertheless, I have no hesitation in saying that the majority of those involved in the peace organisations are motivated by this strange mechanism we introduced into our discussions yesterday – projection. Since they do not possess peace within themselves, they talk at length about international peace.

It is easier to blame the world leaders, the political parties, the presidents and prime ministers than to look into one's own heart and accept individual accountability. Actually the reason why there is so much war and hostility in the world is because, generally speaking, we do not possess peace within ourselves. We create an environment that reflects our inner conflicts – the outside world reflects our inner world. Peace between nations does not guarantee peace within nations, nor does peace between two people guarantee peace within an individual.

FURTHER STUDY
John 14:15-27;
Psa. 29:11;
119:165; Isa. 26:3

1 What keeps us in peace?

2 What does the peace of Christ resolve?

Prayer

Gracious and loving Father, I bow my head in gratitude for the exquisite peace You have given me. Now that I am at peace with You, help me to be at peace with others – and to bring peace to others. In Jesus' Name. Amen.

"What a beautiful day!"

"For he himself is our peace, who has made the two one, and has destroyed the barrier, the dividing wall of hostility …" (v.14)

For reading & meditation – Ephesians 2:11-22

Our meditations over the past few days have shown us that before we can become peacemakers in the true sense of that word, we must first know peace in our own minds and hearts.

The Bible is not content to leave the nature of the peace Christ purchased for us in doubt. Our reading today tells us that Christ made peace by the blood of His cross. He bore the sins of men so that those who know Him and accept His meritorious sufferings on the cross need no longer be troubled by them. The greatest message the world has ever heard – or will ever hear – is this: Christ interposed Himself between sinful humanity and a holy God so that men and women could be eternally redeemed. Have you been redeemed? Have you accepted Christ's sacrifice for you on the cross? If so, good – your mission now in life is to be a peacemaker. You are to share His peace with others.

A little girl who, a few weeks earlier, had become a Christian came down from her bedroom one morning and said to her mother: "What a beautiful day." The surprised mother said: "What do you mean? It's raining like I've never seen it rain before, and the weather forecast is that we are going to have several more days of this. How can you call such weather beautiful?" "But Mother," the little girl replied, "a beautiful day has nothing to do with the weather." In those simple but powerful words, she reconciled her mother to the weather – and had a more beautiful day herself. You see, this is what peacemaking is all about. The peacemakers make a new world around them and within them.

FURTHER STUDY

Matt. 11:20-30;
Ex. 33:14;
Psa. 116:7;
Heb. 4:3

1 What did Jesus promise?

2 What must we do?

Prayer

O Father, help me today to be a peacemaker wherever I go, and to reconcile people, not just to the weather – but to You. That which reaches the heart must come from the heart. Let the peace in my heart overflow. In Jesus' Name. Amen.

Let every Christian begin ...

"... those who are peacemakers will plant seeds of peace and reap a harvest of goodness." (v.18, TLB)

For reading & meditation – James 3:1-18

We continue making the point that we cannot be peacemakers until we first find peace within ourselves. A psychiatrist was interviewing a man full of conflicts. In the middle of the interview the telephone rang, and because the receptionist had put a call through to him when he had given instructions not to be disturbed, the psychiatrist swore. He lost his peace and he lost his patient, for the patient saw that he had little to give except verbal advice.

The fact is that when we lose our peace with others, it is usually the projection of an inner conflict within ourselves. A church in the Far East has this statement engraved over the door: "Let every Christian begin the work of union within himself." This is the place to begin – within yourself. For, as the Chinese saying puts it: "He who has peace in himself has peace in the family; he who has peace in the family has peace in the world."

A prominent member of a peace movement in the British Isles who said he was dedicated to peace wrote a stinging letter to a member of the British Parliament which was published in the press. As a result, his advocacy of peace was blurred. People said: "This man's idea of peace needs an overhaul. It is simply verbal, and not vital." A missionary said: "God and I are not at peace; we seem to be at cross purposes. And my relationships with others are becoming more and more difficult." Of course – for when we are not in harmony with God, then we are not in harmony with ourselves or others.

FURTHER STUDY

John 16:25-33;
Luke 1:78-79;
Rom. 8:6; 14:17

1. What does peace spring from?

2. Why can we take heart?

Prayer

O Father, I long to become so harmonised with You that my life becomes an example of harmony to others. Make me a peaceful and peaceable person. For Jesus' sake. Amen.

What peacemaking is not

"Encourage and rebuke with all authority. Do not let anyone despise you." (v.15)

For reading & meditation – Titus 2:1-15

Today we go a step further and affirm that no one can be spiritually or mentally healthy until they know what it means to have peace in their inner beings. A psychologist says: "If we could only measure the amount of emotional energy that is dissipated within the human personality by lack of peace, we would be surprised to find that physical, mental and emotional loss would represent our greatest deficit within the human economy." He is simply saying that inner conflict tears us apart – physically, mentally and spiritually.

The intriguing thing is that as we make peace with God, a change comes about in our own lives and this, in turn, is reflected in the lives of others. We are not only at peace – we become peaceable. But even more – we become peacemakers. To be a peacemaker means, quite simply, that we become reconcilers. We reconcile people to God and to each other.

We should be careful not to misunderstand the meaning of the word "peacemaker", so let's examine for a moment what it is not. Peacemaking is not just keeping the peace. Some strive to keep the peace because they do not wish to risk any unpleasantness that might be involved in trying to put matters right. They avoid a conflict by smoothing over the surface, but this is not peace. The true peacemaker sometimes has to be a fighter. Paradoxically, he or she is called, not to a passive life, but an active one. Those who pursue this ministry must realise that peacemaking is not patching things up, but getting to the roots of the problem. Peacemakers sometimes have to stir up trouble before they can resolve it.

FURTHER STUDY

Eph. 6:1-15;
Psa. 119:165;
Phil. 4:7

1. What is the essence of the gospel?

2. What keeps our hearts and minds?

Prayer

Father, thank You for reminding me that peacemaking is not cowardice or the love of quiet. Give me the courage I need to risk any unpleasantness that may be involved in the cause of putting matters right. In Jesus' Name I pray. Amen.

Like our Father

*"How great is the love the Father has lavished on us, that we
should be called children of God!" (3:1)*

For reading & meditation – 1 John 2:28-3:11

Peacemaking is a positive attitude that produces good spiritual and mental health, and the one who has this attitude, according to Jesus, is to be envied and congratulated. The promise of the seventh Beatitude is that peacemakers "will be called sons of God". Why *called*? Because they *are* sons of God. This is their lot in life. Dr Martyn Lloyd-Jones put it like this: "The meaning of being called the sons of God is that the peacemaker is a child of God and that *he is like his Father*."

If I were to pick out the one verse that most perfectly expresses the meaning of the Christian gospel, it would be this: "in Christ God was reconciling the world to himself … and entrusting to us the message of reconciliation" (2 Cor. 5:19, RSV). Ever since man sinned, God has been engaged in the positive business of an outgoing love – seeking to reconcile those who did not want to be reconciled. God wants us to do what He does – He commits to us the same task of reconciliation.

Those who are inwardly reconciled to God and seek to reconcile others to Him and to each other are the healthiest and the happiest people on earth. In two outstanding passages in the Bible, we are called sons of the Father – and for the same reason: Matthew 5:9 and Matthew 5:45. What do we conclude from this? We are most like God when we are bringing people together in reconciliation. And those who try to reconcile others are doing the work of heaven – for it is heaven's work to reconcile us.

FURTHER STUDY

Gal. 4:1-7;
John 1:12;
Rom. 8:14;
Heb. 2:10

1. As sons, what have
we become?

2. How are we led?

Prayer

O God my Father, I pray that You will help me become more and more like You. You are a Father who reconciles – make me into Your own divine image. Help me to breathe "peace" upon all I meet. For Your own dear Name's sake. Amen.

When society kicks back

*"For it has been granted to you on behalf of Christ not only to
believe on him, but also to suffer for him."* (v.29)
For reading & meditation – Philippians 1:12-30

We come now to Christ's eighth and final prescription for good spiritual and mental health: "Blessed are those who are persecuted because of righteousness, for theirs is the kingdom of heaven" (Matt. 5:10). The inevitable result of bringing our attitudes in line with Christ's attitudes is that our lives become a silent judgement upon others. And men and women do not like to be judged, so they kick back in persecution. "Society," said someone, "demands conformity: if you fall beneath its standards, it will punish you; if you rise above its standards, it will persecute you. It demands an average, grey conformity."

The true Christian, however, does not conform – he stands out. "Woe to you," said Jesus, "when all men speak well of you" (Luke 6:26). If they do speak well of us, then it could be that we are too much like them. Let there be no mistake about this, the righteous will be persecuted – inevitably so. Once we adopt the principles which Christ presents, the men and women of the world are going to react with hostility and indignation.

Dr E. Stanley Jones was close to the mark when he said that the first thing a person must get used to when he or she becomes a Christian is the sight of their own blood. Are you being persecuted for righteousness' sake at the moment? Is the world venting its hatred and hostility upon you because of your stand for the Lord Jesus Christ? Then take heart – the persecution is the final proof, if one is needed, that you are a true disciple of your Master, a child of God and a citizen of heaven.

FURTHER STUDY

Matt. 10:16-42;
24:9; Luke 21:12

1 How are we sent
out?

2 What was Jesus'
promise?

Prayer

My Father and my God, help me not to miss the deep underlying truth in this, the last of Your prescriptions for happiness. Strengthen me so that I am unafraid of seeing my own blood. In Jesus' Name I ask it. Amen.

Collision course

*"... everyone who wants to live a godly life in Christ Jesus
will be persecuted." (v.12)*

For reading & meditation – 2 Timothy 3:12-17

We continue from where we left off yesterday in saying that persecution is one of the proofs that we are true disciples of the Lord Jesus Christ. Many Christians find great difficulty in coming to terms with this issue of persecution, and because they have never understood that those who reject Christ will also reject those who follow Christ, they become entangled in such things as conciliation and compromise.

If you have never done so before, face the fact right now that when you identify yourself with Jesus Christ, the world will persecute you. The degree of persecution differs from one Christian to another, but in one way or another the world will react against you with hostility and contempt. Once you recognise this, you are nine tenths of the way toward overcoming the fear which cripples so many Christians – the fear of witnessing.

Not long after my conversion, an elderly Welsh miner gave me some advice that greatly helped to overcome my fear of rejection. He said: "Keep ever before you the fact that those who reject Christ will reject you. And the more like Christ you become, the more the world will resent you. Remember also that when they do reject you, it is not you personally whom they are against, but Christ who is alive and who is being seen in you." Never shall I forget the release that came through those wise words. Once I understood that becoming identified with Christ meant I was on a collision course with the world, I came to terms with the inevitability of this fact and was set free from fear. And what happened to me can happen to you – today.

FURTHER STUDY

John 17:1-26;
15:20; 16:2

1. How did the world respond to the first disciples?

2. What was Jesus' prayer?

Prayer

Lord Jesus Christ, I bring to You my fear of persecution and ask You to set me free from it right now. Help me to face the world's hostility in the knowledge that just as it could not overcome You, it cannot overcome me. Amen.

"My neighbours won't talk to me"

"… be wise as serpents and innocent as doves." (v.16, RSV)

For reading & meditation – Matthew 10:1-20

We are saying that many Christians are ineffective witnesses because they attempt to water down their testimony to avoid persecution – and end up achieving nothing. Once we accept that those who reject Christ and His teaching will also reject us, we will then be free to throw our whole weight on the side of Christ and become fully identified with Him.

In following this principle, however, we must be careful that our freedom from fear of rejection does not lead us to become objectionable. I know some Christians who have a hard time from their non-Christian acquaintances, not because of their likeness to Christ, but because of their tactlessness and lack of wisdom. I once met a man who told me he had convincing evidence that he was a true disciple of Christ. I was intrigued to know his reason for thinking this way, and in answer to my question "Why are you so sure?" he replied: "My neighbours won't talk to me and cross to the other side of the road when they see me coming. I take this persecution as proof that I am a true citizen of the kingdom."

Some time later, I had occasion to talk to some of this man's neighbours, who told me that the reason they avoided him was because he continually accosted them with questions like "Do you know you are going to hell?" or "What if you were to drop dead at this moment – where would you spend eternity?" The neighbours thought it good policy to avoid him rather than to be faced continually with his belligerence. The man was suffering, not for Christ's sake, but for his own sake.

FURTHER STUDY

2 Tim. 3:1-13;
1 Cor. 13:3;
Rev. 2:10

1. What is the result of living a godly life?

2. What is promised for faithfulness?

Prayer

O God my Father, I see how easy it is to bring suffering and persecution upon myself by my own tactlessness and folly. Help me to object without being objectionable and to disagree without being disagreeable. In Jesus' Name. Amen.

No compulsions in Christianity

*"If you suffer, it should not be as a murderer or thief or any
other kind of criminal, or even as a meddler." (v.15)*

For reading & meditation – 1 Peter 4:7-19

We continue focusing on the fact that many Christians are persecuted, not because of identifying with Christ, but because of their tactlessness and folly. This eighth Beatitude – "Blessed are those who are persecuted because of righteousness, for theirs is the kingdom of heaven" – does not apply to such people. Let us be quite clear about that.

There is a great difference between persecution for the sake of righteousness and persecution for the sake of self-righteousness. Many Christians are foolish in these matters. They fail to realise the difference between prejudice and principle, and thus bring unnecessary suffering upon themselves. The same applies to those who are over-zealous in their witnessing. They make a nuisance of themselves and interpret the persecution that comes as persecution for righteousness' sake.

The Scripture teaches us to be "wise as serpents and innocent as doves". The writer of the Proverbs puts it powerfully when he says: "He who wins souls is wise" (Prov. 11:30). We are not told in this eighth Beatitude, "Blessed are those who are persecuted because they are over-zealous", neither are we told, "Blessed are those who are persecuted because they are fanatical." I was once asked by a church to counsel one of their members who had a compulsion to witness. The man got into so many difficulties because of this that the church threatened to discipline him unless he agreed to receive counselling. I found his compulsion to witness came not from Christ, but from his own inner drives. He needed to witness so as to feel significant. Witnessing should be a constraint, never a compulsion.

FURTHER STUDY

Acts 9:1-29;
1 Cor. 4:12;
2 Cor. 4:9

1 Who was Saul
really persecuting?

2 What was his early
experience of
proclaiming Christ?

Prayer

O Father, show me how to distinguish between what is a compulsion and what is a constraint. And help me to see that if I don't find my significance in my relationship with You, then I will attempt to find it in other ways. Amen.

A martyr complex

"… you are complete in Him …" (v.10, NKJ)

For reading & meditation – Colossians 2:1-15

We are seeing the suffering and persecution we experience can be due to our own tactlessness and folly. Today I want to go a stage further, and suggest that in relation to this matter of suffering and persecution, some Christians have developed a "martyr complex".

A "martyr complex" is an attitude of mind that finds strange emotional satisfaction in being persecuted. Why should this be? Well, if, for example, a person does not experience a good sense of personal worth, they become motivated to secure that worth in other ways. And one of those ways can be that of making an impact upon their immediate environment or society through taking a stand on some "Christian" issue.

Now I am not saying, of course, that all of those who take a stand on such issues as pornography, violence, and other serious moral problems are motivated to do so because of a "martyr complex". That would be foolish to suggest and foolish to deduce. But it must be seen that some Christians strike out on issues, not because of an overriding concern for Christian values, but because of the satisfaction they get out of being noticed. And when being noticed leads to severe persecution, they draw from this the emotional charge they need to compensate for their low sense of worth. Such people almost court suffering and persecution, but it has to be said that they are not suffering for righteousness' sake – they are suffering for their own sake. May God give us grace and wisdom to understand when we are doing things to meet our own emotional needs, rather than out of love for Him.

FURTHER STUDY

2 Cor. 11:16-33;
2 Tim. 2:8-9;
3:10-11

1. List some of Paul's sufferings.

2. What was Paul's testimony?

Prayer

Father, I see even more clearly that unless my needs are met in a close relationship with You, then I am a vulnerable person – and prone to go astray. Draw me closer to You this day. In Jesus' Name. Amen.

"Xenophobia"

*"… you do not belong to the world, but I have chosen you
out of the world. That is why the world hates you." (v.19)*

For reading & meditation – John 15:12-27

We continue meditating on the eighth and final Beatitude. One of
the questions that has often puzzled people concerning this matter of suffering and persecution is this: Why is it that Christians, when
they do good, are often persecuted, while non-Christians who do the
same kind of good are adored?

One commentator suggests the reason for this is that when non-
Christians do good, other non-Christians find it easy to identify with
them and say to themselves: "These people are just like me when I am at
my best." The thinking that goes on below the threshold of a non-
Christian's mind when he sees other non-Christians doing good is along
the line of: "I am probably capable of the same thing myself if the opportunity came my way." The admiration that is then given is a way of paying a compliment to oneself.

The Christian who does good has about him or her the atmosphere
of another world, and because of this, the non-Christian observes, not
just their act of good, but the different motivation that underlies the act.
They sense that there is something different about this
person, and because they cannot understand or
explain the difference, they react with fear and the fear
then turns to hostility. Psychologists have a name for
this fear – xenophobia. It means fear of someone we
do not know or understand. This is why the scribes
and Pharisees hated our Lord so much. It wasn't
because He was good; it was because He was different.
This is the effect Jesus Christ always has upon the
world. And to the extent that you reflect His spirit, to
that extent you will experience the same reaction.

FURTHER STUDY

Phil. 1:1-14;
Col. 4:3;
2 Tim. 1:7-8

1. How did Paul view
persecution?

2. What was his
charge to Timothy?

Prayer

O Father, I see that if I just try to do good, the world will applaud me, but if I try to
become Christlike, it will hate me. Nevertheless I long to be Christlike. Help me, dear
Father, for apart from Your grace, I know it is not possible. Amen.

Stand – and be healthy

"… I have set before you life and death, blessings and curses.
Now choose life …" (v.19)

For reading & meditation – Deuteronomy 30:1-20

We spend one last day meditating on the eighth and final Beatitude. Some feel that the verses which follow this Beatitude (verses 11 and 12) constitute a ninth Beatitude, but really they are an amplification of what our Lord has been saying in verse 10. It must be pointed out in passing that more is said about this eighth Beatitude than is said about the others – a fact that surely underlines its supreme importance.

The question we ask ourselves today is this: How does this eighth Beatitude contribute to good mental and spiritual health? It does so by encouraging us to stand up and be counted. The famous missionary doctor and scientist Dr Albert Schweitzer, when addressing a group of medical men in Africa many years ago, is reported to have said: "You cannot be healthy unless you stand for something – even at a cost."

The person who unashamedly identifies with Christ and stands up for Him, knowing that their stand will produce, in one form or another, inevitable persecution experiences an inner release from fear that affects every part of the personality in the most positive way. The positive may be persecuted, but they are also the most productive – they survive when others fall by the way. So stop wearing out your nervous system. Cease using up precious energy trying to find ways to make it through this world. Follow God's blueprint as laid out in the eight Beatitudes and yours will be a life which, through the psychology of Jesus, will bring you maximum effectiveness with minimum weariness. Choose any other way and you will experience minimum effectiveness with maximum weariness. I choose life.

FURTHER STUDY

Philemon 1-25;
Eph. 3:1;
1 Pet. 3:15-16

1. How did Paul view his imprisonment?

2. When were you last persecuted?

Prayer

Father, I, too, choose life. Help me to absorb and assimilate Your attitudes until they become my attitudes. Then life will always have to be spelt with a capital "L". With Your help, dear Lord, I'm on my way to real living. Hallelujah!

How do I rate?

"Examine yourselves to see whether you are in the faith; test yourselves." (v.5)

For reading & meditation – 2 Corinthians 13:1-14

As we conclude our study of the Beatitudes it is time for us to take a simple test. Ask yourself the following questions and see how many of Christ's "beautiful attitudes" have been assimilated into your life:

1. Am I trying to grasp things from God's hands or are my hands relaxed and empty so that I might receive?

2. Do I shrink from painful experiences or do I welcome them in the knowledge that they will make me a more sensitive person?

3. Am I so sure of God and His resources that I am free from a spirit of demandingness and over-concern?

4. Is my goal to be happy, or is it to be holy? Am I more taken up with getting pleasure out of God than I am with giving pleasure to God?

5. Do I have a deep compassion and concern for the plight of others?

6. Is my heart clean and pure? Have I experienced an inner cleansing that has reached to the deepest depths?

7. Am I a reconciler – one who seeks to reconcile others to God and, where necessary, to each other?

8. Am I so identified with Christ that I experience the hatred which the world gives to those who remind them of Him?

Don't be discouraged if you can't see all of these "beautiful attitudes" at work in your life. Remember, we *grow* in grace. Ask God, however, to help you absorb more and more of His "beautiful attitudes" day by day. The more you have, the more you are to be envied. Possess them all – and you are truly blessed.

FURTHER STUDY

Eph. 4:1-15;
Heb. 6:1;
2 Pet. 3:18

1. What are we to go on to?

2. What "beautiful attitude" will you reflect today?

Prayer

Lord Jesus, I have listened to Your words and I realise now the Word must become flesh – in me. I want the balance of my days here on earth to reflect, not my attitudes, but Yours. Help me, for Your own Name's sake. Amen.

How to use the Bible

A question I am often asked especially by young Christians is this: why do I need to read the Bible?

We need to read the Bible in order to know not only God's mind for the future but how to develop a daily walk with Him. God uses His Word to change people's lives and bring those lives into a deeper relationship with Himself and a greater conformity to His will. For over four decades now I have spent hours every week reading and studying the Scriptures. God has used this book to transform my life and to give me a sense of security in a shifting and insecure world.

How do we read the Bible? Do we just start at Genesis and make our way through to the book of Revelation? There are many ways to go about reading the Scriptures; let me mention the three most popular approaches.

One is to follow a reading plan such as is included in the *Every Day with Jesus Devotional Bible* or *Through the Bible in One Year*. The great advantage of following a reading plan is that your reading is arranged for you; in a sense you are being supervised. You are not left to the vagaries of uncertainty: what shall I read today, where shall I begin, at what point shall I end?

A second approach is to thread your way through the Scriptures by following a specific theme. It is quite staggering how many themes can be found in Scripture and what great spiritual rewards can be had by acquainting yourself with them. When I started writing *Every Day with Jesus* in 1965 I decided to follow the thematic approach and I wondered how long I would be able to keep it up. Now, over thirty years later, I am still writing and expounding on different themes of the Bible, and the truth is that I have more biblical themes and subjects than it is possible to deal with in one lifetime!

A third approach is by reading through a book of the Bible. This enables you to get into the mind of the writer and understand his message. Every book of the Bible has something unique and special to convey and, as with any book, this can only be understood when you read it from start to finish.

It is important to remember that all reading of the Bible ought to be preceded by prayer. This puts you in a spiritually receptive frame of mind to receive what God has to say to you through His Word. The Bible can be read by anyone but it can only be understood by those whose hearts are in tune with God — those who have come into a personal relationship with Him and who maintain that relationship through daily or regular prayer. This is how the Bible puts it: "The man without the Spirit does not accept the things that come from the Spirit of God, for they are foolishness to him, and he cannot understand them, because they are spiritually discerned" (1 Cor. 2:14).

Praying before you open your Bible should not be a mere formality. It is not the *act* that will make the Bible come alive but the *attitude*. Prayer enables us to approach the Scriptures with a humble mind. The scientist who does not sit down before the facts of the universe with an open mind, is not prepared to give up every preconceived idea and is not willing to follow wherever nature will lead him, will discover little or nothing. It is the same with the reading of the Scriptures; we must come to it with a humble and receptive mind or we too will get nowhere. Prayer enables us to have the attitude that says, "Speak, for your servant is listening" (1 Sam. 3:10).

If we are to grow in the Christian life then we must do more than just *read* the Bible — we must *study* it. This means that we must give time to poring over it, considering it, thinking about what it is saying to us and assimilating into our hearts and minds its doctrines and its ideas.

I have already pointed out that one of the ways of reading the Bible is by taking a theme and tracing it through the various books of the Bible. The pleasure this brings can be greatly enhanced by using this as a regular means of Bible study. When we study the Bible with the aid of concordances, lexicons and so on, we feed our minds but when we study the Bible devotionally, we apply the Word of God to our hearts. Both exercises are necessary if we are to be completely rounded people but we must see that it is at the place of the devotional that we open up our hearts and expose ourselves to God's resources.

Let me encourage you also to take advantage of a reading plan as a further basis of study. Following this will enable you to cover the whole of the Bible in a set period. Those who have used this method tell of the most

How to use the Bible

amazing spiritual benefits. One person who had read through the whole of the Bible in a year said to me, "It demanded more discipline than I thought I was capable of, but the rewards have been enormous." When I asked her what these rewards were, she said, "I used to have a partial view of God's purposes because I dipped into my Bible just here and there as it suited me. Now, however, I feel as if I have been looking over God's shoulder as He laid out the universe, and I feel so secure in the knowledge that He found a place for me in that marvellous plan." There can be no doubt that reading through the entire Bible in a set period enables one to gain a perspective that has tremendous positive spiritual consequences.

The third form of study — reading through a book of the Bible at a time — has the advantage of helping you understand the unity and diversity of the Bible. It is quite incredible how so many writers sharing their thoughts at different times of history combine to say similar things and give a consistent emphasis. Reading and pondering on this gives you such an appreciation of the wisdom of God in putting together this marvellous volume that it fires your soul and quickly brings praise and adoration to your lips.

I have found the best way to study a book of the Bible is to read it through once for a sense of the whole, and then to read it again, making a note of anything that strikes me such as a principle to be applied, an insight to be stored away in my heart, or a thought to be shared with someone who is struggling.

One thing is sure, time spent with the Bible is not wasted. The more one loves God the more one will love the Bible. And the more one loves the Bible the more one will love God. Always remember this unique volume — God's one and only published work — yields its treasures only to those who read it, study it and obey it.

Selwyn Hughes

The Power
of a New
Perspective

"Footholds for faith"

"... I have put my trust in the Lord God ..." (v.28, NKJ)
For reading & meditation – Psalm 73:1-28

We begin today a verse-by-verse examination of one of the great passages in the Bible – the seventy-third psalm. If you were to ask any group of Christians to name their favourite psalm most would probably reply: "The twenty-third." And it is not difficult to understand why. The simplicity and beauty of its language, together with its comforting content, has endeared it to millions. Unfortunately the seventy-third psalm is not so well known, but in my opinion it deserves to be. The truths and insights it contains provide us with some of the most steadying and encouraging revelations to be found anywhere in the Word of God.

The issue with which the psalmist struggles in this psalm is this: Why do the godly suffer so much when the ungodly, generally speaking, seem to get off scot-free? So deeply does this question cut into his soul that he is brought to the point of near despair: "My feet had almost slipped; I had nearly lost my foothold" (v.2). Whilst there, however, he discovers some spiritual principles that bring him step by step to the heights of spiritual assurance.

Are you puzzled by the fact that though you are following the Lord, life is extremely difficult? Do you wonder why those who live in opposition to the Almighty seem to have an easier time than those who are committed to His cause? Take heart. It is possible to find a foothold on this slippery path of doubt. The psalmist found it, and so can you. Follow me day by day through this thrilling psalm and you will discover a few more footholds for your faith.

FURTHER STUDY

Ezek. 18:24-32;
Jer. 12:1;
Hab. 1:1-4

1. What was the complaint of the Israelites?

2. What was the Lord's response?

Prayer

Gracious and loving heavenly Father, help me as I begin this quest for greater light and illumination on life's problems, for I know that a faith which does not hold my intellect will not hold my heart. I would have both held by You. Amen.

A lost emphasis

"Then those who feared the Lord talked with each other ..."
(v.16)

For reading & meditation – Malachi 3:13-18

Although in Psalm 73 the psalmist is beset by doubt, he begins, nevertheless, on a triumphant note: "Surely God is good to Israel, to those who are pure in heart." Preachers usually leave their conclusion until the end of their sermon – but here the psalmist begins with it! It might seem strange to some that the psalmist should begin with a conclusion, but this is often seen in the book of Psalms. And the reason is this: the psalmist is so convinced of the fact that God is good that he decides to start right there. It is as if he is saying: "I want to tell you how I moved from doubt to faith, but the thing I want you to get right away is this: God is good."

Some commentators believe that in the Temple services there was a time of open testimony and worship, similar to that which featured in the old Methodist class meetings, when individuals gave testimonies to their fellow believers of God's dealings with them. This is one of the most powerful ways of building the spiritual life of the Church, but regrettably it does not seem to be widely practised today.

If this psalm was part of the psalmist's testimony during an open time of worship, one can imagine the impact it would have made upon the hearers as he related how he emerged from crippling doubt to renewed confidence in the goodness of God. I know of nothing more motivating in the Christian life than for believers to identify and share the spiritual principles which have enabled them to overcome attacks on their faith. When we ignore this principle we do so at our peril.

FURTHER STUDY

John 3:25-36; 5:39;
15:26; Acts 20:24

1. When was the last
time you publicly
testified to the
goodness of God?

2. When will be the
next time?

Prayer

O Father, show us clearly how sharing with each other what You are doing in our lives not only inspires and motivates us, but greatly strengthens the Body. Help us restore this lost emphasis wherever it is missing. In Jesus' Name. Amen.

How strong convictions come

*"… that you may be mature and complete, not lacking
anything." (v.4)*

For reading & meditation – James 1:2-8

We continue meditating on the first verse of Psalm 73: "Surely God is good to Israel, to those who are pure in heart." The psalmist has gone through an experience of crippling doubt but the great thing is this: he has emerged from it spiritually enriched but with a deeper confidence in the goodness of God. So he starts with that conclusion and then tells us how he got there.

This is one of the great values of the psalms – they reflect and analyse the experiences that we are called upon to face. Ray Steadman says of the psalms: "They are an enactment of what most of us are going through, have gone through or will go through in the walk of faith." Every one of us will be able to understand the psalmist's struggle: we start off with a positive faith in God's goodness and then something happens which causes us to be plagued with doubts. The problem then is how to get back to where we were. This is what the psalmist does in this psalm – he shows us how to return to the place where the soul finds true peace.

We should not forget that the strongest convictions are born in the throes of doubt. The statement "God is good to Israel" is a statement grounded in experience. In a similar vein, Dostoevsky, the famous Russian novelist, could say: "It is not as a child that I believe and confess Christ. My hosannah is 'born of a furnace of doubt.' " Doubts may discourage but they need not demoralise you. It is not what happens to you, but what you make of it that matters.

FURTHER STUDY

Psa. 13:1; 69:3;
119:82

1. What
characteristic did the
psalmist display?

2. What was his
confession of faith?

Prayer

Gracious and loving Father, I pray that You will do for me what You did for the psalmist and help me turn my strongest doubts into my strongest beliefs. I offer You my willingness – now add to it Your power. In Jesus' Name I ask it. Amen.

"A great soul battle"

"I sink in the miry depths, where there is no foothold." (v.2)
For reading & meditation – Psalm 69:1-12

Having shared with us the conviction that God is good, the psalmist now proceeds to tell us what caused him to move away from that belief so that his soul became filled with such desolating doubt: "But as for me, my feet had almost slipped; I had nearly lost my foothold. For I envied the arrogant when I saw the prosperity of the wicked" (Psa. 73:2-3).

Here begins what Spurgeon described as "a great soul battle, a spiritual marathon, a hard and well-fought fight in which the half-defeated became in the end wholly victorious". The psalmist seems bothered by the apparent contradiction between what he had been taught in the Scriptures – that God is good to those who are pure in heart – and his experience in life. He was envious, he says, of the arrogant and deeply upset over the fact that the wicked appeared to be more prosperous than the godly. He had been told that when you were righteous, then God would take care of you and prosper you. Obviously things had not been going too well for the psalmist and when he compared his situation with that of the ungodly who appeared to be so prosperous, he came close to giving up his faith.

FURTHER STUDY

1 Kings 19:1-21;
Psa. 31:10;
42:5-6, 11

1. What point did
Elijah come to?

2. How did God deal
with him?

Am I talking to someone who is in a similar situation at this moment? Is your faith so badly shaken by what you see around you that you are tempted to give up? Then this is the word of the Lord to you today: hold on. It is a dark tunnel you find yourself in at this moment, but God will bring you through. He never fails. Never.

Prayer

Father, thank You for speaking to me today. Help me not to form my conclusions from what I see around – the immediate – but from what I see above, in You, the Ultimate. I wait in quiet confidence for Your word to come to pass. Amen.

Be honest with yourself

"Surely you desire truth in the inner parts ..." (v.6)
For reading & meditation – Psalm 51:1-9

Even the most casual reader of Psalm 73 cannot help but be struck by the openness and honesty of the psalmist. He says: "My feet had almost slipped ... for I envied the arrogant" (vv. 2-3). This again is one of the great values of the book of Psalms – it brings home to us the importance of acknowledging what is going on in our hearts when we are caught up in the midst of conflict. I cannot stress enough how spiritually damaging it is to ignore or deny our true feelings.

There is a form of teaching going around in some Christian circles today which holds that one should never admit or acknowledge a negative thought or feeling – not even for a single second. Life must be lived positively, it is said, and that means refusing to consider or even glance at anything negative. What nonsense! The people who advocate this approach to life can never have read the book of Psalms.

I am all for a positive approach to life, but positivism first involves facing things realistically no matter how negative they may be. How can you know what you need to be positive about until you have clearly seen what is troubling you? Once an issue is faced, and faced realistically, then the matter can and must be dealt with in a positive way. But to try and be positive without bringing into clear focus what is wrong is like building a house on sand. No matter how much cement is poured into the foundations, and no matter how well the walls are reinforced, when a storm comes it will sink without trace.

FURTHER STUDY

Prov. 12:15-22;
Lev. 19:11; Mal. 2:6

1. What word does the Bible use for denial?

2. What delights the Lord?

Prayer

Father, drive this truth deeply into my spirit, for I see that it is not enough to be honest with You and others, I must also be honest with myself. Help me get there and stay there. In Jesus' Name I ask it Amen.

If you're thrown – admit it

"My God, my God, why have you forsaken me?" (v.1)
For reading & meditation – Psalm 22:1-11

We continue looking at the attitude of the psalmist, who does not hesitate to tell the truth about himself. As we saw, he admits that his feet had well-nigh slipped and his faith had almost gone. I find the psalmist's honesty both stimulating and refreshing, especially when compared to the tendency of many in today's Church to pretend that things are not as they are. Dr Martyn Lloyd-Jones said in one of his sermons: "I know of nothing in the spiritual life more discouraging than to meet the kind of person who seems to give the impression that he or she is always walking on the mountain top." I agree.

You see, it is far more important to be honest than to appear to be the sort of person who is never thrown by problems. If you are not thrown, then fine; but if you are then admit it. But can't openness be a form of exhibitionism? Yes, it can. Some people may confess to failure as a means of drawing attention to themselves. But I do not believe that this was the psalmist's motive, for quite clearly he wrote the psalm to glorify not himself but God.

The pathway to spiritual growth begins when we realistically and honestly face up to the struggles that are going on inside us. If we are so concerned about developing or preserving pleasant feelings that we ignore the negative feelings within us or pretend that they are non-existent, then we end up demeaning ourselves. An honest look may involve a struggle, but there is more hope in that for growth than there is in pretence or denial.

FURTHER STUDY

James 5:1-16;
Prov. 28:13;
Acts 12:5

1. What are we to do with our faults?

2. How are we to respond to those who share their struggles?

Prayer

O God, teach me to be unafraid to look at anything – myself included. Make me strong enough in You not to need the defences of pretence and denial. You are on the side of honesty; I am on its side too. Help me. In Jesus' Name. Amen.

Death? Who cares?

"Why do the wicked live on, growing old and increasing in power?" (v.7)

For reading & meditation – Job 21:1-9

Before moving on, we pause to remind ourselves once more of the question with which the psalmist struggles in Psalm 73: Why is it that the wicked seem to prosper while the path of the righteous is beset by so many difficulties? Look now at how the psalmist views the condition of the ungodly: "They suffer no violent pangs in their death, but their strength is firm. They are not in trouble as other men; neither are they smitten and plagued like other men. Therefore pride is about their neck as a chain; violence covers them as a garment – as a long, luxurious robe" (Psa. 73:4-6, Amplified Bible).

What a graphic description this is of the person who has no time for God, yet goes on from day to day with few troubles. It is probably the most perfect picture in all literature of the so-called successful man of the world. Note that the psalmist begins his description of the ungodly with a reference to the way they die: "They suffer no violent pangs in their death." Throughout time the notion has been universally present that a good life ends in a good death, but the psalmist makes the observation that in his experience the reverse is true.

Have you not struggled with these same feelings whenever you have heard of a Christian dying in great agony while a non-Christian passes away peacefully in his sleep? What do you do with those feelings? Ignore them? Deny them? Repress them? Remember, it is only exposed problems that can be resolved. I say again, if you are not willing to face a problem, how can you go about getting it resolved?

FURTHER STUDY

Luke 12:15-21;
16:19-31;
Psa. 14:1; 53:1;
Prov. 12:15

1. What is the danger of worldly prosperity?

2. How did Jesus draw the contrast in his parables?

Prayer

O God, save me from denying the difficult problems and feelings I encounter in life. Help me understand that it is easier to deal with things when they are up and out than when they lie buried within. In Jesus' Name. Amen.

Why we are sometimes drained

"… Clear me from hidden and unconscious faults."
(v.12, Amplified Bible)

For reading & meditation – Psalm 19:7-14

We said yesterday that exposed problems are the only ones that can be resolved. Is this just an interesting theory, or is it something that can be supported from Scripture? Let me see if I can convince you that this statement has a biblical basis.

Come back with me to the Garden of Eden and think again about the questions which God put to the first human pair: "Where are you? … Who told you that you were naked? … What is this you have done?" (Gen. 3:9-13). Does anyone believe that God needed to ask those questions in order to gain information for Himself? Of course not; being omniscient (that is, having all knowledge), He already knew what they had done. Then why did He put those searching personal questions to them? Surely the answer must be that the direct questions encouraged them to face something that they preferred not to look at. God knew that before the problem could be dealt with it must be brought out into the open.

Some people may think that by far the best way of dealing with unacceptable thoughts and feelings is to push them back into the unconscious but, as we are now seeing, that is a fallacy. Problems that are buried inside us rather than brought out into the light work to drain us of spiritual energy. It takes a lot of emotional energy to keep things repressed. This is why people who repeatedly use the defence of repression end up feeling overtired. Healthy people are those who, like the psalmist in Psalm 73, bring their thoughts and feelings into awareness – no matter how "unspiritual" those thoughts and feelings may appear to be.

FURTHER STUDY

Psa. 139:13-24;
1 Cor. 11:27-28;
Lam. 3:40

1. What was the psalmist's prayer?

2. Why is the communion service so important?

Prayer

Father, I now begin to see why You bring me face to face with so many disturbing questions, for You know the havoc that is wrought within when issues are ignored or denied. Help me face anything and everything. In Your Name. Amen.

The roots of some perplexities

"'For my thoughts are not your thoughts, neither are your ways my ways,' declares the Lord." (v.8)
For reading & meditation – Isaiah 55:6-13

We continue examining the psalmist's graphic description of the so-called successful "man of the world": "Their eyes stand out with fatness, they have more than heart could wish, and the imaginations of their minds overflow with follies. They scoff and wickedly utter oppression; they speak loftily – from on high, maliciously and blasphemously. They set their mouths against and speak down from Heaven, and their tongue swaggers through the earth – invading even Heaven with blasphemy and smearing earth with slanders" (Psa. 73:7–9, Amplified Bible).

How perfectly these words describe the person who brazenly flaunts his arrogance and rides roughshod over the rights of others. Note the phrase, "their eyes stand out with fatness", or, as the *International Bible Commentary* puts it: "Their beady eyes bulged through folds of fat as they busily schemed. Superior and cynical, they engaged in malicious talk and threats." We see the same kind of people today – irreligious, self-centred men and women who live only for themselves and view God as an irrelevance.

Why does God allow them to get away with such attitudes and behaviour? Perplexing, isn't it? We must realise, however, that it is only perplexing because we are dealing with the ways of an eternal Being whose thoughts and designs are infinitely greater than our own – as the text at the top of this page clearly tells us. Think about this as you make your way through the day: half our perplexities would never arise if we were prepared *not* to understand immediately the things that God does or the things that God allows.

FURTHER STUDY

Dan. 4:1-37;
Hosea 14:9;
Hab. 3:6

1. How did God deal with Nebuchadnezzar?

2. What was his final conclusion?

Prayer

O Father, what unnecessary perplexities we carry within us because we try to trace the reasons that lie behind Your designs rather than just trust them. Help us in our quest for a more confident faith. In Jesus' Name. Amen.

What's happening!?

"... perplexed, but not in despair ..." (v.8)
For reading & meditation – 2 Corinthians 4:7-12

Today we stay with the thought that half our spiritual perplexities would never arise if we started out by being prepared not to understand immediately the things that God does or allows. We must accept that one of the fundamental principles of the Christian life is the truth that there will be many times when God will work things out in a manner exactly opposite to the way we think He should. If I had been taught this in the early days of my Christian life, it would have saved me from many spiritual struggles. Most of my perplexities arose because I failed to realise that I was dealing with a mind that is omniscient – that God's mind is not like my mind.

The ways of God are inscrutable; His mind is infinite and eternal and His purposes are beyond understanding. When we are dealing with such a great and mighty God it should not surprise us that He allows things to happen which we find perplexing. If we insist that everything in life should be plain, we shall soon find ourselves in the state in which the psalmist found himself – full of doubt, disillusionment and fear.

We should note, however, that perplexity is not necessarily sinful. It only becomes wrong when we allow our perplexity to drive us to despair. The apostle Paul, as our text for today shows us, was perplexed but he was not in despair. Make sure you understand the distinction. It is not foolish or wrong to say: "I don't know what is happening." It is only foolish to say: "God doesn't know what is happening."

FURTHER STUDY

Josh. 1:1-6;
Isa. 54:10;
Heb. 13:5

1. What was God's promise to Joshua and Isaiah?

2. What is God's promise to us?

Prayer

O Father, how comforting it is to realise that I can be perplexed and yet not fall into sin. Help me to keep this distinction clear. Drive the truth deep into my spirit today that You always know what is happening. In Jesus' Name I ask it. Amen.

"I hadn't even seen the accident!"

*"When a land falls into the hands of the wicked, he
blindfolds its judges ..." (v.24)*

For reading & meditation – Job 9:21-35

The more the psalmist contemplates the condition of the ungodly, the
more his perplexity increases. The next verses show him to be upset
over the fact that people treat the ungodly with such admiration:
"Therefore their people turn to them and drink up waters in abundance.
They say, 'How can God know? Does the Most High have knowledge?'
This is what the wicked are like – always carefree, they increase in
wealth" (Psa. 73:10-12). He observes that because they are so well-
admired and well-treated such people say: "Look at how good life is to
us! If there is a God, then He doesn't appear to have much interest in the
way we live."

A Christian tells of a work colleague, a successful man of the world,
who said to him one day: "On my way to work this morning a man
stopped me and said 'Are you a Jehovah's Witness?' Why would he ask
me that? Why, I hadn't even seen the accident!" The man was quite
unaware of who Jehovah was and the question had him completely
puzzled.

This is what troubles the psalmist in this section of Psalm 73 – he
sees people living with no concern for God, yet everything seems to be going so well for them. One can feel
his indignation burning through the words he writes.
Do you feel indignant about this, or a similar problem?
It's not surprising if you do. Be careful, though, that
you don't allow it to become your focus of concentra-
tion, for it is a law of the personality that you become
like the thing you dwell upon.

FURTHER STUDY

Deut. 32:1-15;
Psa. 37:35;
Jer. 5:27-28

1. What did Moses
declare?

2. What did
prosperity do to
Jeshurun?

Prayer

O Father, if it is true that I become like the thing I focus upon, then help my focus
of life not to be indignation at the prosperity of the ungodly but gratitude for the fact
that I am an heir to eternity. Amen.

The heart of the issue

*"Yet they say ... 'Who is the Almighty, that we should serve him?' ...
But their prosperity is not in their own hands ..." (vv. 14-16)*

For reading & meditation – Job 21:11-16

We come now to the heart of the issue with which the psalmist is struggling in Psalm 73: "Surely in vain have I kept my heart pure; in vain have I washed my hands in innocence. All day long I have been plagued; I have been punished every morning" (Psa.73:13-14). Permit me to paraphrase what I think he is saying: "Here I am, living a godly life, keeping my heart and hands clean, avoiding sin, meditating on the things of God and devoting myself to a life pleasing to God, yet despite this I am facing all kinds of troubles. What's the advantage in serving God if He doesn't protect me?"

The problem, then, is not so much the prosperity of the wicked as the fact that he himself is passing through a period of great trial while they are getting off scot-free. We begin now to see the roots of the envy to which the psalmist referred earlier: "For I envied the arrogant when I saw the prosperity of the wicked" (v.3). Envy is born out of two things: ignorance and a wrong comparison.

Take, first, a wrong comparison. "Almost all our problems," said Dr W.E. Sangster, "begin in a wrong comparison." How true this is. We compare our looks, our height, our income, our homes, our training and our abilities with those of others and soon we lose sight of our own individuality and specialness. To compare ourselves with Christ is a healthy spiritual discipline, but to indulge in comparison with those we think are more prosperous and fortunate than we are is the direct road to envy.

FURTHER STUDY

Psa. 37:1-40;
Prov. 3:31; 14:30

1. What is envy?

2. What is the result of envy?

Prayer

O God, save me, I pray, from the habit of wrongly comparing myself with others. Help me to satisfy the impulse I have for making comparisons only in a way that will yield spiritual gain – by comparing myself only with You. In Jesus' Name. Amen.

Don't forget the parenthesis

"He will not judge by what he sees with his eyes ..." (v.3)
For reading & meditation – Isaiah 11:1-9

Yesterday we said that envy is born out of two things: ignorance and making wrong comparisons. Having seen how a wrong comparison can produce envy, we focus now on ignorance. How can ignorance give rise to envy? Far too often our judgments of people are based only on what we see, and we fail to take into account other things that may be going on in their lives. Years ago, A.C. Gardiner wrote a little essay on Lord Simon and spoke at length of his many successes. In one place he described him as "prancing down a rose-strewn path to a shining goal". Gardiner thought that success, in the measure Lord Simon had experienced it, was free of all sorrow. Then he remembered some of the bitter disappointments that Lord Simon had faced and so he added in parenthesis: "I speak here only of his public career."

Many of us forget the parenthesis. We see simply the surface of our neighbours' lives and know nothing of their secret sorrows. If we saw beneath the surface of those lives we tend to envy – the hidden hurts, the emptiness, the heartaches, the guilt and the fears – then I doubt whether the emotion of envy would ever rise within us.

But even if there were no secret sorrows we would still have no reason to envy others. God is the rightful Lord of all life: "It is He who has made us, and not we ourselves" (Psa. 100:3, NKJ). Let us keep our eyes fixed only on Christ and resist all other attempts at comparison. Practise comparing yourself with Him, and only good will come out of it.

FURTHER STUDY

2 Cor. 10:1-18;
1 Cor. 2:13;
Psa. 89:6

1. What is it not wise to do?

2. What is the right way to make comparisons?

Prayer

Blessed Lord Jesus, I see how easily the spirit of envy can filch away my peace and happiness. Uproot this rank weed in my heart and teach me to compare myself with none other but You. For Your own dear Name's sake. Amen.

A recital of experiences

"No temptation has seized you except what is common to man." (v.13)

For reading & meditation – 1 Corinthians 10:1-13

Having spent the past days identifying the nature of the problem which almost caused the psalmist to give up, we pause today to focus on another great value of the book of Psalms – the fact that it presents its teaching in the form of a recital of experiences. We have exactly the same kind of teaching in the New Testament, but there it is presented in a more directive fashion.

Sometimes our hearts grow weary under the stresses of life and we are not open to receiving direct instruction from anyone. I remember when I was a young Christian going to church one evening feeling tired and worn down by the strong temptations I was experiencing. As the visiting preacher announced the title of his sermon – "Fifteen Principles for Overcoming Temptation" – I felt my heart sink within me. His sermon might have been what I needed but at that moment I was too weary to concentrate on principles.

When I got home that evening I turned to the book of Psalms, and as I read the experiences of some of those men and found that they too had been through what I was going through, my strength returned and my spirit revived. This is why the book of Psalms is one of the most important and valuable books of the Bible. Learn to turn to it whenever you feel battered and beaten by the waves of life. You will find, as millions have found before you, that it speaks to your condition because the men who wrote it have been in your condition.

FURTHER STUDY

2 Pet. 1:15-21;
Eph. 1:17-19;
2 Cor. 4:6

1. What is God's Word like?

2. What did Paul pray for the Ephesians?

Prayer

O Father, I am grateful to You beyond words for giving me that part of Your Word that reaches me when perhaps nothing else might reach me. Help me to make good use of it and avail myself of its unfailing resources. In Jesus' Name. Amen.

Starting at the bottom

*"... my soul is downcast within me. Yet this I call to mind
and therefore I have hope." (vv.20-21)*

For reading & meditation – Lamentations 3:19-27

Now we come to the turning point of the seventy-third psalm – the point where the psalmist takes the first step toward the resolution of his problem. We must not forget that the purpose of this psalm is to show us how the writer solved his problem, so that when we get into the same kind of difficulty we can apply the same solutions.

Here, then, is his first step: "If I had said, 'I will speak thus,' I would have betrayed your children. When I tried to understand all this, it was oppressive to me" (Psa. 73:15-16). We see in these words what it was that arrested his feelings of doubt and despair – the thought that if he were to speak out of his discouraged heart he would put a stumbling-block in someone else's path. "If I did that," he thinks to himself, "I would be untrue to the generation of God's children. So, rather than discourage others with my doubts, I will not say anything at all."

Some might regard it as strange that the first step the psalmist took on the road to recovery should be one with such a low motivation. Indeed, there are those who have said it was unworthy of him and that he should not have allowed himself to get into that condition. Similarly, when people in the Church today confess to having "unspiritual" feelings, I am sure you have heard judgmental advice-givers address them with words like: "You ought not to feel like that!" But the point is that they do feel like that, and reality demands that we begin right where they are and not where we would like them to be. Personally, I do not care how low a person's stand might be as long as he or she is *standing* and not slipping.

FURTHER STUDY

Heb. 4:1-16;
Matt. 9:36;
Mark 1:41;
Luke 7:13

1. Why can we come
boldly to the Lord
with our feelings?

2. What will we
obtain?

Prayer

Gracious and loving Father, teach me how to handle myself in a crisis and help me not to be too proud to begin at the lowest level. Better to have my feet on the lowest rung of the ladder than to be struggling in the mire. Amen.

Stop and think!

*"... Everyone should be quick to listen, slow to speak and slow
to become angry ..."* (v.19)

For reading & meditation – James 1:12-20

Yesterday we saw that the first step the psalmist took, the step which helped to save him from spiritual disaster, was most surprising. In the midst of overwhelming temptation, he says to himself: "If I give expression to my doubts and speak out of my envious, discouraged heart, I will put a stumbling-block in someone else's path – hence I will not say anything at all" (paraphrase mine). Now as we said yesterday, many people may find it difficult to accept this as the first step on the road to recovery – but it worked, nevertheless.

Listen to what one commentator says about this first step: "Our reaction to the discovery of what his first step was in his process of recovery will be a very good test of our spiritual understanding." What does he mean? He means that if we fail to see that the steps of faith are sometimes very ordinary, then we are not as spiritual as we imagine. It's all right to have your head in the clouds, but make sure your feet are firmly planted on the earth!

Keep in mind, then, that the thing which stopped the spiritual slide of the psalmist was very simple and ordinary – he made a decision not to say what was on the tip of his tongue. He stopped to think. Rather than spread his unbelief, he determined to keep his mouth shut; rather than threaten someone else's spiritual understanding, he resolved not to act on impulse. It might not have been a particularly high spiritual motive, but it was the thing that prevented him from falling.

FURTHER STUDY

1 Pet. 3:8-15;
Prov. 13:3; 21:23

1. What are we to do with our tongue?

2. How are we to give an answer?

Prayer

Gracious and loving Father, help me grasp this point that sometimes the first step towards spiritual recovery is one that is simple, practical and ordinary. Save me from becoming so super-spiritual that I neglect the commonplace. In Jesus' Name. Amen.

We do what we choose to do

"The tongue has the power of life and death ..." (v.21)
For reading & meditation – Proverbs 18:15-21

We are seeing that the first step the psalmist took to save himself from falling was stopping himself from saying what was on the tip of his tongue. In other words, he took himself in hand.

This is an extremely important issue. What a lot of heartache would be saved if Christians would take heed to this and learn to put a bridle on their tongues. Expressions which convey the idea that the Lord acts unjustly or unkindly, especially if they fall from the lips of men and women who have a long experience in the Christian life, are as dangerous as sparks in a timber factory. Despite his doubts, the psalmist recognised the importance of self-discipline, and that proved to be a saving virtue.

People sometimes claim: "It is impossible for me to control what I say. It slips out before I realise what I've said." This is nonsense, of course, for what we say is the result of what we choose to say. Sometimes we may feel as though we have no control over what we say, but that is all it is – a feeling. Dr Lawrence Crabb, a Christian psychologist, tells us: "The loss of felt choice does not mean the loss of real choice." When you give a person "a piece of your mind", as we say, there is always a moment, albeit a split second, when you can choose to speak out or stay quiet. We cannot hide behind the excuse that our tongue is not under our control. What we do is what we choose to do. The psalmist, though beset by many doubts and difficulties, chose to control his tongue – and so can you.

FURTHER STUDY

James 3:1-18; 1:5;
Luke 21:15

1. What does James teach about the tongue?

2. What are we to ask God for?

Prayer

O Father, help me see that the things I do and say are not the result of compulsion but of choice. I am free to obey or free to disobey. Help me to use my freedom in the right way. In Jesus' Name I ask it. Amen.

"Selective expression"

"How dare you turn my Father's house into a market!"
(v.16)

For reading & meditation – John 2:13-17

We continue thinking about the psalmist's decision to take himself in hand and refrain from relaying his doubts to others. I feel it important at this point to say a further word about repression and expression. Christians, we said earlier, are never to pretend about anything. Whether we worry, covet, resent, hate, we are to acknowledge the reality of who we are at any given moment. Fully admitting to ourselves and to God that we are angry, worried or full of doubts, is not sin. It becomes sin when we constantly focus on it and allow it to drag us down into despair.

But does this mean that in order to experience emotional health we must let everything out and tell everybody exactly how we feel? The clear answer to that question is "No", but it is an answer that must be qualified. For example, when seeking help from a counsellor or minister, it would be right to share exactly how you feel. The principle I suggest we adopt in relation to this is as follows: we may express our acknowledged emotions only when such expression is consistent with God's purposes.

FURTHER STUDY

Luke 24:13-35;
Gal. 6:2-5

1. What did Jesus encourage as He walked with the disciples?

2. How did He bring perspective to them?

This is a critical point and it must be understood. The cure for repression is not to "let it all hang out" but to be selective, expressing only those emotions that are in harmony with God's will. We must freely admit to ourselves and to God what is happening to us, but then we must carefully and selectively consider whether it is right and in line with God's purposes to share what we feel with others.

Prayer

Gracious and loving Father, help me to be honest with my feelings, yet willing to subordinate the expression of them in both timing and manner to Your perfect will. In Jesus' Name I ask it Amen.

A mature response

"But the fruit of the Spirit is ... self-control." (vv.22-23)
For reading & meditation – Galatians 5:16-26

So important is the point we raised yesterday – the need for selective expression – that we will spend another day considering it. Listen to how the Amplified Bible translates Psalm 73:15: "Had I spoken thus and *given expression to my feelings*, I would have been untrue and have dealt treacherously against the generation of your children" (emphasis mine). Notice that although the psalmist experienced strong feelings of uncertainty, he refrained from expressing these emotions because they would have had a negative effect upon his brothers and sisters. He acknowledged his emotions, but he refused to express them because he knew they would hurt and hinder the family of God.

Expression of our feelings with no thought of another's welfare amounts to sinful, selfish indulgence. We must allow ourselves to feel the full weight of our emotions but then subordinate their expression to the purposes of God. Only if it is God's will for us to share those feelings with others must we do so. Thus the apostle could write stinging words of rebuke to the Corinthian church because his words were in harmony with God's purposes.

We have to be on our guard here, because whenever we feel angry, and vent our anger on someone, it is so easy to justify our angry feelings by saying, "God wanted to use me to teach you a lesson." But more often than not, if we examine our hearts we will find that our goal was not the will of God but the desire to get those angry feelings out from inside us. Selective expression of feelings is a mature and spiritual response; indiscrimate expression is immature and unspiritual.

> **FURTHER STUDY**
>
> Eph. 4:15;
> Prov. 16:32;
> 2 Pet. 1:3-7
>
> 1. What is to govern our sharing?
>
> 2. Why are we to be self-controlled?

Prayer

Gracious God and loving heavenly Father, forgive me for the times I have hurt others by the indiscriminate expression of my negative feelings. Help me understand and apply this principle of "selective expression". In Jesus' Name. Amen.

Consider the consequences

"But I said, 'Should a man like me run away? ... I will not go!'" (v.11)

For reading & meditation – Nehemiah 6:9-13

We continue meditating on the fact that the psalmist, though filled with doubts about the goodness of God, nevertheless refrained from expressing those doubts to others. He carefully considered what effect his action might have on the family of God. Nothing that we do in life is without consequences. Someone has put it like this: "Every effect has a cause and every cause produces an effect."

Many of our difficulties in life arise from the fact that we forget the principle that consequences follow our actions. The devil often inveigles us into thinking that the situation we are in is an isolated event, and he gets us to believe that what we do, or are about to do or say, will have little or no effect upon others. He is exceedingly skilful at getting us to become preoccupied with the thing he puts before us. This one thing on which we focus then takes up our whole attention and we become oblivious of everything else, including the results that may follow our actions.

Troubled though the psalmist was, in his heart he considered the consequences of his actions. And this is what Nehemiah did in the passage before us today. A false "friend" came to him and told him that he

FURTHER STUDY

Gal. 6:1-9;
Hosea 8:7;
Isa. 17:11;
James 3:8-9

1. What is the principle of sowing and reaping?

2. What are words like?

should not risk his life. The proposition undoubtedly appealed to him, but Nehemiah considered the consequences and stayed where he was. If he hadn't, the whole course of Israel's history would have been changed. Believe me, this one principle alone – of carefully considering consequences – would be the means of saving us from endless difficulties if we were to take it and consistently apply it.

Prayer

Father, how grateful I am that Your inspired Word teaches me the importance of consequences. Help me absorb this truth and apply it when next I am tempted. May I obey Your Word and not just hear it. In Christ's Name I pray. Amen.

Say nothing unless it is helpful

"Let your conversation be always full of grace, seasoned with salt ..." (v.6)

For reading & meditation – Colossians 4:2-6

From what we have been seeing over the past few days, it is clear that although the psalmist was struggling with doubts about the goodness of God, he took a stand on something he knew to be right. He realised that if he were to speak as he was tempted to speak, the immediate consequence would be the hurt of God's people – so he chose to keep his thoughts and feelings to himself. He was not sure about the goodness of God but he *was* sure it would not be right to be a stumbling-block to God's children – and he held on to that fact.

Dr Martyn Lloyd-Jones said in one of his sermons: "When you are puzzled and perplexed the thing to do is to try and find something of which you are certain, and then take your stand on it. It may not be the central thing; that does not matter." Note the words: "it may not be the central thing". We can struggle in the midst of our doubts, waiting for some great revelation to hit us, and fail to apply the remedy that is immediately to hand. The psalmist saved himself from slipping by saying to himself: "My heart is full of uncertainties and I cannot say with conviction that God is good. But one thing I am certain of: it is wrong to hurt others because of my own doubts. Therefore I will say nothing."

We should be careful about how we express our doubts to other Christians, especially those who are immature. This principle applies also to non-Christian friends, partners, or family members. If we can say nothing helpful we should say nothing at all. The psalmist determined to say nothing until he could say: "God is good to Israel." Then he was entitled to speak.

Prayer

Gracious and loving God, I can do no better today than frame my prayer in the words of Your servant David: "Set a guard, O Lord, over my mouth; keep watch at the door of my lips." Help me, my Father. In Jesus' Name. Amen.

When you fall – others fall

"For none of us lives to himself alone and none of us dies to himself alone." (v.7)

For reading & meditation – Romans 14:5-13

It seems almost unbelievable that the thing which stopped the psalmist's feet from slipping and sliding was not the awareness of his relationship with God but the awareness of his relationship with his brothers and sisters. It might not have been the highest spiritual principle he could have held on to, but it saved him from disaster.

It is this matter – our relationship with one another – that Paul is speaking about in today's passage. You will be familiar, I am sure, with the passages in 1 Corinthians 8 and 10 where Paul enlarges on this subject and where, in a remarkable statement, he says: "I mean for the sake of his conscience, not yours, do not eat it. For why should another man's scruples apply to me, and my liberty of action be determined by his conscience?' (1 Cor. 10:29, Amplified Bible). He is saying, in other words, that you might see no need to refrain from eating meat offered to idols for your own sake, because your conscience is not offended, but what about your weaker brother for whom Christ also died?

You see, "none of us lives to himself alone", so when next the devil tries to convince you that you are an isolated case and that what he is suggesting concerns you and you alone, quote this verse to him. We do not act in isolation; if you fall, you do not fall alone, the whole Church falls also. If nothing else can stop you from doing wrong, remember the people to whom you belong, remember you are part of a heavenly family, and that when you fall, others fall with you.

FURTHER STUDY

1 Cor. 9:15-22;
Acts 20:35;
Rom. 15:1;
1 Thess. 5:14

1. What was Paul's approach to the weaker brethren?

2. What was Paul's word to the Thessalonians?

Prayer

Father, drive deeply into my spirit this truth that I cannot act in isolation, for I am bound up with my redeemed brothers and sisters. Help me experience an ever-growing consciousness of this important fact. In Jesus' Name. Amen.

Use everything you can

"Who despises the day of small things? ..." (v.10)
For reading & meditation – Zechariah 4:1-14

Having followed the experience of the psalmist, who was saved from a spiritual fall by thinking of his brethren, we now ask ourselves: What does all this have to say to us? I think the answer to that question must be this: to stand is more important than to understand.

We said a few days ago that the psalmist took his stand at a very low level on the scale of spiritual values. The principle he followed was this: "If I spread my doubts, I will harm my brethren." I am sure you and I could think of much higher spiritual principles with which to confront ourselves when tempted. What about the principle of reminding ourselves of the blessings of God in times past? Or actually talking to ourselves in the way the psalmist did in Psalm 42:5: "Why are you downcast, O my soul? Why so disturbed within me? Put your hope in God ...".

The psalmist employed none of these, but the one he did employ, low as it was on the scale of spiritual values, worked. And that is the point – use everything you can to stop yourself from falling, however small or insignificant it might appear to be. We are involved in spiritual mountaineering, where sometimes the slopes are like glass. When your feet slip you must reach out and hold on to anything that will stop you in your slide – even though it be only a small branch. Stop and steady yourself. Don't concern yourself about climbing, just concern yourself with stopping your slide. Once you have stopped sliding you can then plan how to climb again.

> **FURTHER STUDY**
>
> 1 Cor. 12:21-31;
> Ex. 4:2;
> Judg. 15:15;
> 1 Sam. 17:40;
> 1 Kings 17:12
>
> 1. What are some of the insignificant things God uses in his purposes?
>
> 2. How does Paul put it?

Prayer

Father, I see that when I am in danger of slipping it is better to take advantage of the smallest foothold than to slide into the depths of despair. Help me grasp the full importance and value of this. In Jesus' Name I ask it. Amen.

A critical position

"These have come so that your faith ... may be proved genuine and may result in praise, glory and honour ..." (v.7)

For reading & meditation – 1 Peter 1:1-7

Today we examine the fact that although the psalmist's feet are no longer slipping and sliding, he continues to struggle inwardly with his problem. Listen to what he says: "But when I considered how to understand this, it was too great an effort for me and too painful" (Psa 73:16, Amplified Bible). It is clear that although he has stopped himself from falling, he is still in great anguish of heart and mind; he is still perplexed over the issue of why the ungodly are prospering while he, a child of God, has to face all kinds of difficulties. He cannot bear the thought of scandalising the family of God, and yet his confusion continues.

Have you ever been in this position in your spiritual life – saved from slipping and sliding but still harassed by a giant-sized spiritual problem? You know enough to stop you falling, but not enough to start you climbing. It is a strange position to be in but one, I must confess, in which I have found myself on many occasions. Perhaps you are there right now – your feet have stopped slipping, but strong emotions continue to rage inside you.

This is a very critical position to be in – critical because the temptation at this point is to quieten the raging emotions within by settling for answers that are less than the real ones. I know many Christians who have been in this position, and because their goal has been to alleviate the pain in their heart rather than find the real solutions to their problem, they have grasped at superficial answers that do nothing more than provide temporary relief.

FURTHER STUDY

Psa. 17:3;
2 Pet. 3:9;
Job 13:1-16

1. What had the psalmist purposed?

2. What did Job declare?

Prayer

O Father, save me from settling for less than the best, even though it means struggling a little longer with some difficult and turbulent emotions. Help me be concerned with maturity, not just temporary relief. Amen.

Staying with the pain

"Though He slay me, yet will I trust Him ..." (v.15, NKJ)
For reading & meditation – Job 13:13-19

We ended yesterday with the thought that the moments after we have been saved from slipping and sliding, but are left with our main problem still unresolved, are exceedingly critical. Why critical? Because, as we said, the desire to relieve the pain that is going on inside us can sometimes lead us to settle for answers that are less than the best. We feel better when we can make sense of the ways of God – even a little sense.

When we are confronted by a spiritual problem that appears to have no immediate resolution and causes strong emotions to rage within us, there are, as far as I can see, just two options: either to live with the troublesome emotions, as Job did, and wait patiently for God to give a clear answer, in His time; or to replace the confusion with some form of understanding. The first option is often difficult, for it demands something which, especially when we are confused, we find hard to do – trust. The second is a lot easier, but potentially more dangerous, for unless we are careful, it can lead us into accepting solutions that are not solutions.

The pressure to move confidently in the midst of ambiguity and uncertainty and come up with "clear" answers is a strong one. But we must be careful that we don't settle for an answer that, although it helps to reduce the level of confusion, is not a real solution. Better to stay with the pain of confusion and uncertainty than to grasp at answers that are not answers because they evade the real problem.

FURTHER STUDY

Prov. 3:1-6;
Psa. 37:5; 118:8;
Isa. 26:4

1. What are we to do?
2. What are we not to do?

Prayer

O Father, help me as I think through this issue. I sense there is something here that I need to learn, but I need Your love and wisdom and insight to support me as I learn it. Come close to me – particularly over these next few days. In Jesus' Name. Amen.

"Why do I cry over nothing?"

"Then you will know the truth, and the truth will set you free."
(v.32)

For reading & meditation – John 8:31-41

Y ou have probably sensed that the issue we have been dealing with is extremely important. In fact, I know of nothing of greater consequence for the Christian Church than the need to resolve the issue of why it is, when facing the tough questions of life, we settle for answers that are not answers. Let me illustrate what I mean.

Many years ago a woman approached me at the end of a prayer meeting and said: "Why is it that I cry so much over nothing?" I replied that there could be a number of reasons and I recommended that if this situation continued she should seek the help of a Christian counsellor. My own feeling was that the problem arose from some unresolved conflicts in her life that needed identifying. Some time later I met the woman again and she said to me: "I still have the problem, but I know now why it happens to me – it is an attack of the devil."

I felt deeply saddened by her conclusion for I sensed that she had settled for an answer that helped to reduce her confusion but was not a real solution. Yes, the devil does attack and harass, but in my opinion something else was going on inside her which needed attention. I gently suggested this to her, but she was adamant that the devil was responsible and that the problem would eventually go. I prayed much for that woman because I saw in her what I see in many parts of the Christian Church – a tendency to reach out and settle for "answers" that help reduce the confusion but do nothing to stimulate spiritual growth and understanding.

FURTHER STUDY

Psa. 51:1-6;
Jer. 17:9;
Matt. 15:16-20

1. What does God require in the inner parts?

2. What is the condition of the heart?

Prayer

O God, I do not want to live my life amid illusions. I want to be real and I want to live really. Help me face the tough questions of life and not be content until I find the true answers –Your answers. In Jesus' Name I ask it. Amen.

Some tough questions

"How long, O Lord, must I call for help, but you do not listen?" (v.2)

For reading & meditation – Habakkuk 1:1-4

We continue thinking through the issue of why it is that we settle for easy answers. Every day we face tough questions as we live our lives for Jesus Christ. Should I let my children watch a certain television programme? Is God leading me into a new job? Why am I so prone to fall under the power of temptation? Should I use anti-depressants as the doctor says I should? These and other questions demand decisions that expose our uncertainty and force us to recognise how deeply confused we are about certain issues.

The Bible addresses some issues clearly, but on others it is not so clear. Sometimes we have to struggle with uncertainty. It is unappealing to be told that we have to go on in the midst of confusion, and we feel a great inner pressure to reduce the confusion to a point where it can be ignored. Motivated by anxiety, we seek to impose an order on our world – and it is at this point that we become extremely vulnerable.

In earlier years I used to be deeply perplexed about why intelligent Christian people bought into the ideas of some of the less responsible healing evangelists, who got them to pledge huge sums of money, give up medical treatment and do the strangest things. But then I realised that these men were providing the people who came to them with hopeful "answers" about their physical condition or that of their loved ones, and this was easier than living with confusion. God does heal, but sometimes He doesn't – no matter how hard we pray. And the way we handle this confusion determines our spiritual maturity.

FURTHER STUDY

James 5:1-7;
Psa. 13:1; 69:3;
119:82; 2 Pet. 3:9

1. What does James say we are in need of?

2. What does Peter confirm?

Prayer

O Father, give me the faith to believe in You in the midst of uncertainty and perplexity. Don't let me settle for an "answer" simply because it relieves my confusion. I know You do have answers, but help me go on even when they do not come. Amen.

The curse of modern Christianity

"… and do not give the devil a foothold." (v.27)
For reading & meditation – Ephesians 4:25-32

There is a price to pay for our desire to grab at easy answers and that price is "trivialisation". Trivialisation is the acceptance of explanations that ignore the difficult questions of life in order to experience relief from confusion. I have no hesitation in saying that this is a curse of the modern Church.

One way trivialisation reveals itself is in the acceptance, by so many, of the view that the major cause of Christians' problems is demonic activity. Demonic activity can be a cause of problems (especially in those who have dabbled in the occult) but it is not the chief cause. The New Testament teaches us the importance of spiritual warfare, but it has much more to say about the influence of our carnal nature on the rise and development of problems.

In the early days of my ministry, when people came to me with problems I would frequently engage in the practice of rebuking the devil, and those prayers often brought great relief. But the mistake I made was not to sit down with the people who came to me and deal with the beneath-the-surface problems which had given Satan a foothold in their lives. By making it appear that Satan was the only problem I trivialised the issue. It's a lot easier (and less confusing) to sit down with a person and "take authority" over Satan than it is to think through together the tough and perplexing issues that lie beneath the surface, and then work towards giving some Biblical perspectives. But that is demanded of us if we are to help each other towards maturity.

FURTHER STUDY

2 Pet. 1:1-6;
1 Cor. 14:20; 13:11;
Heb. 5:14

1. What are we to add to our faith?

2. What was Paul's admonition to the Corinthians?

Prayer

O Father, forgive us for the ways in which we trivialise Your truth in order to avoid facing the tough issues. It feels good to replace confusion with certainty, but help us to be sure that the certainty is Your certainty. In Jesus' Name. Amen.

The first thing to do

*"These things I remember as I pour out my soul: how I used to go
with the multitude ... to the house of God ..."* (v.4)

For reading & meditation – Psalm 42:1-11

Over the past few days we have seen how the psalmist was caught in
the hiatus between the moment when he stopped himself from sliding and the moment when he started to climb again. This, we said, is a
very critical time – critical because it makes us inclined to accept easy
answers. The perplexity did not end when the psalmist stopped himself
from slipping. His thoughts still went around in circles and he continued
to have great anguish of heart and mind.

How, then, were his thoughts concerning the prosperity of the
ungodly resolved? Not by grabbing at superficial answers, but by going
into the sanctuary of God, where he could begin to see the whole situation from God's point of view. Listen to how he puts it: "When I tried to
understand all this, it was oppressive to me till I entered the sanctuary of
God; then I understood their final destiny" (Psa. 73:16-17). The word
"sanctuary" here literally means the physical house of God. Some translations use the phrase, "till I entered the secret of God", but that is incor-
rect. Read Psalm 74 and read Psalm 76 and you will find that they both
refer to the material building where God was worshipped.

Had the psalmist, I wonder, like so many of us
when we are filled with doubt and uncertainty, stayed
away from the sanctuary of God? How strange that the
last thing we want to do when our hearts are filled
with doubts and misunderstandings is meet with our
fellow believers in the house of God. Yet that is the
very first thing we ought to do.

FURTHER STUDY

Heb. 10:19-25;
Matt. 12:9;
Mark 1:21;
Luke 4:16

1. What are we not to
do?

2. What was Jesus'
custom?

Prayer

Gracious Father, I am so grateful that You have ordained that Your people meet
together. Help me understand more clearly than ever the value and benefits that flow
from being with Your people. In Jesus' Name I ask it. Amen.

A redeeming, healing fellowship

"Let us not give up meeting together, as some are in the habit of doing, but let us encourage one another ..." (v.25)

For reading & meditation – Hebrews 10:19-25

Yesterday we ended with the thought that the very first thing we ought to do when seeking to break out of the vicious circle of doubt is to go to the house of God. The psalmist has been prevented from falling by considering the consequences of his actions upon his brethren, so now his next step is to go and meet with them in the sanctuary.

Whether it be in a cathedral or a cottage, how wonderful it is to join with Christian brothers and sisters. It is not so much the place that is important as the redeeming and healing fellowship we find there. Oftentimes people find release just by sitting down among their brothers and sisters and feeling the healing power of their warmth and love. One famous preacher said: "The house of God has delivered me from 'the mumps and measles of the soul' a thousand times and more – merely by entering its doors."

What is it about being among our fellow believers that is so helpful and encouraging? One thing is the very fact that our fellow believers are there. You see, in our private misery and perplexity we could easily run away with the idea that there is nothing very much in the Christian faith after all, and that it is not worth our going on. But when we enter into the Lord's house and see our fellow believers coming together, often our doubts disappear. We say to ourselves, albeit unconsciously: "Here are people who think the Christian life is worth continuing with. My uncertainties must be wrong – there must be something in it after all."

FURTHER STUDY

Acts 12:12-17;
16:12-13;
Psa. 84:10

1. What was the pattern of the early Church?

2. How did the psalmist view God's house?

Prayer

O Father, help me see the power that flows towards me through Christian fellowship. Just as I am encouraged by it, help me to encourage others. In Jesus' Name I pray. Amen.

Others have suffered too

"… the Lord knows how to rescue godly men from trials …" (v.9)
For reading & meditation – 2 Peter 2:4-10

We continue developing the thought that meeting together with our brothers and sisters can bring about a radical change in our perspective. Tell me, have you ever gone to church feeling a little disconsolate or depressed and found, as you have looked round and seen people who have gone through much greater struggles than you, that your heart has been strangely lifted and your burdens have seemed lighter?

You see a widow, perhaps, who has been left with several children, and as you watch her singing praises to God you see your problem in a different light. You notice a man whom you know has gone through the most horrifying experiences, but he is still there worshipping and magnifying God. This again works to change your perspective.

Paul reminds us in 1 Corinthians 10:13: "No temptation has seized you except what is common to man. And God is faithful; he will not let you be tempted beyond what you can bear." One of the things the devil delights to do is to persuade us that the trial we are going through is unique. When you come in contact with others in the family of God you begin to see that is just not true. You rub shoulders with people you know suffered extremely painful experiences – experiences more distressing than you have ever faced. Yet they still continue to sing God's praises. You see, in the church we have an opportunity to evaluate 1 Corinthians 10:13 in a clear light. The truth is seen in its highest form. Others have gone through what we have gone through, and the knowledge of this helps us in our suffering.

FURTHER STUDY

Psa. 10:1-7;
1 Kings 19:10;
19:14; 19:18;
2 Tim. 4:16

1. What did Elijah think?

2. What did God say to him?

Prayer

Father, the more I dwell on the benefits of Christian fellowship, the more I see how wise and considerate are Your purposes. Help me not to neglect this most marvellous and helpful means of grace. In Jesus' Name I pray. Amen.

History is His-story

"In him the whole building is joined together and rises to become a holy temple in the Lord." (v.21)

For reading & meditation – Ephesians 2:14-22

There can be little doubt that meeting together with other members of God's family is a powerful way of bringing about a changed perspective. Another thing that happens when we go to church or meet together in Christian fellowship is that we are reminded that the very existence of the Church in today's world is proof positive that God is on the throne. Voltaire, the French infidel, said: "It required eleven men to build the Church; I will prove that it needs only one man to knock it down."

He was wrong on two counts: first, it was not eleven men who built the Church, it was one man, the Man, Christ Jesus, and second, no one can ever knock it down, for its omnipotent Founder declared: "I will build my church, and the gates of Hades will not overcome it" (Matt. 16:18).

The mere existence of the Church is, I submit, decisive proof that the living Christ is in the midst of it. Voltaire is dust; Christ lives on. Think of the tempests the Church has weathered through the centuries. Think also of the persecutions through which it has victoriously come, and try, if you can, to account for this extraordinary phenomenon apart from the fact that its Founder and Protector is Jesus Christ.

The next time you meet together with your fellow Christians, reflect on the fact that, although every generation has produced people who have predicted the downfall of the Christian Church – it is still here. The realisation of this is yet another thing, I suggest, that helps to put our doubts into the right perspective.

FURTHER STUDY

1 Cor 3:9-17;
Eph. 1:22; 4:15;
5:23

1. What do we know about the foundation of the Church?

2. What does Paul declare to the Ephesians?

Prayer

O Father, how can I thank You enough for the times my own perspective has been changed after meeting together with Your people. I have greater insight now why You commanded us not to neglect assembling together. And I am grateful. Amen.

Life's greatest science

"... that you ... may be able to comprehend with all the saints ..." (vv.17-18, NKJ)

For reading & meditation – Ephesians 3:14-21

We are seeing that once we enter the sanctuary of God our perspective changes. This can happen to us when we are alone, of course, but the chances are it will happen more swiftly in the act of corporate worship. It is a command of God that we meet together, not only that we might come to know each other better, but that we might also come to know Him better. And here's the interesting thing – the more effectively we relate to one another, the more effectively we relate to Him. We come to know God better through the act of corporate worship than when we worship on our own. That is not to say that the shut-ins, or those who for various reasons are unable to meet together in worship, cannot know God intimately, but something special flows out of the act of corporate worship.

Listen to how C.S. Lewis put it: "God can show Himself as He really is only to real men. And that means not simply men who are individually good but to men who are united together in a body, loving one another, helping one another, showing Him to one another. For that is what God meant humanity to be like; like players in one band, or organs in one body. Consequently the only real adequate instrument for learning about God is the whole Christian community, waiting for Him together. Christian brotherhood is, so to speak, the technical equipment for this science – the laboratory outfit."

Christians who neglect attendance at the church, or choose to deprive themselves of fellowship with other Christians, miss out on life's greatest science – learning about God.

FURTHER STUDY

Eph. 2:1-19;
Rom. 8:15;
2 Cor. 6:18;
Gal. 4:5

1. How does Paul describe the Church?

2. What does it mean to be adopted?

Prayer

My Father and my God, I am so thankful that, although I can know You when I am alone, I can know You even better through the fellowship of the Church. Help me to learn about You in every way I can. In Jesus' Name I ask it. Amen.

Changed perspectives in church

*"Were not our hearts burning within us while he talked with us
on the road and opened the Scriptures to us?"* (v.32)

For reading & meditation – Luke 24:28-35

Another thing that brings about a changed perspective when we make
our way to the house of God is the reading and exposition of the
Scriptures. I make this statement on the assumption that the Scriptures
are expounded in your church, for, sadly, in some congregations this is
not so. In the days of the psalmist, of course, they did not have the Bible
as we know it today, but the portions of the Word of God that they did
have they recited and meditated upon.

How many times have you gone to church feeling confused about
God's dealing with you, only to find that as the Scriptures are opened
your view of God and life changes, causing you to leave refreshed and
reinvigorated? Calvin put it like this: "As the elderly, or those with poor
sight can hardly make out the words in a book, but with the help of
glasses can read clearly, so Scripture crystallises ideas about God which
had been very confused, scatters the darkness and shows us the true God
clearly."

You could, and should, read the Scriptures at home, but there is
something special about hearing the Word of God expounded in church.

Merely to hear a well-known text spoken by someone
who emphasises a word which we might not emphasise, can strike us in a way that adds new meaning to
it. Do you have a jaundiced view of God and life at this
very moment? Go to church on Sunday, to a Bible-
believing church, and expect God to speak to you from
His Word. I have it on the highest authority that He
will.

FURTHER STUDY

Luke 4:16-31;
Isa. 11:2; 61:1;
Matt. 3:16

1. What did Jesus do
in the synagogue?

2. What rested upon
Him?

Prayer

Father, forgive me for taking for granted the revelation that flows from Your Word
– whether it comes privately or in church. From now on, whenever I am "talked to"
by the Scriptures, help me to recognise it and to receive it with gratitude. Amen.

Missing from the meeting!

"Now Thomas … was not with the disciples when Jesus came." (v.24)

For reading & meditation – John 20:24-31

We said a couple of days ago that those who choose to deprive themselves of fellowship with other Christians miss out on life's greatest science – learning about God. I heard one preacher say: "People who neglect attendance at the house of God are fools because on some favoured occasion something special and powerful will happen – and they will not be there."

The passage we have read today tells us of that glorious post-resurrection appearance of our Lord to His disciples. The disciples thought He was dead, and although there were rumours of His resurrection, they were not convinced. Suddenly, He appeared to them – they saw Him, heard Him, and felt the impact of His mighty presence. But here is the heart-rending tragedy of it: "Thomas … was not with the disciples when Jesus came."

Why was Thomas missing from that meeting? Many preachers have speculated on the reasons for his absence, and they vary from Thomas not expecting Jesus to be there, to being afraid for his life. My own view, for what it is worth, is that there was something wrong with Thomas himself. The root cause of his defection, so I believe, was his own doubting and denying heart. My experience in the ministry has taught me that those who profess to be Christians and yet deliberately absent themselves from fellowship with their brothers and sisters, are the ones who are usually most in need of this fellowship.

FURTHER STUDY

Matt. 25:13;
Prov. 15:5; 20:24

1. What is the message of the parable of the virgins?

2. How are 5 of them described?

Prayer

Gracious and loving heavenly Father, help me realise that the very time I need to be among my brothers and sisters is when I am at my lowest spiritually. Burn this truth into my consciousness so that it will never leave me. In Jesus' Name. Amen.

Natural versus spiritual thinking

"The man without the Spirit does not accept the things that come from the Spirit of God ..." (v.14)

For reading & meditation – 1 Corinthians 2:6-16

We have been seeing that by going "into the sanctuary" – the place where God had made provision to meet with His people – the psalmist has put himself in a position where his perspectives can be changed. This section of the psalm is probably the most vital part, for it is here that his thinking begins to change from natural thinking to spiritual thinking. He had been thinking like a natural man, considering life from just one perspective, but in the sanctuary he begins to see life from God's point of view.

What is the difference between natural thinking and spiritual thinking? Natural thinking is on the level of the earth – the level of man; spiritual thinking is on a higher level altogether – the level of God. It is surprising that so many Christians think naturally about their problems rather than spiritually. The psalmist was a good and godly man but under the pressure of circumstances he had reverted to thinking naturally about his problem.

We will never learn to live effectively until we understand that the whole of life is spiritual, not just parts of it. In the chapter before us today the apostle asks, in effect, why it was that none of the rulers of this world recognised the Lord Jesus Christ when He was here. It was because they looked at Him from a natural perspective – they saw only a carpenter. Without the Holy Spirit operating upon their minds, they just could not understand. Ultimately, the problems and difficulties of life are all spiritual; so the sooner we learn to think spiritually, the better we will be.

FURTHER STUDY

Isa. 55:1-13;
Rom. 12:2;
Jer. 29:11

1. What did God declare to Israel?

2. How can we be transformed?

Prayer

Gracious and loving heavenly Father, I realise that if I am to become a spiritual thinker I must allow You to think in me. I have given You my heart, help me now to give You my mind. Think in me, dear Lord. Amen.

"Come up on this level too"

"But they do not know the thoughts of the Lord" (v.12)
For reading & meditation – Micah 4:6-13

Yesterday we ended with the statement: "Ultimately, the problems and difficulties of life are all spiritual." What exactly does this mean? Reflect again on the psalmist's problem. He says to himself: "Why does God allow the ungodly to prosper and the godly to go through great trials and tribulations?" He has trouble as he tries to understand God's ways.

Now there is really only one answer to this problem, and it is found in Isaiah 55:8: " 'My thoughts are not your thoughts, neither are your ways my ways,' declares the Lord." Whatever we might think about the ways of God, these words give us the ultimate answer – the Almighty acts in ways that are above and beyond our comprehension. It is as if God is saying: "When you look at My ways you must not approach them on a natural level, because if you do you will be baffled and over-whelmed. I act on a higher level than the natural, and if you want to understand Me, then you must come up on this level too."

How often, however, we persist in thinking naturally about life's situations – even those of us who have been in the Christian life for many years. The difference between natural thinking and spiritual thinking is the difference between heaven and earth. The very first thing we must do when we are baffled by some circumstance in our lives, is say to ourselves: "Am I approaching this on a natural level or a spiritual level? Have I reverted unconsciously to my natural way of thinking about these things." The more we learn to think spiritually about life's problems, the less perplexed we will be.

FURTHER STUDY

Rom. 8:1-6;
Prov. 12:5; Phil. 4:8

1. What does a mind controlled by the Spirit bring?

2. What things are we to think about?

Prayer

Father, I need to adopt and practise many spiritual methods, but none is as impor-tant as that which aligns me to Your thoughts and purposes. Help me come up higher – to Your level of thinking. In Jesus' Name. Amen.

One view of things

"Let this mind be in you which was also in Christ Jesus." (v.5, NKJ)

For reading & meditation – Philippians 2:5-11

We continue meditating on the importance of learning to think spiritually. It is sometimes interesting to listen to Christians discussing together both earthly and heavenly issues. Take politics, for example. When involved in a discussion on this subject, many Christians seem to put their Christianity on one side and bring out all the prejudices and worldly arguments which they have been accustomed to use over the years.

What does this say to us? It reveals the great need we have to break with the idea that life can be viewed on two levels – the natural and the spiritual. The Christian must learn to view everything from a spiritual viewpoint or otherwise he will fall prey to the same problems that the psalmist had. The great preacher C.H. Spurgeon once told a group of theological students that after they entered the ministry they should not be surprised to find that people who prayed like angels in a church prayer meeting could act like devils in a church business meeting. Unfortunately the history of the Church proves his statement to be true.

How can this happen? It's because in a prayer meeting people think spiritually, but in a business meeting they revert to their natural thinking, with all its prejudices and worldly assumptions. They have a party spirit within them and as soon as any one bumps against them – out it comes. Our Lord, as our text for today shows so clearly, saw everything from a spiritual point of view. This is why, in the hour of overwhelming testing, He was able to say: "Not my will, but yours be done" (Luke 22:42).

FURTHER STUDY

James 1:1-8;
Matt 6:22;
1 Cor. 2:16

1. What makes us unstable?

2. What happens when we are single-minded?

Prayer

My Father and my God, forgive me that so often my thinking is based on natural, rather than spiritual, perspectives. I think spiritually about some matters, but not all. Help me, dear Lord. In Jesus' Name. Amen.

Lop-sided Christians

"… if anything is excellent or praiseworthy – think about such things." (v.8)

For reading & meditation – Philippians 4:2-9

We continue to look at the dramatic change in the life of the psalmist when he entered into the sanctuary. It is important to realise that it was not merely the physical act of entering the sanctuary that brought about change. That was important, but something else happened that was even more important. Listen again to how he puts it: "[When] I entered the sanctuary … then I understood their final destiny" (Psa. 73:17). The word to note is "understood". In the presence of God the psalmist was given clear understanding. This is an extremely important point and one which cannot be emphasised too strongly: what he found in the sanctuary was not merely a nice feeling but a new understanding. He was put right in his thinking. He did not merely forget his problem for a little while – he found a solution.

The idea that many Christians have of the house of God or Christian fellowship is that it is a good place to go in order to forget one's troubles for a while. They are soothed by the music and the singing, or perhaps, in some churches, by the beauty of the architecture, and they come away saying, "What a lovely feeling I get whenever I go to church."

There is nothing wrong with that as far as it goes, of course, but the real issue is this: has anything happened to their minds? The psalmist was not changed by the architecture of the Temple; he was changed when his thinking was put right: "Then I understood their final destiny." If the practice of our faith does nothing more than excite our emotions and fails to give us a better understanding of God and His ways, then we will be lop-sided Christians.

FURTHER STUDY

Psa. 48:1-9; 119:59;
1 Sam. 12:24

1. What did the psalmist meditate on in the Temple?

2. What are we to consider?

Prayer

O Father, save me from becoming a lop-sided Christian. Give me not only joy to thrill my emotions but understanding to guide my intellect. In Jesus' Name I ask it. Amen.

Seeing life whole

*"… Always be prepared to give an answer to everyone who asks you
to give the reason for the hope that you have …"* (v.15)

For reading & meditation – 1 Peter 3:13-22

As Christians we ought never to forget that the message of the Bible
is addressed primarily to the understanding; it enables us to understand life. Because of the Bible, we are able to give a reason for the hope
that is within us.

The psalmist found the truth of this. In the sanctuary he discovered
an explanation for the way that he felt. He was not given a temporary lift
that would stay with him for a few hours or a few days – he was given a
solution that would stay with him for the rest of his life. It was this, in
fact, that caused him to write the psalm we are focusing upon day by day.
The words: *"Then* I understood their final destiny" (Psa. 73:17) suggest
that previously he had not been thinking correctly. He had been seeing
things from a partial and incomplete perspective, but now "in the sanctuary" he began to see the whole picture: *"Then* I understood". When?
Then – when he came into the sanctuary.

There is a line in one of Matthew Arnold's writings that goes like this:
"Who saw life steadily, and saw it whole." What a delightful phrase this
is. Nothing can be more wonderful than to see life steadily and to see it

FURTHER STUDY

Eph. 5:1-20;
2 Tim. 1:8

1. How are we to
speak to ourselves?

2. What did Paul
admonish Timothy?

whole. Much of the inner turmoil we go through in life
comes about because we do not see life as a whole.
Prejudice has been defined as "seeing only what you
want to see". People who are prejudiced say: "I have
always seen it that way." That's their problem – their
eyes are fixed on just one facet of an issue and they will
not allow themselves to look at the other sides.

Prayer

O Father, help me, for I don't want to be in bondage to prejudice or bigotry – I want
to see life whole. We must work this issue out together over these next few days, for
apart from You I can do nothing. Help me, Father. Amen.

Restoring the image

*"May your whole spirit, soul and body be kept blameless at
the coming of our Lord Jesus Christ." (v.23)*

For reading & meditation – 1 Thessalonians 5:12-28

We continue meditating on the importance of looking at life "steadily and whole". I venture to suggest that people who are not Christians are unable to see life as a whole. How can they, when their thinking takes place only on the level of the natural? Natural thinking is notoriously partial and incomplete.

Take, for example, the field of medicine. A generation ago doctors treated the symptoms that people presented to them, but now, with a clearer understanding of how the mind affects physical health, they have come to see that this approach was partial. One doctor said: "At long last the medical profession has discovered that the patient himself is important." Medicine is fast moving towards what is described as a "holistic" approach as more and more doctors begin to realise that it is not enough to treat the problem, we must also treat the person. They are still far from seeing that there is also a spiritual element in the person that has to be considered, but perhaps in time that will come.

Christian counselling suffers from the same problem – it does not see the whole picture. I am tired of reading books on Christian counselling that give just one side of the issue and suggest that problems can be resolved by applying one special technique. Man was created as a whole person and he will never be helped back to wholeness unless every part of his being is treated – spirit, soul and body. God wants to restore His image in us: not in part of us but in the whole.

FURTHER STUDY

2 Cor. 4:1-16;
Prov. 20:27;
Eccl. 12:7

1. What is man primarily?

2. What was Paul's testimony?

Prayer

O Father, forgive us that so often we settle for the half view of things rather than the whole. Quicken my spiritual understanding so that I have Your view on all things – the "whole" view. In Jesus' Name I ask it. Amen.

No need for dead reckoning

"I too was convinced that I ought to do all that was possible to oppose the name of Jesus of Nazareth." (v.9)

For reading & meditation – Acts 26:1-18

The place where we can see life as a whole is in the sanctuary of God, or, if you prefer, in the presence of God. There we are reminded of things we have forgotten or ignored. See how the Good News Bible translates Acts 26:9: "I myself thought that I should do everything I could against the cause of Jesus of Nazareth." Here you see the root of Paul's problem: "I myself thought". And is not that the underlying cause of many of our problems too? We say, "I myself thought …" instead of asking: "What does God think?"

Sometimes sailors will attempt to establish the position of their ships by estimating the distance and direction they have travelled, rather than by astronomical observation. This is called "dead reckoning". It is sometimes necessary in foul weather but it is fraught with peril. One mariner has said: "Undue trust in the dead reckoning has produced more disastrous shipwrecks of seaworthy ships than all other causes put together."

There are people who attempt the voyage of life by dead reckoning, but there is no need. God has charted the map for us with loving care in the Scriptures, and our plain duty is to study the chart so that we might become better acquainted with His purposes and His ways. For the better we know the Scriptures, the better we will know God. We cannot ignore the facts of history or science – they help – but if our perspective is not drawn from the Scriptures it will lead us astray. We must not rely on dead reckoning but on divine reckoning.

FURTHER STUDY

Judg. 17:1-6; 21:25

1. What was said of the children of Israel?

2. Can the same be said of us?

Prayer

O Father, just as the art of navigation requires definite and fixed points from which to take a bearing, so does my voyage through life. I am grateful, dear Father, that in You I have all the fixed points I need. Amen.

What says the Scripture?

*"Jesus replied, 'You are in error because you do not know the
Scriptures or the power of God." (v.29)*
For reading & meditation – Matthew 22:23-33

We spend one more day considering the proposition that apart from a relationship with God and an understanding of the Scriptures, we are unable to see life as a whole. The man or woman who knows and understands the Bible will be acquainted with the facts he or she needs to have in order to come to right and sound conclusions.

So immerse yourself in the Scriptures. Understand that human nature is corrupt and that apart from the grace and power of God men and women are unable to live up to their ideals. Realise that the spiritual is more powerful than the material, and unless the spirit is in control we will be driven by carnal desires. When people say humanity is getting better and that sin and evil are just the "growing pains" of the human race – what are the facts? You get them from the Scriptures and only from the Scriptures. What does the Bible tell us about evil? It says it is part of the human condition and can never be rooted out except through the power and the grace of God.

So study the facts of Scripture. Read them, memorise them, and meditate upon them. When next you feel dispirited because you cannot make sense of something, ask yourself: What are the facts? Dig into the Scriptures and draw your perspective from what the Bible says. The root of many of our emotional problems lies in a lack of clear thinking – clear thinking based on Scripture. Think as God thinks about issues and you will feel as God feels about them. For you are not what you think you are, but what you *think* you are.

FURTHER STUDY

2 Tim. 2:1-15; 3:16

1. What was Paul's exhortation to Timothy?

2. What is Scripture profitable for?

Prayer

Father, I see now why so often my thinking about life is confused – my thinking is not based on the facts. Help me draw my deductions not from what I see in the world but from what I see in the Word. In Jesus' Name. Amen.

Where does it all end?

"Enter through the narrow gate. For wide is the gate and broad is the road that leads to destruction ..." (v.13)

For reading & meditation – Matthew 7:13-20

Today we look at the special understanding the psalmist received when he came into the sanctuary of God: "Then I understood their final destiny" (Psa. 73:17). As soon as he considered the final destiny of the ungodly, everything dropped into focus for him. He had looked at the prosperity of the ungodly but he had not looked at their end – he had not taken in all the facts.

What are the facts concerning the end of the ungodly? The passage we read today tells us: the broad road which the ungodly travel leads to destruction; the narrow road which the godly travel leads to life. It is as simple as that. Though this passage was not available to the psalmist, the truth underlying it was most certainly known to him. Listen to this from Psalm 37: "The transgressors shall be destroyed together; the future of the wicked shall be cut off" (v.38, NKJ). The writer of that psalm, King David, described the wicked spreading themselves like a green tree, but when the end came they vanished off the face of the earth and no one could find them.

The trouble with us is that so often we dwell too much on the present and fail to consider the future. Do you look at the ungodly, many of whom seem to be having a marvellous time ignoring moral restrictions, and feel envious of them? Well consider their end. Give some thought to the ultimate outcome. The Bible describes it as "destruction". We ought never to forget that it is not how things are at present that is important; it's how they end that matters.

FURTHER STUDY

Luke 12:15-21;
Prov. 12:15-16; 28:6

1. What did Jesus call the man in his parable?

2. What word keeps occurring in the parable?

Prayer

Father, whenever I am next tempted to compare my life and its circumstances with that of others who do not know You, help me to remind myself of the fact that it is the end that matters, not the beginning. In Jesus' Name. Amen.

"I'm afraid of the dark"

*"Wicked men are overthrown and are no more, but the house
of the righteous stands firm." (v.7)*

For reading & meditation – Proverbs 12:1-8

We continue thinking about the fact that as soon as the psalmist considered the end of the ungodly, everything dropped into focus. Their true position became so clear to him that his language in the rest of the psalm indicates that he not only ceased to be envious of the ungodly but began to be sorry for them. Indeed, the same thing will happen to us too – the more we focus on the ultimate end of the unconverted, the more compassion we will feel for them.

How grim and cheerless is the non-Christian view of life, especially as it relates to the end. Dr Marrett, a rationalist and head of one of the colleges in Oxford, wrote, as he neared the end of his life: "I have nothing to look forward to but chill autumn and still chillier winter and yet I must somehow try not to lose heart." H.G. Wells, who ridiculed and scoffed at Christianity with its doctrine of sin and salvation, said at the end of his life that he was utterly baffled and bewildered. The title of his last book summed up his view of things: *A Mind at the End of its Tether.* When he was dying, a noted atheist asked one of his relatives for a lighted candle to be placed in his hand. "Why a lighted candle?" asked the concerned relative. "Because I am afraid to go out into the dark," was the reply.

How foolish to look enviously at the lifestyle of the ungodly, focusing only on their present successes and the marvellous time they seem to be having, without considering their end. We should never forget that no matter how glittering their lifestyle, the death of the ungodly is a terrible thing.

FURTHER STUDY

1 Tim. 6:1-10;
Psa. 49:10;
Prov. 23:5; 27:24

1. What truth did
Paul reflect to
Timothy?

2. How does the same
truth affect the way
we live our lives?

Prayer

O Father, let this sobering thought not only free me from envy but stimulate within me a deep concern for those who do not know You. May I be used in some way to halt the progress of someone on the road to a lost eternity. In Jesus' Name. Amen.

"It's a dead certainty!"

"Now there is in store for me the crown of righteousness, which the Lord, the righteous Judge, will award to me on that day …" (v.8)

For reading & meditation – 2 Timothy 4:1-8

There can be no doubt that the Bible presents the death of the ungodly as being terrible. How differently, however, does it portray the death of the righteous. Even a hireling prophet like Balaam, bad as he was, recognised that there was something different about the death of the godly. Listen to his words in Numbers 23:10: "Let me die the death of the righteous, and let my end be like his" (NKJ). The book of Proverbs puts the same thought in this way: "The path of the righteous is like the first gleam of dawn, shining ever brighter till the full light of day" (4:18).

I heard one preacher say that the happiest woman he had ever seen was a dying woman. She lay on her bed and clapped her hands at the approach of death. Very many people came to look at her bright countenance. "They tell me this is death," she said. "It's not death at all – it's life." People were converted by her bedside, including her son.

A theologian by the name of W. Cosley Bell, when he sensed that he was about to leave this world, sent these words to the staff of the college where he was employed: "Tell the young men that I've grown surer of God every year of my life, and I've never been so sure as I am right now.

FURTHER STUDY

2 Tim. 1:1-12;
1 Cor. 15:45-58

1. What was Paul's testimony?

2. Why is there no fear in death for the believer?

Why it's all so! It's a fact – a dead certainty. I'm so glad I haven't the least shadow of shrinking or uncertainty. I've been preaching and teaching these things all my life and I'm so interested to find that all we've been believing and hoping is so." That is the way to die. One of John Wesley's proudest claims for the early Methodists was this: "Our people die well."

Prayer

Father, the empty tomb of Jesus makes all our fears lies, and all our hopes truths. That empty tomb is the birthplace of eternal certainty. Because He lives I shall live also. I am eternally grateful. Amen.

Rougher – but more secure

"If only they were wise and would understand this and discern what their end will be!" (v.29)

For reading & meditation – Deuteronomy 32:28-38

We have been seeing that in the sanctuary the psalmist was reminded of the things he had forgotten, and thus his thinking was straightened out. There can be no real change in our personalities until there is a change in our thinking. Counselling that focuses only on changing behaviour and fails to emphasise the importance of changed thinking is partial and incomplete. We may experience some change when we change our behaviour, but we experience the greatest change, as our text for today suggests, when we change our thinking.

In the sanctuary the psalmist's thinking was put right about the ungodly: "Then I understood their end" (Psa. 73:17, NKJ). The next verses indicate how his thinking was also put right about God Himself: "Surely you place them on slippery ground; you cast them down to ruin. How suddenly are they destroyed, completely swept away by terrors" (Psa. 73:18-19). The psalmist's problem, you remember, was not so much that the ungodly prospered, as that God had arranged it that way. Had it happened by mere chance, he might not have had any difficulties, but the fact that the great Designer had planned it like this filled him with perplexity. Now, however, he sees that the divine hand had purposely placed these men in prosperous and eminent circumstances so that they could fulfil the Creator's purposes: *"You"* – note the *You* – *"You* place them on slippery ground." Note, too, the phrase "slippery ground": their position was dangerous. Therefore God did not set His loved ones in that place, but chose instead a rougher but more secure standing for their feet.

FURTHER STUDY

Psa. 16:1-11;
1 Sam. 2:9;
Psa. 18:36;
Eph. 6:13-14

1. Why are we able to stand firm?

2. What did Paul admonish the Ephesians?

Prayer

O God, I am grateful that You have set my feet in a secure place and not on slippery ground. Why I have been chosen to be a recipient of such grace and favour I do not know. Yet it is so. I am deeply, deeply thankful. Amen.

He never leaves the helm

"Surely your wrath against men brings you praise ..." (v.10)
For reading & meditation – Psalm 76:1-12

We touched yesterday on the truth that the reason why the ungodly are set in eminent places is because God arranges it. The psalmist goes on to say that not only does God raise up the ungodly, but He also brings them down: "You cast them down to ruin. How suddenly are they destroyed ..." (Psa. 73:18-19). The hand that led them up to the top of the slope is the hand that also casts them down. Why does God act in this strange and mysterious manner?

One reason is that God is able to demonstrate how unreliable and insecure are the ways of those who choose not to walk with Him. This explains why we so frequently read of some prominent godless person, such as a film star whom everyone is acclaiming, being suddenly removed from the face of the earth. The feet of such people were set in slippery places. Some reading these lines will remember how everyone stood in dread of Adolph Hitler. He had the whole world frightened, but now he is gone and almost forgotten.

The psalmist's words "You cast them down ... how suddenly are they destroyed" are really an exclamation of godly wonder at the suddenness and completeness of the sinner's overthrow. God makes a spectacle of those who persist in rejecting His love and grace. They make a splash for the moment of their lives, but after that they are gone and soon forgotten. Keep that fact before you as you look out upon the world. It may sometimes seem as if God is not in control, but in actual fact His hand is ever upon the helm of human affairs.

FURTHER STUDY

Rom. 1:18;
Rom 3:19-20;
2 Tim. 2:1-19;
1 Pet. 4:18

1. What does the law expose?

2. How is God's wrath averted?

Prayer

Gracious and loving Father, my heart bows in silent wonder as I contemplate the awesomeness of Your ways. Open my eyes that I might see that You are at work all around me and that Your face is constantly set against evil. In Jesus' Name. Amen.

"Hang him on it!"

*"... for the evil man has no future hope, and the lamp of the
wicked will be snuffed out." (v.20)*
For reading & meditation – Proverbs 24:15-22

Today we look at another reason why God allows the ungodly to
flourish – to illustrate by contrast the horror of an eternity without
God. Spurgeon commented: "Eternal punishment will be all the more
terrible in contrast with the former prosperity of those who are ripening
for it." The seeming joy and splendour of the prosperous ungodly actually renders the effect of being cast aside by God more awful, just as vivid
lightning does not brighten but intensifies the thick darkness around.

You will no doubt remember the story of Haman, who prepared a gallows for Mordecai but finished up by being hanged upon it himself. The
ascent to the gallows was an essential ingredient in the terror of the sentence: "Hang him on it!" (Esth. 7:9). The wicked are raised high so that
all might see how great is their fall.

A preacher tells how he read the story of the rich man and Lazarus,
in Luke 16, to a group of young people who were hearing it for the first
time. He stopped at the part where Lazarus lay at the gate, the dogs lick-
ing his sores, while the rich man ate in splendour in his house, and said:
"Which would you rather be, the rich man or Lazarus?" With one voice
the young people shouted: "The rich man." He then
read on, and after telling the story of how both died
and the rich man was in torment while Lazarus was
carried to Abraham's side, he asked: "Now which
would you rather be?" This time they responded more
quietly and soberly "Lazarus." That is the truth the
psalmist saw as he sat quietly in the sanctuary of
God.

FURTHER STUDY

Luke 16:19-31;
Matt. 13:24-30;
13:49

*1. What is Jesus'
teaching in the
parable of the rich
man and Lazarus?*

*2. What is the
message of the
parable of the weeds?*

Prayer

Father, the more I see the whole picture and realise what I have been saved from, the
more I feel like flinging myself at Your feet in adoring worship and praise. Thank You
for saving me, dear Lord. Words cannot fully express my gratitude. Amen.

Alexander the Great

"Surely the nations are like a drop in a bucket ..." (v.15)
For reading & meditation – Isaiah 40:12-17

Now we come to look at a section of the psalm which suggests that the reason why the ungodly continue to prosper as they do is because God is asleep. Listen to the psalmist's exact words: "As a dream when one awakes, so when you arise, O Lord, you will despise them as fantasies" (Psa. 73:20). The truth is, of course, that God does not sleep, but the psalmist has used a figure of speech which pictures our limited human perception of God's actions. God does not sleep, but at times He appears to do so.

But what happens when God stirs from His apparent sleep? The ungodly man, who has seemed so eminent and prosperous, vanishes as a dream. It is as if he had been a phantom or an illusion. The passage before us today puts this whole matter in context when it tells us that the nations are but "a drop in a bucket" to the Creator. Now they may look powerful and mighty, with their stockpiles of nuclear weapons, but when God arises they are as "grasshoppers".

Do you remember being told in your history class at school about Alexander the Great? He was one of the greatest generals of all time and conquered almost the entire known world. Did you know that he is referred to in the Bible? You will not see his name written in the Scriptures, but reference to him can be found in Daniel. Look at what the Bible calls him – a "goat" (Dan. 8:5-8). Walter Luthi puts it like this: "He who to the world is Alexander the Great, is to God nothing more than a he-goat." When God arises, the great become nothing.

FURTHER STUDY

Psa. 121:1-8;
2 Chron. 6:20; 16:9

1. What does the psalmist assure us?

2. How does God show Himself strong?

Prayer

Father, thank You for reminding me over these past few days of Your greatness and eternal power. I so easily forget that I am linked to a God who is not just powerful but all-powerful. Let the wonder of that fact sink deep into my soul today. Amen.

Take an inside look

"A man ought to examine himself ..." (v.28)
For reading & meditation – 1 Corinthians 11:27-34

From what we have seen over the past few days, it is clear that the psalmist has come to the place where his views have changed. He sees that God is ruling over human affairs and that the ungodly are not in such an enviable situation after all. We come now to see that he was not only put right in his thinking about the ungodly and about God, but he was also put right about himself: "When my heart was grieved and my spirit embittered, I was senseless and ignorant: I was a brute beast before you" (Psa. 73:21-22).

What a different view he has of himself now compared to previously, when he so evidently felt very sorry for himself: "Surely in vain have I kept my heart pure; in vain have I washed my hands in innocence" (v.13). Outside the sanctuary, he felt full of self-pity; inside the sanctuary, he had an entirely different view of himself. This is a moment when the psalmist honestly faces himself – something that is very difficult to do.

Most of us don't mind working our way through our problems, but the moment we get relief, we want to stop right there. We do not go on to face up to what caused us to come to the wrong conclusions in the first place. This is why we keep going through the same problems over and over again – we fail to take an inside look. A schoolteacher claimed to have twenty-five years of experience, but her head teacher said of her: "She has just one year of experience twenty-five times." She worked long but learned little.

FURTHER STUDY

1 Chron. 28:1-10;
Jer. 17:10; 23:24;
Psa. 44:20-21

1. What did David reflect to Solomon?

2. What question did the Lord ask?

Prayer

Father, I see why it is that so often I go through the same problems over and over again – I stop short of learning why they happened in the first place. Help me today to think through why it is that I get so tied up. In Jesus' Name I pray. Amen.

"Far too 'healthy' spiritually"

"Search me, O God, and know my heart; test me and know my anxious thoughts." (v.23)

For reading & meditation – Psalm 139:17-24

We said yesterday that the task of honestly facing ourselves in self-examination is often the hardest thing for us to do. We are all very prone to pass quickly over this point. We are quite happy to hear how God has set the ungodly in slippery places but we are not happy to be invited to take a look at ourselves and uncover the things within us that cause us to go astray.

It must be said, however, that two dangers arise whenever the question of self-examination is considered. One is over-emphasis and the other is under-emphasis. Some engage in it too much and become unhealthily introspective, while others fail to look at themselves at all and thus live on the surface. The important thing to remember is this – self-examination should always be carried out in the presence of God. If this is not adhered to, then the exercise can become harmful and counter-productive.

I meet many Christians who strongly oppose the idea of self-examination. They say: "the moment you see that you have sinned and then put your sin 'under the blood' you are all right. To stop and think about it is an indication that you are not spiritually healthy and that you lack faith." Dr Martyn Lloyd-Jones once said: "The trouble with most of us is that we are far too 'healthy' spiritually." He meant by that that we are much too glib and much too superficial. Nothing is more characteristic of a true Christian than a willingness to examine himself; not too much, not too little, but in an appropriate and balanced way.

FURTHER STUDY

Dan. 2:19-23;
Amos 9:3;
Psa. 139:7-8

1. What did Daniel receive from the Lord?

2. How did David feel about God's presence?

Prayer

O Father, the reason I am afraid to examine myself is because I might find something I do not like. However, help me be honest no matter what the cost – honest with You and honest with myself. In Jesus' Name I pray. Amen.

"Emotional reasoning"

"The heart is deceitful above all things, and desperately wicked; who can know it?" (v.9, NKJ)

For reading & meditation – Jeremiah 17:5-13

We continue focusing on the thought that one of the reasons why we go through the same difficulties and problems year after year is that we never stop to examine ourselves and find out what makes us act the way we do. The psalmist examined himself in the presence of God and discovered that three things had led him astray.

First, he saw that he had allowed his heart to rule his head: "When my heart was grieved and my spirit embittered, I was senseless and ignorant" (Psa. 73:21-22). Notice the psychology of this – he put the heart before the head. Many of our troubles are due to the fact that we are governed by the feelings that arise in our hearts rather than the clear thinking that should be going on in our heads. When the heart gets in control, it bludgeons us into believing things that are not true. It makes us stupid. The psalmist thought that his feelings about the ungodly were facts, but this was nothing more than what psychologists call "emotional reasoning" – believing that what you *feel* is the way things really are. The moment the psalmist's feelings were corrected by the facts, the feelings disappeared. There was no real problem at all. He had "worked himself up", as we say, into a self-induced frenzy.

I have done this myself (and so, I am sure, have you) when I have allowed my feelings to dominate me to such an extent that I have begun to believe that molehills were mountains. The real trouble in the psalmist's life was not what was going on in his outer world, but what was going on in his inner world. In other words, the real source of his trouble was himself.

FURTHER STUDY

Mark 2:1-8;
Heb. 3:12;
2 Pet. 2:14

1. What did the teachers of the law fail to realise?

2 What are we to watch out for?

Prayer

Father, I see more clearly every day that most of my problems are the ones I make for myself by my wrong thinking and wrong perceptions. Help me keep my heart under control by biblical thinking. In Jesus' Name I ask it. Amen.

"Think, man, think"

"... be transformed by the renewing of your mind ..." (v.2)
For reading & meditation – Romans 12:1-8

The second thing the psalmist learned about himself as he paused in self-examination was this: "I saw myself so stupid and so ignorant" (Psa. 73:22, TLB). There were things he knew which he had foolishly chosen to forget. He forgot that God was in control. He forgot the temporary nature of success and prosperity. He forgot the whole purpose of godly living. He forgot that God always has the last word. If you and I react as the psalmist did to trials, then there is only one thing that can be said about us – we are stupid and ignorant.

The third thing the psalmist learned about himself was that he had reacted like an animal – instinctively: "I was a brute beast before you" (Psa. 73:22b). What is the difference between a beast and a human being? A beast lacks the faculty of reason. It is unable to stand outside itself to consider itself and its actions. An animal responds to any stimulus instinctively without any interval for thought. The psalmist had been doing that – he had failed to put an interval of thought between the stimulus and the response. Once he did stop to think, and put the situation in a different context, his negative feelings immediately dissolved.

FURTHER STUDY

Psa. 105:5;
Deut. 6:12;
Psa. 50:22

1. What is a basic human tendency?

2. What does the psalmist exhort us to do?

Is not this the value of the Scriptures? As we read them they reason with us. They tell us not to react instinctively to things, but to think them through. They give us a new framework for our understanding, a new context in which to reason. The more we draw our understanding from the Scriptures and learn to think God's thoughts after Him, the more secure and the more effective our lives become.

Prayer

Father, I am grateful that You have made me with the ability to think. My thoughts can lead me astray or they can lead me to You. Help me to draw my thought patterns not from the world but from Your Word. In Jesus' Name I ask it. Amen.

"Nevertheless"

"In my alarm I said, 'I am cut off from your sight!' Yet you heard my cry for mercy ..." (v.22)

For reading & meditation – Psalm 31:19-24

Once the psalmist reached the place of utter abandonment before God there came into his heart an instant reassurance: "Yet I am always with you" (Psa. 73:23). Some translations put it like this: "Nevertheless I am continually with you". Personally I prefer the word "nevertheless" as it conjures up to my mind a movement in the soul of the psalmist that was vital to his spiritual recovery. He did not stop at the point of self-examination and turn in upon himself – he looked into the face of his heavenly Father and realised that he was accepted and loved.

If we end at the point of self-examination and don't remember the next words, "Nevertheless I am continually with you," then we will stay locked into the negative feelings of guilt and self-condemnation. This is why I said earlier that self-examination must not be undertaken except in the presence of God. Many have spent time examining themselves, and because they have judged themselves to be worthless and useless, they have gone out and committed suicide.

Am I talking to someone like that today? If so, put your foot on this next rung of the ladder and realise that although you may be feeling useless and worthless *nevertheless* you are still in the presence of God. He still permits you to come into His presence, even though you have forgotten His promises and misunderstood His ways. God does not cast you away. Let the wonder of this break afresh upon you today. Whatever has gone wrong in your life, confess it to Him and look into His face and say: "Nevertheless I am continually with you."

FURTHER STUDY

Gen. 28:15;
Isa. 43:1-7;
Ex. 33:14;
Heb. 13:5

1. What was God's promise to Israel?

2. What is the assurance we have?

Prayer

Father, how can I sufficiently thank You for giving me the right word at the right time? You knew how much I needed this today. It is a lifeline to my spirit. As I hold on to it let it bind me closer to You. In Jesus' Name. Amen.

What of the future?

"… he who began a good work in you will carry it on to completion until the day of Christ Jesus." (v.6)

For reading & meditation – Philippians 1:3-11

We saw yesterday how the psalmist sensed that despite his doubts and failures he was still accepted by God. But there's more – he realises also that God's restraining hand has been constantly with him: "You hold me by my right hand" (Psa. 73:23). What was it, after all, that prevented him going over the brink? It was the protecting hand of God. God Himself had put it in his mind to go into the sanctuary and had thereby turned him round.

Realising that, he thinks of the future. What is the future going to be like? His conclusion is that the future is going to be just as secure, for: "You guide me with your counsel, and afterwards you will take me into glory" (v.24). Can you sense the psalmist's security as he contemplates the future? He is saying, in effect: "You are doing this now, holding me by my right hand, protecting me, restraining me, restoring me and delivering me, and I know You will keep on doing this right up to the time when I meet with you in glory."

How does God guide us? Through circumstances, through reason, through the fellowship of Christians, but mainly through the Scriptures.

FURTHER STUDY

1 Pet. 1:1-6;
Jude v.24;
Gen. 28:15

1. Of what was Peter convinced?

2. How did Jude put it?

The Word of God, when we consult it, unfolds reality, dispels illusion and guides us safely through the snares and problems of this earthly way until we eventually arrive in glory. The psalmist had seen the end of the ungodly and it had helped to change his perspective. Now he sees the end of the godly and thus his perspective becomes even more clear. And what is the end of the godly? It is glory!

Prayer

O Father, let the prospect of coming glory fill and thrill my soul this day and every day. Help me never to forget that no matter how hard and difficult my earthly pilgrimage may be, it is as nothing compared to the glory that lies ahead. Amen.

No satisfying substitute

"Lord, to whom shall we go? You have the words of eternal life." (v.68)

For reading & meditation – John 6:60-71

We come now to what is without question the topmost rung of the ladder which the psalmist began to ascend when he entered the sanctuary of God. Here, in view of his experience, he can do nothing but give himself to the adoration of God. This is what he says: "Whom have I in heaven but you? And earth has nothing I desire besides you" (Psa. 73:25).

The inevitable consequence of working through our problems in the presence of God is that we worship Him. Countless times I have seen people fall upon their knees at the end of a profitable counselling session and worship God. In fact, this is one of the great purposes of Christian counselling – to enlighten people about their spiritual resources and help free them to draw closer to God. The psalmist has found that there is no one in earth or heaven who can do for him what God has done. He has come to realise that when he plays truant with the Almighty there is simply no way in which he can make sense of life; that, as Othello put it: "Chaos is come again."

Have you come to this same place in your own life? Can you say that you have seen through everything in this life and have come to the conclusion that nothing can satisfy you but God? Then you are in the happy position of the disciples who, pausing to consider how they could replace Jesus, said "Lord, to whom shall we go? You have the words of eternal life." They saw, as hopefully you have seen, that there is no satisfying substitute for Jesus.

FURTHER STUDY

Jer. 2:1-13;
Isa. 55:1-3

1. What had the children of Israel done?

2. What did God offer them?

Prayer

O Father, how can I ever be grateful enough for the realisation that no one can do for me what You can do? You are my centre and my circumference; I begin and end with You. May the wonder of it go deep within me today and every day. Amen.

The desire for God

"My soul thirsts for God, for the living God ..." (v.2)
For reading & meditation – Psalm 42:1-11

Yesterday we looked at the words: "Whom have I in heaven but you?". Now we examine the second part of that text: "And earth has nothing I desire besides you" (Psa. 73:25b). Personally, I find these some of the most enchanting words in the whole of the Old Testament. The first part of the verse is put in a negative, and the second in a positive form. Having looked around and seen that there is no satisfying substitute for the Almighty, the psalmist goes on to make the positive assertion that from the bottom of his heart he desires to know God. He has come to see (so I believe) that it is more important to desire God for who He is than for what He does or what He gives.

In a sense, the psalmist's entire problem arose out of the fact that he had put what God gives in the place of God Himself. The ungodly were having a good time while he was having a bad time. Why was he having to suffer like this? His trouble was that he had become more interested in the things God gives than in God Himself, and when he didn't have the things he wanted, he began to doubt God's love. Now, however, he has come to the place where he desires God for Himself.

FURTHER STUDY

Psa. 63:1; 38:9-10;
Luke 6:21

1. What was the psalmist thirsting for?

2. What is the result of thirsting and hungering?

The ultimate test of the Christian life is whether we desire God for Himself or for what He gives. Each one of us must ask ourselves: "Do I desire God more than forgiveness? More than release from my problems? More than healing of my condition? More than gifts and abilities?" How tragic that our prayers can be full of pleadings that show, when they are examined, that we are more interested in enjoying God's blessings than we are in enjoying God.

Prayer

O Father, forgive me that so often I am concerned more with Your gifts than I am with You – the Giver. Help me to long after You, not because of what You give me, but because of who You are. In Jesus' Name I ask it Amen.

The Rock of Ages

*"To you I call, O Lord my Rock ... if you remain silent I shall
be like those who have gone down to the pit." (v.1)*
For reading & meditation – Psalm 28:1-9

Now that the psalmist's faith is no longer conditioned by material factors, and he is confidently resting in God, he makes this interesting statement: "My flesh and my heart may fail, but God is the strength of my heart and my portion for ever" (Psa. 73:26). Some commentators say he is referring here to the time when his flesh will decay through old age, while others say he was experiencing some physical problems at that very time. Both may be right. When he looks into the future he knows a time will come when he will be an old man when his heart and flesh will fail. He will be unable to look after himself but it will still be all right, says this man, "For whatever may happen, God will still be the strength of my heart."

A commentator who feels the psalmist's words have a direct bearing on his physical condition at that time says this: "You cannot pass through a spiritual experience such as this man passed through without your physical body suffering. His nerves would be in a bad state and his heart would have been affected by the strain. Nevertheless he still affirms that God is his strength."

It is generally agreed that the word which is translated "strength" is the word for "rock", and so the verse may justifiably be translated: "God is the rock of my heart and my portion for ever." What a thrilling thought this is – God is my Rock. As one Welsh preacher put it: "There are many occasions when I tremble as I stand upon the Rock, but there are never any occasions when the Rock trembles under me."

FURTHER STUDY

Isa. 40:21-31;
41:10;
Eph. 3:16-17

1. How are we to
receive strength?

2. What was Paul's
prayer for the
Ephesians?

Prayer

O Father, help me this day to go out into life aware that although I may not know much about the ages of the rocks I know much about the Rock of Ages. And everything I know makes me feel deeply, deeply secure. I am so grateful. Amen.

"Nearer my God to Thee"

"Come near to God and he will come near to you." (v.8)
For reading & meditation – James 4:1-10

The final two verses of Psalm 73 form a conclusion and a resolution. Listen to them once again: "Those who are far from you will perish; you destroy all who are unfaithful to you. But as for me, it is good to be near God. I have made the Sovereign Lord my refuge; I will tell of all your deeds" (vv.27-28). The psalmist has finished his review of the past and is now hammering out a philosophy with which to face the future. He is resolved that no matter what anyone else may do, he is going to live in close companionship with God. He helps us to see the importance of this resolution by putting it in the form of a contrast: "Those who are far from you will perish ... but as for me, it is good to be near God."

Really, when it comes down to it, there are only two positions in life – close to God or far away from Him. I wonder, as the psalmist penned these words was something like this going through his mind: "What caused me so much trouble in recent days and accounted for all my difficulties was the fact that I did not keep close to God. I erroneously believed that the cause of my problems was the prosperity of the ungodly, but having entered into the sanctuary of God I see that this was not the cause of my problems at all. My problems came because I had chosen not to remain close to Him. For me there is now only one thing that matters – staying close to God."

FURTHER STUDY

Psa. 46:1-11;
2 Sam. 22:3;
Psa. 9:9;
Psa 62:1-12

1. What does the
psalmist affirm?

2. What does the
psalmist exhort the
people?

How are things with you at this moment? Do you feel close to God? If you don't, then let me put what I want to say in the words of a wayside pulpit that arrested my attention some years ago: "If you feel that God is far away guess who moved?"

Prayer

Father, I am grateful for the promise of Your Word to me today that when I draw near to You, You will draw near to me. Help me put those words to the test by moving closer to You than I have ever done before. In Jesus' Name. Amen.

Take and tell

"Go ... to my brothers and tell them ..." (v.17)
For reading & meditation – John 20:10-18

Today, on this penultimate day of our meditations on Psalm 73, we face the important practical question: How do we go about the task of keeping close to God? Firstly, we do so by prayer. The person who keeps close to God is the one who is always talking to God. Many definitions of prayer have been given; I add another: prayer is co-operation with God. In prayer you align your desires, your will, your life to God. You and God become agreed on life desires, life purposes, life plans, and you work them out *together.*

Secondly, we do it by constant study of the Scriptures. God's Word is alive with meaning, and when you read it something will happen to you, for "the word of God is living and powerful, and sharper than any two-edged sword" (Heb.4:12, NKJ). Expect it to speak to you – and it will. Faith is expectancy: "According to your faith will it be done to you" (Matt. 9:29). Remember also to surrender to the truth that is revealed: "If anyone wills to do His will, he shall know ..." (John 7:17, NKJ). In a moral universe the key to knowledge is moral response. The moment we cease to obey, that moment the revelation ceases to reveal.

We do it, thirdly, by sharing with others. Remember, nothing is ours if we do not share it. When we share, the things go deeper inside us. We must share what God is doing, both with our fellow Christians and with non-Christians also. The psalmist's last words are these: "I will tell of all your deeds." We take and we tell – we take and we tell; these, we must never forget, are the two heartbeats of the Christian experience.

FURTHER STUDY

Jer. 20:1-9;
Psa. 66:16;
Isa. 63:7

1. What was God's Word like in Jeremiah's heart?

2. What did the psalmist say he would do?

Prayer

Gracious Father, I don't want nearness to You to be an occasional experience – I want it to be a perpetual experience. Help me to pay the price, no matter what it costs. In Jesus' Name I ask it. Amen.

Reflections

"But as for me, it is good to be near God ..." (v.28)
For reading & meditation – Psalm 73:1-28

A tinge of sadness is upon my spirit as I come to this last day of our meditations on Psalm 73. In all my years of writing, never can I remember being so personally blessed. The truth this psalm conveys has gripped my own heart and life in a most unusual way.

Let's remind ourselves of what the psalmist has taught us. Life is filled with many painful and perplexing problems which at times cause us to cry out: "Lord, why don't You intervene?" Yet just as our feet are about to slide, something always comes to us – an idea or a thought, which, if we hold on to it, serves to halt our downward progress. We discover that when we act responsibly and do what is right, even though we do not feel like it, we put ourselves in the way of experiencing inward change.

But it is not God's purpose to bring about only a little change – He desires to bring about a lot of change. How does He achieve this? He does it by bringing us into His presence and revealing to us His Word. There we discover that our greatest problems are not the ones that are outside us but the ones that are inside us – our perspectives are wrong.

FURTHER STUDY

Psa. 57:1-7; 108:1;
112:7

1. What did the
psalmist mean by
"steadfast"?

2. Where is your
heart fixed?

Real change comes about not when our feelings are soothed but when our thinking is changed. Changed thinking leads to changed desires. When our perspectives are controlled by the Word rather than by the world, then we will experience inner peace. The psalmist resolved to draw near to God and stay close to Him so that he could "see life steadily, and see it whole". Let's make that our resolution too.

Prayer

O Father, I see that the secret of effective living is looking at life from Your point of view. I resolve by Your grace to give myself more and more to learning this secret. Help me, my Father. In Jesus' Name I ask it. Amen.

The Corn of Wheat Afraid to Die

No death – no life

"… But if [a grain of wheat] dies, it produces many seeds." (v.24)

For reading & meditation – John 12:20-36

Today we begin to examine one of the most profound truths in the Bible – the principle that life is always preceded by death. It is not difficult to bring together a host of corroborative Scriptures to prove this point, but let the one that is before us suffice for now. The order is unmistakable – it is *only* when a grain of wheat falls into the ground and dies that it produces more seeds. No death, no life – it is as simple as that. Understanding this issue is so important that I would go as far as to say that Christians who don't grasp the concept can easily lose their way spiritually.

Some years ago I read of a pilot whose plane crashed in a field outside a small town in Africa. Investigators looking for the cause of the crash surmised that the pilot thought he was landing at his intended destination when in fact he was approaching a town with a similar name. The difference in spelling was a matter of just one letter. His planned destination was a thousand feet lower than where he actually landed, and he was killed (so it is thought) because he believed he had a thousand feet more than was actually the case. He worked from the wrong map.

If we have the wrong "mental map" of the issue that is before us – that life is preceded by death – then we can miss our way and end up as a spiritual casualty. If we are to live – really live – then we must be willing to die to all self-interest. A missed step here may mean a miss-spent life.

FURTHER STUDY

Rom. 6:1-23;
Luke 9:24;
1 Cor. 15:36

1. What is the significance of baptism?

2. What is "spiritual" death?

Prayer

Gracious and loving heavenly Father, help me I pray not to work from the wrong "mental map". Give me a clear understanding of the fact that life must be preceded by death. In Christ's Name I ask it. Amen.

Caught in the cross-currents

"But striking a reef where two seas met, they ran the vessel aground..." (v.41, NASB)

For reading & meditation – Acts 27:27-44

We made the point yesterday that when we fail to understand, or misunderstand, the highly important issue that life on this sin-stained planet is preceded by death, we could do more than just miss our spiritual destination – we could end up in spiritual difficulty. Am I over-stating the issue? I think not. During my Christian life, I have had many occasions to observe firsthand the struggles of the saints, and if I had to narrow those struggles down to the biggest single problem in Christian experience, I would express it in these words – an unwillingness to die to self-interest and self-concern.

The story of Paul's shipwreck which we have read today is a picture of what happens to Christians who have not understood or come to grips with the truth that we must die in order to live. The New English Bible translates verse 41 thus: "But they found themselves caught between cross-currents and ran the ship aground, so that the bow stuck fast and remained immovable, while the stern was being pounded to pieces."

"They found themselves caught between cross-currents." That is the dilemma in which many Christians find themselves – the bow of their ship is caught up in the Christian cause, but because they have never learned how to die to self-interest, the rest of their life is being pounded to pieces by the breakers. I guarantee you this; if you get hold of the truth around which our present theme is built, you will always find yourself in a manoeuvrable position. Cross-currents may strike you and breakers may pound you – but you will stay in one piece.

FURTHER STUDY

James 1:1-8; 4:8;
Luke 16:13;
Eph. 6:5

1. What causes instability?

2. What makes us stable?

Prayer

O Father, help me not to get stuck in the sands of a half-hearted commitment, so that my life remains fixed and useless. I don't want to go to pieces, I want to go places – with You. Amen.

To die – or not to die?

"… as dying, and behold we live …" (v.9, RSV)
For reading & meditation – 2 Corinthians 6:1-13

Today we ask: What is the meaning of this strange spiritual paradox that before we can live, we must first be willing to die? The best illustration of this truth can be seen in the passage from John 12 that we read on the first day of our meditations and which we will now look at in greater detail.

One day a group of visitors from Greece arrived in Jerusalem, and hearing of the fame of Jesus sought out Philip, one of His disciples, and said to him: "Sir, we would like to see Jesus" (John 12:21). When Philip informed Jesus that some Greeks wanted to interview Him, this precipitated a spiritual crisis in our Lord's heart: "The hour has come for the Son of Man to be glorified … unless a grain of wheat falls to the ground and dies, it remains only a single seed. But if it dies, it produces many seeds" (John 12:24).

Why should the Greeks' simple request precipitate such a crisis in Jesus' heart – a crisis in which dying or not dying seemed to be the vital issue? Could it have been that He sensed that the Greeks were coming with an invitation for Him to bring His message to Athens – the centre of philosophy and learning – where it might be more readily received? Did He sense that in wanting to interview Him, they were going to say: "Sir, if You go on the way Your face is set, the Jews will kill You. Don't stay here in Jerusalem and die: come to Athens and live"? If this was the situation, then how dramatically it would have underlined the issue that was constantly before Him – to die or not to die.

FURTHER STUDY

Gal. 2:1-20;
Rom. 8:36;
2 Tim. 2:11

1. How did Paul view life?

2. What analogy did he use?

Prayer

Blessed Lord Jesus, it is clear that I face a similar issue to the one You faced when here on earth – to die, or not to die. Help me, dear Lord, for I can only face it in Your strength. Amen.

"Come to Athens and live"

*"… Will he go where our people live scattered among the
Greeks, and teach the Greeks?" (v.35)*

For reading & meditation – John 7:25-39

We ended yesterday by suggesting that the issue which the Greeks might have wanted to talk over with Jesus was that of taking His message to Athens – the centre of philosophy and learning. Were they intent on saying to Him: "Put Your marvellous message of the kingdom of God into the medium of Greek thought, and in no time it will spread throughout the world. Don't stay in Jerusalem and die; come to Athens and live"?

We have no way, of course, of knowing for sure that this was the situation, and I am simply suggesting that this is what may have been in their minds. The idea is not as far-fetched as you might imagine when placed against the verse that is before us today: "Does he intend to go to the Dispersion … and teach the Greeks?" (v.35, RSV). Had other nations beyond Israel's boundaries showed interest in His revolutionary approach to life? Tradition says that the king of Edessa once sent a message to Jesus inviting Him to come to his country and present His message concerning the kingdom of God.

Whether or not this was so, one thing is certain – the coming of the Greeks precipitated a crisis in Jesus' soul: "Now my heart is troubled, and what shall I say? 'Father, save me from this hour'? … Father, glorify your name!" (John 12:27-28). He would not rationalise or compromise. He would face the issue to which He had always been committed. It was not to be a philosopher's chair in Athens, but a grisly cross in Jerusalem. He would fall into the ground and die, and bear a harvest richer than anything the world could offer.

FURTHER STUDY

Matt. 16:24-28;
27:32; John 19:17

1. What does the cross signify?

2. What does it mean to "take up your cross"?

Prayer

Lord Jesus, help me to catch something of Your spirit as I face the challenges that lie ahead of me in the coming days. I want to make my life count for the utmost – show me how we can work things out together. Amen.

"A blank cheque"

"Father, if you are willing, take this cup from me; yet not my will, but yours be done." (v. 42)

For reading & meditation – Luke 22:39-48

W e have seen over the past two days how Jesus, when faced with the news that some Greeks wanted to interview Him, appeared to be precipitated into a spiritual crisis. Whatever we make of this incident in the life of our Lord, it is fairly obvious that some deep struggle is going on inside Him. And the terms of that struggle are also clear: "What shall I say? 'Father, save me from this hour'? No, it was for this very reason I came to this hour" (John 12:27). This passage in John 12 underlines most powerfully the humanity of Jesus. We see Him recoiling for a moment – and only for a moment – from the grim ordeal that He was about to face on Calvary, but He comes through to reaffirm His unswerving commitment to His Father's eternal will and purpose.

Note once again the truth that seemed to sustain Him in this dark and crucial hour: "I must fall and die like a grain of wheat that falls between the furrows of the earth. Unless I die I will be alone – a single seed. But my death will produce many new wheat grains – a plentiful harvest of new lives" (John 12:23-24, TLB). He gave a blank cheque to God signed in His own blood. He would fall into the ground and die and bear a rich and bountiful harvest. He aligned Himself with self-giving and not self-saving. The momentous issue with which our Lord struggled in that hour is similar to the one which you and I are being called to face in these meditations – to die or not to die. The way we respond to it will determine our life-direction.

FURTHER STUDY

Phil. 2:1-8;
Psa. 40:8; 143:10;
Eph. 6.6

1. What was God's will for His Son?

2. How did Jesus respond?

Prayer

Father, I sense that quietly things are heading toward a moment of crisis in my life – a crisis of commitment. Help me to see these things, not merely as a matter for discussion, but a matter for decision. In Jesus' Name I pray. Amen.

The greatest loneliness

"I will obey thee eagerly, as thou dost open up my life." (v.32, Moffatt)

For reading & meditation – Psalm 119:17-32

Now that we have seen how crucial is the spiritual principle that life is preceded by death, we move on to consider some of the areas into which God leads us so that this principle may be put to work. If, as we said, this principle is "the deepest law in the universe", then we should not be surprised when God provides us with opportunities to demonstrate its effectiveness.

The first area we consider is *loneliness*. Is this a situation in which you find yourself at the moment? If so, then you can respond to it in one of two ways: you can rebel against it and wallow in self-pity, or you can face it in the knowledge that God is with you in your loneliness and will help you turn it into something positive. Geoffrey Bull, when speaking of his lonely life in Tibet in his book *When Iron Gates Yield*, said: "The Lord had appointed me to stand in solitude upon the threshold of crisis, yet the only loneliness I had need to fear was that of a corn of wheat afraid to die."

A corn of wheat afraid to die – that is the greatest loneliness. Just as there is one sin – the sin of making yourself God (all the rest are *sins*), so there is just one loneliness – the loneliness of being alone with a self that is not surrendered to God. You see, if you do not understand the principle that going God's way is always the best route to spiritual fruitfulness, then loneliness will hold tremendous terror for you. I say again: there is no greater loneliness than a self that is afraid to die.

FURTHER STUDY

Psa. 102:7; 38:11;
John 16:17-33;

1. How did the psalmist feel?

2. What was Jesus' testimony?

Prayer

O God, if You see that I am "a corn of wheat afraid to die", then uproot that fear – in Jesus' Name. May I echo the psalmist's words: "I will obey thee eagerly, as thou dost open up my life." Amen.

"His-appointment"

"Listen to this wise advice; follow it closely, for it will do you good
… Trust in the Lord." (vv.17-19, TLB)

For reading & meditation – Proverbs 22:17-29

Are you afraid of loneliness? If so, then it is likely that there is a greater fear than that in your life – the fear of "a corn of wheat afraid to die". Settle that fear, and all other fears are as nothing in comparison. When our attitude is that of complete and utter surrender to God and confidence in the outcome of His purposes, then we can face anything that comes – good, bad or indifferent.

An extremely prominent minister who was greatly used by God got caught up in a spiritual conflict because he had his eye upon a position in his denomination which he desired for himself. He shared his desire with a prominent laymen and tried to get him to use his influence in securing the position. The layman said: "I do not think it right to use my influence in the way you ask. The decision must be with those who have been selected for that purpose."

The minister was deeply upset by his friend's remarks and became extremely bitter and morose. In due course the position was given to someone else, and the minister, unable to cope with the disappointment, withdrew from the ministry and now lives in a big house all by himself – terribly alone. He was "a corn of wheat afraid to die". Had he been willing to die to the desire for self-aggrandisement, position and prestige, he would have seen the disappointment as "His-appointment". Now he is lonely with the loneliness that comes to all who fail to realise that God always gives the best to those who leave the choice to Him.

FURTHER STUDY

Prov. 3:1-6;
Psa. 37:3-5; 118:8

1. What does "trust" mean?

2. What is promised to those who trust?

Prayer

My Father and my God, I see that there is no greater loneliness than the loneliness that comes from being locked into my own purposes and my own desires. Help me to be continually centred in You and not in myself. In Jesus' Name I pray. Amen

"See Mrs Noby Jo first"

"My food ... is to do the will of him who sent me and to finish his work." (v.34)

For reading & meditation – John 4:27-42

We continue meditating on the thought that the greatest loneliness is that of a "corn of wheat afraid to die".

A story from China tells how a young woman, Mrs Noby Jo, went out into the hills to pray. Soon the Lord began to show her that His plans for her life led in a different direction to her own. Petulantly she cried: "Lord, why do You always have to have Your way; what about my way for a change?" Gently the Lord whispered into her heart: "My child, it is not that your way is wrong; it is rather that My way is best." She surrendered her will to His, and came away with these words ringing in her ears: "You belong to the discouraged and broken people who commit suicide at the bend of the railway track."

Confused by this message, she made enquiries and discovered that outside the town where she lived was a notorious spot at the bend of the railway track where people intent on committing suicide would throw themselves over a cliff into the deep ravine below. She arranged to put up a sign near the spot that read: "Don't: see Mrs Noby Jo first. God loves you." She added her address and the very first day the sign was put up, several people knocked on her door and said they had come in response to the notice. She was "promoted to glory" at the age of 92, having saved 5,000 people from suicide. When she died to her own desires and took God's way, the grain of wheat that had fallen into the ground and died brought forth fruit a hundredfold. It always does.

FURTHER STUDY

Phil. 3:1-21;
Prov. 23:26;
Rom. 12:1

1. What was Paul's attitude?

2. How did he work it out?

Prayer

Father, help me not to get so caught up in my own plans that I become entangled in myself. I want to start with You, not with myself. It is then, and only then, that I will be able to do what You want me to do. Help me – in Jesus' Name. Amen.

"God of remarkable surprises"

"O thou Eternal, thou wilt light my lamp ... thou wilt make my darkness shine." (v.28, Moffatt)

For reading & meditation – Psalm 18:20-40

If you have not yet taken hold of the truth we have been discussing over the past few days, then grasp it with both hands today: the greatest loneliness is the loneliness of "a corn of wheat afraid to die". If we are afraid to die to our own purposes and allow God's purposes to become supreme, then we finish up pleasing ourselves but not liking the self we have pleased. And again, being willing to face any situation that comes with the conviction that God will make it contributive enables us to face life with an inner fortitude and poise.

Understanding this truth and being willing to apply it to all circumstances and situations is one of the greatest safeguards against emotional or personality problems. In fact, I would go further and say that it is one of the greatest defences against reactive depression that I know. I say "reactive" depression because there are some forms of depression which are chemically based and result from malfunctioning of the body's chemical systems. Reactive depression is the depression that comes from the way we interpret the knocks and hardships that crowd into our lives. And what greater hardship can there be than loneliness?

The Bible teaches us, however, that God will never allow one of His children to find themselves in any situation where He is not able to help them – loneliness included. Someone has referred to our heavenly Father as "the God of remarkable surprises". What a fascinating description – and how true. In the midst of life's loneliest moments, God has a way of approaching us and revealing Himself in ways that we would never have conceived possible.

FURTHER STUDY

1 Kings 19:1-8;
Psa. 91:11;
Heb. 1:14

1. How did God deal with Elijah's loneliness?

2. Whom did He send to him?

Prayer

Father – surprise me. In some way today, let the wonder of Your concern and care for me break through the ordered routines and duties of my life. Pull aside the curtain and give me a fresh glimpse of Your face. In Jesus' Name I pray. Amen.

Lonely – but not alone

"… you will be scattered, each to his own home. You will leave me all alone. Yet I am not alone, for my Father is with me." (v.32)

For reading and meditation – John 16:19-33

We spend one last day looking at the issue of loneliness. Our meditations on this subject have made one thing clear – it is in the periods of loneliness that we most abandon ourselves to God and learn how to depend upon Him utterly and completely.

The more I read the biographies of those who have achieved great things for God, the more I realise that their deep knowledge of Him came, in part, out of moments of profound loneliness. It was in such moments that "the God of remarkable surprises" revealed Himself and gave them an understanding of His grace and power such as they could never otherwise have known. Is it not true that God's glory bursts through most powerfully when the sky is at its darkest? Does not His strength uphold us most when we are feeling weak and inadequate? And does not His love penetrate most deeply when we feel unloved or isolated from others?

When we are prepared to die to our own interests and are willing to follow our Lord fearlessly along the path which He sees is best for us, we experience, not just temporal, but eternal rewards. The seed that falls into the ground and dies is the one that yields a rich and bountiful harvest. Many of us fail to be fruitful in our Christian life and experience because we are afraid or unwilling to face the issues which demand a wholehearted commitment to the will of God. We save ourselves – and then what? We finish up by not liking the self we have saved. Make no mistake about it – God's way is best, even though a thousand hardships beset the path.

FURTHER STUDY

John 11:1-46;
14:18; Heb. 13:5

1. How did it seem to Mary and Martha in their moment of loneliness?

2. What did Jesus say to them?

Prayer

O God my Father, give me the courage of Jesus who, despite His loneliness and isolation, went on to achieve Your perfect will. Quicken within me today the sense that when I am walking with You I may feel lonely, but I am never alone. Amen.

"Wait! Wait! Wait!"

*"How great is your goodness, which you have stored up for
those who fear you ..." (v.19)*

For reading & meditation – Psalm 31:1-24

As we move on we start to think about some of the red furrows of life from which we often draw back. At such times we become "a corn of wheat afraid to die". But as we are seeing, where there is no death, there can be no life. Outside the furrow we remain safe, warm, comfortable – and unfruitful.

First we shall consider what I am calling "divine delays" – those periods of life to which God leads us when it seems that nothing is happening and that His purposes for our lives are temporarily shelved. Perhaps you are at this point at this very moment. If so, don't panic – God's delays are not His denials. Our Master has a purpose in everything He does. You must believe that, even though your fears scream the opposite.

One of the most difficult things to do in the Christian life is to wait for God's purposes to come to pass. Sometimes they take so long to materialise that we find ourselves getting vexed and frustrated. Have you heard about the Christian who prayed: "Lord, give me patience ... and I want it right now"? Wouldn't you rather do anything than wait? A man told a Christian counsellor I know: "Waiting for God to bring His purposes to pass is the biggest problem I face in my Christian life; there is something within me that would rather do the wrong thing than wait." As waiting for God to bring about His purposes is more the rule than the exception in the Christian life, we had better learn what God has in mind when His red light flashes out the signal, "Wait! Wait! Wait!"

FURTHER STUDY

Acts 1:4-8; 2:1-8;
Gen. 49:18;
Isa. 25:9

1. What was the result
of the disciples' time
of waiting?

2. What will be the
result of our waiting?

Prayer

O Father, teach me to trust You when Your plans and purposes for my life are seemingly delayed. I confess that impatience is one of the most difficult things for me to "die" to. I cannot do it on my own. Help me, my Father. In Jesus' Name. Amen.

Catching a vision

"If it pleases the king ... let him send me to the city in Judah where my fathers are buried so that I can rebuild it." (v.5)

For reading & meditation – Nehemiah 2:1-10

We ended yesterday with the thought that waiting for God's purposes to come to pass is more the rule than the exception in the Christian life. Does this mean that for most of our Christian life we should do nothing but wait for God to move? No. Clearly there are certain aspects of the Christian life which require immediate and daily attention, and for which we have all the guidance we need. We don't need to wait on God, for example, to know what we should do about forgiving those who have hurt us, or sharing our faith with the unconverted. Those purposes of God are to be seen as standard operating procedure and are clearly set out in His Word.

I am referring here, not so much to His general purposes, but to His individual purposes – those special plans which He wants to achieve through us personally. Every Christian has the responsibility of coming before God to seek to discover just what it is that the Lord wants to achieve through his or her life. And as we are faithful in reading His Word, obeying His commands, and communing with Him in prayer, we can expect Him to reveal those special plans for our lives.

FURTHER STUDY

Gen. 15:1-21;
21:1-5; Heb.2:3;
Prov. 29:18

1. What vision did God give Abraham?

2. How long did it take to be fulfilled?

Take our reading today: Nehemiah served the king faithfully, but when he heard about the disgraceful condition of God's city, Jerusalem, he caught a vision of rebuilding the walls. God then worked in the king's heart to give him a desire to assist Nehemiah in achieving that vision. Have you caught the vision of what God wants to achieve through your own individual life and witness on this earth? If not, why not?

Prayer

Gracious Father, give me, I pray, a clear picture of what You want to achieve through my own personal life and witness for You. I have kept myself in the dark too long; now I want to step out into the light – Your light. Amen.

The special thing

"Where there is no vision, the people perish ..." (v.18, AV)
For reading & meditation – Proverbs 29:1-18

What is the point we are making? It is this: as we are faithful in following the Lord, we can expect Him to reveal His special plan for our lives. Just as Nehemiah caught the vision of rebuilding the walls of Jerusalem, so we, too, if we are ready and alert, will catch the vision of what God has specially equipped us to do.

Many years ago, I asked God to give me a vision of the special thing He wanted me to achieve for Him. He gave me the vision of launching a daily Bible reading programme which is now read by half a million people daily. He also, so I believe, inspired the choice of the title, *Every Day with Jesus*. I sometimes tremble at the awesome responsibility I now have of developing a spiritual theme month by month which will minister to the needs in people's lives.

What if I had not asked God to give me a vision of what He wanted me to do? I might have continued in a ministry that would have been good, but not the best. I believe there are many of you now reading these lines who are living faithful lives for God, but you have never asked Him to show you the special thing He wants you to achieve for Him. And don't think of that special calling in terms of something that will bring you prestige and glamour – to do that will take you right off the track. If you have never done so before, ask the Lord right now to give you a vision of what He wants you to achieve for Him. Who knows – this could be, not just a new day, but a new beginning.

FURTHER STUDY

Acts 26:1-19;
Eph. 1:9; 3:11

1. What was Jesus'
message to Paul?

2. What was Paul able
to testify to Agrippa?

Prayer

O Father, I don't just want to achieve the good – I want to achieve the best. If I have not yet caught the vision of that special thing You want to achieve through my life, then reveal it to me today. In Jesus' Name I pray. Amen.

Everyone is special

"Though it linger, wait for it; it will certainly come and will not delay." (v.3)

For reading & meditation – Habakkuk 2:1-14

A rising out of what we said yesterday – that God has a special calling for each of us – the thought occurs to me that some might view that statement as applying only to those who have the opportunity of working in "full-time Christian service". I don't much like the phrase, "full-time Christian service" – hence the quotation marks. Every Christian is in full-time Christian service – every hour of the day and every day of the week.

Let me make it perfectly clear that in saying God has a special purpose for every one of us, I mean just that – every one of us. The trouble is, when we talk about Nehemiah catching the vision of rebuilding the walls of Jerusalem, or Moses catching the vision of leading his people out of bondage, we tend to think that such visions apply only to those who are specially chosen and gifted.

As you read these lines today ask yourself: "Have I taken the time to ask God what He especially wants me to do?" A man may catch the vision today of a special ministry to other men. A woman may catch the vision of teaching other women how to be discreet, to manage their homes and to love their husbands and children (Titus 2:4-5). A married couple may catch the vision of ministering to singles. And those who are single may catch the vision of embarking on some project for God to which they can give their time and energies in a way that married people cannot. Open your heart and mind to what God is saying to you today. God sees everyone as special, and has a special task for everyone.

FURTHER STUDY

Rom. 12:1-21;
1 Cor. 12:1-31;
Eph. 4:1-16

1. What does Paul teach about the body of Christ?

2. Have you discovered where you fit in?

Prayer

Gracious Father, You continue to stretch my faith and my expectancy. I am so grateful. If I have not yet caught the vision of what You want me to do, then help me to do so today. In Jesus' Name I pray. Amen.

God's wonderful ways

"How unsearchable his judgments, and his paths beyond tracing out!" (v.33)

For reading & meditation – Romans 11:25-36

Now that we have spent a few days discussing the importance of catching a vision of the special contribution God wants us to make through our lives, we ask ourselves: What happens next? Usually, the next step after catching a vision is to see it die. There is a special reason for this: our vision often contains a combination of godly concerns and human perspectives, so God has to engineer a way whereby the godly concerns remain and the human perspectives are changed to divine perspectives. His way of doing this is to cause the vision to die.

This is a Biblical principle that can be traced from Genesis to Revelation. The vision Abraham received of being the father of a great nation "died" when he found his wife was barren. The vision Moses received "died" when he was rejected by his people and was forced to flee into the desert for forty years.

Why, we ask, does God bring a vision to birth and then allow it to die? For this reason: the waiting time in which we find ourselves during the death of a vision is God's classroom for the development of godly character in us. It is in the waiting time, as the vision "dies", that such qualities as patience, persistence, perseverance and self-control are built into us. Has God given you in the past a vision of something that you knew was definitely from Him – but now the vision has died? Then don't be discouraged. This is the way God works. He is using the waiting time to change your ideas to His ideas and your perspectives to His perspectives.

FURTHER STUDY

John 21:1-25; 6:27;
Isa. 55:2

1. What had Peter decided to do?
2. Why did Jesus challenge him?

Prayer

O my Father, I stand in awe at the wonder of Your ways. Forgive me that so often I have viewed the time of waiting as tedious rather than transformative. Now my perspectives are different. Lead on, dear Father – I want to learn more. Amen.

The hour of temptation

"… he rebuked Peter, and said, 'Get behind me, Satan! For you are not on the side of God, but of men.' " (v.33, RSV)

For reading & meditation – Mark 8:27-38

We are seeing that once we have been given a vision of what God wants us to do for Him, the next thing that happens is that the vision dies. The reason for this is that Christian character must be developed in us before God can accomplish His purpose in our lives, and this can only be done by God bringing our vision down into death. Many Christians have been baffled by this strange strategy which God uses to develop Christlikeness in us, but it is yet another illustration of the principle that death must precede life.

An important thing to remember is that Satan is extremely operative at this time, for his purpose is to get you to fulfil the vision by your own human effort. And whenever you do this, you will finish up in conflict. Remember what happened to Abraham? Rather than waiting for God to bring the vision into being at His own time, he tried to "help" God by having a son through Sarah's maidservant, Hagar (Gen. 16:3-4). The result of that was conflict between Isaac and Ishmael – a conflict that has continued to this day.

In our reading today, we see Peter being used by Satan to talk Christ

FURTHER STUDY

Eph. 6:10-18;
2 Cor. 2:11; 11:3

1. How can we
withstand Satan's
schemes?

2. Do it today.

out of facing death on Calvary, but Jesus recognised the true source of his ideas and responded with the words: "Get behind me, Satan!" One writer comments on this passage: "Satan often uses those who are closest to us to 'protect' us from what we know God has called us to do." Even close Christian friends sometimes fail to understand that before we can live for God's purposes, we must die to our own.

Prayer

O Father. I sense that Your ways are written, not only in Your Word, but also in me. Something within me echoes to truth. Help me to be always willing to die to my own purposes so that I can be alive to Yours. Then I will live abundantly. Amen.

The power behind these pages

"I will not yield my glory to another." (v.11)
For reading & meditation – Isaiah 48:1-11

Today we ask ourselves: What happens after God causes our vision to "die", and His purpose of building into us the characteristics of Christ has been achieved? This: He then resurrects the vision and brings it to joyous fulfilment. His purpose in doing this is not just to fulfil the vision, but to do so in a way that points to His supernatural intervention. In that way no onlooker can be in any doubt as to whose power lies behind the success of the ministry – everyone recognises it to be God.

While the disciples were with Christ, they received a vision of the coming kingdom, but on the cross they saw that vision die before their eyes. What happened then? Three days later, they witnessed the supernatural power of God bring Christ back from the dead – an event that turned them upside down.

I referred a few days ago to the vision which God gave me – the vision of putting together a daily Bible reading and meditation programme which would motivate Christians. That took place in 1965. In 1968, three years after the vision was launched, it "died". I do not mean that it discontinued, but for a whole year it was on the verge of collapse. My own enthusiasm for it slowly ebbed away until I came to the place where I said: "Lord, it's not mine – it's Yours." Then came resurrection. From that time to this, God has been seen to have the greatest part in its compilation. The constant stream of letters telling of changed lives, changed families and changed attitudes point to the fact that Jesus Christ is the power behind these pages – not me.

FURTHER STUDY

Isa. 14:12-15;
Micah 6:8;
1 Cor. 1:19-29

1. What was Lucifer's downfall?

2. What was Paul's conclusion?

Prayer

O God, now that I understand this principle of the birth, death and resurrection of a vision, help me to apply it to those periods in my life when it seems as if nothing is happening and Your purposes are temporarily shelved. Amen.

The Christian answer to suffering

"Look, the hour is near, and the Son of Man is betrayed into the hands of sinners. Rise, let us go!" (vv.45-46)

For reading & meditation – Matthew 26:36-46

Yesterday we looked at some of the world's ineffectual answers to the problem of unmerited suffering. In them there are no wounds to answer our wounds, no death to answer our death.

Their so-called answers remind me of a cartoon I once saw which depicted two toddlers in a children's boxing ring. Stripped for action, with nothing on but shorts and boxing gloves, they were ready for the fray. The attention of one of the youngsters was caught by two butterflies flitting just above his head and he stood gazing up at them, exposing himself to the blow which his opponent was about to land on his nose. Gazing at butterflies while in the midst of a conflict is a dangerous occupation. Any system of thought that takes your attention off the grim facts of life by calling attention to butterflies is doomed inevitably to produce pessimism as the blows begin to fall.

What, then, is the Christian answer to this problem? First, we must realistically face the fact that life involves suffering. There is no escaping that fact; to deny it is a denial of reality. I have found from experience that the first thing many Christians do when caught up in a form of suffering is to deny its reality and say something like this: "I don't have any problems, for Jesus is the Great Insulator between me and everything that happens." It is not lack of faith to acknowledge a problem. You don't have to dwell upon it, but before you can deal with it, you must acknowledge it. Remember, you must first be willing to face reality before you can expect to overcome it.

FURTHER STUDY

2 Cor. 4:1-17;
Psa. 34:19-20;
2 Tim. 2:12

1. What is the purpose of our affliction?

2. What has God promised?

Prayer

O God, give me courage to face up to issues and not dodge them. Help me to be open and honest. Father, I look to You now to help me put this into daily practice. For Jesus' sake. Amen.

Is suffering the result of sin?

"Do you think that these Galileans were worse sinners than all the other Galileans because they suffered this way?" (v.2)

For reading & meditation – Luke 13:1-9

Yesterday we ended by making the point that it is only when we realistically acknowledge a problem that we can take the steps to deal with it. The teaching that says you should not admit to having a problem as the negative thought that comes from such an admission will interfere with your ability to deal with it is psychologically and spiritually unsound.

The passage we read yesterday showed how Jesus, in the Garden of Gethsemane, dealt with the problem of His impending death on the cross: He first faced it in His feelings, and then went out to face the fact. "Rise, let us go!" The second thing we must do to deal with suffering is to recognise that not all suffering is due to personal sin. Some suffering is, of course, but not all. The person who violates God's moral laws must not be surprised when these laws kick back. The fact that not all suffering is due to personal sin can be seen from the account in John 9, where Jesus pointed out that personal or parental sin is not always at the back of physical calamities such as congenital blindness.

The point is made even more clearly in the passage before us today, where Jesus points out that calamities can stem from man's inhumanity to man (Pilate's butchering of Galilean Jews) or natural accidents or disasters (the collapse of the tower in Siloam), and therefore the people who suffer from them are not especially sinful. This takes away the self-righteous attitude of those who, being free from calamities themselves, view the problems of others as being the direct punishment of God upon their sin.

> **FURTHER STUDY**
>
> Job 1:1-5; 4:1-5:27; 8:1-22
>
> 1. What does Scripture say about Job?
>
> 2. What did his friends say?

Prayer

Father, I'm relieved to know that suffering is not always the result of personal sin. I'm willing to take my share of the blame for the problems I face, but help me not to become plagued with false guilt. Keep me balanced. Amen.

Turning tests into testimonies

"It will lead to an opportunity for your testimony."
(v. 13, NASB)

For reading & meditation – Luke 21:1-13

We look now at the third step in the process of dealing with unmerited suffering: don't spend too much time trying to understand the reason for suffering – focus rather on how you can deal with it. Notice, Jesus spent very little time trying to explain human suffering, much less explain it away. Had He undertaken to explain it, then His gospel would have become a philosophy – in which case it would not have been a gospel. A philosophy undertakes to explain everything, and then leaves everything as it was. Jesus undertook to explain little, but He changed everything He touched. He did not come to bring a philosophy, but a fact.

What was that fact? The fact was His own method of meeting suffering and transforming it into something higher. Out of this fact, we put together our philosophy – a system of principles and procedures by which we live out our life in this world. Notice that fact comes first, and then the philosophy about the fact. The good news is not merely "good news"; it is the fact of sin and suffering being met and overcome, and a way of life blazed out through them.

FURTHER STUDY

John 17:1-26;
16:33; Rom. 5:3-4

1. What did Jesus promise?

2. What did Jesus pray?

The fourth step is this: remind yourself that in God's universe, He allows only what He can use. In the passage before us today, Jesus gives the nine sources from which suffering comes upon us: confused religionists (false Christs), wars and conflicts in society, calamities in nature, and so on. Then He says this: "It will lead to an opportunity for your testimony." In other words, you are not to escape trouble, nor merely bear it as the will of God – you are to use it.

Prayer

Blessed Lord Jesus, You who used Your suffering to beautify everything You did, teach me the art of turning every test into a testimony and every tragedy into a triumph. For Your own dear Name's sake. Amen.

Gold and silver ...

*"After John was put in prison, Jesus went into Galilee,
proclaiming the good news of God." (v.14)*
For reading & meditation – Mark 1:14-28

Yesterday we looked at the final answer to dealing with unmerited suffering: reminding ourselves that in God's universe, He only allows what He can use. Look again at the words of our text for today: "After John was put in prison, Jesus went into Galilee, proclaiming the good news of God." *After* the finest and truest of prophets had been put in prison and his preaching silenced by a wicked and unjust king, Jesus came preaching the good news about God.

How could there be good news about the God who had allowed such a thing to happen? But that is exactly what Jesus did proclaim – and proclaimed unashamedly. And why? Because Jesus knew that everything God allowed, He would use. By His action, He rejected the idea that a man like John should be exempt from suffering, and that God isn't good when He permits such things to happen.

Can you see now why God allows us to go through suffering? He does it so that, in the fires of affliction, we learn the secret of an alchemy which transmutes the base metal of injustice, and consequent suffering into the gold of character and the silver of God's purposes. In one place in the New Testament, Jesus refers to being "perfected" by His death on the cross (Luke 13:32, AV). Just think of it: the worst thing that can happen to a man – crucifixion – turns out to be the best that can happen to Him – perfection. This is the attitude we must cultivate if we are not only to face, but use suffering.

FURTHER STUDY

Psa. 121:1-8; 50:15;
Isa. 43:2

1. What was David's
declaration?

2. What is your
declaration today?

Prayer

O my Father, how can I ever sufficiently thank You for showing me this way of life? Nothing stops it – permanently. When men and circumstances concentrate on doing their worst – You bring out of it Your best. I see, I follow, and I am unafraid. Amen.

The triumphant attitude

"Do not let your hearts be troubled. Trust in God; trust also in me." (v.1)

For reading & meditation – John 14:1-14

By now it should be fairly obvious to even the newest disciple of Christ that if, like a "corn of wheat afraid to die", we shrink back from being ploughed into the red furrows of suffering, we shall remain alone – alone, and unfruitful. Someone has said, "God never uses anyone unless He puts them through the test of suffering and pain." Strong words. Do you find yourself flinching as you read them? I do. Yet it is not wrong to flinch at the approach of a spiritual test. God knows how you feel.

The issue, however, is not about flinching; it is about following. Are we willing to open our hearts to the Lord and say: "Do to me as You will"? I suggest the only way we will be able to do that is when we have the thought clearly fixed in our minds that God will never allow us to go through anything without providing all the grace we need to bear it, and will turn the test into a testimony that will eternally glorify Him and make our characters more like His.

Jesus, remember, began His ministry here on earth with a wilderness experience, and ended it with an Easter morning. He told His disciples in the text before us today, "Let not your hearts be troubled", not because they were to be protected from troubles, but because they were to "trust in God". Faith in God will not save you from suffering, but it will save you through it – the suffering can be made into an instrument of redemption. Remember, you cannot bless without bleeding, and you cannot succour until you have suffered.

FURTHER STUDY

Matt. 27:27-49;
Luke 9:22;
2 Cor. 1:3-4

1. List the indignities Christ suffered.

2. How many can you identify with?

Prayer

O Father, I see that refusing to pay the ultimate price of surrendering to Your purposes is to choose deadness and death. Today I choose life. I am a "corn of wheat" not afraid, but willing to die. Help me, in Jesus' Name. Amen.

Going – yet not knowing

"And now, compelled by the Spirit, I am going to Jerusalem, not knowing what will happen to me there." (v.22)

For reading & meditation – Acts 20:17-35

We come now to examine another area into which our Lord, eager to obtain fruit from our lives, may be leading us: that of ambiguity and uncertainty. By ambiguity, I mean those situations we sometimes find ourselves in where the Lord's purposes are not clear, and by uncertainty, I mean the feelings we get when we don't know which direction to take on the road ahead.

Are you the kind of person who likes to see the way ahead as far as you possibly can? Do you find yourself getting irritated and frustrated when the Lord unfolds His purposes just one step at a time? If so, then your irritation is saying something about you. What is it saying? Perhaps it is saying that in this area of your life, you are "a corn of wheat afraid to die"; you are fearful of trusting yourself to the unseen and unknown purposes of God.

There isn't a Christian reading my words now who hasn't been called to walk this path of uncertainty and ambiguity, and there may be many who are there at this moment. The apostle Paul, in the verse before us today, was in this situation when he said: "I am going to Jerusalem, not knowing what will happen to me there" (v.22, GNB). What an honest admission: going – yet not knowing. Yet there seems to be no anxiety or apprehension in that statement. And why? Because the great apostle had died to all self-interest and. Having surrendered to God, he was not at the mercy of circumstances, situations, feelings – anything. Sure of God – the one great Certainty – he needed to fear no uncertainty.

FURTHER STUDY

James 4:10-17;
Prov. 27:1; Isa. 55:8

1. What should our attitude be?

2. What picture does James give us of life?

Prayer

O God, I see that unless my certainty is in You – the divine Certainty – I will be at the mercy of all uncertainties. Forgive my little antics of self-dependence. Help me to live in God-dependence. Amen.

"Talking to God all night"

"Therefore, if anyone is in Christ, he is a new creation ..."
(v.17)

For reading & meditation – 2 Corinthians 5:14-21

We ended yesterday by saying that because Paul had died to all self-interest, he was not at the mercy of ambiguity and uncertainty. Sure of God, he was sure of the future. You see, if you don't surrender to God, don't think you don't surrender. Everybody surrenders to something. If you don't surrender to God, then you will surrender to something else – your moods, your circumstances, your fears, your self-centred concerns. And if you do, you will end up becoming downcast and disillusioned.

A doctor tells of being called to see a patient, the head of a large company, who was having increasing attacks of asthma. The doctor could find no physical basis for the asthma, and so he asked the man: "Is there anything troubling you?" The patient replied: "No, doctor, I'm a member of a church, in fact an official in the church – nothing is troubling me."

The next day the patient again sent for the doctor and said to him: "Yesterday I told you nothing was troubling me, but I've been talking to God all night. I looked at the ceiling and saw my own words: 'Seek first the kingdom of God.' Doctor, I've been seeking my own kingdom. I've been a completely self-centred man. But last night something happened to me. I'm seeking first the kingdom of God." The doctor said: "I went away with tears streaming down my cheeks. I had seen the birth of a soul." Surrender means not just the birth of a soul, but the birth of everything – new relationships, new perspectives on life, new power to face whatever comes, and a new sense of certainty and belonging – a new everything.

FURTHER STUDY

2 Cor. 8:1-9;
Matt. 19:21;
1 Cor. 10:24;
Phil. 2:4

1. What was Christ's example?

2. How can we imitate Him?

Prayer

O Father, it is obvious that unless my confidence is placed in the Ultimate, then I will not be able to cope with the immediate. Help me to be a fully surrendered person. For surrendered to You, I need surrender to nothing else. Amen.

The future – safe with Him

"For you died, and your life is now hidden with Christ in God. (v.3)

For reading & meditation – Colossians 3:1-15

We are discovering that when we are surrendered to the certain, we need never surrender to the uncertain. Sure of God, we do not have to be sure of anything else. A Christian who shrinks from walking the road of ambiguity and uncertainty in company with his Lord is saying, in effect: "My trust is in myself and not in Him." We don't like to put it in those terms, of course, because it challenges our self-interest. And if there is one thing we must learn about the self, it is that it does not like to be challenged, confronted or dislodged.

The self, however, must be disciplined to die. It must die to being first in order to live as second. That is why the centre of the kingdom of God is a cross. We must go through spiritually what Jesus went through physically – we must die and be buried in order to experience a resurrection into freedom and fullness of life.

A man who was part of a small group who had met together to deepen their spiritual understanding said: "I see what I need, and I see that I don't want what I need." In those words, he identified the struggle we all have with this business of self. Who is to be first – myself or God? That decision decides all other decisions – it is a seed decision. The moment you fully surrender to Christ, you automatically die to your own intentions and purposes and you gain a new perspective on life. From then on, you live in a state of Christ-reference – not self-reference. You look out at ambiguity and uncertainty and say: "I may not know what the future holds – so what? I know *who* holds the future."

FURTHER STUDY

2 Tim. 2:1-13;
Rom. 6:6;
2 Cor. 4:11

1. Which saying is trustworthy?

2. How does this apply to you?

Prayer

My Father and my God, I see now that I've been out of focus, and all of life's pictures have been blurred and distorted. Help me to see life from a new point of view – Your point of view. In Jesus' Name I ask it. Amen.

Strangers and pilgrims

*"… Therefore God is not ashamed to be called their God, for
he has prepared a city for them." (v.16)*

For reading & meditation – Hebrews 11:8-16

We continue meditating on the fact that one of the reasons why we find it so difficult to cope with ambiguity and uncertainty is because we have never really died to self-interest. We are more concerned about our own purposes than we are about His – hence we are uncertain and insecure.

Today we look at Abraham and the way he handled his situation of ambiguity and uncertainty. He was almost seventy-five years old when God called him to step out on the pathway of uncertainty. There he was, loading up his camel caravan with his wife and nephew, bound for … somewhere. The Amplified Bible puts if most effectively when it says: "… he went, although he did not know or trouble his mind about where he was to go."

Charles Swindoll humorously pictures a conversation between Abraham and his neighbours going something like this: "Abraham, where are your going?" "I'm moving." "Why? Why ever would you want to leave Ur?" "God has made it clear that I should go." "God? You've been talking to Him again?" "Right. He told me to leave. I must go."

"Well, where are you going?" "I don't know; He didn't tell me that." "Wait a minute, you know you ought to go, but you don't know where you ought to go?" "Yes." "Abraham, you really have gone off the deep end." And so it continues. It isn't easy to obey without understanding. It is the same thing that we talked about two days ago: going – without knowing. It might help to remind ourselves of the term God sometimes uses to describe us – strangers and pilgrims. People on the move, free to follow Him wherever He leads – regardless.

FURTHER STUDY

Gen. 12:1-9;
Psa. 25:9, 48:14;
Matt. 1:1

1. What was the result of Abraham's obedience?

2. What followed his first step of obedience?

Prayer

O God, You who wrap me around as the atmosphere wraps itself around my body. Let me respond to You as my physical body responds to its environment – and lives. Help me to trust You even when I cannot trace You. In Jesus' Name. Amen.

A personal word

"But by the grace of God I am what I am ..." (v.10)
For reading & meditation – 1 Corinthians 15:1-11

Today we ask ourselves: Why is it that even though we may have a fairly mature faith in God, we still find it frustrating to be caught up in situations where we have no clear direction or control? The root cause of this is misplaced dependency – we depend too much upon ourselves and not enough upon God.

As I examine my own life, I am constantly amazed that after over fifty years' experience in the Christian faith, I am still sometimes prone to take the way of independence rather than dependence. Do you not find a similar tendency in yourself? I want God's way – so very much – but I want it on my own terms. Granted, this is less of a problem now than it was, say, thirty years ago, but it is still sometimes a struggle nevertheless.

What does this say about me? It says that in this area of my life, there is still a need to die to my own self-concern, and even before these lines were written I had to get down on my knees and acknowledge this before the Lord. I may still have struggles with this issue in the future, but I know for sure that at this moment, my will is more yielded to Him than ever. Perhaps this is the last battle I shall have to fight on this matter, and when I find myself facing situations in the future that are vague and ambiguous without fearing the outcome, I will know the issue has been settled once and for all. I have exposed my heart to you in obedience to the prompting of the Spirit. I need Him as much as you.

FURTHER STUDY

Rom. 8:1-14; 15:1;
Gal. 5:24;
1 Pet. 2:24

1. What happens if we
live according to the
sinful nature?

2. How do we know
we are sons of God?

Prayer

O Father, as we see yet again where we should be centred – in You – help us to die in those areas of life where we have established our independence. Only in You can we be safe and steady and growing. Help us, dear Lord. Amen.

The crucified "self"

"I have been crucified with Christ and I no longer live, but Christ lives in me ..." (v.20)

For reading & meditation – Galatians 2:15-21

If there is one note ringing through these pages, it is this: to the extent that we are afraid to die to our self-interest, to that extent will our Christian lives be unfruitful. We remind ourselves again: "Unless a grain of wheat falls into the earth and dies, it remains just one grain; never becomes more but lives by itself alone. But if it dies, it produces many others and yields a rich harvest" (John 12:24, Amplified Bible). It is easy to say but difficult to put into practice – difficult but not impossible.

Today we ask ourselves: What exactly happens when we "die" to self? Does it mean that the "self" undergoes annihilation? No. The death to which we are called is the death of the false life we have been living, the false ideas and values we have set up, the false world of sin and evil, and the false self, organised around self-concern. When Paul said, "I have been crucified with Christ", he meant that he had died to all the purposes in his life except Christ's purposes.

This whole passage telling of Paul's burial and resurrection is one of the most exciting in the New Testament. He goes on to say: "I no longer live, but Christ lives in me." Paul discovered that life was much more positive and powerful when he pursued God's purposes rather than his own purposes. He got on better with Christ than he did with himself. This may take some thinking through, but the truth is, if you won't live with God, you won't be able to live harmoniously with yourself – nor, for that matter, with anyone else.

FURTHER STUDY

Gal. 5:1-25;
Rom. 6:2; Col. 3:3

1. To what have we been called?

2. How is this achieved?

Prayer

O God, I just can't go through life with this ghastly contradiction – the self – at the centre of my being. I cannot bear this constant civil war within me. Command it to cease and command me to be free. In Jesus' Name. Amen.

"Grace upon grace"

"And from his fullness have we all received, grace upon grace." (v.16, RSV)

For reading & meditation – John 1:1-17

Today we ask: What purpose does God have in leading us into situations which are uncertain and ambiguous? He does so in order that we might learn to depend on Him and not on ourselves. Just as in times of loneliness we learn to realise His presence, so in times of uncertainty we learn to realise His power.

The major reason why our lives are unfruitful lies right here: we depend more on our own strength than we do on His. How can God teach us dependence unless He puts us into situations which are so uncertain that we are compelled either to choose the way of frustration or the way of faith? And if we draw back from entering such situations, we will miss a valuable spiritual education and our lives will become barren.

A statement I came across some time ago sums up what I want to say co.ncerning ambiguity and uncertainty. It is this: "God's purposes are always God's enablings." In other words, when God steers you into strange and uncertain situations, He will keep you very much in the dark concerning His purposes, but He will not leave you bereft of His grace. The purpose of God and the grace of God are two sides of the one coin. If you accept the purpose, you get the grace; if you refuse the purpose, you annul the grace. Anything God purposes for you, He gives you the grace to perform. John speaks in our text for today of "grace upon grace". One preacher I know translates that text like this: "Use the grace I give you and rest assured – there will always be more to follow."

FURTHER STUDY

2 Cor. 12:1-10;
Eph. 2:6-7;
Phil. 4:19

1. How did Paul view his "thorn in the flesh"?

2. What was his attitude?

Prayer

O Father, how wonderful it would be if I could master this lesson today, and become a living illustration of "grace upon grace". May it be so, to the honour and glory of Your peerless and precious Name. Amen.

The final battle

"For the love of money is a root of all kinds of evil ..." (v.10)
For reading & meditation – 1 Timothy 6:3-11

We now start examining some of the areas of life into which we are led by God in order that He might make our lives more fruitful and profitable to Him. First we focus upon the problem of cramped financial circumstances.

No one can deny that money plays an enormous part in our lives. It was Balzac who said more than a century ago: "The final battle for Christian discipleship will be over the money problem: till that is solved there can be no universal application of Christianity." It comes as a great surprise to many new Christians that the Bible talks a good deal about money, and more than one preacher has pointed out that when Jesus was here on earth, this was one of the subjects He talked about most.

One of the most interesting aspects of money to a Christian is that through either the giving or the withholding of it, God is able to steer our lives into the areas in which He wants us involved. Do you find yourself in financial straits at the moment? Does your bank account need month-to-month resuscitation? Then don't panic – God may be allowing this financial stringency in order to teach you some valuable lessons about Himself. Thousands of Christians will testify that God has no more certain way of getting our undivided attention than by withholding money or putting us into tight financial circumstances. How strange that when our pockets are full, often God has to shout to get our attention, but when they are empty, we are alert and ready to hear His faintest whisper.

FURTHER STUDY

James 5:1-5;
Eccl. 5:10;
Jer. 17:11

1. What is avarice?

2. What is the lesson of the partridge?

Prayer

O Father, if it is true that the final battle for Christian discipleship will be over the money problem, then help me resolve this issue once and for all in these next few days. Help me to make whatever I own the instrument of Your purposes. Amen.

God's four purposes for money

"But if we have food and clothing, we will be content with that. (v.8)

For reading & meditation – 1 Timothy 6:6-19

Before we can understand what God may be trying to achieve in our lives by putting us into tight financial circumstances, we must know something of our Lord's purposes for money. Many Christians think that the purpose of money is to provide security, establish independence, or create power and influence, but this is a very worldly view of the subject. The Bible shows us that God has four basic purposes which He wants to achieve through money – and understanding these purposes is crucial if we are to be fruitful and productive Christians.

The first purpose of money is to provide basic needs. It's surprising how little money we need in order to sustain the basic needs of life. These needs can be summed up in the words food, clothing and shelter. And God demonstrates His loving care by assuring us of His help in obtaining these basic essentials: "And why do you worry about clothes? See how the lilies of the field grow. They do not labour or spin … will he not much more clothe you, O you of little faith?" (Matt. 6:28-30).

Since the dawn on time, humankind has tried to become independent of God. There are tendencies in our fallen nature to be self-sufficient and self-supporting. We would much rather pray, "Give us this month our monthly pay cheque" than "Give us this day our daily bread." And why? Because it doesn't bring us face to face with our need to be daily dependent on the Lord. How wise was our Lord in including that phrase in the model prayer He gave His disciples. He knew the recognition of daily needs would help to produce daily dependence.

FURTHER STUDY

Matt. 6:19-34,
10:29-31; 1 Pet. 5:7

1. What are we to seek
first?

2. What will follow?

Prayer

Father, I pray that You will bring me under the complete sway of Your Spirit so that my spiritual dependence will not be year by year, month by month or week by week – but day by day. This I ask in Jesus' Name. Amen.

True contentment?

"But godliness with contentment is great gain." (v.6)
For reading & meditation – 1 Timothy 6:6

We continue meditating on the first of God's four purposes for money – to provide our basic needs. We saw yesterday that God longs for us to be dependent on Him. This is not because God is possessive, but because He knows that we experience our greatest happiness and freedom when we rely on Him alone. When we fail to recognise our need for God, we tend to lose our love for God. And the more we lose our love for God, the more we come to depend upon ourselves.

Permit me to remind you again of the text we looked at yesterday: "If we have food and clothing, we will be content" (1 Tim. 6:8). Contentment is the satisfaction we get from knowing there will be provision for our basic needs. We begin to lose our contentment when we compare what we have with what others have – and then before long expectations dominate our focus. To the degree that our expectations increase, contentment diminishes.

One of the great advantages of being content with basics is that it equips us to resist the alluring advertising which seeks to convince us that we are not able really to enjoy life unless we buy some new commodity. A contented person feels wealthy because he knows that what he already possesses is all he needs for daily living. A veteran missionary, meeting some new recruits to the mission field, surprised them by saying: "The first thing I would like you to do is to make a list of all the things you think you need – then I will spend some time with you showing you how to do without them."

FURTHER STUDY

Phil. 4:1-11;
Prov. 15:16;
Heb. 13:5

1. What was Paul's testimony?

2. How should we live?

Prayer

O my Father, I see that material things can be a good servant but a bad master. Deliver me from the bondage of the material and help me to become a truly contented person. In Jesus' Name I ask it. Amen.

Presumption versus faith

"Be still before the Lord and wait patiently for him ..." (v.7)
For reading & meditation – Psalm 37:1-26

We look now at God's second purpose for money: to confirm His loving direction in our lives. God will use the supply of money or the lack of it to confirm His direction and guidance for many of the decisions we make in our lives. I constantly meet Christians who tell me that one of the biggest lessons they have learned in the Christian life is that of discerning God's guidance through His giving or His withholding of money.

Some years ago, a minister shared with me how he had asked God to guide him over a certain project, and part of his prayer, he said, went like this: "Lord, give me the money to do this, or else it just cannot be done." The money didn't come, so the minister went ahead and borrowed money for the project. A few weeks later, the project got into difficulties and he was declared bankrupt.

I said to him: "Do you know what made you go ahead even though God did not provide the money?" He paused for a few minutes, and said with tears in his eyes: "I had not then learned the difference between presumption and faith." "What is the difference?" I asked. He replied: "Faith is trusting God to achieve His purposes through us, presumption is deciding what we want to accomplish and trying to get God to do it for us." It is so easy to claim that Christ is Lord of our lives, but, as someone put it: "His Lordship is only confirmed when we are obedient to the promptings and limitations which He places on our daily decisions."

FURTHER STUDY

Psa. 46:1-11; 40:1;
Isa. 26:8

1. How can we know
God?

2. How much time
will you spend
waiting on Him
today?

Prayer

My Lord and my God, You know my proneness to "nudge" You when I don't think You are working things out right. Make me sensitive to the promptings of Your Spirit and the limitations that You set upon my life. In Jesus' Name I ask it. Amen.

Generosity generates

"Share with God's people who are in need. Practise hospitality." (v.13)

For reading & meditation – Romans 12:9-21

Today we look at God's third purpose for money: to bless and enrich other Christians. One of the characteristics which God wants to develop in us is that of generosity, for our generosity will determine how much spiritual light we have in our being. Take this verse: "If your Eye is generous, the whole of your body will be illumined" (Matt. 6:22, Moffatt). If your "eye" – your outlook on life, your whole way of looking at things and people – is generous, then your whole personality is illuminated, is lighted up. If you have a greedy or selfish "eye", your whole being will be filled with darkness.

In Acts 11:27-30 we read about a severe famine that caused suffering to many Jewish Christians. The church at Antioch – made up mostly of Gentiles – sent an offering to their fellow believers in Jerusalem, and that offering was an important means of tearing down national and cultural barriers between them, and building bonds of genuine Christian love. God likens generous giving to reaping a harvest: "He who sows sparingly will also reap sparingly, and he who sows bountifully will also reap bountifully" (2 Cor. 9:6, RSV).

FURTHER STUDY

1 Kings 17:8-16;
Prov. 25:21; 11:25;
Eccl. 11:1

1. What is the lesson of the widow of Zarephath?

2. How will you be generous today?

Perhaps the greatest benefit of generous giving to other Christians, however, is this – it results in "an overflowing tide of thanksgiving to God" (v.12, Phillips). Yes, God will give you much so that you can give away much, and when you take your gifts to those who need them they will break out in thanksgiving and praise of God for your help. Giving to the needs of fellow Christians means that many will thank God and fill His Church with praise.

Prayer

O God, help be to become a truly generous person, for I see that when I am generous, then my generosity generates generosity in others. I ask this in the peerless and exalted Name of the Lord Jesus. Amen.

What is a financial miracle?

*" 'Test me in this,' says the Lord Almighty, 'and see if I will
not throw open the floodgates of heaven …' " (v.10)*

For reading & meditation – Malachi 3:1-12

We look now at God's fourth purpose for money: to show His divine power. God is a supernatural God – something Christians seem to forget – and He delights to demonstrate His reality and power among His people. One means through which God has chosen to do this is through His miraculous provision of money.

What is a financial miracle? It is a supernatural event whereby God provides one of His children with the money required to meet a financial need – and usually it involves such precise timing that it cannot fail to point to the Lord's direct intervention. When a Christian prays about a financial need, for example, and an unexpected gift is given to him by someone who knows nothing about the need, the supernatural power of God is demonstrated.

In the days of Elijah, the nation of Israel tried to worship God and serve Baal at the same time. Elijah knew that this would inevitably lead to God's judgment, so he proposed a simple test. The test involved building two altars, one for God and one for Baal, and whichever answered by a display of supernatural power was the one whom they would worship. The prophets of Baal cried out to their non-existent deity all day, but nothing happened. Then Elijah prayed, and in response to his prayer God sent fire from heaven.

One of the biggest of the false gods of this age is money. It has become an idol because people expect from it what only God can give – true security. As the world hankers after money, God wants to prove to those who seek Him that they will not lack any good thing.

Prayer

O Father, help me to see that I grow into the image of the god that I serve. I don't want to be like money – hard and metallic; I want to be like You – gracious and beneficent. Help me to keep my focus only on You. In Jesus' Name I pray. Amen.

The day you "die"

"Take your son, your only son, Isaac, whom you love …" (v.2)
For reading & meditation – Genesis 22:1-14

Having seen God's four purposes for money, we are now ready to ask: What part does money play in our lives? Does it draw us closer to God, or drive us further away from Him? Is our security in silver – or in the Saviour?

Most of us would claim that we are serving God. We would strenuously deny that we have a greater love for money than we do for the Master. God, however, is aware that what we believe to be the situation is not always so. Sometimes He has to bring us into cramped financial circumstances so that we realise where our true security lies.

Although the story of Abraham and Isaac does not have a precise application to what we are saying here, there are certain similarities which I consider do apply. First, God singled out in Abraham's life the thing he most loved – his only son. God often starts His test of our character with the thing that we love the most. Is money one of your greatest loves? If so, recognise and acknowledge it right now.

Second, God pinned Abraham down to a fixed time and place. God's way of doing business always involves a specific time and place.

FURTHER STUDY

Matt. 26:1-13;
Luke 21:4;
Acts 4:34-35

1. What did Jesus say about the woman who anointed Him?

2. What was the attitude of the early Church?

"Sacrifice him *there* as a burnt offering" (v.2). Let the place where you are sitting now be your meeting place with God. God asked Abraham to sacrifice his only son. Abraham could never have lifted the knife over his son unless he had "died" to him in his emotions. Without this emotional break, the offering is only a meaningless ritual. This must be the day on which you "die" to the bondage of money.

Prayer

O Father, Your timing is perfect. Today, by faith, I "die" to all emotional attachments to money, and lay every financial bondage on Your altar. Father, it's done – I'm free. Help me now to live out that freedom. In Jesus' Name. Amen.

Problems? No, prods!

"... God ... is using your sufferings to make you ready for his kingdom." (v. 5, TLB)

For reading & meditation – 2 Thessalonians 1:1-12

We pause at this point to remind ourselves of the principle we are seeking to understand, namely that in God's order of things, life is always preceded by death. A grain of wheat has within it the potential of becoming many grains of wheat, but first the solitary grain must fall into the ground and die. It is only after death that its potential is released, and out of the dying comes an abundant harvest. That principle is not just to be seen as an interesting fact of nature; if our lives are to be fruitful, then we, too, must be willing to die to our own purposes so that we might live to God's.

The next sphere of life we examine is the area of obstacles and opposition. Would you like your life to be free of those potentially frustrating situations that block your way or impede your spiritual development? Then let me say at once, you could be worse off without them. The obstacles and opposition you face can turn out to be prods – prods toward your spiritual growth.

A minister friend of mine who was going through a period of great difficulty once asked me to pray with him that God would remove all the obstacles from his ministry. I put my hand lovingly on his shoulder and replied: "If He does, it will make your ministry less effective." He saw the point, and instead asked me to pray that God would help him to die to his own concerns. I did, and from that day to this, his ministry has flourished and become extremely fruitful. And so, my friend, can yours.

FURTHER STUDY

Phil. 1:1-14;
Acts 5:41;
Rom. 8:17

1. How did Paul view his setbacks?

2. What was the positive outcome

Prayer

O Father, more and more the conviction grows that it is not what happens to me, but what I do with it, that is important. Deepen this conviction within me so that it becomes a controlling one – today and every day. In Jesus' Name. Amen.

Acquiescence – or control?

"I am ready for anything through the strength of the one who lives within me." (v.13, Phillips)

For reading & meditation – Philippians 4:10-20

Day by day, as we unfold this thrilling theme of *The Corn of Wheat Afraid to Die*, it is becoming increasingly obvious that God gives us a choice – a choice of either to live or to die. We can live for the fulfilment of our own desires, or we can die to our desires and live for His.

This is perhaps the moment that we should come to grips with the question which people often ask when this issue of "dying to self" is raised: "Isn't this a terribly passive attitude to life? And doesn't it tend to diminish personal responsibility and self-control?" John Dewey, the famous American educator, held that view. Once, when lecturing to his students, he drew a line down a blackboard and on one side listed those systems of thought which teach control, and on the other those systems that teach acquiescence. On the "control" side he put "science", and on the "acquiescence" side he put "religion".

To be fair, he should have written, "Some forms of religion". The religion of Jesus Christ does not produce passive and acquiescent disciples, but surrendered disciples – surrendered to God, but surrendered to nothing else. They rise from the dust of self-surrender to lay hold on the raw materials of life – good, bad and indifferent – and use them. Would you describe the early Christians as passive and acquiescent? I wouldn't. Surrendered – yes. Acquiescent – no. Surrendering to God so that He may work in and through us may at first seen passive, but actually it represents the most amazingly positive and active method of dealing with life. Other ways are possible, but no other way is as powerful.

FURTHER STUDY

Phil. 2:12-30;
Eph. 3:16;
2 Cor. 9:8

1. What are we able to do when God works in us?

2. What does God's grace produce in us?

Prayer

Gracious and loving heavenly Father, I am so thankful that You show me a way of life that doesn't demean me, but develops me. I fall at Your feet, and lo – I rise to new purposes and new achievements. I am eternally grateful. Amen.

Rise up and walk

"In the name of Jesus Christ of Nazareth rise up and walk."
(v.6, AV)

For reading & meditation – Acts 3:1-16

We said yesterday that when we die to self-interests we rise to meet life, not passively, but actively. In fact, self-surrender is the most amazingly active method of dealing with life.

Take, for example, Peter and John. When they met the man asking for alms, they were, as we say, "financially embarrassed" and unable to help in that way. Most of us would have let the incident go at that, for what can you do if you have no money in a world like this? Not these men, however – they took up this poverty into the purpose of their lives and used it. What do I mean? This: if they had had some money, they might have tossed him a coin and that would have been the end of it – their adequacy on that level would have blocked the higher good.

Instead, conscious that they could not minister to him at one level – the financial – they sought to minister to him at another level – the spiritual. The result was that the obstacle on one level was turned into an opportunity on another. "Rise up and walk," they said to the man – and rise up he did. Nothing passive about that! As one wag put it: "The lame man asked for alms, but instead he got legs!" Forgive me for extending this illustration beyond the bounds of proper biblical exposition, but there are many of us who need to look at the things lying lame around us, and perhaps even within us – higher ministries, spiritual aptitudes – and say to them, "Rise up and walk." Then together we shall walk on into the temple of wider and more effective living.

FURTHER STUDY

Matt. 9:1-8;
John 14:13, 20:31;
Phil. 2:9-11

1. Why is the Name of Jesus so powerful?

2. What will happen one day?

Prayer

O God, forgive me for failing to see the opportunities in every obstacle. Help me to understand that when I am blocked on one level, then I can break out on another. Nothing can deter me when my will coincides with Yours. Thank You, Father. Amen.

Victim – or victor?

"… the immeasurable greatness of his power in us who believe, according to the working of his great might …" (vv.19-20, RSV)

For reading & meditation – Ephesians 1:11-23

Permit me to ask you: What will the obstacles and opposition you meet do to you today? Will they make you bitter, or will they make you better? The last word is not with them, but with you. If your own concerns and interests are well and truly "dead", and you are committed to pursuing God's purposes, then the issue is not so much what your circumstances will do to you, but what you will do to your circumstances.

The Christian who understands this has the power to say to life – do your worst, I have the resources to take every negative and turn it into a positive. Nothing successfully opposes the believer whose life is hidden with Christ in God. Jesus once faced great opposition in His ministry: "They were filled with madness, and began to discuss with one another what they should do to Jesus" (Luke 6:11, Weymouth). Here was opposition in its most terrifying form.

What did Jesus do? Listen again to the Weymouth translation: "About that time He went out … into the hill country to pray" (v.12). Prayer, that powerful means of communicating with God and controlling, not so much the situation as the outcome of the situation, made Jesus, not a victim, but a victor. One of the major purposes of God seems to be that of producing character in His children. Not their ease, not their happiness – except as a by-product – but their character. And how is character produced? One way it is produced is through overcoming difficulties. So don't groan at the obstacles and opposition that face you today – grow in them. They help to sharpen your character – and your wits!

FURTHER STUDY

Rom. 8:28-37; 5:17;
Rev. 1:5-6

1. What are we
through Christ?

2. What should we be
doing in life?

Prayer

O God, forgive me that so often I cry to You for tasks equal to my powers. Help me to pray instead for power equal to my tasks. I ask this, not for my sake, but for Yours. Amen.

Attacked – but not injured

"I am sending you out like sheep among wolves. Therefore be as shrewd as snakes and as innocent as doves." (v.16)

For reading & meditation – Matthew 10:5-20

The gospel of Jesus Christ is the only faith that dares to say to its followers: "Behold, I send you forth as sheep in the midst of wolves" (AV). It is as if Jesus is saying: "You will have as much chance of escaping difficulties and opposition as sheep have in the midst of wolves." If you are a Christian, you can expect people to oppose you – even hurt you. Notice what I say: "hurt" you, but not "harm" you. Sometimes God may not protect us from being hurt, but He will protect us from being harmed.

One writer puts that same thought in this way: "At times God may suffer His children to be attacked, but providing they are fully abandoned to Him and His purposes, He will never suffer them to be injured." He is using the words "attack" to mean physical or verbal abuse, and "injury" to mean the scarring of the soul. In that sense, no attack from without can injure us; we can only be injured from within by wrong perspectives and wrong choices.

Some time ago I quoted a maxim that goes like this: "No man is safe unless he can stand anything that happens to him." A young student wrote to me and said: "Then there aren't many people who are 'safe' – are there?" I point you now to another verse to lay alongside our text for today: "For the Lamb in the midst of the throne will be their shepherd" (Rev. 7:17, RSV). Christ's being on the throne is the pledge that we, too – somehow, some way – shall pass out of the midst of the "wolves" of people and things, to victory over both.

FURTHER STUDY

2 Cor. 4:1-12;
Col. 3:3-4;
Rev. 1:18

1. What was Paul's testimony?

2. How did Paul view life?

Prayer

Lord Jesus, Master of every situation – even on a cross where You dispensed forgiveness to Your crucifiers – give me this mastery over circumstances. Help me to see I am not beaten until I am beaten within. Amen.

"Stay in the kitchen"

*"God ... will not allow you to be tempted beyond what you are able,
but ... will provide the way of escape ..."* (v.13, NASB)

For reading & meditation – 1 Corinthians 10:1-13

We turn now to another sphere of life from which many of us might long to be exempted – the area of strong and unrelenting temptation. Most of us, if we are honest, would like to be excused from having to face temptation, but temptation has its uses: it can work in God's hands to the development of character, and help perfect the image of Christ in our lives. Mark Antony was called "the silver-throated orator of Rome", but he had the fatal flaw of not being able to resist a temptation.

That indictment, I'm afraid, applies not just to Mark Antony, or to the ranks of the unconverted, but to many in the Church also. We all face temptation, and unfortunately far too many of us fall beneath its power. The root meaning of the word "temptation" (Greek, *peirasmos*) is that of testing. The dictionary defines temptation as "the act of enticement to do wrong, by promise of pleasure or gain". Charles Swindoll commented: "Temptation motivates you to be bad by promising something good."

Isn't that just like the devil? Are you facing a particularly fierce temptation at the moment? Then take heart – you have all the power you need to stand up under the blast. Harry S. Truman, a former President of the United States, is famous for saying: "If you don't like the heat, get out of the kitchen." But I've not found anyone who was able to stay strong without spending time in the "kitchen". In coming to grips with the sphere of temptation, my advice is: "If you can't stand the heat, stay *in* the kitchen – and in God's strength, learn to handle it."

FURTHER STUDY

James 1:1-15;
Rom. 8:31;
Heb. 2:18

1. When are we tempted?

2. On what basis can we face and use temptation?

Prayer

O Father, show me how to experience continual victory over temptation. And help me, in this area of life also, not to be "a corn of wheat afraid to die". I face the fire in Your strength, knowing that You never allow what You cannot use. Amen.

"The original quitters"

*"They forgot what he had done, the wonders he had shown
them." (v.11)*

For reading & meditation – Psalm 78:1-11

We ended yesterday with the advice: "If you can't stand the heat, stay in the kitchen – and in God's strength, learn to handle it." The psalm before us today begins by commanding us to listen: "O my people, hear my teaching." You have only to read a few verses of this psalm to see that the psalmist Asaph is recalling the disobedience which characterised the Jews during their forty years' wandering in the wilderness. Then a strange verse appears: "The men of Ephraim, though armed with bows, turned back on the day of battle" (v.9).

These Ephraimites were equipped with all they needed for warfare, but on the day of the battle – that is, the first day of the fray – they "turned back". Although well armed, in the moment of testing they were overcome by fear. Doubtless they paraded well and looked fine as they marched out to battle, but when they came face to face with the enemy, the only weapon they used was a cloud of dust as they retreated en masse – and in a hurry.

A preacher I once heard referred to the Ephraimites in this verse as "the original quitters". What an indictment. The Ephraimites live on, you know; they are to be found in the rank and file of many a modern-day congregation. They look fine in church on Sunday mornings with a hymn book and a Bible in their hands, but let the hot rays of temptation beat upon them – and they run. They surrender to temptation because they have never learned how to surrender to God. As I've said before – when we surrender to God, then we need not surrender to anything else.

FURTHER STUDY

Dan. 1:1-21;
Rom. 6:13;
Eph. 6:13

1. How did Daniel resist the temptation to compromise?

2. What are the results of resisting temptation?

Prayer

Lord Jesus, help me clarify to myself whether I am surrendered or not. For I see that if I do not fall at Your feet, then I fall at the feet of things and circumstances. Show me at whose feet I am lying. For Your own Name's sake. Amen.

"No" to self – "Yes" to God

"… seeing that you have put off the old nature with its practices and have put on the new nature …" (vv.9-10, RSV)

For reading & meditation – Colossians 3:1-17

We continue from where we left off yesterday, saying that the reason why many of today's Christians surrender so easily to temptation is because they have never really learned how to surrender to God. Many (not all) of the people who come for counselling are struggling with the fact that they have never understood how to die to their own purposes and live for God's purposes. Time and time again in counselling, it has been my experience to watch a person slowly recognise that his problem is due, not so much to what is happening to him as his reactions to what is happening to him – and then decide not to do anything about it.

I am saddened by the trend to treat biblical principles as optional rather than obligatory. It is amazing to notice the casualness with which so many approach Scripture and say: "I suppose I shouldn't really be living like this; I had better try to change – if I can." When that attitude is present, there is little hope of change. You see, if there is no experienced death, there can be no experienced life.

When a person does not see the importance of recognising, albeit painfully, that God's way is the way of obedience, irrespective of whether we feel like it or not, and involves death to wrong patterns of thinking and wrong patterns of behaving, there will be no victory and no change. Putting on the new nature requires first putting off the old nature by asserting, with all the conviction possible, that one is going to go God's way no matter how much the carnal nature argues to the contrary.

FURTHER STUDY

James 4:1-8;
Eph. 6:11;
1 Pet. 5:8-9

1. What 3 steps are given in James 4 for overcoming the devil?

2. How would you apply these steps in a practical way?

Prayer

O Father, help me shout a thunderous "No" to anything that is contrary to You, and a mighty "Yes" to all You want to do in my life. And when my carnal nature argues back, help me to put it in its place – under my feet. In Jesus' Name I pray. Amen.

Be a nonconformist

"Don't let the world around you squeeze you into its own mould ..." (v.2, Phillips)

For reading & meditation – Romans 12:1-13

We must spend some more time focusing on the fact that many of today's Christians are like the Ephraimites we spoke of a few days ago – good at parading, but not so good in battle. They cry out for help with their problems, but when confronted with the demands of Scripture, one of which is to die to self, they scurry like rats down the first bolthole they can find. They want a medicine man with a quick cure, not direct advice about how to repent of their egocentricity.

I sometimes wonder to myself whether this trend in today's Church is the result of our being brain-washed by an age that tends to make quitting a way of life. Anna Sklar, in her book *Runaway Wives*, uncovered an incredible statistic of American life when she said that a decade ago, for every woman who walked away from her home and family responsibility, 600 husbands and fathers did so. Today, for each man who does that, two women do.

My purpose in making this statement is not to take sides with either group, but simply to point out that, more and more, the modern trend is to choose the way of escape as the method of dealing with problems. Things that were once viewed by society as a stigma are now accepted without the flicker of an eyelid. "Let's just quit" are almost household words. A marriage gets shaky, hits a few rough patches and the solution is: "Let's get a divorce." How much of today's worldly patterns are affecting our thinking, I wonder? And how much are we letting the world squeeze us into its own mould?

FURTHER STUDY

Matt. 6:19-24;
1 Kings 18:21;
Eph. 6:5; James 1:8

1. What does it mean to have singleness of heart?

2. How does Satan seek to divert us?

Prayer

Father, make me a nonconformist – not in a denominational sense, but in a dynamic sense. Forgive me if I have allowed the world to squeeze me into its own mould. Change my way of thinking to Your way of thinking. In Jesus' Name. Amen.

The greatest temptation

"Jesus ... was led by the Spirit in the desert, where for forty days he was tempted by the devil." (vv.1-2)

For reading & meditation – Luke 4:1-13

I am often asked the question: What is the greatest temptation a Christian faces? My reply is usually this: the temptation to avoid the way of the cross. It was temptation that constantly faced our Lord Jesus Christ, and it is one that constantly faces us:

> *It is the way the Master went*
> *Should not the servant tread it still?*

There were two outstanding periods in Jesus' life when He was greatly tempted to face the sorrow and sin of the world in some way other than the one He took. One such time was the temptation in the desert, and the other was at the coming of the Greeks. As we have already looked at the latter incident – and will briefly examine it once more before we conclude – we shall focus our thinking over the next few days on our Lord's temptation in the desert.

Following His baptism in the River Jordan, Jesus was led by the Spirit into the desert to be tempted (or tested) by the devil. He got away from humanity in order to prepare Himself for the ordeal of giving Himself to humanity. In a sense, the temptation began as soon as He entered the desert. What temptation? The testing of His purposes to see whether, being the Son of God, He would also be the Son of Man. For to be the Son of Man would mean that He would take upon Himself all that falls on the sons of men. Yet on that issue, He never wavered. The Son of God willingly accepted all that was involved in becoming the Son of Man, so that the sons of men might become the sons of God.

FURTHER STUDY

Matt. 4:1-11;
Gen. 3:1-12;
Heb. 4:15

1. Compare the temptations of Jesus and Adam.

2. Why did Adam fail, and Jesus overcome?

Prayer

Lord Jesus, Son of God and also Son of Man, how can I ever sufficiently thank You for aligning Yourself with this sinful human race? I cannot understand it, but yet I stand upon it – and stand upon it for all eternity. Amen.

Feeding on the wrong bread

"... I have come to do your will, O God." (v.7)
For reading & meditation – Hebrews 10:1-18

W e continue looking at Christ's temptation in the desert, but from a slightly different perspective. We are seeing how the temptation was designed to keep Him from identifying Himself with the sons of men. We saw yesterday how, He withdrew from men in order that He might give Himself to men. The issue was not so much whether He was the Son of God – He had heard that confirmed quite clearly at His baptism – but whether, being the Son of God, He would also be the Son of Man.

Once Jesus feels that His period of fasting is over, He prepares to return to feed His weakened body, but the tempter intervenes and tempts Him to turn the stones of the desert into bread. In doing this, is he really saying to Jesus: "Why go back to men? Stay here and feed Yourself. You are the Son of God, isn't that enough"? We cannot be sure, of course, but seen in this light, it is a possibility.

In all spiritual work, there is always the temptation to withdraw, to feed ourselves apart, to rejoice in the fact that we are sons of God and feast upon it. Many Christians down the ages have fallen for this, and have opted for an "escape mentality" in which they attempt to avoid the issue of death via a cross by isolating themselves from it. Mark this and mark it well: a similar temptation will come to you – the temptation to avoid the challenge of going down into the death of your self-life, by focusing on the fact that you are already a son of God, and that there is no need for any further humiliation or pain.

FURTHER STUDY

Eph. 1:1-23;
Gen. 3:15;
John 16:33;
1 John 3:8

1. How did Jesus
destroy the devil's
works?

2. How can we
overcome the devil's
works?

Prayer

Gracious and loving heavenly Father, help me, as You did Your Son, to resist every temptation that tries to keep me from coming to grips with my own personal Calvary. Abide with me, and then I can abide with anything. Amen.

The divine end

"… that I may know him and the power of his resurrection,
and may share his sufferings …" (v.10, RSV)
For reading & meditation – Philippians 3:1-14

If the first temptation contained elements designed to prevent Christ from returning to humanity as the Son of Man, then the second temptation might be seen as an attempt to get Him to take a different attitude to men. Was the devil saying: "If you must go back, then do not take the attitude You took when You began. Don't stand alongside man, but stand on the pinnacle of the Temple. Be worshipped, be honoured and respected. Your place is up there, not down among those wretched multitudes"? A similar temptation will come to you, too. Satan will say: "Stay above all this talk of going down into death; escape the pain by remaining above it. You can descend to help men and women, but then let the angels carry you back to your exalted position."

Then came the subtle third temptation, which seemed to suggest this: "If You are determined to be the Son of Man and to be one with men, then adopt humanity's methods – fall down and worship me. If You are going to be like them, be like them in everything, and take a similar attitude to those who obey me."

Jesus refused this way too. He would be the Son of Man and let everything that falls on men fall on Him. But there would be this difference – He would reach the divine end only by means of the divine method, and by doing the will of His Father in heaven. At that point, He put His feet upon the way that He knew would lead ultimately to the cross. No temptation would divert Him from that. And no temptation must divert you and me either.

FURTHER STUDY

Psa. 37:1-40;
Isa. 12:2;
Luke 12:29

1. What 7 steps of trusting are in Psalm 37?

2. What are the 5 results of trusting?

Prayer

O Father, help me to do with temptation what Jesus did with it – to use it to reinforce my readiness to do Your will. I am so thankful that Your tests are not meant to catch me out, but to spur me on. Help me to meet every test – triumphantly. Amen.

A second look

"Jesus replied, 'The hour has come for the Son of Man to be glorified.'" (v.23)

For reading & meditation – John 12:20-36

Having experienced the principle that life is always preceded by death, we return now to focus again on the incident which launched us into this study – the coming of the Greeks to Jesus.

I firmly believe that this incident has been greatly overlooked by Bible expositors and commentators. We usually take the text, "Sir, we would like to see Jesus" (v.21), and leave it at that. But this is one of the most momentous events in the life of our Lord – an event that is next in importance, in my judgement, to His temptation in the wilderness. In many ways, it was more subtle than the wilderness experience, for the wilderness represents the temptation that comes at the beginning of one's ministry, while the coming of the Greeks represents the temptation that comes as one gets close to the end.

It is often as one gets close to one's goal that the temptation to compromise, or to take an easier way becomes more acute. Just as, in the desert, there was a pull to get Jesus to take another way, so here we see a similar situation. As I said at the beginning of our study, we cannot be at all sure that the Greeks arrived with the intention of enticing Christ to come to Athens, but it is significant that their arrival threw Him into a spiritual crisis. Assuming that to be so, the issue before Him was acceptance in Athens or rejection in Jerusalem. A philosopher's chair, or a grisly cross. A similar issue confronts those of us who are His followers. Do we go the way of the cross, or do we go the way of the crowds?

FURTHER STUDY

Col. 1:1-29;
Psa. 45:11;
Deut. 5:7; 6:13-15

1. What was Satan's aim in tempting Jesus?

2. What did Christ accomplish through overcoming him?

Prayer

Father, my mind is made up – I want to go Your way. Help me to come out clearly on Your side – for You and against everything that is against You. This I pray in Jesus' Name. Amen.

Living by the heartbeat

"… the Son can do nothing by himself; he can do only what he sees his Father doing …" (v.19)

For reading & meditation – John 5:16-30

Although we do not know exactly why the Greeks came to Jesus, it is clear that their arrival aroused powerful emotions. He soliloquises: "Unless a grain of wheat falls into the earth and dies, it remains alone; but if it dies, it bears much fruit" (John 12:24, RSV).

Some commentators think that although there is no record of the Greeks having actually conversed with Christ, they might have sent a message via Andrew and Philip to the effect that He could have a long and fruitful life if He brought His message to their shores. Was this so? We will never know – at least, not this side of eternity. But if it was, this was His answer: life comes through giving life, and fruitfulness through falling into the ground and dying.

Jesus did not live by the hourglass, but by the heartbeat. He knew that when we remain alone by ourselves – when we are like the "corn of wheat afraid to die" – we will find life shallow and fruitless. A refusal to pay the ultimate price – the price of giving ourselves – is to find ourselves paying the price of the deadness of life itself. Again we hear Him cry: "The man who loves his life will lose it, while the man who hates his life in this world [as I must do] will keep it for eternal life" (John 12:25). If the Greeks were coming to ask Him to love His life and save it – and thus save others – they were asking Him to bless without bleeding. Jesus knew that could not be done. There is no life without death, no gain without pain, no crown without a cross, and no victory except through surrender.

FURTHER STUDY

Luke 15:11-32;
Mark 8:36;
Matt. 25:27-28

1. What did the prodigal son have to learn?

2. What is the lesson of the man with one talent?

Prayer

My Father and my God, soon I will leave this theme and focus on another. If I have not yet settled this issue of where my allegiance lies – with myself or with You – then help me to settle it today. For Your own dear Name's sake. Amen.

The hour of decision

"I tell you, now is the time of God's favour, now is the day of salvation." (v.2)

For reading & meditation – 2 Corinthians 6:1-18

Listen to Jesus as He receives the news that the Greeks have come to interview Him: "Now is my heart troubled …" (John 12:27). The Greek word used here for "troubled" is *tarasso*, which implies extreme agitation. And well might He be troubled, for being human as well as divine, our Lord would have felt as keenly as you and I the horror of impending death.

Some of us are not troubled at this point because we fall in with the spirit of the age, and choose acceptance rather than rejection – the plaudits of men rather than the nails of a cross. We are afraid to die, and thus live on to experience only shallowness. Again our Lord cries: "And what shall I say? 'Father, save me from this hour?'" (John 12:27). Would He ask to be excused, from paying the supreme price? Some of us may be asking that at this very moment. We are asking to be "saved from this hour". Listen to how Jesus meets this moment: "No, it was for this very reason I came to this hour" (John 12:27).

Can you see what He is saying? "All the ages have matched me against this moment, all the yearnings of men have brought me face to face with this crisis. I cannot fail now, for I would fail both God and them." Can you sense in your own heart right now that God has been working to bring you to this crisis point? For some of you, particularly those of you who have not yet fully surrendered your lives to God's purposes, this is a moment of destiny. Someone has brought you to this hour – that Someone is God.

FURTHER STUDY

Acts 26:1-32;
Psa. 32:6; 69:13;
Deut. 30:19

1. What was Agrippa's response to the challenge?

2. How will you respond to God's challenge?

Prayer

O Father, what can I say? I feel a struggle going on inside me – the struggle concerning who is to be my soul's rightful Lord. Help me to make the final surrender. I do it now, fully and finally. In Jesus' worthy and wonderful Name. Amen.

"It thundered"

"The spiritual man judges all things, but is himself to be judged by no one." (v.15, RSV)

For reading & meditation – 1 Corinthians 2:1-16

The final words of our Lord in the incident we are considering are these: "Father, glorify thy name" (John 12:28, RSV). What a decision! What a moment! "Father, do not think of what it costs me – only glorify Your name." At that moment, He gave God a blank cheque, blank save that it was signed in His own blood. It is a great moment in our life, too, when we hand God a blank cheque, signed in our own blood, and invite Him to call on us for all we have and all we are.

One person described this moment as "the great renunciation". If that is so, then the moment of great renunciation is followed by a great annunciation. Listen: "Then a voice came from heaven, 'I have glorified it, and I will glorify it again' " (John 12:28, RSV). The moment Jesus made the final response, then heaven spoke. Many of us who complain we are living under a silent heaven would find it vocal with the voice of God if we would choose the Calvary way.

Of course, the bystanders missed what was really going on and "said that it had thundered" (John 12:29). To them, it was the impersonal voice of nature. Others came a little closer to reality, and said: "An angel had spoken to him." To them, it was a little more than the impersonal voice of nature, and yet something less than the voice of God. Anyone who stands on the edges of life as a bystander is bound to give a shallow interpretation of what God is doing. It is only those who have faced the alternatives – to die or not to die – who are really involved.

FURTHER STUDY

Josh. 24:1-15;
Psa. 119:30;
Luke 10:42;
Heb. 11:25

1. What challenge did Joshua bring?

2. What was said of Moses?

Prayer

My Father, I don't want to be a bystander. I want to be in the centre of all You are saying and all You are doing. Here's my cheque – signed with my own blood. Fill it in for everything You want from me. I do it willingly, gladly, happily. Amen.

The last word is *life*

"I have come that they may have life, and have it to the full."
(v.10)

For reading & meditation – John 10:7-18

At the close of our meditations we look at the results of the momentous choice Jesus made when the Greeks said: "Sir, we would like to see Jesus."

Our Lord saw that three things would happen: first, the judgment of this world (John 12:31). What did choosing the cross have to do with that? This – the cross is the judgment seat of the world. I confess that the Man on the cross judges me, convicts me, challenges me. His Spirit of facing the world's sin and suffering makes my spirit tremble like a magnetic needle in a storm. At the cross, His love judges my hate, my selfishness, my desire to live only for myself. His self-sacrifice inspires my self-sacrifice.

The second thing our Lord saw would happen was the overpowering of Satan: "Now shall the ruler of this world be cast out" (John 12:31, RSV). He would overthrow Satan, not by breaking his head, but by letting him break His heart. Third, He would make the cross the magnet by which He would draw all people to Himself: "But I, when I am lifted up from the earth, will draw all men to myself" (John 12:32). His choice was made – and hopefully, ours is also. No longer will we lie on the edge of life's furrow – "a corn of wheat afraid to die" – but willingly roll over into the dark channel of death, knowing, as we do, that from our death will come a life that is well-pleasing to God – fruitful, profitable and productive. Afraid to die? No – afraid to live. For life that is not preceded by death is a life not worth living.

FURTHER STUDY

Gal. 2:16-21;
Phil.1:21;
John 5:24;
1 John 3:14

1.What was Paul's
great declaration?

2.Can you make that
same declaration?

Prayer

O Father, burn the message into my heart that when I try to save my life, I succeed only in losing it. And help me never to forget that the last word is not death, but life. Thank You, Father. Amen.

Heaven-Sent Revival

On heavens

"For I will pour water on him who is thirsty, and floods on the dry ground ..." (v.3, NKJ)

For reading & meditation – Isaiah 44:1-8

$\mathbf{W}$e begin today a study on what is without doubt one of the greatest themes of Scripture – heaven-sent revival. I say "heaven-sent" because real revival is not something that springs up or out of the normal activities of the Church but something that comes down to us from above.

There are, of course, many different and conflicting views on this subject, so I want to begin by looking at a question which I imagine no Christian will have any difficulty in facing: Has God got something bigger in His heart for us than we are at present seeing? What is your response, I wonder? Those who are privileged to be part of a vibrant church, or are actively involved in evangelism, might respond differently from those who find themselves in a spiritual backwater. But the truth is (in my opinion) that no matter how spiritually alive the community in which you work and worship, God is able to do greater and yet more wondrous things. Our God has reserves of power which we, the Church of this generation, have not fully experienced. Surely every Christian believes that.

FURTHER STUDY

Isa. 58:1-11;
Psa. 36:8; 107:9

1. What does the prophet expose?

2. What does God promise?

Although we must not be unappreciative of the fact that God is obviously sending showers of blessing upon His Church, we must not forget either that the God who sends the showers can also send the floods. In fact, revival is just that – God flooding a locality or a community of His people, stirring up the complacent, and producing the conviction and conversion of a great number of people. It has happened at various times in various places throughout history, and as sure as night follows day it will happen again

Prayer

O Father, while I see the need for a greater outpouring of Your Spirit upon Your Church, my initial prayer is not corporate but personal: Lord, send a revival and let it begin in *me*. In Jesus' Name I ask it. Amen.

Defining revival

"... that times of refreshing may come from the Lord." (v.19)
For reading & meditation – Acts 3:11-26

Today we ask: What is revival? Unfortunately the word has no sharp edges and thus everyone who uses the word has to define what they mean by it. The first time I visited the United States (now nearly forty years ago), I was asked by a minister if I would preach at the "revival" his church would be having in a few weeks' time. I remember being overwhelmed by what I thought was his faith in predicting the exact date of a revival, until I was informed by a friend that in that part of America the term "revival" simply referred to a series of special meetings.

In these studies I am using the word in its classic sense to denote the sudden awesome flood of God's power upon a community of His people. D.M. Panton describes true spiritual revival as "an inrush of divine life into a body threatening to become a corpse". Christmas Evans, a famous Welsh preacher whom God used to stir the nation of Wales on several occasions, had this to say: "Revival is God bending down to the dying embers of a fire just about to go out and breathing into it until it bursts into flame." Quite simply, revival means "to wake up and live".

I know of no better definition of revival than that given by J. Edwin Orr who, in his book *The Second Evangelical Awakening in Britain*, wrote: "Revival takes place when we experience 'times of refreshing from the presence of the Lord'." Whichever way we look at it, revival is life at its best, life in all its fulness, life abundant, life overflowing with the grace and power of God.

FURTHER STUDY

Deut. 11:1-17;
Jer. 3:1–25;
Joel 2:23-27

1. What does the latter (spring) rain symbolise?

2. Why did God withhold the latter rain?

Prayer

O Father, this matter of revival has the feel of the real and the eternal upon it. Awaken within me a deep desire for a "time of refreshing from the presence of the Lord" – personal as well as corporate. In Jesus' Name. Amen

What revival is not

"O Lord, revive Your work in the midst of the years!"
(v.2, NKJ)

For reading & meditation – Habakkuk 3:1-19

As it is vitally important to be quite sure what we are talking about when we use the word "revival", we must spend another day defining it. G. Campbell Morgan, the great preacher of a bygone generation, defined it like this: "Revival is the reanimation of the life of the believer, not the unregenerate as they are 'dead in sin'. There can only be revival where there is life to revive."

Revival always begins, not with the conversion of sinners, but with the reanimation of the people of God. That is why it is a mistake to see evidences of spiritual revival in the crusades where hundreds or thousands of people are converted. Evangelism is the expression of the Church; revival is an experience in the Church. Evangelism is the work man does for God; revival is the work God does for man.

Revival is much greater, also, than the restoration of backslidden Christians. There are times in church life, such as during special conventions, large rallies, conferences, camps and other activities, when large numbers of lethargic Christians make a new and deeper commitment to Jesus Christ. This, of course, is highly desirable and is something for which we ought to be deeply thankful – but it is not revival.

Again, some of the large healing services we hear about, where hundreds of people are healed and wonderful miracles take place, are not a sign of revival. We can see people converted, renewed, restored, healed, and yet these happenings fall short of revival. Revival includes all these things yet surpasses them all.

FURTHER STUDY

Isa. 32:1-33:24;
Psa. 80:18; 119:25;
119:40; 119:50;
119:88

1. What will happen
when revival comes?

2. How will this affect
evangelism?

Prayer

Gracious and loving Father, the more I meditate on this subject of revival, the more I long to experience it. You have visited Your people in times past in great and awesome power. Do it again, dear Lord. Do it again. Amen.

Why we need revival

"… But this happened that we might not rely on ourselves but on God, who raises the dead." (v.9)

For reading & meditation – 2 Corinthians 1:3-14

We have seen that revival is "a time of refreshing from the presence of the Lord". Today we examine the question: Why do we keep on needing such experiences? Why can't we hold on to the spiritual highs when they come and not let them go? Why, for example, did the Christians in Wales during the revival in 1904 allow the fire that swept the Principality to die out?

We can find the answer to these questions by looking more closely at the history of God's people as found in the Scriptures and in the records of the Church. In the Old Testament we see that there were times when God's people were lifted to the heights of spiritual blessing, only to plunge later into spiritual apathy and despair. Even after the great out-pouring of the Spirit at Pentecost the Church one generation later lapsed into coldness so that in Revelation 2 and 3 we see our Lord confronting the seven churches of Asia with the challenge to repent and return to their first love. History tells us that there have been periods when the Church has experienced spiritual decay, for instance in the early Middle Ages, before a time of renewal occurred.

Note carefully what I am now about to say: the cause of all spiritual lapse is rooted in the desire for independence. Initially, when we enter into a new relationship with God, we are conscious of a great sense of dependence upon Him, but unfortunately after a while something rises up within us and clamours for independence. And it is this, more than any other single thing, that causes us to let go of what God gives us.

FURTHER STUDY

1 Kings 18:1-39;
Isa. 35:6-7;
Lam.3:40-42

1. In what way is Elijah's experience a picture of revival?

2. Write out your definition of revival.

Prayer

O Father, help me to look within my own heart today and evaluate to what extent the desire for independence rules my life. Show me, dear Lord, that if I do not crown You Lord of all, I do not crown You Lord at all. Amen.

"The swings of history"

"… They have forsaken me, the spring of living water, and have dug their own cisterns, broken cisterns …" (v.13)

For reading & meditation – Jeremiah 2:4-13

We continue meditating on the thought we touched upon yesterday, that one of the major reasons why we experience a spiritual lapse (and thus need to be revived) is our natural and stubborn commitment to independence. Historians talk about "the swings of history", and as far as the people of God are concerned, no swing is more evident in their history than the swing from dependence to independence.

The reason I have chosen the chapter that is before us today is because it highlights, perhaps better than any other passage in the entire Bible, this matter of independence. Note the charge which God brings against the people of Judah: "But My people have changed their Glory for what does not profit" (v.11, NKJ). This indictment bears down on the fact that the inhabitants of Judah were not as loyal to the Almighty as the pagans were to their own gods – a fact so astonishing to God that He calls on the heavens to bear witness to it (v.12). Next, He indicts them for failing to drink from the fountain of living water which He provides for His people and for turning instead to cisterns that can hold no water (v.13).

FURTHER STUDY

Acts 19:1-41;
Eph 1:15-16;
Rev. 2:1-5

1. What did the Ephesian church need?

2. What was it required to do?

Can you see what had happened to the people of Judah? They had started off in absolute dependence on God – worshipping only Him and drinking from His fresh wells – but after a while they had felt within them the urge to take control of their spiritual lives and manage them as they thought fit. And whenever God's people do this, no matter how bright and seemingly happy their religious life may be, they are desperately in need of revival.

Prayer

O God, how it must grieve You that we Your Church, like Judah of old, start off depending on You, but then hanker to put our reliance on things that are more tangible. Forgive us, dear Father. Forgive me. In Jesus' Name. Amen.

The stepping stone

*"Take words with you and return to the Lord. Say to him:
'Forgive all our sins …'" (v.2)*
For reading & meditation – Hosea 14:1-9

Nothing is more abhorrent to God than to see within His people the desire for self-control and self-dependence. This is not because of any egotism in the Almighty that requires Him to be the boss, but because He knows that when we try to run our lives on our own terms we demean ourselves and fall short of His plans and purposes for us. We must face the fact that we are helplessly dependent and that God and God alone is independent. He can exist without us but we cannot exist without Him.

The periods of revival in the Old Testament came at the high peaks of corporate worship in the life of Israel, when the people acknowledged the fact that they could not successfully run their lives on their own terms but were happy and effective only to the degree that they were dependent upon God. In the chapter before us today we see how God called His people back to dependence upon Him by encouraging them to repent: "Take words with you, and return to the Lord." This means (so I believe): "Have a clear idea of what you are repenting of."

The stepping stone from independence to dependence is always repentance. There is simply no other way that it can be done. That is why in all revivals the issue of repentance becomes paramount. In revival God underlines in a dramatic way the truth that the path to a continuous relationship with Him is through repentance. Never forget this. The key to all change is in a returning to God, for every effort to change must invoke at its core a shift in direction – away from dependence on one's own resources to dependence on the living God.

FURTHER STUDY

2 Chron. 7:1-14;
Joel 2:12; Isa. 55:7

1. When will God heal the land?

2. What is God's promise?

Prayer

Father, I see that if I stumble here, over this matter of dependence and independence, I stumble all down the line. Help me not to deny this issue but to face it and repent of it. I do so now in Jesus' Name. Amen.

Pentecost – the God-given norm

> " 'In the last days, God says, that I will pour out my Spirit on all people." (v.17)

For reading & meditation – Acts 2:5-21

We have been seeing over the past few days that revival means "wake up and live". As you know, whenever the prefix "re" is used before a word, as in re-vival, re-animation, or re-turn, it simply means "back again". Revival, then, is the Christian Church going back again to the God-given norm. And what is that "norm"? I suggest it is nothing less than what happened on the Day of Pentecost.

Picture the scene with me on that first Whitsunday. Thousands of people fill the narrow streets of Jerusalem, drawn to the city for the celebration of the Feast of Pentecost. Spiritually, however, the nation is at an all-time low. Except for Jesus and John the Baptist, no prophet has spoken in Israel for over 400 years. The disciples are gathered in a house in secret expectancy, waiting for the fulfilment of the promise which Jesus had given them ten days earlier: "You will receive power when the Holy Spirit comes on you" (Acts 1:8). Suddenly the Spirit comes and transforms the timid disciples into men who are ablaze and invincible. They in turn go out into the streets and witness in such a powerful way that multitudes are swept into a close and thrilling relationship with God. The very atmosphere is impregnated with divine power to such an extent that one feels anything can happen.

This was the "norm" and this is what the Church returns to whenever a revival comes. Indeed, there is clear evidence for the fact that every revival that has taken place over the centuries the Church has been in existence contains some feature of the Day of Pentecost.

FURTHER STUDY

Hosea 6:1-11;
Psa. 80:7; 85:6

1. What was Hosea's exhortation?

2. What 2 things happen when God revives us?

Prayer

O Father, give us we pray another Day of Pentecost. Open the windows of heaven over all countries and all nations, and pour out Your power. In Christ's Name we ask it. Amen.

Christlike power

*"Up to that time the Spirit had not been given, since Jesus
had not yet been glorified." (v.39)*

For reading & meditation – John 7:32-39

Yesterday we said that the pattern for revival is based on what God did
for His people on the Day of Pentecost. But why could the pattern
not be based on the many revivals we read about in the Old Testament
such as those that took place under Nehemiah, Hezekiah or even David?

I believe it was because the Old Testament revivals, while powerful
and reformative, did not contain enough ingredients on which to establish a norm. The Holy Spirit – always the prime agent in any revival –
operated in a limited way. His ministry was special, temporary and inter-
mittent. He came and went, providing temporary infusions of power for
temporary tasks. Also in Old Testament times He came upon people
from the outside as opposed to residing permanently on the inside. It
was said of Samson: "And the Spirit of the Lord began to move him at
times in the camp of Dan" (Judg. 13:25, AV). Yet another reason why the
Spirit's ministry was limited in the Old Testament is the fact there was no
perfect vehicle through whom He could reveal Himself.

The passage before us today draws all these strands of truth together when it tells us that the Spirit could not be fully given until Jesus had
been glorified. Why should this be so? It was because
only through the life and death of Jesus could God's
power be properly seen and understood. Eternal
power must be seen not only in the context of signs,
wonders and miracles, but at work on a cross, dying,
suffering and overcoming sin. The power that fell at
Pentecost, if it is to be the pattern for the centuries to
come, must not be just power – but *Christlike* power.

FURTHER STUDY
John 16:1-16; 6:63; 15:26; Rom. 8:11
1. List several things Jesus said concerning the Holy Spirit.
2. What did Paul say concerning the power of the Holy Spirit?

Prayer

O Father, how can I ever sufficiently thank You for sending Jesus to reveal the truth
about the Holy Spirit, as well as about You? I see now so clearly that not only are
You a Christlike God but the Spirit is a Christlike Spirit. I am so grateful. Amen.

Sanity as well as sanctity

"Let this mind be in you which was also in Christ Jesus ..."
(v.5, NKJ)

For reading & meditation – Philippians 2:1-11

We saw yesterday that the Holy Spirit could not be given until Christ had come to fix the content of the Spirit and make clear to people just what kind of Spirit He is. Jesus reveals not only the nature of the Father but also the nature of the Spirit. If God is a Christlike God, then the Spirit is also a Christlike Spirit.

Men and women have some strange ideas about the Holy Spirit and the way He works in human lives. Over the years I have met some fanatical people in the Church who have claimed that the Holy Spirit has been prompting them to do things which quite clearly were downright absurd, even bizarre. I remember talking to a man some years ago who told me the Holy Spirit had instructed him to leave his wife and go and live with another woman. Clearly his understanding of the nature of the Spirit needed correction.

The nature of the Spirit is determined by what we see in Jesus Christ. This is very important, for in some parts of the Church people have made the Spirit into someone who appears to be peculiar. Why are so many Christians afraid to surrender to the Holy Spirit? They think that to do so will expose them to emotionalism or make them off-balance. The fact that Jesus has fixed the content and nature of the Spirit guarantees that when we surrender to the Holy Spirit we will be made like Christ. If this is not the case then we are not under the guidance of Holy Spirit but some other spirit. Christ is not only sanctity – He is also sanity.

FURTHER STUDY

Acts 2:1-47;
Isa. 40:31;
Zech. 4:6

1. List 7 results of the Spirit's outpouring.

2. How do these relate to revival?

Prayer

Lord Jesus, I am so grateful that You have clarified once and for all the nature and character of the Holy Spirit. Help me never forget that He is like You, and when He comes, He comes to make me like You – balanced and sane and poised. Amen.

"In My Name"

*"But the Counsellor, the Holy Spirit, whom the Father will
send in my name, will teach you all things ..." (v.26)*

For reading & meditation – John 14:15-31

We continue with the thought we considered yesterday, that some people have strange ideas about the work and nature of the Holy Spirit. I once knew a minister who unfortunately had fallen into the grip of alcohol and could not break free. Instead of admitting the bondage he was in and seeking help and support from his fellow Christians, he rationalised the problem and said his heavy drinking opened him up to the Holy Spirit because it lifted his inhibitions and made him more susceptible to divine revelation. I suggested that all that was happening to him was that he was getting drunk. He replied: "Ah, alcohol makes some people drunk, but me it makes more available to God." What nonsense!

How thankful we ought to be that through Christ the nature and content of the Holy Spirit has been fixed. The Holy Spirit is like Jesus. As our text for today says, He is given in Christ's Name. This is why God could only give the Holy Spirit sparingly to people in Old Testament times; he waited until Jesus had fixed the content and character of the Spirit. It is only in Jesus that we see ultimate character revealed.

So take a good look at Jesus before you take a good look at the Holy Spirit, and then you will come out with the right perspectives. There was nothing weird or strange or unbalanced about Jesus. He never laid stress (as do some modern-day Christians) on getting guidance through visions and dreams. He received His guidance through prayer and waiting upon God, as you and I should. Visions and dreams may have their place in the Christian life, but not an unbalanced place.

FURTHER STUDY

1 Cor. 2:1-13;
Luke 12:12;
1 John 2:27

1. What was Paul's testimony?

2. List 5 things the Holy Spirit has taught you.

Prayer

Father, once again I want to thank You for clarifying for me the content and character of the Holy Spirit. Help me not to expect You to exercise or demonstrate in my life any power that is not power Jesus would have exercised or demonstrated. Amen.

Pentecost – the only pattern

"… the place where they were meeting was shaken. And they were all filled with the Holy Spirit …" (v.31)

For reading & meditation – Acts 4:23-37

We continue exploring the thought that Pentecost, and not the Old Testament revivals, is God's norm for the Church. It is imperative that we grasp this, because when they are praying for revival many Christians set their sights on happenings in the Old Testament. But while these contain interesting and helpful insights, they ought not to become our pattern.

As we have seen, the pattern for revival is Pentecost. The Spirit could not have been fully given in the Old Testament dispensation as this would have set a wrong pattern, and for the same reason He could not have been given in the day of our Lord's humiliation. The Spirit could only be given in the time of Christ's triumph – after He had returned to the eternal throne – for that alone was the right pattern. That is why our prayers for revival and our expectation of it must be based on Pentecost – the greatest manifestation of the Holy Spirit the world has ever known.

Do not be swayed by those who tell you that Pentecost was a one-off experience which God does not want to repeat. As I have said, throughout the history of the Church every revival that has taken place has contained one or more of the ingredients of Pentecost. In some the dominant feature has been conviction of sin; in others, abounding joy; and in others, amazing miracles brought about through supernatural power. If God sees fit to send another revival to the world, or parts of the world, perhaps the next one will contain all the ingredients of Pentecost. I don't know about you, but this is something I find myself longing for with all my heart.

FURTHER STUDY

Acts 19:1-41;
Ezek. 36:27;
Acts 10:44-46

1. When the Holy Spirit fell on the 12 men, what were some results in their lives?

2. How did this affect the community?

Prayer

O Father, let my longing for another Pentecost be translated into a deeper and closer walk with You – by prayer, meditation on the Scriptures and sharing with others the concept of Your greatness and power. In Jesus' Name. Amen.

What Pentecost produced

*"And suddenly there came a sound from heaven, as of a
rushing mighty wind …" (v.2, NKJ)*

For reading & meditation – Acts 2:1-4

By now it should be clear that revival is an extraordinary work of God producing extraordinary results among a large group of people. It is vitally important that we see it in these terms, otherwise we will fall for the popular notion of calling any unusual activity of the Church by the name "revival".

Consider with me what the Day of Pentecost produced. First, it produced extraordinary physical manifestations – "a rushing mighty wind" and "divided tongues, as of fire". Almost every revival in history contains accounts of extraordinary physical manifestations. In the 1859 Ulster revival people would fall to the ground in the streets or the fields and would lie there motionless for hours. So astonishing were the physical phenomena that crowds gathered just to see these manifestations take place and many were converted as they witnessed God at work.

The Day of Pentecost also produced extraordinary preaching. One sermon preached by Peter resulted in 3,000 souls coming into the kingdom. Sometimes, today, it takes 3,000 sermons to bring one soul into the kingdom! In revival, preachers experience a strange and extraordinary power pulsing through their sermons. My grandfather, who was converted in the Welsh revival of 1904, told me that many of the ministers of Wales took on a new eloquence and power during the days of revival which quite astonished those who had hitherto listened to them. You may have heard some great preaching in your time, but believe me, it is nothing compared to what one hears when revival comes again.

Simple statements bristle with power; it is preaching from hearts set on fire.

FURTHER STUDY

Acts 16:25-40, 4:31;
8:39; 9:3-4; 12:7

1. List some of the
extraordinary events
of the early Church.

2. What is the last
supernatural event
you remember
witnesssing?

Prayer

O Father, while it is You my heart longs after, not powerful manifestations, I see how these things can make people in the world sit up and take notice. So for their sakes' – do it again, dear Lord. Do it again. Amen.

Detained before the Eternal

*"No-one else dared join them, even though they were highly
regarded by the people." (v.13)*

For reading & meditation – Acts 5:1-16

Another outcome of Pentecost was an extraordinary sense of God's
holiness. Something of this is undoubtedly present in the Church at
all times but when revival comes it is greatly heightened. So great was
the sense of God's holiness in the early Church that, as our text for today
tells us, it was felt even by those who were outside. It would be impossible, I think, to find any revival in history where an extraordinary sense
of God's holiness has not been present. During the days of the revival in
the United States under Charles Finney the sense of God's holiness
became so overwhelming that the entire congregation of 500 rose up as
one crying out, "O God, save us – or destroy us."

Yet another outcome of Pentecost was an extraordinary interest in
prayer and in the reading of the Scriptures. Prior to Pentecost, the disciples, Jews to a man, no doubt spent a good deal of time in prayer and the
perusal of the Scriptures. After Pentecost, however, both prayer and the
study of the Scriptures took on a new and greater importance. The disciples agreed among themselves to hand over their administrative
responsibilities to others in order that they might give themselves
continually to prayer and the study of the Word (Acts
6:2-4).

In revival Christians find no activity more mean-
ingful than praying and reading the Scriptures. Even
those who gave time to prayer and daily Bible reading
prior to revival find themselves gripped with a new
spiritual interest and desire. As they read the Word
they discover that they do not want to pull away. They
are, as Moffatt translates, "detained in the presence of
the Eternal" (1 Sam. 21:7).

FURTHER STUDY

Acts 5:1-11; 8:9-25;
9:31; 10:2

1. What was the sin
of Ananias and
Sapphira?

2. How did the
apostles maintain
holiness in the
Church?

Prayer

Father, the more my mind ponders the great things You are able to do, the more my
heart cries out: "Do it again dear Lord." But don't let my desire to see the extraordinary things blind me to the joys of the "ordinary". In Jesus' Name I pray. Amen.

Dejected melancholics?

"So there was great joy in that city." (v.8)
For reading & meditation – Acts 8:1-8

Yet another outcome of Pentecost was extraordinary fervour and excitement. One has only to read the pages of Acts to feel the throb of excitement and joy that characterised the early disciples. It surfaces in many places, one of which is the text before us today.

The early Church was excited about everything that was connected with God and His kingdom. They were excited about Jesus, about the coming of the Spirit, about the establishment of His kingdom, and about the promise of His coming again. They were gripped by an intense earnestness and a spirit of expectation. The God who had raised up Jesus from the dead had raised them also from their own graves of sin. The power that had elevated Christ to the heavens and placed Him at the right hand of the Father was working in them with all its quickening might.

This is also the way it is in times of revival. Once people have repented of their sins and found peace with God there is invariably extraordinary joy. Let no one think that revival is associated with heaviness and gloom. There is always a period of mourning for sin but this is soon followed by waves of endless delight. It is surely amongst the most tragic misrepresentations of truth that historians should write that in times of revival Christians act like dejected melancholics. The reality is that in revival Christians, like their brothers and sisters in the first century, have to defend themselves against the charge of being drunk. Very few of us come under that dark suspicion nowadays, but it is hardly to our credit that there is rarely any need to stress the distinction.

FURTHER STUDY

Acts 4:1-37, 15:3;
16:25; Rom. 14:17

1. How did Peter and
John stir things up?

2. What was the
response?

Prayer

O Father, as far as it is possible outside of the great wave of revival, let me be gripped with the same spirit of fervour and excitement that pervaded the early Church. For Your own dear Name's sake I ask it. Amen

"The shop is always open"

"So, because you are lukewarm – neither hot nor cold – I am about to spit you out of my mouth." (v.16)

For reading & meditation – Revelation 3:14-22

Having examined some of the ingredients of a spiritual revival we consider now arguments advanced by those (and there are many) who believe that revival is an irrelevant issue in today's Church. Some say the Church is essentially a religious institution not wholly unlike the institutions of law and medicine. And just as the institutions of law and medicine have the resources to meet the needs of those who wish to draw upon them, so also has the Church. The exponents of this view say that the Church possesses everything we need to live an effective life – sacraments, hallowed forms of worship, hymns, fellowship, and so on. If someone is spiritually sick, so they say, all that person has to do is make their way to the Church and they will find there the medicine they need for their soul.

Emyr Roberts and Geraint Davies in their booklet *Revival and Its Fruit* rightly take issue with this view and say of it: "In this sense the Church exists independently of the congregation; if nobody calls, the shop is always open." There can be little doubt that one's view of revival depends on one's view of the Church. Those who see the Church as an institution rather than a community of people brought into being and maintained by the Holy Spirit and the Word will regard revival as irrelevant.

But what is the Church? It is not a building but a body made alive by the Holy Spirit. And the secret of her survival is in continually opening herself to the Spirit who gave her life. She was not only born of the Spirit but survives and thrives by the Spirit.

FURTHER STUDY

Heb. 1:1-14; 8:4-6;
1 Cor. 10:11;
2 Pet. 2:6

1. Why has God given us a historical account of the Church?

2. What is the significance of a shadow?

Prayer

Father, I see that unless the red blood of the Spirit's energy and power flows through the veins of the Church she becomes weak and faint and anaemic. Give us, oh give us, a greater flow of Your life and power. Start in me today. Amen

Too cramped for comfort

"…where the Spirit of the Lord is, there is liberty."
(v.17, NKJ)

For reading & meditation – 2 Corinthians 3:1-18

We continue looking at the view of the Church as a religious or divine institution. Those who see the Church in this light believe (as we said) that the Church exists independently of the congregation. It is easy to see how anyone holding this view of the Church will have little interest in the subject of spiritual revival. They will be interested not in commotion or fervency, but in order and stability. They will not merely regard revival as irrelevant, but as downright messy, even injurious. It interferes with the smooth functioning of the services and cuts across the well-established forms and ceremonies.

The revivals of the past have always been opposed by those who have seen the Church as an institution, for the work of the Spirit cannot be brought under human control. A revival can be untidy and undignified, with people crying out in the midst of a sermon, or striking up a hymn at a seemingly inappropriate time. Whenever institutional Christianity has been faced with a movement of the Spirit that did not fit into its preconceived ideas of how the Church should function, it has immediately set its face against it.

During the Middle Ages, when the Church as an institution was at its strongest, the Spirit tried to break in and reveal Himself to His people, but as history clearly records, the leaders resisted these breezes from the Spirit. As a result, those who felt the Spirit's touch abandoned the institutional church and met together to enjoy Spirit-directed activity and worship. I do not think God despises institutional Christianity; it's just that sometimes it gets too cramped for comfort, and He has to move out.

FURTHER STUDY

Matt. 9:16-17;
Acts 5:12-42; 8:6;
Isa. 61:10;
1 Pet. 1:8

1. What did Jesus teach?

2. What does revival bring with it?

Prayer

O Father, help me to have a right view of the Church for I see that the way I look at this, and every, issue affects all my attitudes. And help me to take Your way, even though it cuts across my nature. Amen

"The pulse beat of all we do"

"So [Samson] ... said, 'I will go out as before, at other times ...' But he did not know that the Lord had departed from him." (v.20, NKJ)

For reading & meditation – Judges 16:1-22

We continue examining the view that the Church is a religious institution. The dictionary defines the word "institution" as "an establishment for the cure of souls". In a sense then, the Church is an institution, but it is not *essentially* an institution. Essentially it is a body through which life and energy must continuously flow. And the life that must flow through the Church is the life that comes from the Spirit. He and He alone gives life. I say "He" for the Holy Spirit is more than an influence. He is a Person who guides, counsels, cleanses, empowers, directs and, most of all, just abides with us. An impersonal influence, an "it", doesn't do that.

Have you ever wondered why it was that at Pentecost the Holy Spirit did not fall in the Temple but in a house? I have thought about this for many years and for what it is worth my conclusion is this: if the Holy Spirit had been given in the Temple, then His coming would be associated with a sacred place, sacred services and sacred occasions. The Holy Spirit came in the most common place – a home. He is not given for special "spiritual" occasions, but for all occasions – for all life.

FURTHER STUDY

Acts 9:1-21;
Gen. 32:24-30;
1 Sam. 16:7; 11:13

1. Why was Saul an unlikely candidate to meet with God?

2. Why was the Damascus road an unlikely place?

The Holy Spirit is not a spiritual luxury to be imported into the unusual but a spiritual necessity at work in the usual. He is to be the pulse beat of all we do – the Life in our living. And when He is absent or not permitted to have full control, the Church, like Samson in our text today, might shake itself and make a great fuss but will accomplish nothing.

Prayer

Gracious and loving Father, I am so grateful that I do not have to wander from sacred place to sacred place in search of Your Spirit. You come down to me wherever I am and turn all my seculars into sacreds. Amen.

A scandal to Christianity

"Do not quench the Spirit." (v.19, NKJ)
For reading & meditation – 1 Thessalonians 5:12-22

Today we look at another argument advanced by those who think revival is an irrelevant issue. It is sometimes stated in this fashion: "A religious revival is nothing more than a manifestation of crowd hysteria." For example, one critic of the Welsh revivals says: "Welsh people are easily moved. Their fiery nature and love of singing makes them easy prey to the emotional and the melodramatic." There is some truth in those words of course, but it takes more than emotionalism to explain the fact that during the 1904 revival in Wales crime dropped to such a degree that many of the courts were closed and some of the public houses went out of business.

Peter Price, a strong critic of the Welsh revival, saw in it nothing more than tumult, noise, play acting and imitation. Those who believe that religious worship should not contain any show of emotion are offended by the ferment of spiritual revival. Thomas Morgan, a nonconformist minister writing about the Methodists of his day said: "It appears to all true and serious Christians that they [the Methodists] are stark mad and given to a spirit of delusion, to the great disgrace and scandal of Christianity."

But those who condemn revival for what they call its extremes of emotion would do well to reflect on those occasions in Scripture when men and women appear to be beside themselves in the presence of God. Whilst we must not hesitate to condemn all excess of emotion we must make equally sure that we do not quench the Spirit by our intellectualism and our unwillingness to accept the supernaturalism that is everywhere portrayed in the Scriptures.

FURTHER STUDY

Acts 4:13-22; 5:12-16; 14:1-18

1. How did the rulers, elders and scribes react to the early disciples?

2. What effect did this have?

Prayer

O God, help me not to be one who quenches Your Spirit. Whatever it may be that causes me to draw back from asking and believing for greater and bigger things, then root it out of me today. In Jesus' Name I ask it. Amen.

The poorer language

*"But the natural man does not receive the things of the
Spirit of God ..." (v.14, NKJ)*

For reading & meditation – 1 Corinthians 2:6-16

We spend another day examining the objection we looked at yesterday, that revival is merely a manifestation of crowd hysteria. One
eyewitness of a revival meeting in Anfield Road Chapel, Liverpool, in
1905, says: "... crowds were pressing against the chapel doors trying to
push their way in, elderly ladies were climbing over the railings to get to
the door and falling on the others, and some were being thrown inside
by the police like sacks of flour."

Critics who read such reports ask: "Is there any difference between
the religious madness seen in times of spiritual revival and the frenzies
and ecstasies associated with the rock and pop groups of the present
day?" On the surface there appears to be little difference; the immediate
sensations and the conscious nervous impressions may be very similar.
But, as C.S. Lewis pointed out in *Screwtape Proposes a Toast*, the tongues
phenomenon on the Day of Pentecost might also have appeared to an
onlooker to be nothing but an expression of nervous excitement or hysteria.

When we try to express the spiritual through the natural it is like
translating from a richer to a poorer language. In the
poorer language you have to use the same word to
express more than one meaning, and it is the same
when you try to express the richer world of the spirit
through the poorer medium of the physical frame. We
have only laughter to express both ribald revelry and
godly joy; we have only tears to express the most selfish, worldly grief and the most godly sorrow. Therefore
we must not be unduly surprised that spiritual rejoicings are mistaken for rejoicings of a very different kind.

FURTHER STUDY

Dan 3:13-30;
Num. 22:21-35;
Ex.7:20-21;
Acts 28:1-6

*1. How did
Nebuchadnezzar
respond to the
manifestation of
God's power?*

*2. In what ways did
God reveal Himself?*

Prayer

Gracious and loving Father, give me that inward look, the ability to think through
and see the reason for things. Quicken my spirit so that I am able to recognise the
truth. In Jesus' Name I pray. Amen.

An excitement going somewhere

"One generation will commend your works to another ..."
(v.4)

For reading & meditation – Psalm 145:1-13

I remind you that the question we are looking at is this: Is revival a man-ifestation of crowd hysteria? We have seen that though on the surface there may appear to be little difference between the scenes reported at meetings where revival has broken out and the frenzy and excitement observed in many of today's pop and rock concerts, underneath there are great differences.

Let me deal with just one difference – the matter of final outcome. A crowd coming together for a pop concert experiences a high degree of emotion and excitement, but what does it result in? A family member of mine who is not a Christian and who attended a pop concert said to me afterwards: "It was tremendously exciting being there but the trouble is, the excitement doesn't go anywhere." Compare this with the excitement and fervour that was evident on the Day of Pentecost. It was excitement and fervour that went somewhere.

Charles Foster Kent says: "On the Day of Pentecost this pent up feel-ing broke out into an irresistible wave of spiritual enthusiasm that marked the beginning of the world-wide Christian missionary move-ment." I have a little problem with his phrase, "a pent up feeling broke out into an irresistible wave of spiri-tual enthusiasm", for it was not an enthusiasm worked up by circumstances but an infusion of the Holy Spirit. However, he is right when he says it "marked the beginning of the world-wide Christian missionary movement". When God moves in revival power the fervour and excitement goes somewhere – it influ-ences and affects not just the present but also the com-ing generations.

FURTHER STUDY

Psa. 33:11; 45:17;
72:5; 79:13;
Acts 2:1-21

1. What was the psalmist's testimony?

2. What did Peter reaffirm?

Prayer

O God, whatever excitement or fervour fills my soul as a result of my contact with You – let it go somewhere. Grant that it might not stay in my feelings but be trans-lated into light and energy by which I might walk. In Jesus' Name I ask it. Amen.

Don't get tipped off balance

"… so that the man of God may be thoroughly equipped for every good work." (v.17)

For reading & meditation – 2 Timothy 3:16-4:5

We look now at another argument advanced by those who see the issue of revival as unnecessary and irrelevant. It goes like this: "Encouraging people to believe for a revival serves only to make them spiritually discontent. They become so preoccupied with praying in a revival (which happens only infrequently) that they fail to get on with the task at hand." I have some sympathy for this argument as I too have been concerned for years over those Christians who talk a lot about a coming revival but avoid the day-to-day responsibilities of Christian living.

Many years ago, when I was a minister in Wales, I knew a church whose leaders believed that they should cancel all their activities and hold a prayer meeting every evening of the week until God sent revival to their community. Once committed to this seemingly spiritual but rather misguided idea, they simply had to keep going. They continued holding prayer meetings every evening for over a year, after which the congregation were so tired and bewildered they were obliged to call a halt. The church has never recovered to this day.

FURTHER STUDY

Luke 11:1-13;
2 Chron. 7:14;
Deut. 4:29;
Isa. 55:6

1. What is promised to those who sincerely seek?

2. How did Jesus illustrate this?

Think of all the opportunities the church missed in evangelism and outreach because they had an unbalanced view of the subject of revival. They thought they were being guided, but they failed to see that their commitment to pray every evening until revival came was more an obsessive demand than a deep spiritual desire. When the issue of revival becomes an obsession that tips us off our spiritual balance then there is something seriously wrong.

Prayer

O Father, help me differentiate between the demands that arise out of my own nature and the spiritual desires which arise out of Your inner prompting. For I see that one is an open road; the other a cul-de-sac. In Jesus' Name I pray. Amen.

Is revival an obsession?

*"Now to him who is able to do ... according to the power
that works in us." (v.20, NKJ)*

For reading & meditation – Ephesians 3:14-21

Yesterday we looked at a church whose commitment to pray every evening until revival came was more an obsessive demand than a deep spiritual desire. This raises the question: What is an obsession? An obsession is a repetitive or persistent thought or idea which crowds into the mind and thus helps to relieve one's basic anxiety. It is really a defence mechanism which enables the personality to avoid anxiety by focusing not on the anxious feelings but on the continuing or recurring thought instead.

Some years ago I talked with a young psychologist who told me that he had made a study of the temperaments of people who continually wrote and talked about spiritual revival and had found an interesting pattern – all of them tended to be obsessive. I offered to take the psychological test he had devised and it showed that although I was determined and single-minded, I was also able to change – something an obsessive person cannot do. When I saw he was convinced that I was a fairly well-adjusted person, I talked to him about my own preoccupation with revival. And he said I was the exception that proved the rule!

I have no doubt that by reason of their temperament some Christians can become obsessed about anything – including revival. But I also know that around the world there is a growing army of well-adjusted Christians who are discovering within their hearts at this vital time in history a deepening desire to see God work in great and mighty power. Some may see it as an obsession; I see it as a possession – the thoughts of God taking hold of the thoughts of man.

FURTHER STUDY

1 John 5:1-15;
Rom. 8:25;
Heb. 10:22;
1 Pet. 1:3

1. What motivates us to pray for revival?

2. What does the word "hope" mean in Scripture?

Prayer

O Father, while I do not want to be the victim of an obsession, I most certainly want to be the recipient of divine possession. I give You the freedom to occupy my whole being and to think and feel in me day by day. Amen.

How to wait for revival

"Do business till I come" (v.13, NKJ)
For reading & meditation – Luke 19:11-27

We continue looking at the argument that encouraging people to pray for revival serves only to make them spiritually discontented, so much so that they fail to get on with the tasks at hand. I recognise that this can happen, but it need not happen if clear biblical teaching is given.

Permit a personal testimony here: I have been talking and writing about revival ever since I came into the ministry nearly fifty years ago, and although it has been a major preoccupation of my life (not an obsession!), I have always encouraged people not only to pray for revival but also to be sure that other responsibilities, such as evangelism, fellowship, and Bible study, are not neglected.

In the text before us today our Lord tells us: "Occupy till I come" (v.13, AV). I take this to mean that He wants us to get on with the task of representing Him to the world no matter what may be the conditions around us. Those who say, "Let's give up working and just wait and pray for God to send revival," are violating Scripture. Evan Roberts prayed several hours a day for thirteen years for God to send revival to Wales,

FURTHER STUDY

James 2:14-26;
Heb.10:24;
1 Pet. 2:12

1. What does James admonish us?

2. What are the pagans to see?

but he still went about his daily tasks and made sure that nothing was left undone. The same can be said of others who have figured greatly in past revivals.

A good motto to follow is one that was given to me early in my ministry. Like most mottoes, it has some flaws but it makes good spiritual sense nevertheless: Work as if it all depended on you, and pray as if it all depended on God.

Prayer

Gracious and loving heavenly Father, make me a responsible and balanced person, I pray. Help me to keep up my prayer life without neglecting the other responsibilities that You have given me. I want to keep occupied until You come. Amen

Taking a qualitative look

"The Lord reigns for ever, your God, O Zion, for all generations. Praise the Lord." (v.10)

For reading & meditation – Psalm 146:1-10

We look now at yet another argument advanced by those who see revival as unnecessary. Put in its simplest form it goes like this: fruits of revival do not last.

Admittedly not all who make a profession of faith during a time of revival continue to follow Christ after the fire has subsided. It would be foolish to deny that some of the fruits of revival do not last. Critics claim that out of the many converts won to Christ in the United States during the 1859 revival, only a small proportion could be found in the Church ten years later.

How do we answer this argument? The fruits of revival, I submit, ought to be looked at qualitatively and not just quantitatively. Take, for example, my native Wales. I believe that if it had not been for the revival that stirred the Principality in 1904, the Christian presence there today would be almost non-existent. During revival sometimes only one member of a family is converted, but that one person often influences a whole family.

I regard myself as a product of revival. My grandfather was converted to Christ in the Welsh revival of 1904. He influenced my mother who, together with my father, greatly influenced me to give my life to Jesus Christ. How many families who are now in the Christian Church might be outside had it not been for the fact that some distant relative or ancestor was won to Christ during a time of revival. The duration of a revival may be comparatively short and brief but its results spill over into succeeding generations.

FURTHER STUDY

Acts 8:1-40; 10:44-48; 11:19; 13:3

1. How did the coming of the Holy Spirit spread beyond Jerusalem?

2. What were the results?

Prayer

Father, I am beginning to understand that there is more to revival than I first thought. Thank You for helping me see that the influences of revival never stop – they pass from one generation to the other. I am grateful. Amen.

Fruit that lasts

*"... we will tell the next generation the praiseworthy deeds of
the Lord ..." (v.4)*

For reading & meditation – Psalm 78:1-8

W e continue considering the argument that the fruit of revival does
not last. While it is true that some of the fruit does not last, it is
not true that none of the fruit lasts. When revival is measured qualitatively and not just quantitatively we see that its benefits spill over into
the next generations.

Some of the greatest preachers have been men who were converted
during the time of revival. It was said that at the funeral of Daniel
Rowland of Llangeitho in October 1790 (the man who was greatly used
by God to bring revival to Wales in the eighteenth century) over one
hundred ministers were present, many of them having been won to
Christ during the days of that revival. Sidney Evans, a man who has written a good deal about the subject of revival said: "The revivals of past history have often safeguarded the Christian ministry for a whole generation." And when you consider the influence ministers have in inspiring
young men to enter the ministry you can see that a revival safeguards the
ministry not just for one generation but for many generations.

Then take the staggering number of converts who have been swept
into the kingdom of God during times of revival. The
revival in America in 1859 claimed a million converts
and a further million in the British Isles, 110,000 of
these in Wales alone. These numbers are staggering,
and even allowing for the fact that not all may have
been genuinely converted, it is obvious to a fair-mind-
ed person that the spiritual impact of these large numbers of converts cannot help but have an influence on
future generations.

FURTHER STUDY

Acts 3:11-26; 4:13;
9:29; 14:3; 19:8;
Matt. 7:29

1. How was Peter's
message far-
reaching?

2. What was the
central focus of the
early Church's
message?

Prayer

Father, help me to understand that the river of revival never really stops. It may
disappear for a while but it continues to flow on – underground. Thank You, dear
Father. Amen.

Why things are not worse

*"Let this be written for a future generation, that a people not
yet created may praise the Lord." (v.18)*

For reading & meditation – Psalm 102:18-28

A lthough the Church of Jesus Christ is sometimes in a sad and sorry state, things might well be worse were it not for the fact that the influence of previous revivals still reverberates in our midst. The same, I think, can be said of the secular world. Here in the British Isles our society is in a bad way, morally and spiritually, but I believe things would be much worse were it not for the continuing influence of the great revivals of history.

This must not be taken to mean that the prayer life and godly living of present-day Christians make no contribution to our world, for clearly they do. We the people of God in this present generation provide "the salt and light" that makes it more difficult for evil to prosper. That said, however, the impact of past revivals can still be felt at work in our generation – even in our Houses of Parliament.

Several years ago I was part of a small group who visited the Houses of Parliament to present a specially produced Bible to the prime minister of the day – Harold Wilson. While there, we had the opportunity to talk to several Christian MPs who, among other things, informed us that the origins of many of the laws and statutes by which our land is run can be traced back to the times when our nation was in the midst of spiritual awakenings. I know it is a sobering thought with which to begin the day, but we might well ponder what kind of society we would find ourselves in at this moment were it not for the great spiritual awakenings of the past.

FURTHER STUDY

Acts 16:1-40; 10:19;
Rom. 8:14

1. How did the early Church revival spread to Europe?

2. How were the early apostles directed by the Holy Spirit?

Prayer

Gracious and loving heavenly Father, how can I sufficiently thank You for the way You have revived Your people at intervals throughout history? I sense the past at work right here in the present – and I am grateful. Amen.

Mixed experiences

"But grow in the grace and knowledge of our Lord and Saviour Jesus Christ …" (v.18)

For reading & meditation – 2 Peter 3:10-18

We examine one more reason why some people regard revival as unnecessary and irrelevant – the fact that emotions kindled in revival are not unmixed spiritual experiences. Critics point out that revival brings to the fore not only the spiritual side of human nature but the baser and more carnal side too.

Here again we must listen to the truth in this criticism before attempting to answer it. It is true that in revival the spiritual is often mixed with the carnal. Williams put it like this: "When our soul came to taste the feasts of heaven, the flesh also insisted on having its share, and all the passions of nature aroused by grace were rioting tumultuously." And this was at the high point of the Methodist revival when none can deny that the Holy Spirit was mightily at work. Revival does not abolish in one fell swoop human carnality or the defects of our nature.

In the years immediately following the great outpouring of the Spirit at Pentecost there were clear evidences of carnality at work. Paul's letters are full of exhortations to resist carnality and subdue the works of the flesh. The great revivalist Jonathan Edwards said that if the Corinthian Church had been left to themselves they would have torn themselves to pieces – yet clearly the Spirit was at work in their midst. The apostle greets them as "the church of God … called to be saints" (1 Cor. 1:2, AV).

We will never understand revival until we understand its primary purpose. And what is that? It is not to bring saints to perfection in a day, but to wake up the drowsy.

FURTHER STUDY

Rom. 8:1-17;
Gal. 5:25; 6:8

1. What does Paul teach about the Spirit and the flesh?

2. What new law does he talk about?

Prayer

Father, thank You for reminding me that revival, like conversion, does not produce "instant" saints. Help me understand that although character may come out of a crisis, more often than not it is the result of a process. In Christ's Name I ask it. Amen.

The Delectable Mountains

"… you rejoice with joy inexpressible and full of glory …"
(v.8, NKJ)

For reading & meditation – 1 Peter 1:3-12

We continue considering that the primary purpose of revival is not to bring saints to perfection but to wake up the drowsy. "The cultivation of Christian virtues, and the building of sound and sane Christian character," says Emry Roberts, "is the work, under the blessing of God, of the pastor and the teacher." Sublime and joyous feelings, however, have their place, and these are felt most keenly during revival.

Listen to what one person says about his experience of revival: "Thursday night the 22nd December 1904 will be inscribed in letters of fire on my heart for ever! Don't ask me to describe what I felt that night – I can never do it! All I can say is that I felt the Holy Spirit like a torrent of light causing my whole nature to shake. I saw Jesus Christ – and my nature melted at His feet. I have done nothing since Thursday night but to sing to myself that hymn: 'O, the love of Jesus'. And today I feel I belong to everybody. Oh how the love of Christ expands a man's heart."

We readily agree with the critics of revival that such an elevated emotional state cannot last, and it would be misguided to expect that one could live continuously in the fever of such exaltation. This does not mean, however, that there is no point to such feelings. One supporter of revival says of such experiences: "They are like a walk on the Delectable Mountains from whose heights we are given a glimpse of Mount Zion. We have to walk generally by faith and not by sight but on our pilgrimage it is no small thing to catch a glimpse of the heavenly city and to know a foretaste of its felicity and bliss."

FURTHER STUDY

Eph. 3:14-21;
Isa. 12:3;
John 15:11; 16:20-
28; Psa. 16:11

1. What do we need to
do for our joy to be
full?

2. What was Paul's
prayer?

Prayer

O Father, day by day my appetite for revival is being whetted. I see that only an invasion from heaven can produce the impact to turn both the Church and the world in Your direction. Grant that it may come soon. In Jesus' Name I pray. Amen.

No need for a fire extinguisher

"For Demas, because he loved this world, has deserted me ..." (v.10)

For reading & meditation – 2 Timothy 4:9-18

The fact that Christians can come down from the ecstatic heights experienced during times of great spiritual awakening and lose their first love and joy is not a valid argument against revival. As we have seen, we have only to examine the New Testament to find that following the outpouring of the Spirit at Pentecost there were some who seemed to lose their joy. Yet none can deny the reality and genuineness of the power that surged in their midst.

Critics also draw our attention to the fact that revival can induce great spiritual pride – especially in the young. Revival history contains many accounts of young men being carried away by pride after a high peak in their spiritual experience. William Williams says of one: "He was a raw youth whom no one would entrust to shepherd his sheep and is riding high in a boldness of spirit much superior to old ministers who have borne the burden and heat of the day." But then, were there not such people in the Church that emerged after the Day of Pentecost? In one place Paul warns against appointing a novice in the faith to office in the Church, "... lest being puffed up with pride he fall into the same condemnation as the devil" (1 Tim. 3:6, NKJ). It is a failing that must be expected and guarded against.

Revival is full of dangers – let us not argue against that – but all the dangers can be handled through the principles set forth in the Word of God. When a coal falls out of the fire no reasonable person rushes for a fire extinguisher. They simply pick up the tongs and return the coal to the grate.

FURTHER STUDY

1 Cor. 4:15-21;
Prov.11:2; 28:25;
Rom. 14:17

1. How did Paul describe the kingdom of God?

2. How did he describe himself?

Prayer

O Father, help us as Your Church not to draw back from praying for revival because of the obvious dangers that accompany it. Show us that when we keep close to You we are equipped to handle anything that comes. Thank You dear Father. Amen.

Getting ready for revival

*"… exhorting one another, and so much the more as you see
the Day approaching." (v.25, NKJ)*

For reading & meditation – Hebrews 10:19-25

We spend a final day reflecting on the argument that the emotions kindled in revival are counter-productive to an effective Christian life. The answer, as we have seen, is that this can be so – but it need not be. When sound Christian teaching is available to channel the emotion seen in times of revival into productive purposes, then the sky's the limit.

Many who witnessed the 1904 Welsh revival say that it could have continued longer and made an even greater spiritual impact if there had been more teachers to lead the people into the deeper things of God. When I first learned this (just after becoming a Christian in my mid-teens), I immediately committed my life to doing everything I could to ensure that future revivals would not suffer for lack of teaching resources.

In 1965 I founded the Crusade for World Revival (now called CWR) with the primary objective of encouraging people to pray for both personal and corporate revival and deepen their understanding of the Word of God. Other objectives have been added to these over the years, but the primary goal is still that of helping God's people prepare for revival. I like to think that day by day as you follow these meditations and read the set Scriptures, you are not only building up your own spiritual resources but preparing yourself for a deeper and more effective ministry to others – now and in the future. Who knows but that in addition to your present and daily ministry for Christ you may have a part in establishing someone who has come to know Him in a time of revival?

FURTHER STUDY

2 Tim. 2:1-15;
Heb. 3:13;
Rom. 15:1

1. What was Timothy
to do with the things
he heard?

2. What was he to do
personally?

Prayer

O Father, how wonderful it would be to witness a revival – and have a part in it. But whether I will or not, help me take the knowledge I gain from You day by day – and pass it on. In Jesus' Name I ask it. Amen.

What good is light without life?

"... when the enemy comes in like a flood, the Spirit of the Lord will lift up a standard against him." (v.19, NKJ)

For reading & meditation – Isaiah 59:9-21

From what we have been saying, it is quite clear that revival brings not only unlimited blessing but very real dangers. It is also clear that despite the dangers, the very survival of the Church depends on the timely and reviving work of the Holy Spirit.

There are some who think the Church does not need revival. A magazine article I read a few years ago said: "The Christian Church is stronger now than she has ever been throughout her entire history. Numerically, there are more people in the Church today than at any other period of her existence. She is well represented in almost every nation under the sun and if she would become aware of her strength and size and draw upon it she could dominate the world and have it sitting at her feet."

The words sound good but what are the facts? The Church may be numerically strong and well represented in different parts of the world but since when has her strength been in her numbers? The source of her strength and power is in the Holy Spirit. Without His presence in the Church, energising and reviving, there may be plenty of light, but little life. And it is *life* – the life of the Spirit – which the Church so easily loses.

Generally speaking, the Church has been good at protecting its theological position, but not so good at preserving life. That is why at certain times and in certain generations God mercifully breaks in upon His people to revive and refresh them by the Spirit. In every century the Christian Church has stood in need of a new invasion of that life. But perhaps never so much as now.

FURTHER STUDY

Matt. 23:23-39;
2 Tim. 3:5;
Isa. 29:13

1. How did Jesus deal with pharisaism?

2. How did Paul put it?

Prayer

Father, help me see that no matter what else Your Church has, if it does not have life – the life of the Spirit – then it is nothing more than a religious club. Breathe upon us for we want not only to be living – but lively. In Jesus' Name. Amen.

How do revivals begin?

"Will you not revive us again, that your people may rejoice in you?" (v.6)

For reading & meditation – Psalm 85:1-13

Now that we are at the half-way point in our meditations on revival we pause for a moment to remind ourselves of some of the points we have been considering. Revival, we have said, is God bending down to the dying embers of a fire just about to go out and breathing into it until it bursts again into flame. The pattern for all revivals is Pentecost, which was an extraordinary visitation of God accompanied by extraordinary happenings. God is after the recovery of a fully-orbed New Testament Christianity and He has invariably used revivals to this end. The reason why we need revival is because the Church turns from its first love and falls into decline. And when revival comes it achieves, sometimes in a few weeks, what could never have been achieved in years of normal Christian activity.

The next question we must consider is this: How does a revival begin? Is it something that forms in the minds of devoted Christian people and is then brought into being through powerful intercessory prayer? Or is it something that originates in the mind of God and comes down to earth irrespective of the desires or the prayer life of His people?

I have no hesitation in saying that in my opinion revival begins in the mind of God. It is something that God plans; men and women have little to do with it. There are many things that Christians, by dedicated and committed spiritual effort, can bring to pass in the Church, but revival is not one of them. For instance, evangelism, preaching, teaching, and counselling is work that we do for God; revival is work that God does for us.

FURTHER STUDY

Ezek. 18:1-32;
Isa. 55:7;
Acts 17:30

1. What does God demand before He will send revival?

2. What does this involve?

Prayer

Father, let the wonder of Your sovereignty and power sink deep into my soul today. Help me see how much bigger and greater You are than my imagination could ever conceive. In Christ's Name I pray. Amen.

The place of prayer

"Ask the Lord for rain in the time of the latter rain ..."
(v.1, NKJ)

For reading & meditation – Zechariah 10:1-8

We continue considering the question: How do revivals begin? A revival is a sovereign act of God in the sense that it is initiated by Him and not by the Church. It is at this point – the sovereignty of God – that Christians tend to differ in their thinking. One school of thought says: "Revival is a sovereign act of God and there is absolutely nothing that man has to do with it. God sends revival when He wills and does not consult or confer with any of His creation." Many of the great Welsh revivalists, such as Christmas Evans, Daniel Rowlands, John Elias, Thomas Charles Edwards, and John Evans subscribed to this view.

Another school of thought says: "Revival can happen any time the Church wants it – providing she is willing to pay the price." The great revivalist Charles Finney believed this. "The Church," he said, "can have a revival whenever it wills, for revival is like a crop of wheat – the farmer sows and then in due course the wheat comes up. When we are willing to sow the seeds of prayer and travail in the red furrows of God's fields then as sure as night follows day – we will have a revival."

The truth, so I believe, lies somewhere between these two views. Revival is a sovereign act of God in the sense that He alone can produce it, but I believe that He deigns to hand over to His people the responsibility of bringing it down from heaven by fervent believing intercession. Every great outpouring of the Holy Spirit – Pentecost included – began in the mind of God but it broke through on earth at the point of passionate and persevering prayer.

FURTHER STUDY

Gal. 6:1-10;
John 12:24;
Eccl. 11:1;
2 Cor. 9:6

1. What is the principle underlying sowing and reaping?

2. How does this relate to revival?

Prayer

O Father, if so much depends upon prayer, then wake me up to its power and its importance. Help me this day to catch a new vision of what it means to be an intercessor. In Christ's Name I ask it. Amen.

Involved in government

*"... that now, through the church, the manifold wisdom of
God should be made known ..." (v.10)*

For reading & meditation – Ephesians 3:1-13

Today we ask: What does it mean when we say that God is sovereign?
Sovereignty simply means to possess supreme power. What we have
to be careful about when we talk of the sovereignty of God is that we do
not fall for the idea (as some have) that this is God's *greatest* attribute;
His greatest attribute is love. And because He is love this means (so I
believe) that He delights to have His redeemed children become involved
with Him in bringing His purposes to pass.

Anyone who writes on the subject of revival has to come to a point
where these two great and important truths – the sovereignty of God and
the involvement of man – have to be harmonised. I am at that point right
now. A way of thinking about this issue which has always satisfied me is
to see these two thoughts like two rails that run from one end of the
Scriptures to the other. One rail is the sovereignty of God and the other,
the involvement of man. If you try to keep to only one rail you finish up
being derailed. Those who focus only on the sovereignty of God
inevitably result in minimising the responsibility of man. And those who
focus only on the responsibility of man end up minimising the sovereignty of God.

When we move along both rails, making sure that
we do not place a disproportionate emphasis on either
truth, then we are more likely to arrive at sound judge-
ments and correct conclusions. God is sovereign but
He is also a *loving* Sovereign and by virtue of this fact
delights to involve His people in the affairs of government.

FURTHER STUDY

Acts 12:1-19;
Luke 1:10;
Acts 1:14; 4:24

1. What was the
result of corporate
prayer?

2. How did the
believers respond to
Peter's appearance?

Prayer

Gracious and loving Father, how can we Your Church sufficiently thank You for the
fact that You love us enough to involve us in Your government? Help us to see that
we are there not because we deserve it, but because You desire it. Amen.

"Except through prayer"

"Devote yourselves to prayer ...." (v.2)
For reading & meditation – Colossians 4:2-15

A single sentence written by the great John Wesley has helped me more than anything else to balance the two great truths we referred to yesterday – the sovereignty of God and the responsibility of man. Here is the statement which Wesley made: "God does nothing redemptively in the world – except through prayer."

Permit me to put into my own words what I think he was saying: whenever God wants to bring His purposes to pass here on earth He does not act arbitrarily, but touches the hearts of praying people and then ushers in His purposes across the bridge of prayer. God may be sovereign but He is not dictatorial or capricious. He can no more act against His nature and the principles He has established in the world than He could make a square circle or an aged infant. There are some things impossible even for God, and acting independently of the principles of prayer is one of them. This is why prayer and revival are so inseparably linked. I know of no revival that is not connected in some way with powerful, believing, intercessory prayer.

This, then, is how I see God's sovereignty and man's responsibility being brought together in harmony: when God decides that in the interests of His people a spiritual revival is necessary, He lays a burden of prayer upon the hearts of His children – it may only be comparatively few – so that their prayers become the bridge across which revival power flows. Let Wesley's famous statement ring in your heart once again: "God does nothing redemptively in the world – except through prayer."

FURTHER STUDY

2 Kings 19:1-37;
Prov. 21:1;
Ex. 17:8-13;
Rev. 19:6

1. What caused Hezekiah to act as he did?

2. How did God show His sovereignty?

Prayer

O God, I see that Your purposes are not arbitrary or capricious but the expression of Your nature – a revelation of Yourself. Amid the splendour of Your majesty I feel a heartbeat – a heartbeat of love. Thank you, dear Father. Amen.

The wider context of revival

*"… if my people … will humble themselves and pray … then will I
hear from heaven and will forgive their sin …"* (v.14)

For reading & meditation – 2 Chronicles 7:12-22

We continue meditating on the question: If revival is a sovereign act
of God (and it is), does this mean that the people of God have no
part to play in it? My answer to that question is a categorical "No".
Revival is a sovereign act of God in the sense that He sends it where and
when He wills, but a study of revivals of the past, both in Scripture and
in the history of the Church, shows that revival always follows the pre-
vailing prayers of God's people.

The central condition of the verse before us today is, "if my people
… pray …". When Evan Roberts was asked the secret of revival he said:
"There is no secret: ask and you shall receive." Matthew Henry, the
renowned Bible commentator, wrote a good deal about this particular
point and summed it up in this powerful statement: "When God intends
a great mercy for His people, the first thing He does is set them a-pray-
ing." God is the only one who can produce revival, but the fervent
believing intercession of His people is the ramp over which it flows into
the Church.

It must be recognised that sovereignty is not the *only* thing at work
in revival – love is also at work. We are dealing with a
God who is beneficent as well as omnipotent. Once we
see revival in this wider context – the context of love
– we begin to understand why God inspires strong
intercessory prayer in the hearts of His people prior to
revival. He just loves His children to be involved with
Him in bringing about His purposes.

FURTHER STUDY

John 15:1-17;
Jer. 29:13;
Mark 11:24;
1 John 3:21-22

1. When can we ask
for whatever we
want?

2. What is one of the
conditions of
answered prayer?

Prayer

O Father, I am grateful that You are a God who not only hears our prayers but
delights to respond to them. Cause our prayers to be Spirit-inspired that we may pray
aright and help build Your Kingdom. In Jesus' Name I ask it. Amen.

The burden of revival

"And the burden of the Lord shall ye mention no more: for every man's word shall be his burden ..." (v.36, AV)

For reading & meditation – Jeremiah 23:33-40

We ended yesterday by saying that God loves His children to be involved with Him in bringing about His purposes, and that it is not in God's nature to ignore the great principle of prayer which He Himself has established in the universe. At the risk of being tedious, let me make the point again: although revival begins in the sovereign purposes of God, it comes into the world through the doorway of believing prayer.

John Wallace, principal of the Bible college I attended prior to entering the ministry, used to say: "Before somebody can experience a blessing, somebody has to bear a burden." He used to illustrate the point in this way: "Before deliverance came to the nation of Israel when they were in Egypt, Moses had to bear a burden. Before the great Temple of God could be built in Jerusalem, Solomon was called to bear a burden. Before the sins of the world could be removed Christ had to bear a burden. Before somebody can experience a blessing, somebody has to bear a burden."

This is a principle that can be traced throughout the whole of the Bible – from Genesis to Revelation. It can be seen at work, too, in the history of all religious revivals. Before God comes from heaven to work in extraordinary ways He places the burden of revival on the hearts of His people. And who does He choose to carry this burden? You can be sure that they will be men and women who are drawn to prayer and understand something of its power and potential. Would you, I wonder, be one?

FURTHER STUDY

Psa. 21:1-13; 38:9; 73:25; Isa. 26:9; Mark 11:24

1. What will God grant to us?

2. How can a desire become a burden?

Prayer

Gracious Father, You know how my heart shrinks from such a great challenge as this. All I can say is – I am willing to be made willing. Help me, dear Father. In Jesus' Name. Amen.

God works through authority

*"... who has blessed us in the heavenly realms with every
spiritual blessing in Christ." (v.3)*

For reading & meditation – Ephesians 1:3-10

Another reason why God takes great care to involve His people when He initiates a revival is because He is committed to working through His Church – not behind her back. I said earlier, you might remember, that our view of the Church will greatly influence our view of revival, and now I must make the point again.

The Church (so I believe) is God's agent in the world through which His purposes are demonstrated. She is here to model the kingdom of God to the world. God is committed to working through her and not around her, and no matter how lethargic His people become, He will not withdraw from that commitment. If God wanted to exercise His sovereignty (and nothing else) then He could burst in upon His Church in times of declension without regard to anyone. But, as we have seen, there are other characteristics in God beside sovereignty – love and respect being just two.

If there is one thing above all others that impresses me about God's dealings with people in the Bible it is the fact that He greatly respects the authority He establishes, even though that authority does not act in the way He desires. It would have been easy for Him to have swept aside the Old Testament kings and priests who failed to do His bidding, but patiently and lovingly He worked to involve them in His purposes. If God did that with His earthly people, Israel, then I cannot conceive of Him doing any less with His heavenly people, the Church. He will make sure the Church is represented and involved in every single spiritual project in the universe.

FURTHER STUDY

Hosea 10:1-15;
Deut. 4:29;
Psa. 105:4;
Isa. 55:6

1. What did the prophet exhort the children of Israel to do?

2. How can we break up our fallow ground?

Prayer

Gracious Father, Your commitment never to go behind the back of Your Church to accomplish Your purposes amazes me. My heart says: a God who works like this can have all there is of me to have. Amen.

"Revival praying"

"Oh, that you would rend the heavens and come down ..."
(v.1)

For reading & meditation – Isaiah 64:1-12

Now that we have seen the place which prayer plays in bringing about revival, without doing any injustice to the sovereignty of God, the next question we must face is this: What kind of praying is it that seems to precipitate a mighty and extraordinary move of God?

A phrase which crops up time and time again in revival literature is the phrase "revival praying". This is a term used to describe the special type of praying which observers have noticed takes place in the months or years preparatory to the outbreak of revival. Over the next few days I want to examine with you some of the characteristics of this phenomenon known as "revival praying". By doing so I hope to deepen our understanding and awareness of this mysterious but important subject.

First, "revival praying" is zealous praying. People pray with fervour and passion. It is not that they look with disdain upon formal prayers but, almost as if they cannot help it, their prayers catch alight and are uttered with what appears to onlookers to be uncharacteristic energy and enthusiasm. They become not only enthusiastic about their prayers but eager in the pursuit of them. They pray whenever they can, wherever they can and with whomsoever they can. Prayer becomes less of a duty and more of a delight. I am sure you have occasionally touched something like this in your own prayer times but prior to a revival it is not something that happens periodically but something that happens regularly, not just in a few scattered places, but generally.

FURTHER STUDY

Joel 2:1-13;
Psa. 34:18; 51:17;
Isa. 66:2;
2 Cor. 7:10

1. How should we turn to the Lord?

2. What does it mean to "rend your heart"?

Prayer

Father, I long to experience more zealousness and passion in my prayer life. I throw open every pore of my being to You today. Move into the whole of my life, but especially my prayer life, and set my prayers on fire. In Jesus' Name I pray. Amen.

The story of Jeremiah Lanphier

"... zeal for your house consumes me ..." (v.9)
For reading & meditation – Psalm 69:1-15

We continue thinking about zealousness, which we said yesterday is one of the characteristics of "revival praying". An example of what I mean by zealous praying comes out of the story of the great revival which hit New York in the middle of the nineteenth century.

On 1st July 1857 a man by the name of Jeremiah Lanphier, described as "a quiet and zealous businessman", took up an appointment as city missionary in the Dutch Reformed Church in New York. He decided to hold a noon-day prayer meeting and distributed a few handbills inviting others to join him during the lunch hour every Wednesday. At the first meeting six people were present. The second week there were twenty and the third week over forty. It was then decided to hold the prayer meeting every day. Within months 10,000 people were gathering in the city every day to pray. Thus began in New York the spiritual awakening which eventually spread through America and in 1859 crossed the seas to the British Isles. Zealous praying – the kind that precedes revival – usually begins with one person in an area and then spreads to others. I know of no revival where this has not happened.

How can we explain this strange "spirit of prayer" that grips God's people prior to revival? What makes them want to be present at as many prayer meetings as they can get to and pour out their hearts in earnest supplication to God? There is only one convincing explanation – it is a supernatural phenomenon. The heart of revival is beyond psychological or sociological explanation. It has been well said that if in prayer we have great intention, then God gives greater attention.

FURTHER STUDY

Acts 3:1-10; 4:24;
12:12; 21:5

1. Where were Peter
and John going?

2. What was the
result?

Prayer

Father, I have already asked You to give me more zealousness in prayer; now I must go further and take it. I reach out with empty hands to receive the fullness of Your Spirit. From now on my prayer life shall be Spirit-taught and Spirit-wrought. Amen.

"Great prayer warriors"

"... I will not let you go unless you bless me." (v.26)
For reading & meditation – Genesis 32:22-31

We look now at the second characteristic of "revival praying" – tenacity and persistence. Read the record of revivals and you will find that this quality is also present. In the days prior to revival people not only pray zealously but they pray persistently. For over a period of thirteen years Evan Roberts prayed for revival to come to Wales. "There was never a day," he says, "when I didn't fling myself before God and cry out for Him to send the Holy Spirit to my native land." Dafydd Owen also prayed every day for over ten years for a great outpouring to come to the Principality. And concerning David Morgan it was recorded "that for ten years before 1858 a petition for the outpouring of the Holy Spirit was never absent from his prayers".

We must recognise that often this persistence was not something that was natural but was given by the Holy Spirit. It was said of Evan Roberts that when he was a boy, "he hardly ever saw anything through and would give up a task most easily".

Listen to what Jonathan Edwards, another great revivalist, had to say about the importance of persistence and perseverance: "It is very apparent from the Word of God that the Lord is wont often to try the faith and patience of His people, when crying to Him for some great and important mercy, by withholding the mercy sought for a season; and not only so but at first to cause an increase of dark appearances. And yet He, without fail, at last succeeds those who continue instant in prayer with all perseverance and will 'not let Him go except He blesses'."

FURTHER STUDY

Luke 18:1-8;
James 5:13-18;
1 Thess. 5:17

1. What did Jesus teach on prayer?

2. What did Elijah demonstrate?

Prayer

O Father, search my heart today and see if there is any hidden thing in me that holds me back from persistent and perservering prayer. Bring it to the light so that I can deal with it. I ask this in Jesus' Name. Amen.

"A revival is on the way"

"And pray in the Spirit on all occasions with all kinds of prayers and requests ..." (v.18)

For reading & meditation – Ephesians 6:10-20

We continue looking at the quality of tenacity or persistence as a component of "revival praying". Prior to a revival this characteristic is seen even in those who were not naturally persistent or tenacious people, and this is fairly clear evidence (so I believe) that something supernatural is at work.

When the news of the American 1857 revival reached the shores of Great Britain many churches (especially those in Northern Ireland and Wales) became gripped with a desire to see the same thing happen here. William Jenkins, the minister of a church in one of the Welsh valleys, said in 1858: "Ever since the news of the outpouring of the Spirit upon the American churches reached our country I longed and prayed that the Lord would, in His infinite mercy, visit poor Wales. I immediately brought the subject before the church and earnestly exhorted them to 'seek the Lord'. I related every fact and incident I could glean ... in order to produce in the minds of my people the desire for a similar visitation. Some of our members prayed and *continued to pray* as I have never heard them pray before. A new burden seemed to press upon their hearts. They became persistent almost to the point of being obsessed. Even before revival came there were no less than eighty-five added to the church in about six months" (italics mine).

Examples of persistent and tenacious praying gripping the people of God prior to a revival can be multiplied. They have made such an indelible mark in history that those who observe their occurrence are able to say with confidence: "A revival is on the way."

FURTHER STUDY

Rom. 8:22-28;
Matt. 26:41;
John 16:24

1. What help do we get in prayer?
2. What did the disciples find?

Prayer

O Father, I cannot help but echo the words of Your disciples: "Lord, teach us to pray." In this area I confess I am weak, but help me see that in You I am able for anything. So I shed my weakness and take Your completeness. Amen.

God – sleeping on the job?

"Awake, O Lord! Why do you sleep?" (v.23)
For reading & meditation – Psalm 44:13-26

A third characteristic of "revival praying" is boldness or directness. Here again I have been struck, as I have read and researched this subject, by the daring and direct language used by God's people when pleading with Him to send revival.

We can see something of this in the verses that are before us today. The psalmist appears to be accusing God of sleeping on the job. Listen to the graphic language used in the Moffatt translation of this passage: "Bestir thyself, Eternal one! Why sleep? Awaken! ah discard us not for ever! Why art thou hiding thy face, forgetful of our woe and our distress? For our soul is bowed to the dust." This language of the psalmist is forceful and direct but it is the kind of attitude and language that prevails with God.

Notice I say *attitude* as well as language. You and I can come before God and use similar language but if it is not accompanied by the kind of holy desperation that the psalmist felt, then it will sound false and hollow – even impertinent. Such was the spiritual decline around him that it looked to the psalmist as if God was asleep and needing arousing. His

FURTHER STUDY

1 John 3:16-22;
Heb 4:16; 13:6

1. Why can we come to God with confidence?

2. What can we say with confidence?

deep concern over the declining conditions with which he was surrounded made his language appropriate and permissible. When we feel as strongly about the moral and spiritual bankruptcy that surround us as the psalmist felt in his day, then we can speak as strongly as he did. We dare not copy the words unless we are also prepared to copy the psalmist's deep spiritual concern.

Prayer

O God, my concern at this moment is not so much whether You are awake but whether I am awake – awake to the urgent needs that lie all around me. Wake me up, dear Lord, and help me pray with boldness. In Jesus' Name I ask it. Amen.

Prayer God delights to answer

*"O Lord God Almighty, the God of Israel, rouse yourself to
punish all the nations ..." (v.5)*

For reading & meditation – Psalm 59:1-8

We must spend another day looking at this quality of boldness which seems to be a characteristic of all "revival praying". There is a fine line, of course, between impertinence and concern. To some it may appear that the psalmist has crossed this line. Telling God to rouse Himself hardly seems to be a reverent or respectful way of approaching Him. But, as we said yesterday, it is the spirit underlying the words that makes it permissible.

I have often heard people in prayer meetings try to copy the strong language of the psalmist and other Old Testament characters, but only on a few occasions have I felt that they had the psalmist's same burning concern. And lacking that concern, their prayers came across as empty and hollow. One biographer tells of listening to the great Christmas Evans praying before the outbreak of revival in a certain part of North Wales. This is what he said: "Wake up, O Lord, and shake Yourself. Can't you see what is happening to Your Church? It's shameful that You allow things to go on like this. Do anything – do something – and do it soon "

The biographer went on to say: "Those who heard him caught their breath and wondered why God did not strike him dead for his impertinence. But what they did not know was that Christmas Evans had earned the right to talk to God in this way." He was not just using language – he was expressing through that language the deep concern of his heart. And when those two things combine – passion and daring – you have the ingredients of the kind of prayer that God delights to answer.

FURTHER STUDY

Dan. 10:1-21;
Psa. 65:2; Jer. 24:7

1. How earnest was
Daniel?

2. What does "all
their heart" mean?

Prayer

O Father, once again I have to confess that my feet stumble on the path of prayer. There is so much to learn, so help me over the hard places. This is life and I must learn it. In Jesus' Name I pray. Amen.

"Pleading the promises"

"… Revive me according to Your word." (v.25, NKJ)
For reading & meditation – Psalm 119:25-32

Now we look at a fourth characteristic of "revival praying", which I am calling persuasiveness. As the word is sometimes used to convey the idea of being coercive, permit me to give it a more precise definition. One of my dictionaries defines it thus: "The art of being able to marshall one's arguments in a convincing way so as to leave the other person or persons little or no option." This exactly sums up what I have in mind when using the word in relation to "revival praying".

Here again, when examining the great prayers that precede revival, I have been struck by the way in which the men and women concerned build and develop their arguments on the basis of what God has said in His Word. You might have already noticed in the psalm before us today that the psalmist founds his plea for divine quickening on the fact that God has promised it in the Scriptures: "Revive me according to Your word." Some people call this "pleading the promises" – taking a clear promise which the Lord has made, reminding Him of it and insisting that He be held to it.

Charles Spurgeon, when teaching on prayer, used to say: "Every promise of Scripture is a writing of God which may be placed before Him in reasonable request, 'Do as Thou hast said.' The Creator will not cheat the creature who depends upon His truth; and far more, the heavenly Father will not break His own word to His own child." Our forefathers discovered that prayers which plead the clear promises of a covenant-keeping God are guaranteed success – it is time we discovered it too.

FURTHER STUDY

2 Cor. 3:1-18;
Heb. 10:16;
Rom. 2:14-15; 7:22

1. Where does God want to write His law?

2. How does He do it?

Prayer

Father, the concept that You are a covenant-keeping God fires my faith and energises my spirit as nothing else can. You are showing me a way of prayer that is breathtakingly powerful. Help me know how to use it. Amen.

What is a promise?

*"And now, Lord God, keep for ever the promise you have
made ... Do as you promised ..." (v.25)*

For reading & meditation – 2 Samuel 7:18-29

Yesterday we ended with the thought "prayers which plead promises
are guaranteed success". This raises this question: What is a
promise? A promise has been defined as, "a written declaration that
binds the person who makes it to do or forbear from doing a specified
act." When used of God, it is His pledge or undertaking to do or refrain
from doing a certain thing. Such promises form the basis of the prayer of
faith.

The validity and dependability of a promise rests on the character
and resources of the one who makes it, just as the validity of a bank
cheque depends on the honour and bank balance of the one who signs
it. It is the holy character and faithfulness of God that makes all His
promises credible. "Not one word has failed of all the good promises,"
said King Solomon (1 Kings 8:56). Those who have studied the great
prayers of the Old Testament are struck by the way in which the prayer
warriors continually reminded God of the promises He had made. We
see this, for example, in the passage before us today: "Do as you
promised".

It is not presumptuous to take God at His Word,
providing we are sure that the promise applies to our
particular situation. Note that last statement, for it is
extremely important. The requests in verses 25 and 26
of today's passage are built on the promises in the previous verses. In "revival praying" men and women
stretch their desires to the width of God's promises and
hold God to the pledge He has made that times of
refreshing *shall* come from the presence of the Lord.

FURTHER STUDY

1 Pet. 1:1-9;
Heb. 6:17; 11:17-19

1. What have we
become partakers of
through the
promises?

2. What did Abraham
prove?

Prayer

O Father, I see that this throws open infinite possibilities to me. But I see also the
danger of holding You to a promise that is not relevant or applicable. Give me the
wisdom to know the difference. In Jesus' Name. Amen.

"Are my hands clean?"

"O Lord, we acknowledge our wickedness and the guilt of our fathers ..." (v.20)

For reading & meditation – Jeremiah 14:17-22

A fifth characteristic of "revival praying" is contrition. Even the most casual reader of the Old Testament cannot help but notice that when the leaders of the people approached God with the plea of revival they usually began by acknowledging their own sin and the sins of the people. Jeremiah does this in the passage before us today: "We acknowledge, O Lord, our wickedness and the iniquity of our fathers ... Remember, do not break Your covenant with us" (vv.20-21, NKJ).

Every carefully researched report of revival I have read contains the record of people coming before God prior to the revival and openly confessing their sins. The Hebrides revival which took place in 1949 is a classic illustration of this. A group of people gathered to pray in a barn about twelve miles north of Stornaway. Kneeling in the straw one of them, a young deacon, opened up his Bible and read from Psalm 24: "Who shall ascend into the hill of the Lord? or who shall stand in his holy place? He that hath clean hands, and a pure heart ..." (vv.3-4, AV).

After reading the passage twice the young man said: "Brethren, it is just so much humbug to be waiting thus night after night if we are not right with God. I must ask myself: Is my heart pure? Are my hands clean?" And at that moment something happened. Let Duncan Campbell, the man who wrote the account of the Hebrides revival, finish the story: "God swept into the barn, whereupon the group moved out of the realm of the common and the natural into the sphere of the supernatural. And that is revival."

FURTHER STUDY

2 Cor. 7:1-10;
Psa. 34:18; 51:17

1. What is godly sorrow?

2. Who is the Lord close to?

Prayer

Father, I see that prayer holds challenges for me which only a full and determined commitment can meet. I have come a long way with You, Lord. Now help me go further. In Jesus' Name. Amen.

A sure sign of revival

*"Then I acknowledged my sin to you and did not cover up
my iniquity …" (v.5)*

For reading & meditation – Psalm 32:1-11

We are seeing that prior to revival the prayers of God's people are characterised by contrition and a desire to break with all known sin. The closest I have ever come to witnessing this came during a visit to South Korea in 1958. As you know, Korea has been experiencing religious revival since the beginning of the 60s, but in the year that I was there, although the people were greatly expectant, the Church could not be described as being in revival.

One morning I participated in a 4 am prayer meeting. As I entered the prayer venue – a large school assembly hall – I was conscious that I was about to witness something unusual. The place was crowded and there was a tense reverent expression of attention on every face. There was no singing and at a given signal people knelt for prayer. At first there was silence but soon the people began to pray aloud, one after the other, until within seconds their voices became a crescendo which then stopped as suddenly as it had begun. A man's voice rose in high-pitched tones and my interpreter told me that he was confessing his sins and the sins of the nation. No words of mine can adequately describe the intensity that was in his voice, the agony of his sobs and the penitence that seemed to grip him. Within minutes the same spirit of penitence swept through every heart in the audience – my own included.

I came away from Korea sensing that I had witnessed the first stages of a spiritual revival. When later I heard that revival had broken out I was not surprised. The signs had told me so.

FURTHER STUDY

Luke 15:1-21;
Prov. 28:13;
1 John 1:9

1. How did the prodigal son show penitence?

2. What is the result of confessing sin?

Prayer

O Father, help me never forget that Your Name is called Jesus because You save Your people from their sins. I know I am saved but now I ask – save me to the uttermost. In Christ's Name I pray. Amen.

"Labour pains"

"... I sat down and wept, and mourned for days; and I continued fasting and praying before the God of heaven." (v.4, RSV)

For reading & meditation – Nehemiah 1:1-11

We look now at the sixth and final characteristic of "revival praying": spiritual desperation. My one-time pastor, David Thomas, used to say to me when I was a young Christian: "If ever there is to be another revival in our nation, then it will be borne in on the shoulders of desperate men."

One of the best illustrations I know in the Old Testament of a person who experienced spiritual desperation is Nehemiah. When he heard of the pitiable condition of his fellow countrymen he reacted deeply. He was told: "The survivors there in the province who escaped exile are in great trouble and shame; the wall of Jerusalem is broken down, and its gates are destroyed by fire" (v.3, RSV). Look at the reaction of Nehemiah when he received this news: "When I heard these words I sat down and wept, and mourned for days; and I continued fasting and praying before the God of heaven" (v.4).

We do not read of many of the Jewish exiles reacting in this way. Nehemiah could easily have turned his attention to other things, but his heart was so sensitive to God that he became spiritually desperate.

FURTHER STUDY

Ezra.10:1-6;
Joel 2:12; Acts 13:2

1. What motivated Ezra to fast?

2. What happened when the early disciples were fasting?

Arthur Wallis, commenting on Nehemiah's reaction to the news that the walls of Jerusalem were reduced to rubble, says: "His feelings ... were the labour pains out of which a new movement of God was born."

Nehemiah was so desperate to see God work that he not only prayed but fasted as well. People have to be pretty desperate to go without food! How desperate are you in connection with the need for revival? Desperate enough to do something about it?

Prayer

Father, You are probing deep. But I know You do it not to demean me but to develop me. Help me, I pray, to know something more of what it means to be spiritually desperate. In Jesus' Name I ask it. Amen.

"Desperate men"

"I spread out my hands to you; my soul thirsts for you like a parched land." (v.6)

For reading & meditation – Psalm 143:1-12

We continue looking at the characteristic of spiritual desperation which, we have been saying, usually makes its presence known in all "revival praying". I believe it was Karl Barth who once said: "We do not read our Bibles aright until we read them like desperate men." He meant, I think, that until we become spiritually desperate ourselves we will not be able to recognise the desperation that flowed in the hearts of the men and women who are portrayed in the Scriptures.

I wonder, as you read the psalm that is before us today did you feel the desperation that is present in the heart of the psalmist? Commenting on this psalm, C.S. Lewis said: "The first eleven verses were written in a strain that brings tears to the eyes. He is obviously a desperate man." Of course, the psalmist here is praying for personal revival and not national revival, but the principle to get hold of is this: desperate praying brings powerful and positive results.

Permit me once again to ask you a personal question: Have you ever felt desperate enough about the moral and spiritual conditions around you to spend a few days praying and fasting? Most people's response to the idea of fasting is: "Well, things are not desperate enough to demand *that!*" There's an old saying that goes: "Desperate situations demand desperate measures," I don't know how you view the world situation, but it seems obvious to me that things are in a desperate state. And they will only change as the desperation in the world is met and countered by a holy desperation in the hearts of the men and women who constitute the Christian Church.

Prayer

O Father, use the facts that I have read today to drive me to Your feet in a spirit of holy desperation. I cannot escape them – nor do I want to. Make me desperate – desperate enough to be a "fool for Christ" if that is necessary. In Jesus' Name. Amen.

Are you available?

"... I did not immediately confer with flesh and blood ... but I went to Arabia, and returned again to Damascus." (vv.16-17, NKJ)

For reading & meditation – Galatians 1:11-24

Over the past days we have been looking at some of the marks of "revival praying" – the special characteristics that appear in the intercessions of those who feel deeply burdened for revival. We have examined six of these characteristics (though of course there are many more): first, zealousness; second, persistence; third, boldness; fourth, persuasiveness; fifth, contrition and sixth, desperation.

We now ask: What is it that causes these characteristics to manifest themselves? Is it something that God puts into people's hearts or is it something that arises out of the conditions that are around? Probably it is a combination of both. Oswald Chambers has the key to it, I think, when he says: "Whenever God plans to send revival blessing He first lays a burden for it on the hearts of those who make themselves available to Him." Note the phrase: "those who make themselves available to Him". Oswald Chambers tells the story of how an aged saint came to his pastor one night and announced: "We are about to have a revival." The pastor asked him why he thought this, whereupon the old man replied: "I went into the stable to take care of my cattle two hours ago, and the Lord has kept me in prayer until just now. Because of this I just know we are going to have a revival." Oswald Chambers continues: "Sure enough, a revival followed just as the old man had predicted."

Are we similarly available to God? Would we be spiritually sensitive enough to know when God is breaking in upon us to lay a burden of prayer upon our hearts for revival? Is this perhaps the real reason why revival tarries?

FURTHER STUDY

John 3:1-8;
Rom. 8:14;
Acts 10:19-20

1. What did Jesus say of the Holy Spirit?

2. What was Peter's experience?

Prayer

Gracious and loving heavenly Father, once again You have Your finger on a nerve centre in my life – and I wince. Help me not to draw back, for I know that here are the issues of life and death. Help me be available. In Jesus' Name I pray. Amen.

"The spirit of prayer"

"And I will pour out on the house of David and the inhabitants of Jerusalem a spirit of grace and supplication." (v.10)
For reading & meditation – Zechariah 12:1-14

One of the insights I discovered many years ago which threw a whole new light upon the subject of revival came from the phrase found in the verse before us today: "a spirit of grace and supplication". The passage refers to the days of Christ's return when God will pour out His Holy Spirit upon the people of Israel so that they recognise the One they crucified as their one true Messiah. As a result of the Spirit's work in their hearts, they will be able to approach God with a degree of prayer and supplication that they never before experienced.

I believe something similar happens in the hearts of those who carry a great burden for revival. They are lifted out of themselves into a new dimension of praying, so that their prayers become filled with a passion and an urgency that is greater than anything they ever before knew. Sometimes this is referred to in revival literature as "the spirit of prayer" or "the spirit of intercession".

Over the past few days I have asked you some deeply personal and challenging questions. Permit me to ask yet another: Are you willing to let God put upon your heart a burden for revival? Would you be prepared to be enrolled in the company of those who know what it means to be involved in what we have been calling "revival praying"? Think long before you answer, for the cost is great in terms of time, dedication, energy, commitment and effort. Keep in mind, however, that the rewards are worth more than the cost and no one can give anything to God without experiencing something greater in return.

FURTHER STUDY

Jer. 23:33-40;
Num. 11:11

1. What had Israel lost?

2. How did they make light of it?

Prayer

Father God, help me see as I face yet another challenge that You not only set before me extremely high demands but You also provide the power by which I can meet them. In Jesus' Name. Amen.

Don't wait for feelings – begin

"Call to me and I will answer you and tell you great and unsearchable things you do not know." (v.3)

For reading & meditation – Jeremiah 33:1-11

Following what we said yesterday about the "spirit of prayer", it occurred to me that some might conclude that unless one feels strongly impelled by the Spirit to pray for revival there is no real need to do so. But as our text for today implies, whenever we see that there is a need for revival, as there was in Jeremiah's day, we are instructed to pray for it. We must be careful that we do not wait for any special "moving" of the Spirit to do what the Word of God plainly tells us is our spiritual duty.

I have come across many Christians in my time who believe that prayer is of no value unless one "feels like it". They seem to think that the efficacy of prayer depends on the emotional keenness one feels as one prays. This is nonsense. D.L. Moody said: "When it is hardest to pray, we ought to pray the hardest." When we pray and do not really feel like it we bring to God not only our prayers but a disciplined spirit as well. We must be willing to recognise feelings but not to depend on them. Feelings fluctuate with our health, the weather or the news, and our communication with heaven must not depend on something as flimsy as feelings.

FURTHER STUDY

Isa. 65:17-25; 58:9;
Zech. 13:9

1. What did Isaiah prophesy?

2. What has God promised when we call on His Name?

Having said that, however I must make the point that many of those who in their prayer times begin to take up the need of revival often find themselves being gripped and seized by a depth of passion and feeling they have never known before. They begin in the natural and are caught up into the supernatural. The important thing, however, is to *begin*.

Prayer

Father, show me even more clearly that I do not need to experience a "spirit of prayer" in order to pray for revival. If the spirit of prayer comes as I pray, then so be it. If it does not, I will pray anyway. Help me – in Jesus' Name. Amen.

"The magnetism of heaven"

*"… they were cut to the heart and said to Peter and the other
apostles, 'Brothers, what shall we do?' " (v.37)*

For reading & meditation – Acts 2:36-47

An important and final question which we must look at before we
close our meditations on revival is this: How great is our need at this
moment in history for a great spiritual awakening? I would say that in
most countries of the world it is very great. If revival is an extraordinary
movement of the Holy Spirit bestowed upon the Church by a sovereign
God, then when is God most likely to demonstrate this extraordinary
work? Is it not at a time of extraordinary need? Such a time, I suggest, is
upon us now. If I understand contemporary Christianity at all, then it is
my conviction that the need for revival is not only great but urgent and
desperate.

Take, for example, the issue of evangelism. It should be a matter of
the deepest concern that with all its evangelistic efforts the Church is
only touching a small proportion of the community. The fact that some
are being converted should not obscure the fact that great masses of people remain unreached. We expend great effort and spend large sums of
money on evangelistic crusades, which is right, but the results are rarely
what deep down in our hearts we long for. We are thankful, of course,
for those who are being won to Christ but surely it
must concern us that in proportion to the population
the results are but a drop in a bucket.

Revival would change all that. Although revival, as
we saw, is different from evangelism, you can be sure
that when revival comes the unconverted will crowd
into the churches, drawn not by human persuasion
but by the magnetism of heaven.

FURTHER STUDY

1 Kings 8:1-11;
Ex. 24:17; 40:34-35;
John 1:1-18

*1. What happened
when the glory of God
filled the Temple?*

*2. What are 2
characteristics of
God's glory?*

Prayer

O Father, give us another Pentecost so that as in Bible days preachers will not call on
sinners, but sinners call on the preachers asking: "What must I do to be saved?" In
Christ's Name we ask it. Amen.

"A time of spiritual tragedy"

*"... Jesus went out to a mountainside to pray, and spent the
night praying to God." (v.12)*

For reading & meditation – Luke 6:12-19

A nother issue in today's Church which makes the need for revival
urgent is the way in which the Church, generally speaking, has
become more activity oriented than prayer oriented. There can be little
doubt that today's Church has learned a good deal about how to organ-
ise events, how to get the best results from advertising, how to research
and target specific objectives, how to identify trends and make predic-
tions based on those trends ... and so on. What it is not so good at is
teaching people how to pray – to pray powerfully for God to make His
mighty presence known in the world. I would point out again that I am
speaking generally, for I know there will be many reading these lines
who come from churches which are exceptions to what I am saying.

Now do not hear me speaking in condemning tones of the prowess
of today's Church in the areas I have mentioned. It is good to research
and study underlying principles, such as, for example, what makes for
effective evangelism or how churches grow. There can be little doubt that
the study of these things has greatly contributed to the life and development of the Church in this generation.

FURTHER STUDY

Prov. 6:1-11;
Eph. 5:14;
Rom. 13:11;
1 Thess. 5:6

*1. What can we learn
from the ant?*

*2. What is the danger
of over-activity?*

Here, however, is the problem: it is so easy for us
to become satisfied by our successes in the field of
study and research that our satisfaction deadens our
desire and robs us of a sense of need to see God work
in a sovereign and extraordinary way through revival.
We are in a time of spiritual tragedy when our activity
becomes a blockage to His activity. Only prayer can
keep our eyes fully upon Him.

Prayer

O Father, forgive us that we so easily let our successes move our focus away from
what You can do, to what we can do. Bring us to our knees – metaphorically and literally. In Jesus' Name we pray. Amen.

When we become god

"Pride goes before destruction, and a haughty spirit before a fall." (v.18)

For reading & meditation – Proverbs 16:17-25

Another issue in today's Church which makes the need for revival urgent is unconscious self-dependence. I say "unconscious" because most Christians do not know they have this attitude – but they do, nevertheless.

This is how it develops: we learn ways of doing things for God that make us feel good. At first, the more important thing is not the feelings we get but the significance of the task in which we are engaged. Gradually, however, we become preoccupied with the good feelings that our actions give us and the significance of what we are doing takes second place. Subtly the tables have been turned – we have moved from depending on God for our significance to depending on the good feelings we get from what we are doing. Can you see the danger in this? And whatever we depend upon to hold our lives together and make them work – that is our god. So it can be said that when self-dependence rules our hearts then *we* become god.

Revival would change all this. In times of great spiritual awakening unconscious motives are brought into consciousness and men and women see themselves as they really are. The proud become humble, the arrogant become unassuming, and the self-dependent become God-dependent. One of the most difficult tasks of a Christian counsellor is to help people realise how they are hiding behind the defence mechanism of denial and come out from behind it. It sometimes takes months, even years, to get that point across. In revival God does it in one fell swoop.

FURTHER STUDY

Psa. 139:13-24;
1 Chron. 28:9;
Jer. 17:10

1. What was the psalmist's prayer?

2. What were David's words to Solomon?

Prayer

Gracious and loving heavenly Father, I don't want to wait for a revival in order that I might become a more real and aware person. You have my permission to do it this hour. Give me my own personal revival – today. In Jesus' Name. Amen.

The battle for the Bible

"For ever, O Lord, Your word is settled in heaven."
(v.89, NKJ)

For reading & meditation – Psalm 119:89-96

Yet another issue in today's Church which makes the need for revival urgent is a growing loss of confidence in the Scriptures. Not all churches have moved away from the authority of the Scriptures, but we must face the fact that many have.

"We are slowly reaching the position," says one writer, "where the Christian who is orthodox in his beliefs and convictions, who stands on the Bible and in the central tradition of the Christian faith is considered to be a dogmatic reactionary, a stubborn anti-intellectualist, an obscurantist to be pitied and derided. The gospel which brings men to a personal knowledge of Christ and to the joyful experience of the new birth has to be fought for in the very inner councils of the historic denominations. In conditions such as these it would be a glib and shallow mind that dared to say a revival is not our greatest need."

Revival brings with it a new confidence in the Bible. People who are moved upon by the Holy Spirit in times of great spiritual awakening invariably find their faith and understanding of the Bible being greatly quickened. An Irishman who was involved in the revival in Ireland in the mid 1800s said: "I used to read the Bible before revival came, but after I came in touch with the Holy Spirit the Bible became a new and different book. It was as if God had taken it up to heaven, rewritten it and handed it back to me. I now know it is inspired because it inspires me."

That is not the only reason, of course, why we know it is inspired but it is a good reason nevertheless.

FURTHER STUDY

2 Tim. 2:1-15;
Psa. 119:1-16;
Acts 2:42

1. What was Paul's exhortation to Timothy?

2. What did the early Church continue to do?

Prayer

Father, it is difficult to see how the battle for the Bible can be won apart from a mighty deluge of Your Holy Spirit. Your people need to be revived, refreshed and enlightened. Let it happen, dear Lord – soon. In Jesus' Name. Amen.

"The sound of marching"

"... when you hear the sound of marching in the tops of the mulberry trees, then you shall advance quickly ..." (v.24, NKJ)

For reading & meditation – 2 Samuel 5:17-25

Having recognised the urgent need for revival, we must ask: Will we see another great spiritual awakening in our own day? I cannot say with certainty, but I most definitely feel so. There are clear signs that a revival is on the way, but before looking at them, pause with me to focus on the passage before us today.

Soon after David had been made king over Israel he was threatened by the Philistines. His first concern was to find what God wanted him to do about it. After getting divine permission to proceed, he led a bold frontal attack that carried the day. Later, however, the Philistines returned and took up the position that they had occupied before. Without presuming on past guidance David again sought God's direction and obtained permission to attack. However, this time he was led to make a detour and take up a position behind the enemy, near the mulberry (or balsam) trees. God said: "When you hear the sound of marching in the tops of the mulberry trees, then bestir yourself; for then has the Lord gone out before you, to smite the army of the Philistines" (v.24, Amplified Bible).

These two battles illustrate the difference between the normal activity of the Holy Spirit in the Church and the way He operates in revival. In the first we see David acting under God's direction and with His enabling. In the second it is God who takes the field and David follows on behind gathering up the spoils of victory. We have witnessed for decades the normal operation of the Spirit; the time has now come to prepare for revival.

FURTHER STUDY

Psa. 85:1-13;
Hab.3:1-19

1. What was the psalmist's prayer?

2. What was his expectation?

Prayer

O Father, quicken my faith to believe for an outpouring of the Spirit as great if not greater than at Pentecost. I want to live in Your Word and Your Word to live in me. Fill Your Church with Your glory – and let it overflow. In Jesus' Name I ask it. Amen.

Three signs of coming revival

"… Zion … For Your servants take pleasure in her stones, and show favour to her dust." (vv.13-14, NKJ)

For reading & meditation – Psalm 102:1-17

We saw yesterday that before God came down and intervened in the battle against the Philistines He gave David a sign that He was about to move in a supernatural way against the enemy. I am emboldened to say that I believe God is giving us at this hour in history some clear signs that He is about to move in great power throughout the world.

The first sign I see is an increasing interest in the subject of revival. Almost every Christian leader I have spoken to recently has talked to me about his or her concern for a spiritual revival. I hear it also in the new hymns and songs that are being written for the Church. God is touching the hearts of His people in a fresh and wonderful way to pray and expect a great Holy Spirit revival.

The second sign I see is a deep desire amongst Christians to forget denominational differences and identify themselves simply as brothers and sisters in Christ. The preparation of the first disciples at Pentecost came as they were all "with one accord" in one place (Acts 2:1, AV). A third sign I see is a growing desire in the hearts of believers everywhere to pray and intercede for revival. It is one thing to be interested in revival; it is another to be interested enough to give time to pray and intercede for it. When God finds those who are as concerned for revival as God's people were about the stones and dust of Zion (as our passage for today points out), it will not be long before those who mourn are comforted – by divine intervention.

FURTHER STUDY

Acts 2:1-7;
John 17:1-26;
1 Cor. 1:10

1. What was the prayer of Jesus?

2. What did Paul beseech the Corinthians?

Prayer

My Father and my God, deepen my conviction that revival is not just a dream but a reality. You have sent revival before and You can do so again. I believe – help Thou my unbelief. In Christ's Name I ask it. Amen.

"The watchman on the walls"

"Behold ... new things I declare; before they spring forth I tell you of them." (v.9, NKJ)

For reading & meditation – Isaiah 42:1-9

There is a vital faith element which is always in evidence in the days preceding a revival," says Arthur Wallis in his book *Rain from Heaven*, and the stimulus for that faith is provided by those whom we may call "the watchmen on the walls".

In Bible times watchmen stood on the walls of Jerusalem during the night so that they could report any signs of enemy activity. These watchmen were also the first to see the dawn and in its light assess the situation in a way that those in the city could not.

Just as Jerusalem had its watchmen, so too does the modern-day Church. They are the seers, the prophets, the intercessors, who are constantly on watch and report to us their findings. I do not regard myself as one of this favoured group, but I do know many who are. They tell me that like Elijah of old they see "a cloud the size of a man's hand" scudding across the heavens and know that soon we shall see a deluge such as we have never seen before. I believe them, for my own spirit witnesses to what they say.

Charles Finney tells the story of a woman in New Jersey who felt that God was about to send revival to her town. She encouraged the leaders to arrange some special meetings and when they refused she went ahead herself, getting a carpenter to make seats so that she could have meetings in her house. He had hardly finished before the Spirit of God fell upon the community. How could this woman have been so sure? She was a watchman – a watchman of God.

FURTHER STUDY

Rev. 2:1-7;
Acts 3:19; 8:22;
17:30; Luke 15:21

1. What was Jesus'
message to the
Ephesian church?

2. What does
repentance mean?

Prayer

O Father, I may not be in the category of a "watchman" but help me keep so close to You that I will be able to hear Your faintest whisper. This I ask in Christ's peerless and precious Name. Amen.

"Keep your eyes on the tide"

"Your troops will be willing on your day of battle ..." (v.3)
For reading & meditation – Psalm 110:1-7

On this our final day we ask again: Has God something bigger for us than we are at present seeing? I hope I have convinced you that He has! How can we be open to receiving it? It comes at the precise moment God appoints but it is carried down from heaven on the wings of fervent believing prayer. Dr A.T. Pierson said: "From the Day of Pentecost until now, there has not been one great spiritual awakening in any land which has not begun in a union of prayer though only among two or three, and no such outward or upward movement has continued after such prayer meetings have declined." Revivals are born in prayer and sustained by prayer.

Just as there are signs concerning the second coming, so there are signs that the Lord is not far from reviving His whole Church. In the early days of the Salvation Army in France, the eldest daughter of General Booth, known by her French rank as the "Marechale", found herself at one point in an extremely discouraging situation. She wrote to General Booth asking for his advice, which came in these words: "Take your eyes off the waves and fix them on the tide."

FURTHER STUDY

Ezek. 37:1-14;
2 Kings 3:16-17;
Isa. 40:3-5;
Rev. 22:1

1. What was God's message to Ezekiel?

2. What will you do to bring about revival?

I give you now that same advice. Don't let your eyes become focused on the waves, with their advances and retreats. Keep your eyes on the tide and ask yourself: Is it rising? If you look with the eye of faith I think you will see that it is. When it breaks I pray that it will not find you or me unprepared, but that we shall be a people who are willing in the day of God's power.

Prayer

Father, I don't know whether I will live to see a world-wide revival but I want to live to experience a personal revival. Take me on from this point to know You in a much greater way. In Christ's Name I ask it. Amen.

Index

Index

Index

Index

EVERY DAY WITH JESUS – ONE YEAR DEVOTIONAL

CWR, Waverley Abbey House, Waverley Lane, Farnham, Surrey GU9 8EP

Editions of *Every Day with Jesus* were previously published as follows: The Vision of God 1992, From Confusion to Confidence 1987, The Beatitudes 1986, The Power of a New Perspective 1989, The Corn of Wheat Afraid to Die 1986, Heaven-Sent Revival 1989.
© Selwyn Hughes
Revised edition in this format 1997 © Selwyn Hughes
First published 1997 by CWR
Reprinted 1997, 1998, 2000, 2002, 2003

Design: CWR Production
Typesetting: David Poyser
Printed by W.S. Bookwell, Finland

ISBN 1-85345-121-5

Unless otherwise indicated, all Scripture references are from the Holy Bible: *New International Version* (NIV). Copyright © 1973, 1978, 1984 by the International Bible Society.

Waverley Abbey House, Waverley Lane, Farnham, Surrey GU9 8EP.

NATIONAL DISTRIBUTORS

UK: (and countries not listed below)
CWR, Waverley Abbey House, Waverley Lane, Farnham, Surrey GU9 8EP.
Tel: (01252) 784710 Outside UK (44) 1252 784710
AUSTRALIA: CMC Australasia, PO Box 519, Belmont, Victoria 3216.
Tel: (03) 5241 3288
CANADA: Cook Communications Ministries, PO Box 98, 55 Woodslee Avenue, Paris, Ontario
Tel: 1800 263 2664
GHANA: Challenge Enterprises of Ghana, PO Box 5723, Accra.
Tel: (021) 222437/223249 Fax: (021) 226227
HONG KONG: Cross Communications Ltd, 1/F, 562A Nathan Road, Kowloon.
Tel: 2780 1188 Fax: 2770 6229
INDIA: Crystal Communications, 10-3-18/4/1, East Marredpally, Secunderabad – 500 026.
Tel/Fax: (040) 7732801
KENYA: Keswick Books and Gifts Ltd, PO Box 10242, Nairobi.
Tel: (02) 331692/226047 Fax: (02) 728557
MALAYSIA: Salvation Book Centre (M) Sdn Bhd, 23 Jalan SS 2/64,
47300 Petaling Jaya, Selangor.
Tel: (03) 78766411/78766797 Fax: (03) 78757066/78756360
NEW ZEALAND: CMC Australasia, PO Box 36015, Lower Hutt.
Tel: 0800 449 408 Fax: 0800 449 049
NIGERIA: FBFM, Helen Baugh House, 96 St Finbarr's College Road, Akoka, Lagos.
Tel: (01) 7747429/4700218/825775/827264
PHILIPPINES: OMF Literature Inc, 776 Boni Avenue, Mandaluyong City.
Tel: (02) 531 2183 Fax: (02) 531 1960
REPUBLIC OF IRELAND: Scripture Union, 40 Talbot Street, Dublin 1.
Tel: (01) 8363764
SINGAPORE: Armour Publishing Pte Ltd, Block 203A Henderson Road,
11–06 Henderson Industrial Park, Singapore 159546.
Tel: 6 276 9976 Fax: 6 276 7564
SOUTH AFRICA: Struik Christian Books, 80 MacKenzie Street,
PO Box 1144, Cape Town 8000.
Tel: (021) 462 4360 Fax: (021) 461 3612
SRI LANKA: Christombu Books, 27 Hospital Street, Colombo 1.
Tel: (01) 433142/328909
TANZANIA: CLC Christian Book Centre, PO Box 1384, Mkwepu Street, Dar es Salaam.
Tel/Fax: (022) 2119439
USA: Cook Communications Ministries, PO Box 98, 55 Woodslee Avenue, Paris, Ontario,
Canada
Tel: 1800 263 2664
ZIMBABWE: Word of Life Books, Shop 4, Memorial Building,
35 S Machel Avenue, Harare.
Tel: (04) 781305 Fax: (04) 774739

For email addresses, visit the CWR website: www.cwr.org.uk
CWR is a registered charity – number 294387

Every Day with Jesus

With over three-quarters of a million readers, *Every Day with Jesus* is one of the world's most popular daily Bible study tools.

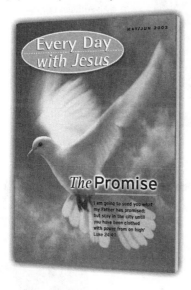

- Get practical help for life's challenges
- Gain insight into the deeper truths of Scripture
- Be challenged, comforted and encouraged
- Study six topics in depth each year

Price: £1.95 each
£11 annual subscription (UK)

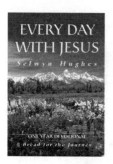

Bread for the Journey

The All-Sufficient Christ,
The Pursuit of Excellence,
The Wondrous Cross,
The Treasures of Darkness,
The More Excellent Way,
The Care of the Soul

ISBN 1-85345-224-6
Price: £5.99

Treasure for the Heart

The Songs of Ascents,
The Divine Eagle,
The Lord's Prayer,
The Armour of God,
Hinds' Feet on High Places,
Your Father and My Father

ISBN 1-85345-151-7
Price: £5.99

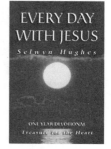

Light for the Path

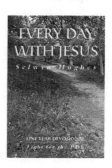

The Uniqueness of Our Faith,
The Search for Meaning,
The Twenty-third Psalm,
The Spirit-filled Life,
Strong at the Broken Places,
Going Deeper with God

ISBN 1-85345-134-7
Price: £5.99

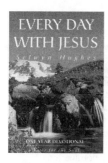

Water for the Soul

Staying Spiritually Fresh,
Rebuilding Broken Walls,
The Character of God,
When Sovereignty Surprises,
The Fruit of the Spirit,
Seven Pillars of Wisdom

ISBN 1-85345-128-2
Price: £5.99

Every Day with Jesus for People in Search of God

When it comes to those hard, demanding questions people want clear, thoughtful answers. Here Selwyn Hughes offers an intelligent and helpful perspective on those big issues, including:

- What is life all about?
- Is there life after death?
- Who is God and what is He like?
- How can we know God?
- Why does God allow suffering?

ISBN 1-85345-226-2 **Price:** £1.99

Content is revised from the popular evangelism book *Every Day Light – Light of the World*

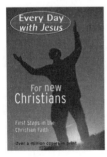

Every Day with Jesus for New Christians

Every Day with Jesus for New Christians is a powerful and relevant handbook for people new to the Christian faith or for people who need the basics presented to them clearly and dynamically. A favourite with churches of all denominations.

ISBN 1-85345-133-9 **Price:** £1.99